Change Mummified

Change Mummified

Cinema, Historicity, Theory

Philip Rosen

University of Minnesota Press
Minneapolis • London

The University of Minnesota Press gratefully acknowledges the assistance provided for the publication of this book by the McKnight Foundation.

Chapter 1 draws from material originally presented in "History of Image, Image of History: Subject and Ontology in Bazin," *Wide Angle* 9, no. 4 (winter 1987–88): 7–34; copyright Ohio University, Athens Center for Film and Video; reprinted by permission of The Johns Hopkins University Press. Sections of chapters 2 and 3 originally appeared in "Traces of the Past: From Historicity to Film," in *Questioning Paul Ricoeur*, edited by David Klemm and William Schweiker (Charlottesville: University Press of Virginia, 1993); reprinted with permission of the University Press of Virginia. The original version of chapter 5 was published as "Disjunction and Ideology in a Preclassical Film: *A Policeman's Tour of the World*," *Wide Angle* 12, no. 3 (1990); copyright Ohio University, Athens Center for Film and Video; reprinted by permission of The Johns Hopkins University Press. A version of chapter 6 originally appeared in *Theorizing Documentary*, ed. Michael Renov (New York: Routledge, 1993); reprinted by permission of Routledge and Taylor and Francis. An early version of chapter 7 was originally published as "Making a Nation in Sembene's *Ceddo*," *Quarterly Review of Film and Video* 13, nos. 1–3 (1991): 147–72; copyright OPA (Overseas Publishers Association) N.V.; reprinted with permission from Gordon and Breach Publishers. The original version of chapter 8 was published as "Old and New: Image, Indexicality, and Historicity in the Digital Utopia," *Iconics* 4 (1998): 5–45; republished with permission of JASIAS (*Iconics* is the international edition of the journal of the Japan Society of Image Arts and Sciences).

Published by the University of Minnesota Press
111 Third Avenue South, Suite 290
Minneapolis, MN 55401-2520
http://www.upress.umn.edu

Library of Congress Cataloging-in-Publication Data

Rosen, Philip
   Change mummified : cinema, historicity, theory / Philip Rosen.
      p. cm.
   Includes bibliographical references and index.
      ISBN 0-8166-3637-0—ISBN 0-8166-3638-9 (pbk.)
      1. Motion pictures and history. 2. Motion pictures—Philosophy.
   I. Title.
   PN1995.2 .R66 2001
   791.43'658—dc21
                                        2001001010

Printed in the United States of America on acid-free paper

The University of Minnesota is an equal-opportunity educator and employer.

11 10 09 08 07 06   10 9 8 7 6 5 4 3 2

For my mother, Kail Blumenthal Rosen, and
the memory of my father, Max Rosen

Contents

Acknowledgments

At various stages, this project has benefited from the encouragement, pointers, references, and advice of a number of distinguished scholars, including Richard Abel, Dudley Andrew, John Belton, Manthia Diawara, Anne Friedberg, Marvin D'Lugo, Teshome Gabriel, Tom Gunning, Miriam Hansen, Marsha Kinder, Neil Lazarus, Richard Maltby, Hamid Naficy, Michael Renov, Michael Rogin, Robert Scholes, and Linda Williams. I feel lucky to know all of them as colleagues and many as friends, and I am grateful for their generosity. I also am grateful to Edward Dimendberg, for substantive suggestions, encouragement, and editorial persistence.

Early work for this book was supported by a grant from the National Endowment for the Humanities. Rosalind Galt assisted with conversions of data between computer systems. Brown University film archivist Richard Manning was invaluable in the researching and reproduction of stills. My thanks also to Linda Lincoln for intelligent and sensitive copyediting.

Mary Ann Doane has been an irreplaceable presence in my life. For this project, she helped in ways that were specific and concrete, but also in ways that cannot be easily or quickly expressed. Hannah Doane Rosen made the period spent on this book a source of indelible memories.

I have dedicated this book to my parents, Max Rosen and Kail Blumenthal Rosen. They first taught me respect for the intellect and instilled intellectual honesty in me. They gave me cause to wonder at the attractions of the past. I would also like to include a note of love to my aunt, Ida Rosen, who has given me love for my entire life.

Introduction

This book addresses film theory, filmic textuality, and film history in relation to the modern category of history, or rather, modern historicity. In my view, there are significant interrelations, connections, and overlaps between cinema as we usually know it and modern historicity as we usually know it. It seems to me that ideas about those relations have not been pushed conceptually or categorically as far as they could be. By pushing harder, I hope to say some interesting things about cinema and its theory, a little about its history, and something about historicity. Thus, the phrase in the title of this book, "change mummified," is a translator's rendering of a figurative definition of cinema offered by André Bazin. But, I will argue, it also registers modern historicity. For it rests on a notion of temporality as a threateningly dynamic force, a threat registered especially in the high valuation placed on stabilizing relations between present and past; and these are assumptions definitive of modern historicity.

For the sake of terminological clarity, I make a distinction between historiography, history, and historicity. By historiography, I mean the text written by the historian (historio-graphy). By history, I mean the object of the text, the "real" pastness it seeks to construct or recount in and for the present. This entails the definitional proposition that historiography always has referential ambitions. By historicity, I mean the particular interrelations of the mode of historiography and the types of construction of history related by it.

When I say the book is about cinema and *modern* historicity, this in itself implies a history or histories: histories of historiography, histories of constructions of history, histories of historicity. What I take to be the skeletal attributes of modern historicity will be discussed in greater detail in Part I, but this reflexive implication of the demand to historicize stems from them. In turn, this suggests that using some kind of category of history remains necessary if we are to discuss historicity. Whatever else happens in this book, this necessity, which is implicit in modern historicity, serves as an inescapable limit on any critiques of modern historicity. I will therefore refer to historians of historiography as often as I refer to theorists of history. And my general position in this regard is that the category of history, as inherited from the later modernity that crystallized in the nineteenth-century West along with full-fledged industrial capitalism, remains an unavoidable one.

Part of what film theory can do is unfold and interrogate basic understandings of what films are supposed to do. This book reformulates some of those basic understandings, but portions of it are also devoted to basic understandings of what histories are supposed to do, in order to suggest ways one can conceive of the two as intertwined. I intend the phrase "are supposed to do" in a doubly normative sense: not only what cinema and historiography are required to do to produce "proper" films and histories, but also what it is generally supposed that they do. This is to say I continue to treat both cinema and historiography as social and cultural operations as much as technological or epistemological structures. Often I use a term like *ideal* or *sociocultural ideal* as a reminder of this.

That said, it should be acknowledged that the immediate intellectual contexts in which this book is situated include not only film and media theory and historiography, but also recent theories of history that have in some sense deauthorized modern historical thinking. For some time now, much of the most important textual and cultural theory and critique has treated modern historicity as a conceptually problematic enterprise. The arguments and issues are too intricate to be covered in depth in an introduction, but a standard view would trace this theoretical deauthorization back to the onset of structuralism and semiotics in the humanities, with the understanding that it subsequently extended far beyond those particular approaches.

For a reminder of the flavor of this deauthorization, one can refer to a canonical signpost of its emergence, Claude Lévi-Strauss's critique of Jean-Paul Sartre in the concluding chapter of *The Savage Mind*, published in 1962. This was not only a famous structuralist attack on the predominance of existential phenomenology in France, but also established an attitude and claims about historicity. Here are four of Lévi-Strauss's assertions in this regard:

1. Historical thinking divides the world between dynamic historical societies and unchanging "peoples 'without history.'" This is to say it establishes an unscientific "other" in order to privilege a scientific, historicizing "self" defined precisely by the power to position the other in history. Writing during the breakup of the French colonial empire, Lévi-Strauss noted that this division between nonhistoriographic and historiographic societies was intimately intertwined with rationales—that is, ideologies—of colonialism.[1]

2. Historical thinking compulsively privileges temporal continuity. By coherently ordering purportedly real occurrences in time, it makes continuity an ontological attribute of a genuinely historicized reality; however, the attribution of continuity to the real cannot be explained or sustained except in relation to the mythic functioning of historiography.

3. Relatedly, historical discourse establishes its claims to a referential, explanatory continuity by assuming an illegitimate degree of transparency for its linguistic forms. For example, on the basis of his analytic, structuralist conception of language and codification, Lévi-Strauss argued that historical discourse methodically obfuscates the artificial character of its temporality, for it can only express its continuities by means of linguistic elements that are necessarily discontinuous (signifiers of temporality, including classes of dates such as years, months, days).[2]

4. Historical thinking is built on, and builds, what other kinds of social

and cultural theorists would soon label a masterful subject-position, and which Lévi-Strauss conceives as a universalizing humanism that is in fact a culturally specific, mythical product. On the basis of the presumption of temporal continuity, for example, the historicizing subject is able to posit *itself* as a persistence, a continuity; hence historical thinking stabilizes a positionality of consistent and coherent subjectivity and/or identity. As the implicit self–other division of historical thinking already suggests, the prestige that the modern West accorded to historical knowledge was not only a cultural but a sociopolitical process. The "supposed totalizing continuity of the self," Lévi-Strauss wrote in response to Sartre, "seems to me to be an illusion sustained by the demands of social life."[3]

These four themes—the inescapable immersion of historiography in socio-ideological rationales, the insupportability of the temporal continuities it constructs, its necessary ignorance of its own linguistic means and their implications, and the illegitimate universalization of the humanist subject-position it constructs and upon which it depends—will by now seem very familiar to those conversant with contemporary cultural theory and critique. But this is surely because Lévi-Strauss hit on one of the central epistemological and cultural nerves of the later twentieth century. In the decades since the publication of *The Savage Mind*, a deliberate and critical distance from supposedly dominant or workaday conceptions of historiography has become common in the academic humanities.

We could say that there are two extremes to this distancing. One takes the form of a complaint that conventional historiography is built on a system of exclusions—exclusions of certain kinds of events or populations, for example. It results in a demand for rectification. This kind of critical stance has perhaps been strongest within movements and approaches that most directly define themselves as politically oppositional, such as feminism, identity politics, and certain sectors of postcolonial studies, but it is also connected to some elements of the historiographic profession, such as the *Annales* school of historians in France. At the other extreme, however, that critical distancing is manifested in radical and intensive interrogations of modern historicity per se. Here the forms, terms, and very possibility of asserting secure knowledge about history may come into doubt. Instead of a demand for rectification of particular historiographies, this may lead to a call for a complete reconceptualization of historicity, and for some could even imply the rejection of the very idea of a coherent historiography. Of course, these two poles might intermingle at any point along an imaginary line between them, for another argument is that the only way to recover the elements excluded from conventional historiography is to reject its forms and terms.

Beginning in the 1960s, an influential generation of thinkers, more or less aligned with the second pole and working from a variety of philosophical positions, formulated highly developed accounts and forceful critiques of Western historicity. While this tendency at first seemed to be headquartered in Paris, it had international impact in cultural and social theory. If quick references are useful, the following were some of the best known of these thinkers: Althusser, with his reconceptualization determination by the social whole and a complex historical temporality for Marxism; Derrida, with his Heidegger-influenced, poststructuralist deconstruction of such dominant notions as linear temporality, origin, and identity; and Foucault, with his Nietzschean reformulation of historical time and transition into genealogy through a notion of networks of power.[4]

Crucially for theorists of history, there was also highly influential work manifesting the Lévi-Straussian theme of close attention to the representational and discursive procedures of historiography, with the goal of unpacking the artifices, subterfuges, and implications of its linguistic and rhetorical forms. The most influential exemplars of this tendency were probably Roland Barthes and Hayden White, who in the 1960s and 1970s published seminal accounts of historiography that drew on structural linguistics, theories of narrative, and theories of rhetoric. They did not seek to unpack and adjudicate proper and improper forms of historiographic logic in comparison with accounts of scientific logic, as had the analytic philosophers who dominated post–World War II philosophy of history. Rather, they sought to uncover the ways in which the linguistic

and representational practices of modern historicity necessarily but sur-
reptitiously slip into a structuring illogic associated with a rhetoric of
address, with broad social and ideological determinations, and with
implicit desires and fantasies. Both the referential aspirations of the currently dominant and canonical form of historiography as well as its production of coherent explanatory meanings, it was now argued, should be
understood as socially and culturally functional discursive constructs.[5]

If placing modern historicity under radical conceptual suspicion has
now become a commonplace of advanced cultural theory, powerful
reconceptualizations of historiography informed by these impulses have
also been produced. However, even they tend to incorporate certain of
the characteristics attached to historiographic form in recent textual and
cultural theory. For example, one of the most highly developed tendencies has been to revivify the old association between historiography and
narrative, to accept certain aspects of newer accounts of narrative that
question its validity as referential form, but then to assert the validity of
narrative as a tool for knowledge of states of affairs over time. This strategy was adopted by two of the most crucial thinkers with a stake in historicity, Paul Ricoeur and Fredric Jameson. Ricoeur confronts the crisis
of historical theory by defining narrative as the figuration of temporality,
within a view that promotes figuration or tropology and the hermeneutic
consciousness it entails as a primary and productive form of human
knowledge. Of course, figuration is usually associated with the connota-
tive aura of fiction and the poetic, rather than with the denotative aura of
direct empirical representation, and Ricoeur explicitly incorporates such
thinkers as White and Michel de Certeau into his own theory. Jameson
erected a historicizing Marxism that uses a range of recent cultural theories under its own subsuming, totalizing dialectic, while simultaneously
acknowledging a projective, imaginary component or drive even in the
most valid social cognitions. Again, narrative and figuration loom large.[6]

But meanwhile, elements of the critique of the authority of historiography have overspilled the boundaries of the theory of history. By the
1980s, certain of these theoretical themes commonly appeared in generalized descriptions of the dominant direction of contemporary (usually

first-world) cultural production and social formations. This move is often identified with postmodernist cultural theory. To take a much-invoked example, Lyotard's distinction between modern legitimation by grand narratives—his chief examples of which are historiographic—and post-modern "incredulity towards metanarratives" was originally part of a con-ceptualization of the production of knowledge. But it has been employed by others to help define contemporary cultural practices as postmodern.

More broadly, qualities often said to define postmodern culture cor-relate with many themes associated with the theoretical deauthorization of historical thinking; for example, awareness of the conventional, arbitrary quality of representation, along with a rejection of, or irony toward, the quest for referential language or codes; or a tendency to understand sub-ject-position as arbitrary, multiple, and/or changeable, which implies sus-picion not only of profoundly rooted subjective interiorities, but also of claims for consistent sociocultural identities as a position from which to construct historicities; or an aesthetics that privileges temporal fragmen-tation as opposed to the complex but coherent temporalities that could give "metanarratives" their reach as knowledge and their sociocultural appeal. Jameson himself, having identified the connectivity of historical knowledge with narrative, went on to argue that a defining characteristic of postmodern society is the devaluation of both. However, he explicitly treated this shift as itself "historical."[7]

Of special interest here is the fact that many who believe that an attenuation of modern historicity is a general tendency in contemporary culture give prominence to the impact of media of technological produc-tion and reproduction. On the plane of society and economics, such media are defined in part by their compatibility with mass reproduction and therefore mass distributability. On the plane of representation and per-ception, the most pervasive "new media" technologies of the past two centuries have tended to be media of images and sounds: photography, technologies of mass magazine illustrations, phonography and its descen-dents, cinema, television, and video. Most recently, aspects of computeri-zation involving digitally encoded images and sounds can be added to this sequence of the appearance and dissemination of new technological media.[8]

Let me make three points as an introductory signal of my own attitude toward the idea of associating the proliferation of such media with the thesis of a general deauthorization of the historical in cultural practices. First, I do not believe this media culture is necessarily hostile to modern historicity. On the contrary, much of its development and diffusion coincided "historically" with the development and diffusion of modern historicity. "History" as we know it became established as a central component of social and cultural theory, as well as a master discipline of the emergent modern university during the nineteenth century, which also saw the dissemination of photography and mass magazine illustrations and led to the invention and widespread deployment of cinema and phonography. Perhaps this is why those who argue for a general cultural deauthorization of modern historicity tend to locate it at some point in the later twentieth century. At the very least, then, they must correlate that deauthorization not with media culture per se, but with the passing of some kind of threshold in the expansion of media culture. And, incidentally, they must explain the fact that modes of thinking promoted as historical research and argumentation remain normalized scholarship to this day.

Second, it seems to me that claims, assertions, or presentations about pastness, not to mention representations of it, remain common currency in the nonacademic media culture that is now universally recognized as a definitional fact of contemporary life. It also seems to me that these still partake of modern historiography, in at least some senses to be explained in the body of this book. Even postmodernist cultural theory and critique acknowledge this situation when it propagates notions such as "nostalgia for history," "hyperreality," and so forth. However productive these are in certain ways, I find them ultimately unsatisfactory. They appear to be designed to explain the persistence of something they proclaim is passé.

This is not to deny offhand claims for cultural changes in the status and components of historiographic forms, but rather to insist that there have also been continuities. To emphasize the former at the expense of the latter is to evade their interplay, the mixtures of old and new, the temporal hybridities that constitute the present. Such temporal hybridity ought to be constitutive of historiographies that oppose themselves to the alleged linear coherence of modern historiography. To the degree that they ignore or downplay this hybridity, such accounts contradict their own theoretical premises, and this contradiction revolves around their understanding of historicity.

But my third point is that such notions are extraordinarily useful in one respect. They extend questions around historicity throughout a broad continuum of cultural forms, including this nonacademic media culture, although academic historiography has undoubtedly been at the most epistemologically prestigious extreme in this continuum. This brings us back to cinema. I believe that cinema has occupied a special "historical" position in this media culture. Scholars of the emergence of cinema have often paid attention to how cinema draws on precedent media and genres—painting, photography, optical toys, various narrative modes, and so forth. However, it is possible to see it in a prospective as well as a retrospective way. The commercially viable appearance of moving photographic images, soon with synchronized recorded sound, can now be understood as a kind of threshold. As the first globally disseminated medium of two-dimensional moving images with synchronized sound, cinema became the terrain of a field of signifying modules and, in complicated ways, models for other, subsequent media with which it has became intertwined, such as radio, television, and the digital realm. Once established, of course, these have had and continue to have their own specific effectivities in shaping and transforming the overall "field" of images and sounds (including elements of cinema). The same could be said for the economics in which these various media participate, as well as their social and cultural functions. Hence, my interest in arguing that cinema bears a special relationship with modern historicity is connected to a view of the history of, and the historicity implanted in, modern media culture, as well as the history of historiography. And so, although this book is centered on film theory, filmic textuality, and film history, it will sometimes be necessary to remark on the status of other media with respect to historicity, including television and the digital.

———————

If one context or setting for this book is the problematicity of modern historicity in textual and cultural theory, another is Film Studies itself. Although efforts to legitimize the study of film as an academic field began earlier, the "take-off" of Film Studies as an academic institution was only solidified during the 1970s. The leading intellectual developments in film scholarship during these years were dominated by the emergence of what we may now call 1970s film theory. This was a self-consciously radical and controversial transformation of the grounds of thinking about cinema across a sometimes contradictory conjunction of structuralist and post-structuralist semiotics, anti-illusionist textual politics, neo-Marxist ideological analysis, psychoanalytic theories of signification and subjectivity, and feminist theory. In its actuality, 1970s film theory was a tissue of inter-secting, sometimes mutually contestatory arguments and discourses about cinema among several individuals, often conducted on the basis of overlapping but not necessarily identical premises. It developed in several directions over just a few years. But as a recognizable intellectual constel-lation, it set the terms of advanced debate in film scholarship for over two decades, arguably even for those who reject every aspect of it and have claimed to supercede it.[9]

Nineteen seventies film theory also had significant influence on more general cultural critique and was closely related to the kind of cul-tural and textual theory that deauthorized modern historicity. Indeed, in spite of the claims of some of its most important figures to be construct-ing a historical materialist approach to cinema, it seems fair to say that new theories of the text in relation to subjectivity were much more devel-oped in 1970s film theory than were new conceptualizations of film histo-riography, much less historicity. But on the heels of 1970s film theory, concern with historicity persisted on at least three broad scholarly fronts.

The first was within 1970s film theory itself. Sometimes claims were made about the revolutionary effects this theoretical thrust should have on understandings of film history. The early 1970s saw some important attempts to reconceptualize film history or the history of filmic textual-ity in ways that took into account the fields of subjectivity and ideology central to the new developments in film theory. Some film scholars were attracted to the idea of rethinking the allegedly linear histories in which film history had been cast in favor of a stratified, nonlinear historical temporality.[10]

The second front has been an intensification of research into the history of cinema, which is ongoing. The institutionalization of Film Studies soon gave rise to a new kind of scholarly grouping, self-identified academic film historians, usually with doctorates in Film Studies or at least teaching in Film Studies programs. Their articles have generally appeared in peer-reviewed journals of film scholarship and their books have been published by university presses; by the 1980s, they had produced something very much like a subdiscipline. Going beyond revising standard accounts of the history of filmic textuality, the new generation of film historians paid close attention to the economic and social aspects of film, studying written sources that had previously been untapped or unavailable. That is, these new film historians were more likely than their (often nonacademic) predecessors to follow established protocols of disciplinary historiography, basing their arguments on critically evaluated, written primary source materials. The sense of increased rigor compared to previous film historiography was reinforced not only by closer adherence to conventional kinds of protocols and venues of academic historiography, but also by a carefully developed self-consciousness about the kind of arguments and concepts they were bringing to bear, perhaps provoked by the importance of 1970s film theory to the field as a whole.

In fact, the relation of their work to 1970s film theory was diverse. Some of the new film historians manifested explicit awareness of theoretical discussions. At least some concepts privileged in film theory could be objects for productive historical investigation (classical cinema was one such concept); some of the conceptions of filmic textuality developed in 1970s film theory could be integrated into institutional histories of cinema (as happened in the remarkable historiographic rethinking of preclassical cinema, a little of which will be invoked in Part II). On the other hand, almost as if in response to the contemporaneous critique of modern historicity, at least some film historians expressed suspicion of the abstract generalizations of theory as opposed to the concrete, particularities sought by historical method—thus reproducing the most traditional of modern disciplinary debates. For the opposition between theory and history is a version of that between "philosophy of history" and critical historical method (discussed in chapter 3), dating back to the rivalry between students of Hegel and Ranke at the foundations of the modern discipline of "History."[11]

The third front on which history remained a significant category in film scholarship after 1970s film theory was the study of narrative films that purport to represent history—that is historiography *in* film. This has been a topic rather than a subdiscipline, which means it has not been as self-consciously rationalized or organized as historiography *of* film. But since the 1970s, there has been an intermittent though continuing production of significant scholarly studies of historical representation in film. Being defined by textual characteristics—how and why claims to represent history on film were implemented at different points in the history of cinema—such studies were likely to register awareness of the main lines of 1970s film theory and later developments and debates stemming from it. In fact, already in the mid-1970s *Cahiers du cinéma*, one of the leading organs of 1970s film theory, went through a phase when historical filmmaking came to the foreground. Since then, various filmmaking contexts have received attention in this regard: contemporaneous filmmaking, individual films or filmmakers, national cinemas, occasionally historical representation as such in cinema. Thus, even while critiques of explanatory and referential claims of modern historicity were current, some scholars conversant with 1970s film theory and usually with those critiques were paying new kinds of attention to instances of historical representation in the history of filmic textuality.[12]

In this book I do not pretend to cover these three fronts in any systematic way, but at different points awareness of one or more of them is manifest, and examples of each will be invoked. At this point, I can say that, taken together, they indicate to me how difficult it is to think about film and media without thinking about notions of historicity in a modern sense. I mean not only that one must historicize cinema (or media), which is basic but too easily becomes a shibboleth that affects neither the conception of cinema, nor the conception of history with which one begins; I also mean to suggest the need to think about how the category of history penetrates the representational and discursive modes that have characterized the history of filmic textuality. Perhaps notions about historicity are in some way embedded in the dominant uses to which cinematic technology has been put, as well as how it has been theorized. And if trying to conceptualize the interpenetration of cinema and history can enrich film theory—and help historicize *it*—it may also contribute to the understanding of what it is to historicize.

My mode of proceeding is to interrogate examples and exemplary cases. The book is divided into two parts. Part I revolves around rethinking the centrality of modern temporality for film theory and film in relation to a number of concurrent Western cultural practices pegged onto the value of pastness, including professional, disciplined historiography. Chapter 1 is the "purest" reading of film theory in the book, though even this reading has elements that are more or less historiographic. It deals with the work of André Bazin, the canonical film theorist subject to the most critique in 1970s film theory. I argue for the coherence and force of his emphasis on cinematic indexicality, pastness, and a defensive subject, while still relating this to certain incoherences or contradictions in his logic around temporality and historicity.

Chapter 2 pulls back from the hermetic focus on one theorist, arguing that the conjunction of pastness, the indexical trace, and a defensive subject posited by Bazin can be found in a number of nineteenth- and twentieth-century cultural practices. These range from museum villages and theme parks to science-fiction literature and architectural debates. It borrows an opposition from the last to derive a polarity or dialectic between preservation and restoration, which defines the vicissitudes of indexicality on the plane of representation and subjectivity.

In chapter 3 I move to foundational conceptualizations of disciplinary historicity as professionalized in the university. This historicity

(a) seeks security in basing its claims about the past on a version of the indexical trace, namely primary documentary evidence; (b) embodies a distinctive temporal form; and (c) entails classic epistemological aporias that were well known among historians by the early twentieth century and that entailed a search for stable standpoints or subject-positions from which to comprehend time and pastness. One theme of Part I is that modern temporality poses threats, not only representationally and epistemologically, but socially. Chapter 3 begins and ends with reminders about the social history of labor time and leisure time, which leads back to cinema as social institution as well as text.

Part II consists of a series of case studies that treat historical representation as central to various aspects of the history of filmic representation. In chapter 4 I try to formulate a basic problematic of the inscription of history in mainstream cinema in order to trace out some vicissitudes of indexicality, which emerged as a key term for modern historiography in Part I. From this perspective, the rationalization of production in the classical studio system appears as a rationalization of the indexically imprinted detail. I reinflect canonical definitions of mainstream cinema established in 1970s film theory by defining it against the actuality film, a "primitive" or preclassical film genre that was suppressed in the normalization of the fictional feature film and the development of the Hollywood economic and sociocultural institution. I propose a dialectic between the documenting and the spectacularizing levels of the film image in the mainstream "system," and I conceive of levels of critical spectatorial "activity" expected by the films in order to control indexicality, even as they try to keep it in check in the name of centered social order. I speculatively conceptualize this activity on the basis of utopian projections of subjectivity in Barthes. While I draw on crucial aspects of 1970s film theory, it repressed the constellation of indexicality, the real and pastness, whose sociocultural importance is the basis of my argument here.

Chapters 5 through 7 turn to nonmainstream examples of texts and discourses bearing on cinematic aspirations to the real and historicity. Chapter 5 builds on the emphasis on the transition to the mainstream feature film in chapter 4. It is a close study of a preclassical film aimed at elaborating on the pressures toward centered sense-making as a means of controlling indexicality registered in its textual strategies.

Chapter 6 deals with discourses and conceptions of documentary cinema as a supposed alternative to mainstream film. Comparing disciplined historiography based on the document to documentary filmmaking as two practices aimed at conveying something of the real, this chapter argues that the classical documentary tradition was never predicated on a so-called naive realism. In this it evinces kinship to mainstream cinema, for it envisions a filmic indexicality seeking centered sense-making and a temporality controlled by a social or cultural expert. Certain kinds of postmodern cultural theory concerned with imaging miss the persistence of this process into the present. Certain kinds of leftist theorists and filmmakers quite properly embrace that process as an arena available for contestation.

In chapter 7, I examine a postcolonial film (*Ceddo*) as an example of a strategy taken by a different kind of "expert," the postcolonial intellectual or artist. This film textualizes what I call a radical historicity. Among other things, this involves a rethinking of temporality and historical representation in cinema, hence both sequenciation and indexicality, but it does not pretend to evade any of these. It is motivated to construct a radical historicity because of its explicit political positionality, which may also be conceived as a historiographic positionality.

In chapter 8, I consider contemporary polemical and theoretical discourses that radically oppose indexical and digital imaging as old and new. The discourse of the digital utopia embraces an absolutizing idea of radical novelty, crystallized in its claim to have surpassed indexicality and reference. Having already touched a little on television in chapter 6, I argue that a utopian conception of the digital sets up a cluster of social, economic, and ideological ideals that register the persistence of earlier media and modern historicity. In obscuring this persistence, the digital utopia must obscure the hybridity of historical temporality. This temporal hybridity, closely tied to the notion of a radical historicity, underlies modern historicity and must therefore be a component of any historicization.

Part I.   From Film to Historicity

CHAPTER 1

Subject, Ontology, and Historicity in Bazin

From Bazin to History

It has been said that in the 1940s, a new generation of film directors looked freshly at the possibilities of narrative cinema. Their innovations consisted of exploring various ways that stylistic and formal manipulations of camera and editing could be used to convey a sense, a feeling, for the material put or found in front of the camera for filming. This respect, not just for the integrity of subject matter but for what film scholars now call the profilmic field, had a wide and varying range of manifestations. On the one hand, in the Italian neorealism of a Rossellini or a De Sica, there were novel emphases on the possibilities of location shooting, the occasional use of nonprofessional actors, and a certain equanimity of moral tone. On the other hand, even in the highly controlled production situation of Hollywood studio cinema, new tendencies were developed following the lead of such directors as Welles and Wyler. When they used such devices as extreme deep focus cinematography with long take and/or traveling camera, this not only evinced stylistic experimentation with the continuity of time and space; it served significantly distinctive aesthetic and sometimes moral and political values.

Anyone familiar with film theory and scholarship will recognize this as a position developed by André Bazin concerning the filmmaking of his own day. One summary appears in his famous synoptic essay on the history of film style, "The Evolution of the Language of Cinema" (*WC*,

1:23–40).[1] In Bazin's view, even as early as the 1920s there had been a few directors whose preferred filmic strategies were centered on revealing qualities of the profilmic, such as Stroheim and Murnau; however, the leading aesthetic interests of silent cinema tended strongly toward a fascination with using it as malleable raw material. A major example of this latter tendency was the distorting, "Caligaristic" mise-en-scène of German expressionist cinema, but its most long-lasting impact could be traced in the broad outlines of a history of editing. The Soviet montage school, led by Eisenstein, demonstrated that meaning intended by the artist and signified in no individual shot or the profilmic in itself could be communicated by the determinate juxtaposition of shots. And by the 1930s, Hollywood cinema had perfected an analytic form of editing, which breaks down the profilmic into spatial fragments in order to subordinate it to the dramatic and psychological logic of the fiction (for example, the close-up of a doorknob slowly turning during a suspense-filled scene); yet it does impart a convincing illusion of spatiotemporal continuity, a kind of virtual image of a time and space that had never before existed. The economic power, aesthetic influence, and cultural unification of Hollywood cinema were such that Bazin labeled it "classical."

Bazin's concerns were by no means restricted to camera style. But he did celebrate the development of the long take in the narrative sound film, including films of Jean Renoir in the 1930s and culminating in its arrival as a viable stylistic option in 1940s Hollywood. Seeing the long take as a dialectical negation—a sublation—of the history of editing to that point, he believed that it acknowledged and exploited a general principle at the heart of all filmmaking. Editing inevitably interrupts the real spatiotemporal continuum imprinted as a shot on a strip of film, and classical editing rejoins chopped-up bits of that continuum into an illusory but dramatically full continuity. The choice between cutting and the long take is thus one between two attitudes toward profilmic reality, namely manipulation and respect. The first manifests the prerogative of the artist to plan a significance for the spectator prior to the encounter of camera with the profilmic, something evinced by the very style of the film. In that case, the task of the spectator is to derive or experience the filmmaker's communicative intentions. The other attitude, also evinced by the film's style, suggests greater respect for the actual existence of the profilmic prior to the act of producing meanings from it. In that case, there may be a semantic ambiguity, an excess over any meanings attributed by the filmmaker to the profilmic, and this in turn entails openings for the spectator's own apprehension of the encounter with the profilmic. In fact, a recognition of the indefiniteness, the ambiguity, of reality with respect to the meanings that humans inevitably pose for it, is the mark of a more authentic engagement with the real. The vicissitudes of this engagement, this realist impulse, ground the history of cinema.

It may seem late in the day to be reviewing this canonical position from the history of film theory. True, Bazin's writings were the single most innovative and influential combination of film theory and critical analysis produced anywhere during the 1940s and 1950s, and they remained a dominant theory of cinema in the 1960s. Furthermore, certain of his chief aesthetic and stylistic categories continued to appear for decades in formal analysis and critical work on films, as well as in textbooks and histories of cinema. Examples include the opposition between expressionism and realism; his distinctions between Soviet montage, analytic editing, and the long take; and his conception of Hollywood studio cinema as a classical cinema. A founder and early guiding intellect for *Cahiers du cinéma*, he is often treated as a kind of godfather of the epoch-making French New Wave. A great contemporary spokesperson for Italian neorealism, his careful explications of the various projects of that movement within the history of cinema are still major text-critical and historiographic achievements. The same is true for many of his studies of other movements and directors. Furthermore, although he emphasized the stylistic response of individual artists to a complex, multifaceted reality, Bazin never looked down on what he saw as the workshop atmosphere of mainstream filmmaking. He therefore could lay the groundwork for (and with reservations participate in) that massive revaluation of Hollywood studio cinema called auteurism. The list could go on.

But my inquiry in this book deals with relations among conceptions of historicity, film theory, and cinema. Even given the "historical" importance and resonance of his arguments, why begin with Bazin? There are at least two preliminary answers to this question. The first stems from the fact that since the late 1960s, a rejection of Bazin and the general kind of attitude his work manifests has tended to structure dominant film-theoretical conceptions. I believe the terms of this rejection were complicit with the difficulties 1970s film theory had conceiving of historicity and dialectically taking into account the resistances, impulses, and opportunities historiography offers to film theory. This rejection has affected socially and politically engaged film theory since then. More will be said about this, but in one sense, this first chapter is a reconsideration or nuancing of film theory's opposition to Bazin, which was institutionalized in the 1970s.

The second reason has to do with my sense that Bazin's thought is entwined with historical thinking in profound and exemplary ways. Of course, his theoretical and critical formulations usually position films within specific historical contexts, treating even the most specific elements of cinema as temporally localized. But more indicative is his general conception of the history of filmic textuality as an ongoing, never-completed dialectical sequence of representational strategies attempting to move toward total flexibility and completeness in encountering the real. I would emphasize two related temporal assumptions of this mode of thinking: first, the present is always already different in some respect from the past, and second, reality is definitionally temporalized, in the sense that it always involves change or at least the consistent potential for change. In chapter 3, we will see that these are fundamental assumptions of modern historicity.

In addition, the notoriously realist impulse of Bazin's film theory is itself congruent with a historicizing cast of mind. For present purposes, this point can be made terminologically. Let us say that any *historicity* is realized as a combination of two moments. One is *historiography*, the writing of history ("historio-graphy"). The other is *history*, the actual past that the writing claims to convey. In that case, knowledge about history can only be constructed and conveyed through historiography. But clearly there might be different approaches to historiography, and in any given context, only a certain mode or range of modes of historiography is likely to be conceived as legitimate. Thus, different modes of writing history often imply different ways of conceiving of or understanding history. There may also be a variety of conceptions of relations between historiography and history, which means a variety of historicities.

However, there is one constant: historiography always purports to be referential. That is, the construction that is history is necessarily to be read against some standard of the real. This is so even if historiography is envisioned as an art rather than a science, or (as in more recent formulations) as a narrative text rather than a report or list, or as a discourse rather than a transparent representation, or as a figurative act rather than a denotative one. It does not matter how much a text claiming to relate or analyze history is made up of formal, aesthetic, or discursive procedures associated with the imaginary, the fictional, or the rhetorical; nor does it matter how self-conscious or reflexive it is about its own inevitable inadequacies. If its overt ambition is to be historiographic, then by definition it must be claiming to tell us something about events, persons, states of affairs, and/or discourses that had some type of *actual* existence at some point in the past. Otherwise it would have to be read as, precisely, a fictional text. Let me emphasize that there are many degrees and notions of reference. My point is only that any attempt to conceptualize historicity in theory or practice must explicitly or implicitly acknowledge the referential ambitions of any historiography.

There are other elements that should be added, especially the concern with pastness. But when an insistence on asserting referentiality combines with a grounding emphasis on temporalization and the constant potential for change, one is in the realm of historicities (or at least, as later chapters will specify, modern historicities). Bazin's film theory is, broadly speaking, on intellectual terrains where modern intellectuals have conceptualized historicity. In this chapter, I reread Bazin not to "recover" or "save" him, but to highlight and interrogate certain of his central categories and emphases and the logic organizing them. This will introduce, at a fairly high level of abstraction, a description of cinema that will lead toward imbrications of cinema and historicity.

A Film Theorist from France: Subjects and Objects

And so, we can begin this reading by recalling the rejection of Bazin. In the 1970s, the field of film theory was explosively remapped. Some of the chief impulses in cultural theory in which 1970s film theory participated are well known in film scholarship; they include structuralism, semiotics, Althusserian Marxism, some tendencies in poststructuralism, psychoanalytic theory, and feminism. A network of arguments and theoretical discourses established central debates and discussions around such problems as subject-positioning, the filmic enunciation, ideology, desire, sexual difference and sexuality, and so forth. One thing this internally diverse network of arguments and discourses almost always assumed in common was a principled antirealist conception of representation and textuality.

There had been previous critiques of Bazin, but Bazin-bashing now became widespread and even fashionable in French, British, and U.S. film theory and scholarship. These attacks ranged from complete dismissal to measuring a respectful distance from his positions. Some writers mapped his work onto bourgeois and/or reactionary ideals, or charged it with being inextricably implicated in theological or undesirably metaphysical premises. Some subjected it to logical analysis and discovered debilitating internal contradictions. Most complexly, his realist cinema aesthetic was reviewed at the service of an argument that any realist theory must hypostatize human subjectivity out of the very processes that form and define it. In this atmosphere, it is not surprising that even those who found useful elements in Bazin's work tended to detach themselves from his overall arguments and positions, arguing, for example, that his partial insights had to be integrated into a more comprehensive theory that excluded objectionable elements of his thought. Sometimes, for example, Bazin's immersion in certain forms of French phenomenology was said to give his work a certain descriptive advantage, but no explanatory value.[2]

Since then, Bazin's notion that cinema has a special referential capacity has most often seemed outdated, even quaint. But the insistent film-theoretical return to Bazin as the "other" to be attacked was also a kind of tribute. Somehow, Bazin's history of style, his critical work, and his explications of realism in film, beginning with what he calls an ontology of the image, have all remained required reading for anyone with a serious interest in cinema. Even given his rhetorical utility as an opponent, the repeated appearance of Bazin when referentiality was under such suspicion in critical and theoretical discourses is striking.

Despite local disagreements, the following reading of Bazin is informed by such commentaries on him. But dismissal of Bazin has too often become a facile, settled premise, rather than an earned conclusion. Insofar as my own reading includes critique, it does not start from an initiating condemnation or an unmediated outlining of contradiction, but rather from the forms of coherence by which Bazin's writings can claim our attention—appeal to us—as theoretically sophisticated. It is all too easy, having found something with which to disagree in a position or large-scale argument, to stop thinking about it. But what is then missed is the relation between forms of coherence and contradictions that can place an argument symptomatically, which is also to say "historically." (That I must use this last term, which is an object of interrogation, may itself be considered such a symptom.)

Now, the claim to coherence of Bazin's project is often said to begin from its stance as a phenomenological theory of film. Bazin established the mature foundations of his phenomenological view of cinema with the publication of "The Ontology of the Photographic Image" and "The Myth of Total Cinema" in 1945 and 1946. Some care is needed in understanding this "ontology." Any phenomenology involves an account of a relation between a human subject and objects with which it is concerned. But the "ontological" basis Bazin established in these essays has sometimes been too quickly read as a kind of technological finality, whereby the objective world (materiality) is directly captured by the lens (*objectif*) of the photographic/cinematic apparatus for the subjective (human).

It is useful to recall that 1946 also happened to be the year that Jean-Paul Sartre's noted lecture, "Existentialism Is a Humanism," was published. In this lecture, even while insisting on his radical differences with

Descartes, Sartre said: "[A]t the point of departure, there cannot be any truth other than this, 'I think, therefore, I am.'" Dudley Andrew has emphasized that Bazin was conducting a debate with Malraux and Sartre.[3] However, what is important here is the common territory that was the ground of this debate: the *activity* of the subject, the central premise of all phenomenologies. If Bazin's theory invokes the classic subject-object relation so familiar in the history of continental philosophy, a phenomenological resolution of that split would take place on the ground of subjective intentionality. That is, any reading of Bazin on the image should begin from Bazin's view of the subject. Furthermore, this would have to be an intending subject, in the sense of philosophical phenomenology.

In the 1970s, the need for a "theory of the subject" became something of a catchphrase in Anglo-American film theory. It became so as a result of the intervention of continental sources, most intensively French textual theory and philosophy, but not only that. For example, Jacques Lacan's work (where awareness of Hegel is manifest) was a crucial source for psychoanalytic theories of the filmic subject. Lacan makes the Cartesian cogito an explicit target, seeking to divert not only psychoanalytic thought, but also the course of French intellectual history by demystifying the allegedly fundamental nature of that category. On the other hand, in the institutional and pedagogical processes of the Anglo-American tradition, the role of the Cartesian cogito as an explicit, formal heritage was a less immediate issue than the practical dominance of empiricist and positivist standards in the human sciences generally, and this affected readings of Bazin. Thus, while certain ways of receiving Bazin were not exclusive to Anglo-American commentaries, they could sometimes become accentuated in them.

For example, in a 1976 critique that is enlightening for emphasizing the place of subjectivity, Colin MacCabe argued that Bazin's realism posits an empiricist subject, which values direct perception of an object as the basis of secure knowledge. MacCabe objected that by thus making knowledge a matter of static transparency between subject and object, Bazin reifies the subject out of the processes that form it. A counterexample is the 1971 critique of Bazin by the continental materialist, Jean-Louis

Comolli, who read Bazin's "The Evolution of the Language of Cinema" in terms of the *search* by the subject, faced with exteriority, for secure definition and positioning. Despite his heavily politicized conceptual framework, the antirealist materialist Comolli places the antirealist film theorist Jean Mitry under even more severe critique than the realist Bazin. According to Comolli, Mitry is formalist and technicist (in the English-speaking world, we might say empiricist and positivist); yet, while Bazin is a philosophical idealist, his idealism at least has the crucial virtue of exposing the struggle of the subject as a central issue. On the other hand, MacCabe is able to make an argument that seems especially pertinent in the English-speaking theoretical tradition by placing the term *empiricism* under critique and applying it to Bazin. But this polemical pertinence prevents MacCabe from fully confronting existential phenomenology in one of its founding claims, which Comolli recognizes: the primacy of the activity of the subject.

An opposition between continental and Anglo-American rejections of Bazin should not be overstated. The real point is to emphasize the relevance of the mode of thought in which Bazin worked. The subject's struggle for security, knowledge, and/or position is a problem not only for a psychoanalytic or social subject, but also for the philosophical subject. It was a central issue posed in French philosophy from Descartes through at least existentialism and much of poststructuralism (often, however, in a negational mode), and it is Bazin's intellectual "context."

This is to begin considering Bazin from the classic opposition or relationship between subject and object. Bazin's theory of cinema contends that film has special capacities to convey something of reality, and it is certainly true that one must always read him with awareness of his emphasis on the pre-givenness of the concrete, objective real. However, another fundamental aspect of Bazin's theoretical work needs emphasis, and I would put it as strongly as possible: the processes by which human subjectivity approaches the objective constitute the basis of his position.

Of course, Bazin believes in the necessary coexistence and interaction of both objective and subjective aspects in the making and receiving/experiencing of films. However, what should not be ignored are the terms of this interaction. Bazin is quite consistent in his phenomenological solution to the subject-object split. For his phenomenology, the subject's *projections* toward exteriority are definitive, and Bazin can almost always be read as analyzing the status of the objective *for* the subject. That is, "objective" here can be put in quotes with greater clarity, for the "objective" is always inflected by the "subjective," never available except through the processes of the latter. Bazin often expresses this with the terminology of abstract and concrete, which should again remind us of his continental philosophical heritage: the world can never present itself or write itself apart from the abstracting drive of the subject to find meaning; the pure, brute concrete real in its totality and apart from the intentionality of a subject is simply unavailable as such to humans. (This should not be confused with a quasi-automatic perceptual/mental processing of information, as in gestalt psychology, to which some important phenomenologists appealed.)[4]

This complicates Bazin's film theory and any realist aesthetic that it proposes or that is attributed to it. Bazin's theory is famous for arguing that cinema manifests a special, intimate relation to reality. But for this theory, any answer to the question "What Is Cinema?" could just as well begin from the *limitations* of objective cinematic "realism." Illustrations can be found in some of his most important critical work, such as "The French Renoir" and "An Aesthetic of Reality: Neo-realism":

> Given the fact that this movement toward the real [i.e., "realism"] can take a thousand different routes, the apologia for "realism" *per se*, strictly speaking, means nothing at all. The movement is valuable only insofar as it brings increased meaning (itself an abstraction) to what is created. . . . There is no point in rendering something realistically unless it is to make it more meaningful in an abstract sense. In this paradox lies the progress of the movies.[5]

> The same event, the same object, can be represented in various ways. Each representation discards or retains various of the qualities that permit us to recognize the object on the screen. Each introduces, for didactic or aesthetic

reasons, abstractions that operate more or less corrosively and thus do not permit the original to subsist in its entirety. At the conclusion of this inevitable and necessary "chemical" action, for the initial reality there has been substituted an illusion of reality composed of a complex of abstraction (black and white, plane surface), of conventions (the rules of montage, for example), and of authentic reality. It is a necessary illusion. (*WC*, 2:27, my emphasis)

Such passages would seem to stand in direct contradiction to Bazin's notorious discovery of cinematic perfection in *Bicycle Thieves*, "no more cinema." However, even that phrase, virtually always quoted out of the context of the essay and even the sentence in which it appears, refers to "the perfect *aesthetic illusion* of reality" (*WC*, 2:60, my emphasis). So there is something inevitably illusory in this apparently complete concreteness. Given the necessary abstraction, the physical-technical limitations of even cinema (e.g., black and white, plane surface), Bazin insists realism is an aesthetic, or rather, various realisms are various aesthetics. If readers are sometimes confused on this point despite Bazin's explicit insistence, it is perhaps because Bazin seems to propose that one can distinguish among various kinds of abstraction from reality, and that some illusions of reality are to be valued over others. Is this not finally the point of his most influential essay, "The Evolution of the Language of Cinema," where the final paragraph proposes as exemplar neither Rossellini nor Welles, but Hitchcock(!), whose stylistic flexibility serves as an example of what the progressive realisms of the 1940s have made possible (*WC*, 1:39)?

Bazin is a master of stylistic commentary, but formalistic distinctions can never be absolute for him; nor can the standards differentiating among kinds of illusions be held to an absolute criterion, a single view of reality. Even his noted postulate of reality's "ambiguity" works, among other things, to refuse the finality of constant criteria. (This parallels his film-historical tenet that cinema will never quite achieve its own telos of grasping the real in all its concreteness.) But if formal and stylistic procedures cannot provide an actual, unmediated access to the objective, then the basis for evaluating those procedures is located elsewhere than in the relation of text to its referent. Bazin's idea of referentiality must go back to the processes of the subject, its modes of postulating and approaching "objectivity."

Thus, if we read Bazin in terms of the subject-object opposition, there is a fundamental move that must always be kept in mind: the "no more cinema" is by and for the subject. Bazin generally assumes a "subjective" assigning of significance to the concrete real, an activity that is abstract, but inevitable with respect to the concrete. But the opposite term of this abstraction from the real is not an absolute concrete objectivity that cinema can somehow make immediately available. It is rather a subjective striving, a subjective investment in the image precisely as "objectivity." This subjective projection is what serves Bazin's ontology in defining a cinematically specific phenomenological intentionality; and it is the stake of his analyses and his history of filmic style. It is a premise that can help maintain the complex interest of his work even after 1970s film theory.

Space and Time: From Perspective to the Indexical Trace

For example, consider what Bazin has to say about the import of Quattrocento perspective in his foundational essay, "The Ontology of the Photographic Image." This is useful in evaluating his current status, because central, one-point rectilinear perspective has often been put forward as a key format for representing depth on a two-dimensional plane, and for three decades it has often been invoked in film-theoretical discussions of realisms, illusionisms, and basic spectatorial apprehensions. In 1970s film theory, figures such as Comolli and Stephen Heath made claims for its dominance in image technology (from the Renaissance camera obscura to "normal" cinema lenses). They connected this persistence to the appeal of a "centered" subject-position, whose geometrical construction in perspective they understood through certain kinds of historical materialism and psychoanalysis. In this kind of 1970s film theory, perspective becomes a visualized epistemological ideal, manifesting a standard of reliable visual knowledge and the imagination of a stable subjective position, which is incorporated into cinema even as perspectival composition is integrated with other elements of filmic space, such as movement.[6]

It is not surprising that those who objected to 1970s film theory made perspective a major area of engagement. For example, David Bordwell has proposed a cognitivist understanding of perspective as just one possible perceptual-cognitive schema, which spectators experience primarily as an inferential comprehension of "a layout of objects in an environment" rather than as a socioculturally generalized or idealized structure of subjectivity. This means that even in normalized photographic or narrative film images, the depth cues of a visual "layout" can diverge from central perspectival projection.[7] Another recent alternative is Jonathan Crary's more or less Foucauldian position. While agreeing with 1970s film theorists such as Comolli that perspective constructs an ideal subjectivity, or position of "the observer," he argues that by the time cinema appeared in the nineteenth century, the Renaissance spectatorial ideals emphasized in 1970s film theory had already eroded. The notion that it was possible to objectively or reliably map space according to the procedures of scientific optics (philosophically associated with the camera ob-scura and its successor mechanisms) had been replaced by another, more relativistic model. This model was associated with research on perceptual illusions, the bodily temporality of perception, and so forth. It was part of a discursive field staked on the thesis that there is always a subjective shaping of objectivity in visual and other perception, as opposed to a single ideal position of knowledge.[8]

These recent positions on perspective and cinema differ on many contentious questions, from how spectators appropriate representational artifacts, such as films, to the status and nature of cultural norms in cinema. But notice that they have something in common: even when they analyze "cues" for perception, all three tend to assume a distinction between the apprehension of actual spatial depth and its perspectival representation. They must therefore account for spectators' finding enough in the basic iconic design of the image to invest in it as a sign or record of space. That is, discussions of perspective have tended to define its appeal beginning from the comparison of "real" and pictured space, even if that comparison is ultimately to be bypassed. Bordwell explicitly calls on cognitive psychology, but at points even Heath draws on Arnheim's gestaltist account for a description of the experience of the film image. One would expect Crary to bracket comparison of perspectival and real space because he treats all accounts of perception as components of discursive formations; nevertheless, he ends up depending on this comparison simply because the theories of illusion on which he draws depend on it.[9]

There is something different about the function of perspective in Bazin's theory, however, and this difference leads to the heart of his claims about cinema and referentiality. It is true that passages can be found where his writings deal with the photographic and/or cinematic image by reference to perceptual-spatial accuracy or lack of accuracy. What needs highlighting, however, is how the centrality of this concern is ultimately diminished in the overall framework of his theory. In fact, the function of perspective in Bazin's theory invites us to displace consideration of the special appeal of cinematic "realism" from spatial similarity or dissimilarity between image and world to issues of temporality.

In "The Ontology of the Photographic Image," Bazin actually seems at first to exemplify the view taken up by 1970s film theory and opposed by Bordwell and Crary. He presents the development of Quattrocento perspective as a key moment in the history of the representational arts, and the camera obscura as the direct ancestor of the photographic camera. In the history of culture, according to Bazin, the power of this system for painting does at first lie in its apparent spatial accuracy. Since photography and cinema can replicate it, they serve as automated, "superior" developments of perspective and thereby liberate painting from achievements founded on spatial accuracy. Thus, Bazin describes perspectival representation of space as "the first scientific and already, in a sense, mechanical system of reproduction" (WC, 1:11). And yet, a basic thesis of his other crucial "ontological" essay, "The Myth of Total Cinema," is that scientificity had little to do with the development of cinematic technology, which was instead motivated by a mythic ideal of complete reproduction of the world. Is there a contradiction between these two essays?

Actually, even in "The Ontology of the Photographic Image," Bazin's early comments on perspective turn out to be ironic. We have already seen that Bazin was not afraid to remind his readers of the limits of cinematic representation, one of which is the distinction between a real space and the planar surface of the film image. In "The Ontology of the Photographic Image," however, he draws a surprising conclusion from this. The importance of perspective as road to the real diminishes only a few paragraphs after its introduction. Bazin explains that with the dominance of perspectival representation,

> [p]ainting was forced, as it turned out, to offer us illusion, and this illusion was reckoned sufficient unto art. Photography and cinema, on the other hand, are discoveries that satisfy once and for all and in its very essence, our obsession with realism. (*WC*, 1:12)

In the distinction between likeness or mere illusion and the satisfaction of an obsession lies a key to Bazin's thought. The terms of satisfying an obsession can never be decided on the side of a concrete object; such satisfaction can by definition only be decided on the side of the *subject* whose obsession it is.[10] Bazin consistently associates the need for realism with what he here calls "psychology" rather than "aesthetics"; hence "reality" itself is not the primary term of his ontology of the image, except insofar as it is an object of the obsession. An emphasis on the subject ("psychology") is what allows Bazin to indicate a surprising break between perceptual likeness to reality (usually associated with perspectival illusion) and the ontological status of the photographic image. That ontology is in operation, Bazin tells us, "no matter how fuzzy, distorted or discolored" the image may be (*WC*, 1:14).

The impression of visual likeness through perspective, then, becomes merely a kind of prop, historically necessary for the development of the mechanically produced image. This historical function can almost be described by saying that perspective provides a sort of credible code— to put it in necessarily oxymoronic terms, a reliable illusion—whose credibility can then be lent to automatically produced images. But then, by a peculiar inversion, it ultimately becomes the mechanical process that was previously a supplement to the spatial illusion of likeness, which, once established, lends *its* credibility, a new kind of credibility, to the spatial

distinction, what is necessary to the special credibility of automatically produced images is not an apparently unmediated record of how reality appears, but rather markers of indexicality itself, which signify the presence of the referent at some point in the sign production. But this would mean that that special credibility depends on a certain prior knowledge on the part of the spectator—not so much of what the object actually looked like, but of how signs of a certain type or appearance are generated and what such genres of signs look like. The process of diffusing that prior knowledge generally, of making known the presuppositions necessary to the workings of indexical signification, is not directly addressed by Bazin. It is possible to attribute it to cultural configurations. In chapters 2 and 3 I will attempt to explore some major cultural underpinnings of indexicality.

For now, consider a related aspect of this line, a point about temporality that bears directly on photography and cinema. Some of Peirce's examples of an indexical sign, such as a weather vane or a sundial, attest to the action of a referent occurring at the moment one apprehends the sign. Others, such as the rolling gait of a sailor, require a reading based on a kind of history of the sign, for at least some of the referential presence occurred before the time of the reading. When Bazin compares cinema to such indexical signs as a fingerprint, a mold, a death mask, or the Holy Shroud of Turin, his examples consistently turn out to be the kind in which the referent was present in the past. I will call this subcategory of sign the *indexical trace*. Photographic and filmic images have normally been apprehended as indexical traces, for their spatial field and the objects depicted were in the camera's "presence" at some point prior to the actual reading of the sign. The indexical trace is a matter of pastness.[14]

This already makes it appear that the image is in some way "historical." The spectator is supposed to read pastness in the image, not only a past as a signified (as in, say, a historical painting), but also a past of the signifier, which is in turn that of a signifer-referent relation as a production. This is consistent with lessening the importance of a comparison between perception of film space and perception of real space. The referential credibility of indexicality assumes something absent from any immediate perception: a different *when* from that of the spectator. Since this different *when* cannot be immediately present, it must be "filled in," "inferred," "provided" by the subject. Thus, if indexicality is a crucial aspect of the image, we must assume some active capacity at work beyond perceptual activities, be it memory, mental activities, subconscious investment, rational inference, the effectivity of cultural discourses, or whatever. But this capacity must include a knowledge about how the signifier was supposed to be produced.

To summarize: Bazin must assume that the special credibility of photographic and cinematic images is based on the subject's prior knowledge of how any such images are produced. Furthermore, that production is apprehended as coming from some past moment, which makes temporality a crucial component of the process for the subject. Bazin links both of these assumptions to the idea of a subject obsessively predisposed to invest belief in such an image.

Subject and Representation

This tie between subjective obsession and temporality is crystallized in Bazin's most famous metaphor, the "mummy complex," with which he begins "The Ontology of the Photographic Image." In this trope, the ancient Egyptian mummies reveal a universal, unconscious human need that all cultures must confront through ritual, religion, art, or some other way. This is the need for some fantastic defense against time. For any human subject, the passage of time is the approach of death, the ultimate material limitation on subjectivity. On the one hand, the existential desire to defeat death is clearly an impossible one; hence, it can only continue to exist as an obsession, not a rational project. On the other hand, with greater or lesser degrees of conscious purpose, individuals in different cultures require imaginative indications of the possibility of defeating time to defend their existence, their subjectivities: "Civilization cannot ... cast out the bogy of time" (*WC*, 1:10). It can only construct modes of coming to grips with it, of engaging it, of countering it. The mummies thus supply Bazin with a carefully chosen symptom, a founding desire.

Within a mode of argument that appeals to origins, Egyptian culture provides him with a handy, quasi-figurative starting point for Western art history and, more pertinently, for a sketch of the history of visual media. This subjective project—or subjective projection—finds increasingly intensive satisfactions in a long-term, progressive succession of representational technologies. Bazin jumps from the mummies and sculpture to Renaissance painting, the camera obscura, photography, and cinema. But the trope of the mummy complex thereby generalizes the subjective project that grounds that sketch all the way back to the foundation of the plastic arts and image culture. (Thus, while this putative origin of Western visual representation is located in a religious context, it is not necessarily a Christian one, since the model is a paganism.)[15]

The first vehicle of this subjective project is maintenance of the body against decay in the context of a belief in an afterlife, amounting to an obsession with the problem of "embalming time." Thus, we can call the founding obsession *preservative*. The history of the representational arts can then be seen as sublimations of this impossible impulse to defeat death:

> It is no longer a question of survival after death, but of a larger concept, the creation of an ideal world in the likeness of the real, with its own temporal destiny . . . , man's . . . last word in the argument with death by means of the form that endures. (*WC*, 1:10)

When photography appears in this historical development, its indexicality adds the appeal of endurance through time to the impression of likeness in painted perspective. Crucially, "likeness" is not given epistemological or cognitive value in itself, but rather is being invoked as a support for fundamental needs of the subject vis-à-vis time. And cinema adds duration to the embalming of a single temporal instant in still photography. As Bazin puts it in "The Myth of Total Cinema," this makes cinema the realization of a perennial compulsion, a virtually ageless dream of perfect realism, which would have to include duration. But, as with any wish fulfillment, such preservation of the real object is projectively converted into the preservation of the subject. Always, for Bazin, cinema achieves its specificity through the relations of the subject.

But also, and more complexly, if its character as indexical trace gives the automatically produced image a special appeal, this appeal is inseparable from the limitations of such images with respect to the perfect reproduction of reality. As we have already seen, Bazin freely acknowledges these limitations. In fact, since it is grounded on subjective obsession, Bazin's ontology could not exist without a *gap* between referent and signifier; hence his oft-noted assertion of an asymptotic relation between film and reality. This gap is determined by the inevitable abstraction from reality inherent in the effort to form representations that make contact with it. This gap serves central functions in Bazinian realism. It is precisely this gap that is filled in variable manifestations of human imagination, which are in effect subjective projections. This imagination is obsessively drawn to discover types of signs that can be invested with the credibility of the real in order to maintain itself. The subjective project requires an objective gap as a field for its actions and realizations.

The mummy complex and the break between film and reality are the interlinked premises leading to Bazin's accounts of various components of the filmic process. They ground his accounts of both spectatorship and filmmaking or authorship. At the level of spectatorship, it is from the desire to counter threats to its own existence, its own being, that the spectator is drawn to investing an unprecedented credibility in the image in spite of its perceptible differences from the referent in full, three-dimensional space; the spectator may thus affirm his or her own subjective being.[16] In a parallel way, Bazin's writings on the history of filmic textuality suppose that the artist responds to this universally anxious condition of the human subject by artistic means, especially through his or her style, including narrative form. These necessarily embody an attitude toward the world, since they respond to the objective inadequacies of the signifier (the gap between film and reality) in the face of the subjective desire for a fantastic control over materiality (locus of causation of death).

So what is usually regarded as Bazin's ontology describes a subjective intentionality for automatically produced images based on a preservative obsession. Now, of course this means that the relations between such images and the physical world remain crucial for his theory: the special appeal to the subject rests on the preexistence of concrete objects, a pre-existence offered by their preservation via indexicality. Nevertheless, once it is emphasized that the referential force of such concreteness exists only for a subject, the relation of indexical trace to the preexistent takes on a broader function. It can become a pervasive *ideal* or privileged model—that is, a manifestation of certain ambitions of subjectivity vis-à-vis represen-tation beyond the basic level of the relation of a film image to its referent.

There are many illustrations of Bazin's recourse to this relation as an ideal representational model rather than a literal description at key points in specific arguments. In his 1955 defense of Rossellini, for example, he defines Italian neorealism not by the physical appearance of the image and its likeness to some reality, but by the subjectivity of the artist, which (he believes) necessarily filters out aspects of literal reality. He then expli-cates the consciousness of the neorealist by analogy to the indexicality of a black-and-white photograph: "a true imprint of reality, a kind of lumi-nous mold in which color simply does not figure" (*WC*, 2:98).

One of the most striking and complex examples of indexicality as ideal model is his approach to literary adaptation as it unrolls in the dense, revealing essay, "The Stylistics of Robert Bresson." In it, Bazin's praise of Bresson's realism in literary adaptation occurs as a variation on the gen-eral theoretical and critical themes for which he is noted, beginning from his famous opposition between a predetermining, substitutive use of the profilmic and an ex post facto respect for its preexistence; however, the novel figures in the place of physical reality. According to Bazin, Bresson renders Bernanos's novel, *Diary of a Country Priest*, as if it were the face of an actor, that is, (1) an objective preexistent, a "pure reality." Now, by the conventions of narrative cinema, faces can be filmed, but not Bernanos's writing, at least not in any literal sense. Consequently, we have (2) a gap between the filmic sign and a literal transmission of its object; hence, as always in Bazin, (3) abstraction from the preexistent reality is unavoidable. But (4) the stylistics of Bresson fill in the gap by manifest-ing a subjective relation to the novel. This relation is not the artistic sub-ject of Bresson's assertion of his own capacity to construct a substitute for the preexisting reality, and he does not impose his own categorical preconceptions. Such overweening assertions of the artist's subjectivity are found in a negative example, the film adaptations of Aurenche and Bost that Bazin denigrates.[17] Rather, while Bresson's stylistics inevitably embody a mode of abstraction, it is a mode of abstraction aimed at minimizing the gap by evincing (5) respect for the prior, independent existence of the novel and through this subjective relation of respect, the film establishes a special bond with it.

Interestingly, a certain specificity having to do with time devolves on cinema in order to justify the analogy between adapted novel and the profilmic. Bazin writes that a film about a painting "cannot pretend [either] to be a substitute for the original or to share its identity." But novel and film "are both narrative arts, that is to say temporal arts...." This recalls the differentiations among media with respect to the subjective ambitions of indexicality in the ontological essays. But also, note how indexicality ("share its identity") remains an ideal pervading even an argument about literary adaptation. For Bazin, Bresson demonstrates that it is possible "for the existence of the novel to be affirmed by the film, and not dissolved into it. It is hardly enough to say of this work ... that it is in essence faithful to the original because, to begin with, it *is* the novel" (*WC*, 1: 142–43).

The hyperbole of "it *is* the novel" corresponds to Bazin's more noted hyperbole about *Bicycle Thieves*, "no more cinema." The central grounds in Bazin's account of the experience of reality through cinema, and hence of an auteur's style, is not physical reproduction, but the nature of the relation of a preexistent to the film. That relation is inseparable from preservation as an obsessive issue for the subject. Thus, the Bazinian questions for adaptation may be phrased in a way consistent with his entire mode of thought: what are the various sorts of subjective projection toward the literary work, as they can be read within the history of filmic textuality?

Bazin's classic history of filmic style in "The Evolution of the Language of Cinema" begins with a distinction between faith in the image and faith in reality. The essay is mostly about cinematic "language," considered as historically shifting stylistic and formal systems, which must be employed given the unavoidable minimum of abstraction from the object in any representational instance. The dialectical drama of the history is that this cinematic language is always confronted by "faith." Or rather, the kind of faith in operation is readable in the progressive evolution of formal and stylistic systems, such as that of editing, through its histori-cally significant strategies to the long take. But one can here recall Bertrand Russell's remark to the effect that faith is belief in something for which there is no evidence. Since the ground for Bazin's position is an account of a generalized subjective obsession, he must finally make imag-ination, fantasy, the illogical a root of any true realism. In "The Ontology of the Photographic Image," he even remarks on the affinity of photogra-phy with surrealism (*WC*, 1:15–16).

Faith can move mountains—into the movie theater. This is why Bazin believes it is legitimate to invoke the fantastic and the religious as kindred to those forces subtending the work of both the most distinctive realist artist and the spectator, and why what Bazin sometimes calls "psy-chology" is the foundation of his ontology. It explains the extraordinary subjective investment in indexicality that is presupposed in his theory and his critical work. But if the irrational leap of faith is the basis of Bazin's ontology of the cinema, then what must follow are accounts of the specific vicissitudes of this fundamental subjective investment. Bazin's construc-tion of an evolutionary account of "film language" and his often brilliant analyses of the stylistics of individual filmmakers begin from here. He also treats this intentionality as having various manifestations as a collective, a cultural and/or social, phenomenon that he often calls "myth," to which I will shortly return.

But at this point, simply note the supple utility of Bazin's mode of proceeding from the phenomenologist's concern with an essential subjec-tive project: the theorist of cinema's basic realism became the most influ-ential producer of stylistic categories for two generations of historians and critics, as well as the godfather of auteurism. The herald of the special significance of photography and cinema for the modern world did so by means of sympathy for supposedly timeless needs met by fantasy, faith, religion, and myth.

A Temporalized Stylistics

Reading Bazin from the centrality of subjectivity leads one to emphasize the founding place of the preservative obsession and the mummy complex in his corpus; that is, time becomes central to his overall theory. If we turn from his theoretical premises to his analyses of films, this may seem odd, and not only because many film and media commentators generally and vaguely associate "realism" with spatial resemblance. It is also the case that some of Bazin's most important work can leave the impression that he is giving analytic priority precisely to spatial configurations and manipulations in film, as in his much-cited metaphor of the film frame as window. Indeed, Bazin's sensitivity to mise-en-scène and camera work points up the importance of those instances when Bazin defines spectatorship spatially. One need only recall his canonical and controversial thesis that the spatial continuity of deep-focus long takes in a Welles or Wyler film brings the spectator's vision into a regime of greater spatial freedom than in classical continuity editing, because it makes available a degree of choice as to where in the image to look. Bazin argues that the greater range of choice places the spectator in a more "realistic" relation with the profilmic, because actuality is only ever available to the human in an ambiguous state. He also attributes moral and political significance to this strategy.[18]

Yet, even where Bazin at last seems to illustrate his contentions about deep focus by comparison to perception of real space, time is introduced to subtend the activities of the subject. Consider the following from his crucial 1948 analysis of William Wyler: "In reality, in fact, our eye adjusts spatially, like a lens, to the important point of the event which interests us; it proceeds by successive investigations, *it introduces a sort of temporalization on a second level by analysis of the space of a reality, itself evolving in time*."[19]

To say such a passage demonstrates that for Bazin space and time are inseparable would be correct enough, but bland and not very informative. However, the way temporalization is introduced here—the spectator chooses when as well as where to look—is an aspect of the metaphysical *partis pris* related to the ambiguity of reality, in the sense of its unfixedness.[20]

Any real existent in space—the object—is by definition in a temporalized state, a state of change. Given that *partis pris*, a happy coincidence of subjective processes and object seems possible, for the perception/apprehension of the concrete on the part of the subject is also a perpetual experience of temporal flux. Epistemologically, this proposition might enable a correspondence or reflection theory in the structures of subject and object on the common ground of time. This subjective given—the sense of time passing, of duration and the constancy of transformation—is also a sense of the actual structure or founding process of reality.

Yet, Bazin's account of the subject in his ontology, crystallized in the mummy complex, provides a more complex, challenging, and telling extrapolation. Bazin's subject is essentially defensive. Time passing, duration, and change are exactly what Bazin's ontological subject is driven to *disavow*, for they raise the problem of death. The lure of automatically produced images is attributable to subjective obsession precisely because time is a threat. It threatens the stable existence of the subject (death, decay) as well as the object (degradation, transformation). Hence, the paradox: On the one hand, automatically produced images fundamentally appeal to a desire that the concrete be preserved, stopped in time as reality. This desire leads to the special attraction and epistemological possibilities of cinema, insofar as it can move the subject toward opening itself to a revelatory experience of reality. But on the other hand, reality itself evolves in time, and is even perceived in the flow of time, which means that reality in some sense goes against that which motivates the desire to engage it.

This may be why respect for reality is such a cinematic value for Bazin. In the genuine realist attitude the impulse to control time is both exploited and checked. That is, the desire to master reality is activated yet somehow sublimated, so that the self-protective mechanisms motivating the projection toward the real are diverted from their defensive stance. Realism becomes an act of heroism. But this also throws into doubt the idea of realism as correspondence of subject and object on the grounds of temporality. For the subject's first interest in representations of time is in overcoming temporality itself. It is in order to deal with the continual onset of the future, which holds material death, that an investment in the possibilities of freezing the past is incorporated into the desires and imaginative projections involved in Bazin's cherished realism.

Of course it would be nonsense to say that space is not also a basic Bazinian category. However, even a sentence such as "Our experience of space is the structural basis of our concept of the universe" (WC, 1:10) is best understood in terms of the special—temporal—levels of representation and engagement that automatically produced images bring to spatial representation. (In fact, immediately after this sentence, Bazin goes on to note that spatial correspondence between image and world is not the point.) Bazin insists on the pregivenness of the universe to the human. The indexicality of mechanically produced images makes it possible to experience that pregivenness in the realm of representation, through the temporal relation of the profilmic to the camera. For Bazin the photographic or cinematic image always provides the spectator with absolute brute knowledge that the objects visible in the frame *were at one time* in the spatial "presence" of the camera, that they appear from an irrefutable past existence. Furthermore, this "presence" of camera to object lasted *for a certain amount of time.*[21]

This makes not only the temporality *of* the image, but also the representation of temporality *in* the image (and sound) crucial to any stylistics of cinema. In fact, the imprinting of a length of time is the particular contribution of cinema to the evolution of image-production. Photography preserves an instant of time for a subject, but cinema preserves a fragment of time that can be experienced as actual duration. Time itself seems captured.

In this regard, it is worth insisting that the theoretical consistency Bazin brings to his concern with film stylistics goes well beyond the usual examples of the long take. Brian Henderson has usefully emphasized its seeming contrary, Bazin's rarely noted interest in ellipsis.[22] Finding significant virtues in Bazin's analysis of narrative ellipsis in Rossellini (e.g., WC, 2:34–38), Henderson goes on to object that Bazin illegitimately applies the classical concept of narrative ellipsis to reality, seeing this as part of an overall contradictoriness in Bazin's corpus. Contradictions there may ultimately be, but, as with all Bazin's accounts of stylistic and formal usages, temporal manipulations must be read through the special investment in the credibility of cinema by the subject. This is not definable in strictly formal or objective terms, but is a condition of the cinematic experience prior to any specific instance of it, and indeed, is based in the gap rather than in the perfect match between film and reality.

In a film, not only is continuous temporal flow possible, but also its *interruption* is unavoidable. Henderson is puzzled when he finds in Bazin a suggestion to the effect that all cinema is based on ellipsis, but cinema always interrupts any literal impression of "real" temporal continuity. Even a hypothetical one-shot film must begin and end. So Bazin's often-quoted praise of Stroheim is doubled-edged: When he writes, "One could easily imagine a film by Stroheim composed of a single shot and as long-lasting and as close-up as you like" (*WC*, 1:27), he points to what is imaginary, an ideal. All realisms play on a psychological, subjective premise. But in Bazin's dialectic they must engage with their opposing term, aesthetics, because the myth of total cinema is impossible to realize objectively.

Consequently, various cinema aesthetics involve various modalities of playing temporal continuity against its inevitable interruptions, whether what is involved is diegetic, narrational, and/or (at another level) the purportedly referential time of a shot. A good cross-reference for Bazin's interest in narrative ellipsis in Rossellini is his commentary on *Kon Tiki* (1951) in "Cinema and Exploration." Here Bazin claims that realism is manifested by the film precisely because, at a moment where the filmmakers are depicted as being in danger, a chunk of time encompassing the events of most interest must be omitted. This frustration acts to draw a greater quotient of belief from the spectator, for the interruption serves as evidence that the danger was real. This reading hinges on indexical pastness (the camera and filmmakers were actually present at the moment of danger) and the special credibility of cinema for the subject. It is thus no accident that when Bazin concludes this essay with a comparison to another film, *Anapurna* (1953), we find a constellation of familiar figures: mummy, religion, indexicality, and objective endurance of the preexistent —a virtual invocation of the mummy complex:

[T]hen begins with long Calvary of the descent, with Herzog and Lachemal strapped like mummies to the backs of their Sherpas. This time the camera is there like the veil of Veronica pressed to the face of human suffering. Undoubtedly the written account by Herzog is more detailed and more complete. Memory is the most faithful of films—the only one that can register at any height, and right up to the very moment of death. But who can fail to see the difference between memory and that objective image that gives it eternal substance? (*WC*, 1:162)

Thus, while I have been arguing for the priority of temporality in Bazin's theory, his aesthetics of style cannot be reduced to the promotion of a restricted set of filmic devices associated with continuity (emblematically, the long take). Yet, his analytic flexibility and openness to a variety of filmic strategies do not derive from the willful theoretical slackness of a cinematic enthusiast, but from the prior centrality of temporality as inseparable from the status of subjective projection, which underpins cinema per se and its specific modes of indexicality. The essential "realism" of this mechanically reproduced image lies in the relation of the subject to the future by something like a hallucinatory control over the past. This is registered in one of his definitions of cinema, which derives from the mummy complex: "change mummified" (*WC*, 1:14–15). In oxymoronically yoking together change with stasis, this trope crystallizes the founding paradox of Bazin's cinematic subject, which grounds the coherence of his corpus.[23]

The priority of temporality is necessarily manifested at another level, however, where the theoretical coherence of Bazin's work does become problematic. This level has to do with historiography.

Change Mummified

In Bazin's work generally, the explicit concern with the flow of time and the various ways a subject obsessively apprehends the past is pertinent not only for the filmic subject, but for the theoretical/critical subject—such as Bazin himself. In Bazin's critical writings, filmic procedures are consistently conceived within the history of cinema, film style, and, to some extent, their wider contexts. His critical practice is therefore inseparable from his historicity.

The teleological impulse underlying his stylistic histories—the inexorable evolution toward greater and more flexible realisms—may justifiably draw suspicion. But it is useful to recall that they consistently imply asymptotic, pseudo-teleologies, since their endpoints always remain unattainable. Thus, they retain their own subject-object, sign-referent gaps. In the logic of his film theory, such gaps are what attract the special kind of subjective investment that founds the invention of cinema and implications of cinematic style. In that case, the ontological centrality Bazin attributes to the relation between the subject and "pastness" in film—the preservative obsession—may well be refracted into his own work, which takes in the existence of cinematic signification in time, "film history," as *its* object. Bazin's mode of theoretical and critical work leads directly to problems of historiography—the "shapes of time."[24]

In this light, we may not only ask whether Bazin's account of the subjective compulsions of film is acceptable, and not only if his account of those compulsions should be a fundamental factor for understanding film history as he argues; we may also ask whether his work does not include a subtext on the compulsions and fascinations of history, the sublimations and attractions of the past, even outside cinema. Since this latter question rarely receives any overt treatment by Bazin, it will illuminate his position in unanticipated ways. It will enable us to shift from comprehending the general coherence of his corpus, for which I have been arguing, to a more symptomatic reading of that coherence.

It is possible to section Bazin's interest in historicity, considered as manifestations of the human concern with "pastness" in cinema carried to the prestigious knowledge claims of historiography. The most obvious and influential sector of this interest is surely his dialectical-evolutionary history of filmic styles. Outlined most directly in "The Evolution of the Language of Cinema," this film history asserts itself in some of his most important critical work, for example, "An Aesthetic of Reality" and the essay on Wyler; as we have already seen, vicissitudes of filmic textuality are here accounted for by appeal to a fundamental subjective project. But another sector of Bazin's historical concerns is not often enough interrogated. This is what some kinds of Marxists might call the construction of "second nature" and what Bazin often calls "myth." Myths function in his writings as particular kinds of social or cultural usages of cinema that embody what we can tentatively label a *collective* subjectivity. It is clear that the word *myth* does not in itself carry necessarily negative or positive connotations for Bazin. In addition to the more universal "myth of total cinema," he is sympathetic to localized "myths," such as those embodied in the American Western and certain periods of Soviet cinema. Yet he is hostile to others, such as the mythic representations of Stalin in Soviet film.[25]

Like an auteur's style, which embodies individual subjectivity within the overarching myth of total cinema, these collective subjectivities may or may not respect the pregivenness of the concrete in its ambiguity. That is, these myths can employ the abstracting side of subjectivity either to the detriment or benefit of that side that projects toward concrete objectivity and to which indexical image-production makes its special appeal. For an analysis of a myth that goes too far toward the abstractive side, and one that reveals how a special relation between cinema and history might be embedded in Bazin's thought, consider his essay, "The Stalin Myth in Soviet Cinema."[26]

The key symptom from which Bazin unpacks the Stalin myth is the fact that even while Stalin is living, he is constructed in Soviet cinema as a perfect subject, identified with the objective course of history. Stalin is alive, a historical being with the limitations that implies, yet he is represented as omniscient; hence he embodies the end of contingency within history. This makes Stalin as subject the ultimate telos of human history because he is given as being in a perfect relation of knowledge to objectivity. This is a way of describing the ideal direction of any myth for Bazin: if "no more cinema" is the goal of the myth of total cinema, for example, that slogan implies a subject no longer alienated and threatened by objectivity (with the threat figured as "death") but rather in perfect communion with it.

Bazin's analyses of myth thus highlight the conjunction of a transcendent, ontological function with an actual existent—here, the person of Stalin. In this case, however, contradiction is not converted into one of Bazin's beloved revelatory paradoxes, and it is therefore refused entry into his dialectic. Why? *In this myth, there is no asymptote—with the subject-object split suppressed, the gap between sign and referent is closed off.* For if subject and object were united as the objective course of history in the person of Stalin, then telos has been already objectively attained, and the desires of the subject perfectly realized. Such a victory of subjectivity would leave no place for further processes of subjectivity, and thus no basis for realism.[27] So Bazin argues that this cinema is actually imposing telos by politically motivated fiat; it marks a fatal imbalance, whereby the side of subjectivity that projects toward the objective concrete is overwhelmed by the abstractive side of subjectivity.

The implications of the Stalinist cultural strategy are especially high-lighted by its embodiment in cinema. In the present context, we can note Bazin's comment that the realistic appeal of cinema is used "to fix his [Stalin's] essence forever." This is explicitly compared to mummification, as Bazin dates the beginnings of this process from the embalming of Lenin's body.[28] But *this* mummy complex, culturally and politically imposed on cinema, hypocritically validates itself by laying claim to the achievement of an absolute, closed subjective (epistemological) security; that is, by pre-tending to abolish the original mummy complex, it suppresses the always unfinished aspiration that defines the appeal of "pastness." The peculiar project of these films—historical films that abolish history—can thus be explained as a "bad" paradox: the claim to objective realization by a myth means that the myth suppresses the gap that stimulates the necessary imaginative projection toward actual, concrete objectivity.

So this conjunction of myth, mummification, and the relation to a past returns us to Bazin's ontological essays. Clearly, Stalinist cinema diverts the founding myth of total cinema. The irony and precision of Bazin's examination of religious attitudes in the decadent socialist realism of late Stalinism show that the appeals of cinematic realism could be put to what an existentialist would call bad-faith uses. But it also highlights the extent to which, as Comolli indicates, Bazin's theory is a theory of the struggle of the subject to maintain itself in the face of materiality. In

Stalinist cinema, an undesirable hypertrophy is manifested in the representation of history, but it is a hypertrophy of a condition that pervades all cinema: the subject defends itself against time, seeking (among other things) to tame temporality. The extremism of Stalinism is that it purports to be a victorious conquest of the problem.

This is the special danger of a medium that, as we have seen, claims an ontological purpose that is to be realized in paradoxical struggle with its ontology. If time must be captured because it is a threat, then the ultimate victory for subjectivity might seem to be to do away with time, to make it irrelevant. But for Bazin the phenomenologist, this must be a perversion—a perversion that can occur in relation to historical representation as well as properly cinematic instances. As the case of Stalinist cinema makes clear, filmic and narrative strategies are readable for Bazin not only at the level of the individual subject (artist), but also at the interconnected level of culture and societies; subjectivity is both individual and collective.[29] On both levels, the gaps between subject and object, sign and referent, and the inevitability of realizing myths only asymptotically must be maintained; then contingency, subjectivity, cinema—and phenomenology —may all continue to exist, and can register temporality in ways that keep the subject open to its fundamental action in reality.

Stalinist cinema, as one kind of limit case of the struggle of the subject, shows that human subjectivity cannot be posited as outside of time and outside of history. This principle returns us once more to "The Ontology of the Photographic Image" and "The Myth of Total Cinema." There Bazin establishes a historically shifting hierarchy among image-producing media, based on their relative capacities to appeal to the human desire for security against death. Further, in the medium of cinema, the shifting relations among styles, developed or referred to in many of Bazin's essays and definitively outlined in "The Evolution of the Language of Cinema," are similarly hierarchized on the basis of the types of credulity the aesthetic strategies elicit, given the mummy complex. Thus, it is precisely a *history* of subjectivity that is to be read off of shifts in this hierarchy among media and/or styles. In fact, this historiographic project is the connection between Bazin's ontology and his critical work.

Now, this means that there are not two, but three coexisting levels at which the history of subjective investment in images manifests itself. We have noted those of the individual subject (artist, spectator) and the collective subject (social and/or cultural myth, with the Western and Stalinist cinema as relatively pure examples). Throughout Bazin's writings, these are subsumed by a third, which, in effect, mandates the other two and functions as a universal, dating back to the origins of representation: the fundamental preservative impulse of the subject to overcome time, with the consequent desire for "objective" representation. But if Bazin is driven by his project and his logic to posit a universal, the question arises whether his history of subjectivity has truly evaded the dilemma of Stalinist cinema with its abstractive hypertrophy of the atemporal. Has not the desire to control time taken over his own formulations, perhaps from the other side of subjectivity, which projects toward the concrete?

For even if there are individual and cultural variations in the ways that this projective desire of subjectivity is met, the desire is itself posited outside of change and history. Whether in ancient Egypt, Renaissance Florence, or post–World War II Italy, the force of that desire remains consistent, not just the premise of an obsession but an obsessional premise explaining the pull of the image as realistic representation. Histories, cultures, and technologies may develop in various ways, and individual artists may propose distinctive, revelatory utilizations of representational possibilities, but that subjective obsession is always the ground. It serves Bazin's theory as a perpetual phenomenological intentionality, a constant existential projection of the subject into the material world, where it cannot find satisfaction—so therefore, into representations of the world that are materially distinct from that world and yet can be diverted toward a special credibility.

What kind of historian, then, is Bazin? Certainly he is not one who allows an emphasis on the vicissitudes of a fundamental phenomenological intentionality to blind him to economic, social, and technological determinants of film history and textuality; on the contrary, he often insists on their pertinence. However, the terms of that pertinence are in the last instance secondary. For example, in "In Defense of Mixed

Cinema," his noted geological metaphor of an equilibrium profile of form and style is embedded in something close to a technological determinism. He argues that a period of novelty in technique and form that lasted from the invention of cinema through the innovation of sound has been succeeded by an "age of the scenario," whose technical and formal equilibrium will only be shattered by some further technological innovation, such as an advance in color or in stereoscopy (WC, 1:73–74). But how could Bazin explain the technological development that could have such a result? Even in "The Evolution of the Language of Cinema," when he announces that the equilibrium profile has undergone a vast disturbance associated with the profusion of deep focus cinematography and the new kind of realism it manifests, Bazin himself declares that the reasons for the shift cannot be found in technical determinants (WC, 1:30). But then, how does one explain why the shift to a categorically new realism occurred when it did—in Hollywood, Renoir, the Italians?

This illustrates a fundamental difficulty in Bazin. The insistence on a historicized outlook in his notions of a succession of media and styles within media—intimately connected to the centrality of temporality in his theoretical work—must raise the question of the determinations of transformations within those successions; yet, there is ultimately little theoretical space that would allow for explanations of even his own skeletal outlines of *change*. For example, "The Myth of Total Cinema" identifies a historiographic issue in the delay of the profusion of optical machines synthesizing movement until the nineteenth century, because the necessary principles had been known for centuries. At first this issue is handled by reference to the innovations of image chemistry (photography), which is said to have manifested a dominant impulse of "the imagination of the [nineteenth] century." But this tentative move toward temporally localized historical explanation is then blocked, for the final claim organizing the essay is that the *idea* of cinema—of perfect, lifelike reproduction—long preceded its materialization. He compares it to the idea of flight, which "had dwelt in the soul of everyman since he first thought about birds" (WC, 1:22).

The universality of the ambition for perfect reproduction of the world is the universality of the preservative obsession, the characterization of the subject that is Bazin's founding theoretical axiom. The axiom here finds reconfirmation in history. But the consequence is a waffling on any historical explanation of transformations among media and styles. In this case he seems to embrace the idea that nineteenth-century technological, industrial, and economic developments were important conditions for the emergence of cinema; yet he finally accounts for that emergence only by vague reference to a conjunctural convergence of obsessions (scientific, industrial, economic) into the general preservative obsession. It appears that every new realization of the fundamental preservative obsession described by the mummy complex can only be explained on the basis of a circular reference to that obsession.

There may well be no way that Bazin can satisfactorily answer questions proper to historical studies—about change. In his case this would require accounts of shifts in the hierarchy of media and/or styles. For example, he cannot with theoretical consistency resort to the idea of an independent technical development of various media, with which he occasionally flirts. This would separate the history of technology from subjectivity, and hence his ontology, as well as the coherence of his critical work with the ontology, would collapse. At the crucial historiographic point, Bazin must suppress the temporal.

Yet, the omnipresence of time and change is inextricable from the virtues of the irrational projection toward the concrete basic to Bazin's account of subjectivity. This shows up in his often insightful impulses on levels to integrate a more historicized consciousness on certain local levels, especially when he embeds subjects in specific societies and cultures. This is the case not only with respect to the social mythifications associated with collective subjectivities; sometimes it appears even in the analyses of individual subjects, such as those cinema artists working in postwar Italy. Nevertheless, in the last instance Bazin's historical accounts remain variations on an ontological theme. Distinctions among periods and cultures there may be, but not radical, qualitative differences in the premises of human subjective activity.

"Change mummified" indeed. Bazin's oxymoron aptly crystallizes his view of the relations of cinema for the subject by registering the illogical processes and desire for *permanence* (of subjective existence, of identity), which can paradoxically open the spectating subject to the concrete, hence the flow of time and the fact of *change*. But this oxymoron may also describe a fundamental inconsistency or aporia in the relations of Bazin's own historicity. We have seen how his account of the irrationality at the heart of the cinematic experience takes on a static quality, the character of an unchanging law. Thus, as the figure of the mummy complex assumes the logical position of a valid description, Bazin's historiographic discourse presumes the function of a rational metalanguage. In this it is like much modern thought. By analyzing the illogicality or irrationality of a phenomenon, it establishes its own logical and epistemological security, its superiority. The surest way to achieve such security is to establish generally applicable laws or premises, from which the conditions of specific cases can be produced.[30] Cognitive efficacy becomes rooted in an imputed universality.

For film historiography, there is something enabling about this. It follows from the claim for the universality of the mummy complex that the historian would share with all humans in all periods basic aspects of film viewing—those described by the mummy complex. (There may be limitations to such empathy insofar as some components of a film are historically localizable in Bazin, but their extent is open to discussion.) So, there is a theoretical basis for identification between subjects of the past who are objects of historical investigation, and subjects of the present who may be conducting the investigation, no matter what the differences are between present and past. Some have argued that such identification is the basic assumption of historical writing.[31] Yet, it seems less of a delicious Bazinian paradox than a critical contradiction that, in the aspirations to a kind of knowledge crucial to his mode of thought, namely historical knowledge, Bazin desires a kind of security that would disjoin his historiography from his film-theoretical presumptions about the limitations of subjectivity vis-à-vis pastness.

A Bazinian might respond that the mummy complex has to do with the experience of iconic or figurative representation, and the writing of history is a paradigmatically linguistic act, whose cognitive rather than irrational claims define it. For some this might be true enough, but for Bazin this would split off the centrality of temporal experience in cinema from the centrality of temporal understanding in his writings about cinema. He would have to give up the theoretical rationale for the compulsive insistence, even in his critical work on individual filmmakers, on an overall evolutionary, teleological, and/or dialectical account of film history.

So it is difficult to see how the appeal of pastness and temporality to Bazin's historiographic subject could be completely divorced from the preservative obsession and the characteristics he attributes to the cinematic experience. But in that case, we find in Bazin himself a hypertrophy of abstract rationalization, the blockage of the static. In his own terms, it is as if temporality were as fascinating a threat to Bazin the historian as it is to the cinematic subject, so that temporality must be both figured and mastered. Ultimately, if Bazin's analysis has shown how the Stalin myth becomes a kind of "second nature" for Soviet filmmakers, then so does the myth of total cinema for Bazin as historian; and is the ultimate ideological consequence, the abstract transcendence of historical time, that dissimilar? Bazin's attempt to negotiate temporality through a timeless subjective intentionality has as its consequence a theoretical blank spot around history.

From one point of view, it may seem that much of this is only to say, with 1970s film theory, that Bazin is an idealist thinker. Yet, the extraordinary critical power, intelligence, and influence of his idealism, including his subject-based account of realism, brings us back to the difficulties of simply dismissing all his work on the basis of a theoretical a priori. Thus, several years ago such a self-proclaimed anti-idealist as Comolli could suggest we consider the possibility that Bazin's obsessional premise, with its pull toward the ahistorical, might well reveal something crucial about the *historical* regime of the filmic.[32] And indeed, one could argue that a theoretical blank spot around history was also a problem in the very 1970s film theory that institutionalized the rejection of Bazin.

In conclusion, then, we find in Bazin the postulate of a subject existing in a time-filled universe, one predisposed to a defensive stance against time. On the plane of representation, this institutes an impossible desire to make the past present, a pursuit of referential pastness that will make the time-filled universe timeless. The privileged signifying mode of such a subject is the indexical trace, which involves a persistence from the past to the present. "Change mummified" is the trope intertwining the time-filled with the timeless, and Bazin formulates it as a key specificity of cinema. But this same trope contradictorily insinuates itself into his own historiography, although from the side less valued by Bazin. It disavows the force of time and change within a logic that makes this force basic to reality. Most important here, this suggests parallels between cinema and historicity in Bazin, or to put it more strongly, some kind of kinship between the two, and defensiveness about time is a nodal point in their intrication. Just as Bazin conceptualizes the appeal of cinema as a defense against time at the service of subjectivity, so it can appear that there is something defensive in his own historicity.

One way to develop these issues would be to attempt to reinstall history at the point where change stops in Bazin's logic. That is where indexicality meets subjective obsession. But what would it be to historicize what Bazin requires as an ahistorical constant? For one thing, it would mean beginning not from the image, but from what precedes the image in Bazin—the preservative desire, the obsession with pastness that his work universalizes. Is this simply an essentialist premise to be dismissed by those who oppose his phenomenology, or can it be located more specifically? If the latter is the case, we can propose an interrogation of the media of automatically produced images that starts by asking when and how this sense of time becomes culturally central and fatal, in many senses, for conceptions and experiences of human subjectivity. But this necessarily leads back to the cultural privilege of historicity and hence historiography, which is the basis for the question in the first place.

CHAPTER 2

Entering History:
Preservation and Restoration

She said, "What is 'historicity'?"

"When a thing has history in it. Listen. One of those two Zippo lighters was in Franklin D. Roosevelt's pocket when he was assassinated. And one wasn't. One has historicity, a hell of a lot of it. As much as any object ever had. And one has nothing. Can you feel it?" He nudged her. "You can't. You can't tell which is which. There's no 'mystical plasmic presence,' no 'aura' around it."

"Gee," the girl said, awed. "Is that really true? That he had one of those on him that day?"

"Sure. And I know which it is. You see my point. It's all a big racket; they're playing it on themselves. I mean a gun goes through a famous battle, like the Meuse-Argonne, and it's the same as if it hadn't, unless you know. It's in here." He tapped his head. "In the mind, not the gun. . . ."

"I don't believe either of those two lighters belonged to Franklin Roosevelt," the girl said.

Wyndam-Matson giggled. "That's my point! I'd have to prove it to you with some sort of document. A paper of authenticity. And so it's all a fake, a mass delusion. The paper proves its worth, not the object itself!"

"Show me the paper."

"Sure." Hopping up, he made his way back into the study. From the wall he took the Smithsonian Institute's framed certificate; the paper and the lighter had cost him a fortune, but they were worth it—because they enabled him to prove that he was right, that the word "fake" meant nothing really, since the word "authentic" meant nothing really.

—Philip K. Dick, *The Man in the High Castle*

Call 1-800-HISTORY.

—Television advertisement for Colonial Williamsburg

Restoring Context

In Philip K. Dick's novel *The Man in the High Castle*, history has taken a different turn: the Axis won the Second World War. A problem for a major character in occupied America becomes contacting the author of *The Grasshopper Lies Heavy*, a detailed, convincing novel in which the Allies won the war; however, *The Grasshopper Lies Heavy* still includes significant differences from the history known as actuality to the reader of *The Man in the High Castle*. In this novelistic confrontation of counterfactual conditionals, historicity is not so much debunked, as it is defamiliarized and explored from inside its inescapabilities, its fragilities, and its fascinations.

Throughout *The Man in the High Castle*, historical knowledge always circulates around the search for authenticity. This is illustrated by a major fascination, and fragility, of historicity for the Japanese, who are occupying the Western United States. Dick's victorious postwar Japanese culture is Americanophile, and it has made collection of the remains and detritus of prewar U.S. popular and material culture into an exquisite social and metaphysical practice. Triumphant Japanese bureaucrats, officers, and merchants are attracted by cultural artifacts preserved after the death of the culture that produced them. These artifacts therefore take on economic value—which enables various frauds and rackets on the part of some Americans—but they also take on a quality of *aware* for the Japanese. There is a moment when a sympathetic administrator, Mr. Tagomi, is thrown into a semitrance from contemplating not a historical artifact, but a new piece of American handwrought jewelry of original, aesthetically significant design. Its claim to a kind of contemporary authenticity without recourse to pastness is something unprecedented in his experience. Meditating on it, he slips briefly into our own postwar world and is appalled by the ugliness of an unfamiliar and massive artifact from this other history, a freeway overpass. Its lack of any claim to historicity, of "mystic plasmic presence," of "aura," is a shock to Mr. Tagomi's subjectivity and through him to the fabric of the fictional universe itself.[1]

What is a genuine historical object and what is its use? Dick's novel locates historicity in a line running from authenticity of artifact to both subjective experience and the seemingly more secure, transsubjective knowledge of past occurrences as it is written in the history textbooks. This is a line full of claims to rigorous knowledge and encounters with ambivalent knowledges. The past is to be comprehended and constituted on the basis of perceiving something of it—seeing, holding, reading, contemplating objects in the present that actually existed in the past. Characters run into problems of historicity and the object everywhere, in power politics and cultural politics, exchange value and ontology, industrial technology and art, empirical data and mystical faith. By thematizing the status of preserved artifacts, *The Man in the High Castle* foregrounds historicity as convention, as social practice and as instrumental worldview, and yet one that can abut a certain mysticism. (The other authoritative text routinely consulted by characters is the *I Ching*, which, it is revealed, was used to formulate the plot of *The Grasshopper Lies Heavy*.)

Here, subjective relations to pastness are routed through investment in objects preserved from the past, an investment that hovers between proper epistemological standing and quasi-religious faith. In the present context, parallels to the preservative obsession one finds in Bazin are striking. But there is no reference to film or media. Dick's novel therefore points toward a wider attraction of pastnesses and the historical, and this meditation on their attraction comes from a science-fiction writer at that. This suggests how the idea of a preservative obsession is susceptible to more general cultural, theoretical, and "historical" contextualization, all in relation to historicity itself. In the next chapter, this will lead us to the foundations of modern, professionalized historiography. But Dick's fictional construction of the preservative obsessions is a reminder that formations of historicity are not limited to the products of an elite occupational caste called historians.

This chapter aims to do two things. First, it provides some indications of the cultural range of notions related to a preservative impulse or obsession in the modern West, and the historicity with which it is associated. Second, this chapter will reveal something more about the vicissitudes and organization of the category of the indexical trace, along with the experiences and subjective positionality it is supposed to entail. It proceeds from discourses and practices having to do with buildings and built environments pegged onto the value of pastness during the nineteenth and twentieth centuries. This cultural arena was chosen in part precisely because it belongs neither to cinema, nor to written historiography (which will be discussed in the next chapter). But to keep at least some of the connections toward which we are working in mind, let us begin from the bon mot that concludes Bazin's Bresson essay: "After Bresson, Aurenche and Bost are but the Viollet-le-Duc of cinematographic adaptation."[2]

This invidious comparison in Bresson's favor turns on a pejorative reference to one of the most prominent architectural thinkers of the nineteenth century. As a practicing architect, Eugène-Emmanuel Viollet-le-Duc is most notorious for the restoration of cathedrals such as Notre Dame in Paris (in a typical reference, Susan Sontag goes out of her way to refer to him sarcastically as "that indefatigable improver of French architectural treasures").[3] But Viollet-le-Duc also dealt in written principles, as an architectural historian and theorist. In fact, he was later admired by Frank Lloyd Wright, who read Viollet-le-Duc as promoting a version of functionalist rationalism. Of particular interest here is the association of his name with the concept of architectural *restoration*, and the critique of his position in favor of an alternative called architectural *preservation*.

In the nineteenth century, the disposition of old edifices became an important architectural issue in Western Europe. Many buildings dating from the Middle Ages and even further back included additions and alterations constructed by those who had used the structures in later eras. Sometimes such buildings had not even been completed by the generation that originally designed them and initiated construction. As succeeding generations continued the construction, the original plan was often modified to accord with current practices. As a result, a revered old building might appear, by standards drawn from an organicist aesthetic, to be a stylistic hodgepodge. In such situations, given what appeared to be a virtual continuum of architectural work and adjustments from a large segment of the past, what should be the precise standards guiding the rapidly increasing number of projects commissioned to renovate, say, a medieval cathedral?

In his major theoretical essay on restoration, Viollet-le-Duc characterizes this as a completely modern problem, arising in the first quarter of the nineteenth century. Only then, he believes, did it become necessary to invent principles to guide the architect in such cases, something he proposes to do. Viollet-le-Duc became associated with a general line whose theoretical slogan was *l'unité de style*. With historical learning and research, the architect could ascertain the dominant style in which the building had originally been intended, or at least hypothetically infer the one that was most probable in the period of the original construction. He argued that modern architects should restore buildings as aesthetically valid entities according to those unifying stylistic tenets, derived from a periodization of architectural history.

But in practice, this conception of the authority of the past could have odd results. It tended to justify razing more recent components of a building in order to reconstruct it with stylistic unity; yet, some of those demolished portions might themselves be centuries old. This was accentuated by the fact that the rationale flourished during the Gothic Revival, when medieval styles were most often privileged against those of more recent eras. In fact, in many cases restorationism meant unifying the building according to an "original" period style *even when the building itself had never actually existed in that style.* In addition, this principle served as a standard justifying the common restorational practice of using new materials and modern methods to replace parts of the building, original or otherwise, that had been worn down over the centuries.

Now, this is a quick, extremist summary of sometimes vaguely formulated rationales for restorationism in the first half of the nineteenth century, and in his writings Viollet-le-Duc was often not an extremist. He intermittently inveighs against hypothetical renderings. He repeatedly provides examples that require pragmatically balanced architectural choices based on such considerations as the building's constructive stability, its current usefulness, respect for original remains (with which he wants any new construction to harmonize), and the historical or aesthetic value of parts of the building originating in different periods. Nevertheless, he does begin his article on restoration with the following sentence: "To restore a building is to reestablish it to a completed state which may never have existed at any particular time." Furthermore, he conceived the architect as making judgments about stable construction, social function, and beauty in and for the present. This insistence on a present-oriented pragmatic flexibility along with his actual architectural practice enabled commentators then and now to align him with the view that restoration could mean to construct, on the shell of the old, a modern ideal substitute of an ancient thing. (Hence Bazin's analogy, making him an example of "inauthentic" film adaptation.)[4]

By the second half of the century, notably in Great Britain, there had appeared a resistance to the dominant attitudes in architectural restoration theorized by Viollet-le-Duc. While some scattered voices had previously been raised against standard restorational practices, the most famous early spokesperson of this opposition was John Ruskin. This resistance is often said to have achieved a lasting ideological victory on the European continent as well as Britain, spearheaded by The Society for the Protection of Ancient Buildings, founded in 1877 under the leadership of William Morris. Morris summed up its attitudes toward refinishing old surfaces by nicknaming it "the Anti-Scrape Society." Put briefly, the Ruskin-Morris position was that in restoration, new construction becomes destruction: To replace what succeeding ages have added to a building, especially in order to match a supposedly "original" style that was often only a hypothetical ideal anyway, was in effect to evacuate historical actuality. The proper response to the aging of buildings was not restoration as commonly practiced and as theorized by Viollet-le-Duc, but *preservation:* maintaining the old, prolonging its existence as long as practically possible.

The rhetoric by which the Ruskin-Morris line appealed for preservation as opposed to restoration has significant resonances. When Ruskin sounded the battle cry in 1849, he explained his position through figures of life and death. Thus, declaring the very ambition of physically perfect restoration absurd, he writes:

> [I]t is *impossible*, as impossible as to raise the dead, to restore anything that has ever been great or beautiful in architecture.... Another spirit may be given by another time, and it is then a new building; but the spirit of the dead workman cannot be summoned up, and commanded to direct other hands, and other thoughts.[5]

This figure of life and death therefore makes the past absolutely Other to the present. Yet, respect for remains left by the dead across time enables contact with the past:

> [I]t is no question of expediency or feeling whether we shall preserve the buildings of past times or not. *We have no right whatever to touch them.* They are not ours. They belong partly to those who built them, and partly to all the generations of mankind who are to follow us. The dead still have their right in them....[6]

Such passages construct a temporality that conjoins two divergent impulses. On the one hand, there is the fundamental *separation* between past and present, likened to that between death and life; the past is irreducibly different from the present and cannot be reproduced. The power of time is understood as a certain loss, the unrepeatability of the past.

Thus, Ruskin's language expresses a profound insistence on the transformative, indeed corrosive, power of temporality. On the other hand, he emphasizes that that power is itself unending, a kind of constant. Historical actuality consists in a *continuity* of effectivities between any point in the past and the present, and this will somehow admit of a degree of contact with the past over the gap between present and past. This allows Ruskin to impose on the present a duty toward the past. The fundamental deficiency of any newly constituted replica of the old is with respect to the sheer continuousness of the passage of time. Thus, Ruskin finds "the greatest glory of a building" in its age, which makes its walls "lasting witness against men, in their quiet contrast with the transitional character of all things, in the strength which through the lapse of seasons and times, and the decline and birth of dynasties, and the changing of the face of the earth ... connects forgotten and following ages with each other, and half constitutes the identity, as it concentrates the sympathy, of nations."[7]

In opposition to the spatial aesthetic coherence that was the principle of *l'unité de style*, then, Ruskin emphasizes respect for time's passage. This leads him to value the wear on the surface, which marks a building as genuinely old, as a crucial, irreplaceable asset:

> As for direct and simple copying, it is palpably impossible. What copying can there be of surfaces that have been worn half an inch down? The whole finish of the work was in the half inch that is gone; if you attempt to restore that finish, you do it conjecturally; if you copy what is left, granting fidelity to be possible (and what care, or watchfulness, or cost can secure it?), how is the new work better than the old? There was yet in the old *some* life, some mysterious suggestion of what it had been, and of what it had lost; some sweetness in the gentle lines which rain and sun had wrought.[8]

The dead cannot be brought back to life, but reverence for their remains can keep them alive in memory. Restoration cannot replicate the historical actuality of a building, which is its existence in time, but preservation can provide an encounter with that actuality by refusing to interrupt its passage through time. Ancient buildings should therefore remain untouched, becoming something like monuments to the dead, preserving their spirits in a kind of architectural afterlife. Here the genuine surface of the old building is perceptible in the marks of its gradual deterioration over the years, which thereby becomes an indexical trace, not just of an origin but of its entire existence over a real temporal span. As such, it makes available a certain kind of subjective experience for the onlooker in the present, a "mysterious suggestion" or experience of the reality of past existence.

In a landmark 1877 manifesto announcing the principles of the new Society for the Protection of Ancient Buildings, Morris forcefully articulated the implications of the preservationist line. It is worth a lengthy quotation:

> [T]he Restoration of ancient buildings: a strange and a most fatal idea, which, by its very name, implies that it is possible to strip from a building this, that and the other part of its history—of its life, that is, and then to stay the hand at some arbitrary point, and leave it still historical, living, and even as it once was.
>
> In earlier times ... [i]f repairs were needed, if ambition or piety pricked on to change, that change was of necessity wrought in the unmistakable fashion of the time: a church of the eleventh century might be added to or altered in the twelfth, thirteenth, fourteenth, fifteenth, sixteenth, or even the seventeenth and eighteenth centuries; but every change, whatever history it destroyed, left history in the gap, and was alive with the spirit of the deeds done amidst its fashioning. The result of all this was often a building in which the many changes, though harsh and visible enough, were by their very contrast interesting and instructive, and could by no possibility mislead. But those who make the changes wrought in our day under the name of Restoration, while professing to bring back a building to the best time of its history, have no guide but each his own individual whim to point out to them what is admirable and what contemptible; while the very nature of their task compels them to destroy something, and to supply the gap by imagining what the earlier builders should or might have done. Moreover, in the course of this double process of destruction and addition the whole surface of the building is necessarily tampered with; so that the appearance

of antiquity is taken away from such old parts of the fabric as are left, and there is no laying to rest in the spectator the suspicion of what may have been lost; and, in short, a feeble and lifeless forgery is the final result of all the wasted labour.[9]

This makes the implications of the preservationist position clear with respect to aesthetic totality and what we might as well call subjectivity. As to the first, the preservationist position is willing to subordinate organicist harmony of spatial style to the disordering work of time. On this view, restorationism entails removing or covering up traces of both natural wear and the reworkings of old buildings over the centuries in the interests of unity; it thereby denies part of "the life" of the building and kills it. The restorationist may consider the historical conjoining of several period styles as an aesthetically offensive disunity, but the preservationist finds in this apparent discord an index of the continuous temporality of the edifice—which is what he or she also finds in the gradual reduction of an external surface due to weather. Indeed, perhaps to the regret of some of its proponents, a rigorous preservationism implied that no period, not even the cherished medieval, could be privileged. In theory, at least, the preservationist would have to respect all the work of all times. (The preservationist tolerance of a disjunctive set of period styles in the same building might seem strangely akin to recent postmodernist rationales, but a crucial difference is that preservationism supposes that the styles actually come from various periods in the past to the present. Preservationism is thus an affirmation of authenticity in time rather than the ironic negation of authenticity.)

Second, there is the matter of subjectivity. Morris is absolutely clear that his position on the architectural totality depends on a conception of reception, the point of which he calls the spectator. Ruskin's empathy-inducing "mysterious suggestion" of being in the presence of the past must be an appeal to the imaginative faith of an onlooker in the historical actuality of the building. It therefore hangs on the spectator's active investment, which must be solicited in the experience of the ancient edifice. When the restorationist substitutes a harmonious model of what he or she infers the "original" might have looked like, the consequence for this spectator is suspicion rather than faith. But the stylistic disunity of a preserved edifice, encountered as a clashing conjunction of differing architectural periods, draws the spectator into a more authentic encounter with the past as the work of time. It brings the spectator into engagement with the corrosiveness of the ever-continuing work of temporality.

While Morris's position certainly partakes of the broad nineteenth-century reaction against architectural neoclassicism, its specific mode of justification lies in connecting the subject with evidence of real temporality and the reality of temporality. In the present context, Morris's account of the preservation-restoration opposition could be rewritten in quasi-Bazinian terms. His remark about restoration arousing the spectator's "suspicion of what may have been lost" could be likened to Bazin on editing and on modalities of the film spectator's desire to believe in the reality of the shot. More, the reverence in preservationism for the surface of the edifice makes it into an indexical sign that offers paradoxical contact with a preexistent, and in that might be compared to Bazin's ontology of the image. The preservationist promotion of stylistic disunity could be compared to Bazin on Rossellini or *Kon Tiki*. The opposition between restorationism, associated with the name of Viollet-le-Duc, and the Ruskin-Morris preservationism, is said by the latter to be an opposition between a substitute and a reality, and might bear comparison to the Bazinian opposition of respecting a temporalized reality and constructing a disavowing substitute for that reality. It is also an opposition between the abstractly ideal and the concrete, between a priori organicized conceptions of a building and a posteriori respect for what the building is and has been in time—and therefore, we might say, between the building's hypothetical essence and its actual, historical existence. It is as if, in the Ruskin-Morris view, the existence of a medieval cathedral precedes its essence.

Presumably the inference to be drawn from such homologies between a twentieth-century film theory and a nineteenth-century architectural controversy is not that Ruskin and Morris were existential phenomenologists or Italian neorealists. But there is some usefulness in the comparison if we move back one step, in a more generalized direction that implies thinking of Bazin in a wider context. For these nineteenth-century debates over building restoration define more than opposing architectural schools. They hook into widespread sociocultural concerns. This can be illustrated by the fact that these seemingly specialized architectural discussions extend throughout nineteenth-century language, institutions, organizations, and even laws.

Take some examples from Great Britain: In language, the term *restore* had previously meant repair (restoring what is broken). Only in the nineteenth century, and in specific connection with architectural restoration, was its current sense of returning something to a past condition established. Perhaps more tellingly, nineteenth-century institutions pertaining to the past could themselves be the topic of a good-sized book. Just consider the impressive number of archaeological and architectural societies. The years between 1838 and 1846 saw the foundation of at least ten national organizations in Britain alone, followed in the 1850s and 1860s by many more; and several of these sponsored publications that were read and discussed on the continent and in the United States, where similar organizations and publications were initiated. (By 1879, Morris's manifesto had already been translated into French, German, Dutch, and Italian.) Furthermore, the widespread interest in scientific investigations of the past, with which such organizations generally allied themselves, had a flip side. In Great Britain, the Gothic Revival was linked to renewed interest in the heritage of the High Church and Catholicism. This was especially important for restorationist and preservationist movements in architecture, because one of their major concerns was cathedrals. According to one count, 7,144 British churches were restored between 1840 and 1873.[10] This explains why many preservationists felt a sense of emergency, and in later years Thomas Hardy recalled "the craze for indiscriminate church-restoration" of this time.[11] While such numbers can leave one with the impression of a mania, they also indicate something like a legitimated social movement for which the past had become a crucial object.

This impression is strengthened by considering legal developments and the state. For example, one can trace out legislative attention to the heritage of the past from side effects of Britain's Church Building Act of 1818 to the Ancient Monuments Protection Act of 1882 and a number of succeeding acts of Parliament. In the late nineteenth century, comparable laws were passed in several Western countries. These are highly significant because they embody a crucial factor in historiography and the promotion of pastness as an ideological value, a modern political and even governmental interest in "the national heritage." What is often said to be the earliest legal document mandating modern principles of preservation—an 1818 decree of Louis X, Grand Duke of Hesse—begins by defining the history embodied in architecture as belonging to the nation.[12] We have already seen that Ruskin himself links the desired continuity to past and present to the identity of something he calls the nation.

All of this suggests that the preservation-restoration debates were situated within a widely receptive sociocultural and political context, and much more could be said. For example, given that the iconography of the ruin pervaded nineteenth-century romanticism, even a biographical account of the two most emblematic figures in the architecture debates would lead us to a wide range of cultural references with respect to pastness. The great weight placed by Viollet-le-Duc on historical research and old models was part of a fascination with medieval architecture that he felt as a young man and that led him, within a romantic context, to emphasize the study of the past. On the other side, of course, it is often noted how important Ruskin's trips to the continent and the direct experiences of ruins were to his own thought.

But beyond biography and even beyond restoration and preservation, in Western European architectural theory and practice, the relation of the present to older building styles was a central issue from at least the mid-eighteenth century through much of the nineteenth. The debate over the proper way to treat genuinely ancient buildings was only one aspect of a larger discourse in the architectural field, for the past was also directly pertinent to the construction of *new* buildings. Dominant alternatives in architecture drew on the ever-increasing number of antiquarian studies, which, beginning in the seventeenth and eighteenth centuries, gradually developed into the disciplines of art and architecture history.

This was the period of "Revivals" (again, the figure of resurrection): Elizabethan, Jacobean, Romanesque, and, above all, the reaction of the Gothic Revival against classicism, itself followed by neo-Renaissance, neo-Baroque, and so forth. Textbooks came to label the dominant architectural impulse of this era historicism, an attitude whereby "architectural scholarship abandoned aesthetic theory and concentrated on historical research."[13]

This has not been a very nuanced presentation of the preservation-restoration debates. I have not dealt with claims for architecture as a unique human activity that makes issues of preservation and restoration especially important. The appearance of terms like nationalism, romanticism, and historicism at this point is a brief signal that very broad connections might be drawn. But my discussion has introduced a contrast general enough to be useful in other fields and other times. In this regard, there is one particular nuance that needs emphasis. My discussion of restorationism and preservationism as extremes has not considered the many kinds of mixed arguments and cases that are crucial to the deployment of these notions. It is more accurate to characterize these two terms as a polarity subject to a spectrum of admixtures. This kind of dialectical polarity between the two conceptions will be as important in what follows as the opposition itself.

In the end, these debates allow us to crystallize one of the crucial parameters for understanding what it means to claim to present the past. For the nineteenth-century debates over building restoration occurred on the basis of assumptions common to all sides. In particular, the argument was never about whether to recover the past, but about the rationales, definitions, and practices of such recovery. The restorationist-preservationist dispute reflects a seemingly pervasive premise of much of Western intellectual and cultural practice of this period, positing the power of temporality and, within that, the fundamental value of interrogating pastness. It is therefore not surprising that the debate may also be read as one between two classic views of temporality. For the restorationist, time was conceived as a directional series of segmentable points, such that the best access to history became the rational, inferential re-construction of a given point or sequence of points based on evidence available in the present. For the preservationist, time was a continuous, uninterruptable flux, so that the best access to history became a more experiential sense of the unending flow of time through objective remains from a vanished past.

The general concern with these issues is indicated by the cultural ambit of the indexical trace. In *The Clothing of Clio*, a brilliantly suggestive study of nineteenth-century British and French cultural practices, Stephen Bann argues that representational media and genres during the nineteenth century as a whole were pervaded by "effects of resurrection."[14] He convincingly demonstrates that an ideal of representation as the transparent re-creation of a preexisting referent was a dominant, long-term aspect of post–eighteenth century Western cultural formations bearing on a significant number of influential representational forms and technologies, institutions, and cultural practices innovated or transformed during this century. His coverage includes not only historiography, but painting, the museum, architecture, photography, literature (the historical novel from Scott to Thackeray and James), and even taxidermy (think of both Bazin and the trope of bringing the dead to life). Importantly, he also shows that this widespread impulse was not monolithic, but was subject to a variety of diachronic developments and differences, not only among diverse representational practices but within them. For example, he finds that by the 1840s, the ideal of the lifelike recovery of a lost past was already so well established that ironic or parodic treatment of it was possible. Of special interest here is the inevitable importance to his discussion of the innovation and diffusion of a number of image technologies, among them lithographs, dioramas, various photographic inventions, and, by the end of the century, cinema. Indeed, as Bann hints and as we will see, these concerns continued to be manifest in at least some cultural sectors, such as tourism and cinema, long after the period Bann studies.[15]

But even earlier, according to Bann, photography and cinema were not unique projects, but responses to a representational problem that pervaded cultural practices by the first half of the nineteenth century, namely responding to an ideal of perfect re-presentation of something real from the past:

> The evidence goes to show, therefore, that photographic reproduction aroused no absolutely new types of response. On the epistemological level, photographs appeared to present no distinctive and unprecedented vision of the external world. Or rather, whatever was novel about them could be contained within the existing framework of responses to [purportedly] non-mediated forms of representation, which were already becoming established by the later eighteenth and early nineteenth centuries.

The interdisciplinary expanse of his analysis thus puts him in a position to conclude that "the unique 'testimony' of the photograph remained as the extreme boundary of a continuum of forms of historical representation."[16]

A continuum of *historical* representation: the polarity of preservation and restoration delimits one of the key dimensions forming the problematic of historicity and its compulsions. This is a problematic that includes the relations of preserved remains of the past to its "spectator" (Morris's term). This is precisely the field of indexical traces, "effects of resurrection." These terms, *preservation* and *restoration*, were developed in nineteenth-century architectural controversies, but they may be used to understand the range and implications of ideals of indexicality and authenticated pastness in general. The rest of this chapter will elaborate on some vicissitudes of the desire to preserve or restore, to make the historical past present, in order to illustrate just some of the ways the polarity between preservation and restoration remained applicable in the twentieth century.

Living History

Today in Sturbridge, Massachusetts, there is an enterprise called Old Sturbridge Village. Pay an admission fee, and you enter what purports to be an authentic display of New England village life from the first half of the nineteenth century. You can walk through a small water-powered gristmill and a sawmill; a cooperage, kiln, schoolhouse, bank, and so forth;

and a farm with livestock, worked with early nineteenth-century implements. In so doing, you encounter a number of peripheral details, such as horse-drawn carriages and proper period costumes for those working at the various trades. It is claimed that, to the extent possible, the place is self-contained; for instance, barrels used in some of the village undertakings come from the cooperage, where you can watch barrels being made. The major activities are seasonally correct, so that tourists coming in the spring can see planting, in the summer haying, in the fall harvesting and harvest festivals.

Throughout, there is respect for the ideal of preservation, an invitation for the tourist to engage in the kind of relation with the past envisioned by Ruskin and Morris. This is especially the case with the buildings making up the village. A number of them are actual nineteenth-century structures moved from their original sites, repaired, and re-erected at Old Sturbridge Village. Their authenticity is communicated in a number of ways, from the direct claims of the tourist literature to more immediate manifestations. Take the building surfaces so valued by Ruskin. On the schoolhouse walls are generations of graffiti and names carved by students. The schoolhouse originated in 1800 in New Hampshire, and its walls—and the personalized indexical traces left in them by the acts of those long since dead—have been preserved for us to see and touch.

Yet the project assumes that compromises must be made, and to that extent the gap between past and present is not met purely with preservation. For example, there are the legal constraints of current building codes, and much of the food served visitors is not from the farm because of current health regulations. A portion of what you see, including elements of some buildings and perhaps costumes, has been fabricated with modern methods. But the most evident manifestation of this gap is the "interpreters," people in the guise of village inhabitants from the past. You can engage in conversation with them in their roles as early nineteenth-century Americans, but they also slip out of those roles to answer questions from a contemporary viewpoint, like good guides to any kind of exhibit. That is, they both act out their roles (one meaning of "interpreter") and they also explicate the significance of things (another meaning of "interpreter"). This means that their dress is not a simple appeal to imagine them as authentic figures from the past; they are only an exhibit of what the past looked *like*. They do not represent particular historical individuals, as is the case at another Massachusetts museum village, Plimouth Plantation. Rather they are conceived as historical types whose presence is nevertheless a form of resurrecting the past. According to one travel section newspaper story, "The gossip, the banker, the tinsmith, the guys in the grist mills and sawmills, the man shooting a musket, the potter, the women working in the gardens, the shoesmith—they bring the place alive."[17] This is a way of handling the fact that they are at best representations of the past, people actually alive in the present serving as tokens of the kinds of people who lived in the past.

Indeed, Old Sturbridge is itself an assemblage of buildings from various locations rather than an integrally preserved site. Despite being composed of preserved buildings, Old Sturbridge as a whole is a replica, a substitute, something like a restoration. Or rather, the invitation of Old Sturbridge to the past is less to a pure restoration or a pure preservation than to a fluctuating mix. What is crucial is the shifting and variable dialectic of the two extremes.

Old Sturbridge is interesting here not as a unique phenomenon, but as an example of a genre. It was conceived between the two World Wars, when this genre—variously called the "outdoor museum," the "museum village," or the "living history museum"—also appeared as a significant national phenomenon in the United States. A forerunner was the outdoor museum of Skänsen in Stockholm, which became a model that spread throughout Europe. Skänsen collected various Swedish buildings, artifacts, and craftspeople, promoting the craft practices of prior periods. In this, the Skänsen movement was in alliance with the fascinations assumed by the historic preservation movement. This merger developed most intensively and influentially in the United States in the 1920s, when both John D. Rockefeller Jr., and Henry Ford became heavily involved in projects that established the genre, Colonial Williamsburg in Virginia and Greenfield Village in Michigan.[18]

A most useful analysis of their development has been provided by the social historian Mike Wallace. In 1923, both John D. Rockefeller Jr. and Henry Ford were attracted to different public preservation projects, Rockefeller to the restoration of Versailles (!) and Ford to saving an inn in Sudbury, Massachusetts. Ford was drawn into spending between three and five million dollars on land and a small collection of buildings that became one of the earliest museum villages. His interest in earlier lifeways piqued, Ford had employees around the country acquire artifacts and edifices to add to his existing collection of outmoded mechanical devices. As this project mushroomed, he eventually arranged for his collection and additional period buildings to be transported to Greenfield, Michigan. As Ford put it, he sought "the things people used" in order "to show how our forefathers lived and to bring to mind what kinds of people they were." Greenfield Village opened to the public in 1929. Ford had gathered a miscellany of objects displayed in an industrial museum, and buildings ranging from a New England windmill and firehouse to the courthouse where Lincoln argued law and Thomas Edison's Menlo Park laboratory. Greenfield Village also includes nineteenth and early twentieth century crafts and manufactures shops with demonstrations.

Having already demonstrated interest in maintaining French antiquities, Rockefeller was recruited to the idea of restoring Williamsburg, Virginia, by a local minister, W. A. R. Goodwin, who sought to retain "[t]he spirit of days long ago [which] haunts and hallows the ancient city and the homes of its honored dead." Rockefeller eventually engaged Goodwin as his agent in a buyout of local properties. Rockefeller enthusiastically participated in the ensuing restoration of an American town of the 1790s that was effectively completed by the mid-1930s, insisting on intensive scholarship and precise, accurate detail. ("No scholar must ever be able to come to us and say we've made a mistake," he is reported to have said.) While pre-1800 buildings still extant were preserved as much as possible, hundreds of post-1800 buildings were razed in order to allow twentieth-century contractors to restore eighteenth-century edifices over their original foundations.

Between these two projects, then, there were differences in both ideological proclivities and constructive attitudes. In Wallace's convincing reading of their ideologies, Ford's Greenfield Village excluded achievements of the professional and upper middle classes (bankers, lawyers, and so forth). It was thereby able to represent historical progress as a consequence of the activities of inventors and entrepreneurs, who embodied the individualistic work ethic rooted in pioneer virtues associated with a previous age. The diverse objects and environments of Greenfield Village could display them as exemplary in the present. Rockefeller's Colonial Williamsburg also manifested a class-based vision of utopia built on older virtues, but it was different from Ford's. In it, a plethora of accurate details coalesced around a perfect town populated only by hardworking craftspeople and responsible patricians. That is, productive, unalienated workers lived in satisfied harmony with the socioeconomic elite. The result was a preindustrial, precorporate utopia of a working town, sponsored by one of the most famous capitalists of the industrial age. Colonial Williamsburg did not even acknowledge the existence of slavery until the 1970s, when it was first depicted but relegated to a reconstructed plantation six miles from the main village.[19]

On the level of constructive attitudes in the design of environments appealing to a desire for pastness, these two museum villages define a generic axis delimited by strategic extremes. Ford collected aspects of the old that exemplified his individualist-progressivist ideology of history; he was less interested in a perfect replication of an original context validated by scholarship than in preserving the tools, artifacts, and edifices associated with admirable figures and types of actions from the past. In Greenfield Village, the tourist could walk through both an 1839 doctor's office and the actual "invention factory" of Edison. As a result, Greenfield Village is more like the kind of museum that houses genuine, preserved entities but from a jumble of times and places. In Colonial Williamsburg, on the other hand, Ruskin's dictum that restoration is destruction was literalized. Rockefeller had all buildings constructed later than the 1790s demolished to make way for an organically totalized reconstruction of an idealized eighteenth-century town that could nevertheless claim scholarly accuracy. Dissatisfied with the preservation of isolated edifices from different places and different periods, Rockefeller desired, in his own words, "to restore a complete area and free it entirely from [historically] alien or inharmonious surroundings."

Thus, discussions of the two enterprises often seem to invoke not only historiographic but recognizably aesthetic criteria circulating around issues of totality. Greenfield Village has been criticized as an admittedly impressive collection of preserved authenticities that is ultimately a mélange without definite temporal or spatial shape. Colonial Williamsburg, on the other hand, explicitly represents a specific town during a restricted temporal span, claiming a level of utmost historical accuracy; however, its pursuit of unity has been charged with promoting a vision of history that is falsely harmonious, aestheticized, and/or sterile. Such critiques reflect issues that extend beyond these specific examples. Debates among professional historians and curators concerning living history museums typically encompass such problems as the nature of relations of the individual exhibitionary elements to the surrounding environments, narrativization, and so forth. That is, they have to do with questions of the proper limits and proper means of implanting significance and totalization in the engagement with pastness.[20]

I have suggested that the distinction between the Ford and Rockefeller approaches is a generic axis of the museum village. This axis defines a polarity between the disunified collection of preserved historical elements and unification in the name of complete restoration or replication of a hypothetical original. This seems very much like a variation on the preservationist-restorationist controversies of the previous century, for the two poles embody two attitudes toward materials from the past and toward keeping and arranging them for the perception and historiographic contemplation of a spectator-tourist in the present. However, as a generic axis, variations on this polarity are readable within many kinds of individual instances of the genre. Old Sturbridge Village is typical in that it is a kind of compromise formation between the extreme strategies of Greenfield Village and Colonial Williamsburg. While Old Sturbridge does supposedly replicate the daily life of an entire farm village during a given period, its temporal span (1790–1840) is more vague than that of Colonial Williamsburg. While many of its edifices are genuine preservations, they have been imported from several areas of New England with the express purpose of making up a *model* nineteenth-century community. All of this is to say its spatial unity is justified by a crucial degree of abstraction or ideal-typicality, rather than in the past existence of a specific village in a highly limited, specific temporal span.

This mediating approach extends throughout Old Sturbridge and generates various configurations. The farm's livestock provides an irresistible example. As Old Sturbridge experts explain it to journalists, sheep raised on an early nineteenth-century New England farm would probably have been a breed called Wiltshire-Dorsets, but this type has since been interbred into extinction. In the name of authenticity, therefore, Old Sturbridge has bred phenotypes, sheep that are genetically unrelated, but that physically resemble the now nonexistent Wiltshire-Dorsets.[21] This practice extends the preservation-restoration problematic from built environments to biology. Genuine preservation would provide us with an individual animal of a certain genuine identity because it was produced from a gene pool extending continuously in time back to the early nineteenth century. The extinction of that gene pool breaks the continuity of time, opening up a materially unbridgeable gap between past and present. But facing this gap, Old Sturbridge resorts to a restoration of Wiltshire-Dorsets. This produces a replica. Temporal continuity and the identities it supports have been irretrievably lost, but they are replaced by a substitute with an appearance of the original, whose correctness is substantiated by scholarly research and scientific knowledge. The sheep are not authentic Wiltshire-Dorsets come down to the present in an unbroken genetic chain, but they look as much as possible like authentic Wiltshire-Dorsets.

It is worth emphasizing that this goes beyond verisimilitude in the sense of avoiding conflict with a tourist/spectator's preexisting sense of the real past. After all, how many visitors to Old Sturbridge would recognize a deviation from the correct type of sheep? The attention to detail, the desire for accuracy here begins to border on compulsion or obsession. Yet, because this restorationism is a compromise formation, it evinces the victory of preservationism. The preservationist goal of imaginatively and perhaps mysteriously *being* in the presence of the past through the mediation of authentic objects remains significantly dominant; it would have been better to have actual Wiltshire-Dorsets. In their absence, however, that goal has been diverted into a restorationist satisfaction with seeing or experiencing what the past should have looked like. But that word *like* opens the gates to a multitude of slippages, since it continually highlights the resort to resemblance rather than sameness, iconicity rather than indexicality, and the annealing of breaks between past and present through substitution, rather than continuity from past to present through identity.

Strategies for dealing with such slippages involve documented justifications by experts, appeals to scholarship, the authority of knowledgeable historical research. That is, authoritative attestation comes into play not just to prove that an object is a genuine, preserved one, but even when the object is *not* authentically from the past, for it can alternatively assert exactitude of appearance. The job done by research specialists goes beyond the libraries and the production of the exhibit, for they must inform journalists and the public about the very quest for accuracy. It is again important that this task of reassuring audiences goes beyond any postulated public knowledge about a specific artifact or exhibit. Indeed, it is assumed that public expectations might be contradicted by superior scholarly expertise. But even this is part of a process of constant reassurance that the gap between past and present is always being minimized, a reassurance that is an important function for such expertise. Thus, Sturbridge "inhabitants" may proudly tell visitors of a research library of well over 20,000 volumes that, along with the various educational projects associated with Old Sturbridge Village, become in turn supplementary signs of accuracy.[22] The assumption is not necessarily specific prior knowledge on the part of the public, only a generalized desire for contact with the past.

However, the fascination with the past presupposed here is grounded in the dream of a perfect preservationism. Ideal resemblance constructed in the present—that is, restorationism—is only a backup strategy. Absent the requisite temporal, indexical continuity, then, this fascination can be engaged by an overwhelming impression of exactitude supplemented by an aura of scholarship. A kind of compulsive precision validated by scholarly authority may come into play when restorational replication displaces preservative authenticity. This marks a moment when preservation encounters its limits, and the supreme value of recovery of the past—which is shared by Ruskin and his symbolic opponent, Viollet-le-Duc, and also by all rationales for and variants on the museum village—is turned toward the substitutive, the restorational.

But the theoretical point is surely that preservation must *always* encounter its limit. In practice, there will never be enough artifacts remaining from the past to completely reproduce it. Imagine what would happen if all materialities from the past were preserved. Spatially, the situation would be akin to Borges's famous map; there would be no room for those of the present. Temporally, such a perfect preservation would entail canceling the gap between present and past, so that the rationale for preservation would become nonsensical. It is in this gap that Morris's "spectator" of an ancient edifice and the tourist of the museum village operate their fascination with the past. At some point and to some degree, preservation must always give way to restoration, for (like Bazin's total cinema) total preservation is an impossibility.

This is a nicely Derridean twist: the backup strategy, a kind of supplement, takes over the center, because the preferred value, preservation, can only achieve its appreciation of the past by recourse to some element of present-mindedness, incompleteness, restoration. If Old Sturbridge composes a totality, it is one that never existed in reality—a *model* village. True, it includes preserved elements and only such replicas as necessary to complete the model. To that extent it partakes of the Greenfield Village generic pole; however, as a composite whole, it is itself a new entity, made for purposes of the present. Here is where the Colonial Williamsburg generic pole comes in: exactitude also validates this new totality, offering experience of the old that includes elements of the new.

Preserving for What?

The polarity of preservationism and restorationism is partly defined according to the kind of totality that is its consequence, from the stylistically and therefore temporally unified to the stylistically and temporally disjunctive. This leads to a question that can only be answered on the plane of ideology: a totality of what and for what? Even in the preservationist polemic à la Ruskin-Morris, the ultimate goal was imaginative, or spiritual, contact with the past. That is, principles of material authenticity are in the service of immaterial ends, objectivity is in the service of subjectivity. This is related to the slippages possible in the restorationist goal of "looking like." If the value of authenticity is as a means rather than an end, deviations from absolute authenticity or accuracy might be justified in the name of such ends. But perhaps the ends are not always those explicitly expressed in the rationales for authenticity and accuracy.

As an example, consider Old Sturbridge Village's own history. First open to the public during the post–World War II tourism boom, it had been originally conceived and developed during the interwar period. Much like Greenfield Village and Colonial Williamsburg, it proceeded with the enthusiastic patronage of agents of industrial capital, the Wells family, who had acquired their wealth from an optical manufacturing business founded in the nineteenth century. The key figure for Old Sturbridge seems to have been Albert Wells, who, along with a brother, was an enthusiastic rather than a systematic collector of antiques. Early in the existence of what was first called Old Quinebaug Village, Wells faced a visit from a group of connoisseurs from the antiquarian Walpole Society. He felt compelled to write a booklet explaining why authenticity of artifact was not always his controlling principle:

> Old Quinebaug Village will be a living museum where the arts and industries of early rural New England will be preserved and taught anew.... It will make no apology to the expert who examines each board and nail with a critical eye to historial exactness.... This purpose, briefly, will be to preserve the ever-good things of New England's past in a manner that will teach their usefulness to the people of the present and the future. By "good things" of the past is meant not merely antique objects, but rather everything these objects imply—how they were made, how they were used, what the people and conditions of life were that made them necessary and influenced their designs; above all, how virtues and ideals expressed in them can be applied to life and work today.[23]

This rationale for Old Sturbridge is not the literal preservation of buildings and artifacts in and for themselves. Rather, preservation is a means of supporting a past way of life in the present, a way of life involving older values of unalienated craftsmanship, a certain spirit of work in early New England—"virtues and ideals." What is sometimes presented as if it were a purely anthropological concern with older lifeways therefore has a more utilitarian significance. Wells seems to have imagined a stream of potential industrial workers who would first serve as crafts apprentices in Old Sturbridge and be educated in early nineteenth-century values. This resonates with the concerns of Ford and Rockefeller, in its ambition to inculcate values from a mythical good old days of allegedly greater craftsmanship and social harmony into the labor force.

Not only does this accord with projects of Wells's socioeconomic compatriots, but it also continues the nonmaterial, nonliteral elements of the preservationist rationale for material preservation expressed in Ruskin and Morris. Wells wishes to make the attitudes and culture underlying the activities of the dead people of an earlier period live in the present. He hoped Old Sturbridge would provide examples and educational projects to that end, and makes it clear that this goes well beyond the antiquarian preservation of material historical objects, which may be a starting point but cannot in itself control every aspect of the project. Yet, the fact that Wells felt the need to respond to preservationists indicates the rhetorical and ideological strength of preservationism by the 1930s.

This strength was part of a strong "historical" tendency. Even in the United States, the theme of recapturing the spiritual values of the virtuous dead through the medium of their continuously lasting products and tools runs through the entire history of the preservation movement. The beginnings of organized preservation in the United States are often dated back to a successful 1850s campaign to save Washington's home, Mount Vernon. Initiated by a group of wealthy women, many of whom traced their ancestry back to the Revolutionary War, the campaign enlisted politicians and other public figures. In a speech delivered 139 times, the popular orator Edward Everett argued that a preserved Mount Vernon would offer "a common heritage for the estranged children of a common father, the spell of whose memory will yet have the power to reunite them around his hallowed sepulchre."[24] Claims about the unifying power of the tomb of the Father notwithstanding, the success of the Mount Vernon campaign was quickly followed by the Civil War.

Despite this unfortunate counterevidence, the impulse to recover the past gained momentum in the years after Reconstruction, and the growing number of increasingly visible organizations and crusades for historic preservation remained the province of well-off, ideologically respectable social strata. Wallace identifies four American social groups who provided leadership as well as financial and political support to the cause of historic preservation between the 1880s and the 1940s. First, descendants of established New England textile and merchant families found self-confirmation by supporting genealogical and historical societies. Second, by the 1920s descendants of the pre–Civil War planters were enthusiastically engaged in protecting the artifacts and environments of their ancestors. Third, a small but significant number of multimillionaire individuals and families such as Ford and Rockefeller (and Wells), whose wealth was generated from industrial capitalism, became heavily interested in this kind of historical philanthropy. And finally, a different kind of group emerged, not from wealth and its heritage, but from the professionalized middle class. A stratum of professionals and managers supplied talent and intellectual energy for the notion of rational, conservationist management of environments and resources, and eventually spawned the preservation professional, whose entire occupational life and training was built around the concept of historic preservation.[25]

This is an impressive set of high-status groups that, after the mid-nineteenth century, sought from different perspectives to make preservation a public value. Given their varied social and financial resources, it is not surprising that the ideal of preservation, with its inevitable restorationist components, has been established as a touchstone for sociological, political, and discursive processes associated with built environments. This touchstone remained effective, often as a fulcrum for critique, even at the height of modernism in architecture and the urban renewal movement. Of course, powerful economic forces could also be marshaled against

preservationism in any specific instance. Fluctuating and sometimes fric-
tional relations between real-estate interests, preservation lobbies and
historical societies, and local governments have become a standard aspect
of planning and zoning. Since the 1960s, however, the built-in rivalry
between real-estate developers and preservationists has been sometimes
ameliorated by a growing belief that the preservation and/or restoration
of old houses could add to the value of a property, for some buyers were
willing to pay as much or more for a "historic" building than for a new
building on the same site. This could become an advantage for real-estate
business strategies in some older neighborhoods and a consideration in
urban renewal, but any alliance between development and preservation
would always be tenuous, something evident in the Reagan-era real-estate
boom of the 1980s.[26]

At any rate, today there is scarcely a medium-sized American city
that does not have an informal or formal "historic district." (The use of
zoning laws to create such districts was one of the tactics introduced by
preservation groups in the 1930s.) In the deep South one can visit ante-
bellum mansions where the tour guides are young women in hoop skirts.
In the far West one can tour Spanish colonial missions established by
Father Serra. In the West and on the Great Plains, one can amble through
"ghost towns." Throughout the United States, walking through environments tinged with pastness and advertised as such has become a conventional tourist activity, one that is intertwined with local economies and
economic planning. And the framework of preservation and restoration is
supposed to define the ground rules establishing that pastness.

Some commentators believe that a chief impetus for preservationism in the United States came from the New Deal, and government participation all the way up to the federal level has intermittently contributed
to this normalization. However, even here an emphasis on well-off
socioeconomic and professional groupings deserves more emphasis. For
example, although Congress established the National Trust for Historic
Preservation in 1949, it was privately financed. The key to its activities was a $2,500,000 endowment from the Mellon family in 1957, and it
has also been supported by sources such as the Duponts and the Lilly

Foundation.[27] Even for the National Trust, the concrete successes achieved by preservationist rationales are inseparable from economic sources associated with high status groups and interests.

The support of major industrial and finance capitalists for preservationism links it with the museum village, and both are components of a broad historical context of concern with built environments based on pastness. Considering them not only as individuals but as situated socioeconomically, the depth of their commitments is striking. Estimates of the pre–World War II expenditures by Ford and Rockefeller on their definitive projects range from twenty-five to seventy-nine million dollars *each*, and the passion and involvement of such figures as Wells, Ford, and Rockefeller in acquisition, planning, and construction decisions is well documented. This makes something noted by some commentators especially intriguing. Although the concept of the museum village entails no particular restrictions of historical period, museum village projects most often tended to privilege objects, activities, and periods that predate modern industrial capitalism by just a couple of generations at most.[28]

Wallace therefore reads Greenfield Village and Colonial Williamsburg as evincing anxiety about the social relations of modern corporate capitalism. As we have seen, both construct a thematized vision of the past through selections of buildings and artifacts that idealize the activities of certain historical social strata. Greenfield Village highlighted individuals of the two or three previous generations, often technological innovators, who rose from an industrious common people to determine history. Colonial Williamsburg is set much more precisely, in the 1790s—"just before that junction at which artisanal production succumbed to capitalist social relations," in Wallace's words. It sought to demonstrate how a beneficent planter elite, as forerunner of the twentieth-century corporate elite, presided over a society based on an order of craft production that was supposedly free of socioeconomic discontent and conflict—in short, free of history. It is true that such constructions were subject to dispute over the years, not only among museum professionals but also in the wider public sphere. This was so especially after the political turmoil of the 1960s and the subsequent rise of a "new social history" among academic U.S. historians; however, it remains debatable whether and how much this basic structural framework changed.[29]

At any rate, the ambition expressed by Wells certainly applies to the conceptions behind all the paradigmatic museum villages discussed here. The spirit underlying a well-functioning community of some superior past time was to be resurrected beginning from its objects, monuments, and edifices, which would then serve to display virtues and ideals applicable to life today; hence the crucial importance of making the past somehow present. Of course the notion of a past "golden age" is unique neither to this genre nor the society that produced it. It is also unsurprising that dominant social types or groups find means to construct their own versions of the past and of a perfect society. But it seems less predictable to find not just, say, descendants of a declining planter elite compulsively saving or erecting and displaying utopias of the past, but also scions of a triumphant and dynamic industrial capitalism. And this after a century in which that capitalism had transformed much of the world.

An underlying assumption that goes hand-in-hand with this anxiety has to do with historicity itself. Modern historiography is an ordering of time that always evinces the possibility of change.[30] Paradoxically, the need to construct the past seems to lead to a form of historiography—as the discursive construction of a history in the present—that must function to overcome history. According to Wallace, a certain knowledge of the present is being displaced by the museum villages: that social discord and friction can lead to a destabilization of social and economic hierarchies in the present that define the powerful positions of capitalist-businessmen. In that case, the ideological impulse behind the founding of the museum village genre is realized in a drive to defang the possibility of transformation inherent in the temporality of capitalist modernity. These museum villages aim to immobilize historical temporality. One might say they seek to mummify change.

Wallace thus describes a defensive subjectivity manifested in the historiography of the museum village. There may be something evocative about this historicity not only for a film theorist who sees a certain kinship to Bazin, but also for the psychoanalytic textual theorist. The historical "just before" of Rockefeller's Williamsburg bears comparison to the "just before" in Freud's much-cited account of fetishism. Recall that in Freud's scenario, the little boy's perception of the woman's body generates a knowledge that the woman does not have a penis, which raises the threatening specter of castration. This threatening knowledge is a metaphor for the tenuousness of a unified totality, and must be countered in order to sustain the subject's coherent identity. The mechanism of this warding off is an obsessive overvaluing, a fetishization, of something that spatially adjoins the threat and henceforth becomes a focus of the subject's sexual pleasure. The classic fetish objects are nongenital parts of the woman's body or clothing associated with them, which are subconsciously remembered as having been perceived "just before" the threatening perception.[31]

Suppose we consider the authentic, preserved historical object in analogy with a fetish object. There are at least two points about this scenario that resonate with our account of the museum village. First, the fetish object is a "part" of the woman's body that, in the fantastic logic of the symptom, restores it as a "whole" body (one not subject to castration). This is a structure of metonymy-as-synecdoche: a bordering "part" (the fetish object) replaces the missing "part" (the penis), so as to symbolize a complete "whole." Similarly, if one fixates on an authenticated, preserved object as a trace of a vanished past that brings one into contact with it, that object is just one fragment or part of a postulated total past. As noted earlier, it is impossible for there to exist enough preserved objects to reconstitute the whole set of existents from a given instant or period in the past; nevertheless, preservationism values such objects as the royal road by which a subject may imagine a reconstituted past. The construction of historiographic environments in the museum village in a range of mixed deployments of preservationism and restorationism (which, again, implies that the two extremes are dialectically necessary to one another) is thus tied to questions of a totality, albeit one that can bear the weight of a corrosive temporality. Thus, there may seem to be vast differences between the Ford and Rockefeller models, with Greenfield Village emphasizing those genuine parts that survive, at the cost of a disunified or incomplete totality, while Colonial Williamsburg emphasizes the reconstitution of the whole at the cost of fully authenticated parts. But this difference is not fundamental, for each postulates and seeks to recover something nonmaterial, an underlying *spirit* that unified the earlier time. Colonial Williamsburg is simply more literalistic about it. Both posit a "just before," such that their differing compositional strategies both evince knowledge of present discord, which is a threat to a social subject's self-image and social situatedness.

Second, the fetishistic overvaluation of a "part" in Freud's scenario is a process of disavowal. Disavowal is not mere erasure of the offending memory, but something more complex. Subsequent and repetitive fixations on the fetish object would not be necessary if the threatening knowledge had been obliterated. Fetishism therefore assumes a constant underlying awareness of the threat that must be constantly warded off. This suggests that the fetishist retains some awareness of the impossibility, and hence the artificiality, of the solution. In that case, there may be knowledge value embedded in the structure of the fetish. Similarly, it need not be assumed that preservationism and enterprises that come in its wake, such as the museum village, completely obliterate knowledge of the contradictory and conflictual social relations associated with industrial and corporate capitalism, which engender a fear of historical change. On the contrary, they constantly manifest the problem of what might be called socio-economic maintenance, and they link it with historicity. The high valuation—the fetishism—of authenticated survivals from the past and other practices I have associated with preservationism can therefore register this knowledge. That is, conceiving of the recourse to preserved objects through a concept of disavowal suggests that such fascination with pastness may also have knowledge value. After all, what is here being disavowed is history itself, and so the very critique of the operation expressed by someone like Wallace must value historiography, albeit a more radical one.

The analogy of fetishism highlights the notion of a defensive subject, with respect to temporality and historicity. In later chapters I will have cause to return to the structure of fetishism and historical representation. For now, it is enough to remark upon such representatives of massive economic power disavowing the present through a commitment to historical constructions that are at least partly susceptible to description as fetishistic structures. Of course, while support for the preservationist cultural tendency (with its unavoidable admixture of the restorationist pole) has not always been unanimous among such high status or class groupings, it has provided major reservoirs of resources and energy to make historic preservationism a potent ideal to this day.

However, precisely because of the long-lasting strength of this tendency, it is important to insist on a range of variability in the kinds of enterprises it generates. This might not be evident from my discussion to this point, which has been focused on the museum village in the wake of preservation and restoration, so I will conclude this section with three qualifying points. First, it should be emphasized that this overall tendency has been an international one. This point can be made with respect to the museum village. As a genre, it crystallized in the United States, but it has by no means been limited to this country. Inspired by the crafts exhibits of the European Skänsen movement, and established with the interest and monetary support of privileged U.S. socioeconomic strata, the museum village was reimported back to the different financial and administrative context of Europe. By then, architectural pastness had long been an element of serious cultural debates and theories in a general Western context. (Of course, the same could be said about the institution of the museum, and the museum village is part of that history also.) On the one hand, this means that there have been significant local variations. On the other hand, this also suggests that it may well be possible to extend the notion of socially defensive subjectivity more widely.[32]

Second, not only have preservationism and the museum village spread geographically, but they also have a certain temporal expanse. It has been roughly 150 years since Ruskin crystallized the preservation-restoration debates, and the U.S. museum village genre has been in existence for about three-quarters of a century. The quest for genuine historicity and authenticity is itself "historical" in the sense that it is subject to changing configurations and overdeterminations over time. This is certainly true of the particular version of this quest one finds in the museum village, which constitutes itself as a built environment enabling one to enter and perceive the historical. Its languages of self-conception, justification, argument, and even publicity have always drawn on the rhetorical reservoir of the nineteenth-century restorationist-preservationist debates; however, these are subject to continual readjustment, reformulation, and refunctioning.

For example, *The Seven Lamps of Architecture* concludes with a plea for the benefits of laboring by hand on churches and houses as opposed to building railways. Moreover, in what might be Ruskin's ultimate insult to restorers, he likens them to a mob—connotatively, the democratic masses—in their destructiveness. The correlation of mid-nineteenth century preservationism with a general tendency toward medievalism found a culturally resonant outlet in Ruskin's and Morris's promotion of handicrafts, and it can clearly be treated as one more example of social disavowal. Here also, the instabilities and changes of the present are to be countered in a socially meliorative fashion by contemplation of and reference to artifacts and practices of an age prior to ascendant capitalism and its modern technologies.[33] Yet, while the museum villages conceived in the 1920s drew on some of Ruskin's rhetoric, they did not simply reproduce his anti-industrial yearning for idealized medievalist cooperativism. Instead they tended to idealize some version of productive virtue and enterprise just prior to industrial-corporate capitalism. Furthermore, they were not formulated by and for intellectual and cultural elites (even if sometimes disaffected) whose exemplary figures included Viollet-le-Duc, Ruskin, and Morris. Instead, they attracted practical, monied elites such as Ford, Rockefeller, and Wells, and as the twentieth century progressed, these were increasingly abetted by historical and museum professionals. After World War II, the U.S. museum village was often supported by philanthropic foundations or public-service institutions and aimed at the mobile middle-class tourist market of the postwar leisure-time boom. Yet, this is not to say that the museum village finally escaped its association with the desire for a prior social harmony. Writing in a more international context in the 1990s, Tony Bennett could still note that contemporary tourist literature and practices consistently make the past "something to get away to," citing Dean MacCannell's thesis that the logic of historical tourism is to make of the past modernity's other.[34]

Since the appeal to authenticity connected to a structure of dis-avowal seems to be so widely undertaken, it may be tempting to treat it as uniformly reactionary, but this is a mistake of the sort that itself banishes history. For example, in an intervention at a conference on historical pre-servation, George Mosse once pointed out that the desire for stabilized social harmony underlay nineteenth-century discussions of authenticity. A historian of German nationalism, he then associated this constella-tion with the twentieth-century European political Right, and ultimately argued that any postulate of such an ideal is polluted with the reactionary romanticism that valorizes a corporate, *volkisch* nation.[35] But we might instead regard the terms proposed by early figures in the preservationist-restorationist debates as a kind of ideological module that could be appro-priated, adjusted, reconfigured, or put to other uses at other places and times.

This brings us to my third point, that the pursuit of authentic past-ness may instead include elements of a more dynamic consciousness of temporality and a different kind of politics. Even in the exemplary preser-vationist figure of William Morris, one can find a more complicated reac-tion to industrial capitalism, which included an attraction to socialism. Mosse brushes aside Morris's socialism, for it suggests the possibility of contest on the terrain of imaginative and imaginary relations to the past. It calls into question the idea that a vision of harmonious social totality is necessarily impregnated with reactionary social and political attitudes. Indeed, Leftist historians have often thought it possible and necessary to intervene in arenas with labels like popular memory and public history. How could they not, since the genealogy of their politics is intertwined with privileging historical analysis? In fact, it is arguable that even a reac-tionary historiographic formation at least places history in play, for dis-avowal involves an underlying knowledge that provokes it, including the impossible nature of the pursuit evoked by the fetish object.[36]

The fascinations of pastness and cultural practices around historic-ity encompass a range of practices, including but not limited to architec-tural monuments, museum culture, tourism, and historiography itself, as well as the special concern of this book, the screen media. To absolutize the mystifications associated with the pursuit of authenticity such that the only alternative is complete rejection of every aspect of it is to abandon a massive terrain of cultural and intellectual discourses by which historicity is constructed. This terrain may be defined by certain inescapable premises, for example around temporality itself, and it certainly has its dominant historical tendencies and directionalities, stemming in part from socioeconomic power. But it can nevertheless be understood as a terrain where contestations and struggles over modes and uses of authentication and the authority of pastness can occur.

Postscript: Modern-Day Time Traveling

A periodical tourist guide to Old Sturbridge Village describes it thus:

> Only a few hundred yards separate the past from the present. On one side … sit hundreds of cars and buses carrying thousands of time travelers 150 years and more into the past. On the other side move "ancient" New Englanders carrying on the tasks and chores … familiar to area residents six generations ago.
>
> It's not a pathway into the Twilight Zone. It's the entrance to Old Sturbridge Village.

Or, as the back cover of a guide to museum villages urges us: "Become a modern-day time traveler." It explains: "Unlike a visit to a typical museum, where the exhibits are protected in glass cases, the exploration of a historic village enables you to be a time traveler, nearly an active participant in the past."[37]

By the late twentieth century, it may seem that something has again changed in the tropology of recovering the past. The language of science fiction seems to replace the language of spirits and the defeat of death, and it might be reasonable to decide that the appeal of preservationism and the museum village has been transformed. Yet, it would be premature to conclude that our age, so often described as "postindustrial" or "postmodern," has completely broken with the obsessions with the past and the problem of controlling time inherited from the nineteenth century. Certainly the languages of preservationism remain evident well into the television age as a self-consciously continuous heritage of principles. (For example, in 1963, "A Report on Principles and Guidelines for Historic Preservation in the United States" still quotes with approval an antirestorationist maxim that was well-known in the 1840s: "In treating surviving old buildings, generally speaking it is 'better to preserve than repair, better to repair than restore, better to restore than reconstruct.'")[38] The contemporary museum village was conceived during the interwar period and is associated with elite social strata "looking backward," but its heyday as a tourist attraction was the post–World War II period and it continues internationally to the present. But most pertinently, the discursive currency of the notion of time travel itself stems from the later nineteenth century, much like the practical currency of historic preservationism.

Previously used as a literary device for the representation of utopias, the premise of time travel was at that time taken over by socialist-oriented writers. Edward Bellamy's novel, *Looking Backward* (1888), was only the most famous of many socially and politically allegorical time travel tales.[39] Between its publication and World War I, as many as two hundred such novels may have been published in the United States, as well as dozens of utopian and anti-utopian narratives in Germany. Even such recognized eminences as Mark Twain employed the time travel plot (in his 1899 attack on ideologies of progress, *A Connecticut Yankee in King Arthur's Court*). Its impact in Britain was felt by the generally stipulated progenitor of modern science fiction, H. G. Wells.

There are two aspects of Wells's work that are suggestive here. First, Wells linked such socially speculative fiction to notions of scientific procedure popularized in the nineteenth century. Thus, unlike the utopian novel, *The Time Machine* proposed that an apparatus had to be devised to carry the Time Traveler. As Darko Suvin puts it, "He invented a new thing under the sun in the time-travel story made plausible or verisimilar by physics."[40] This means that a drive for plausibility and a certain accuracy of detail (no matter how hypothetical), already familiar from historiographic concerns, helped to constitute modern science fiction. Second, and crucially for current purposes, Wells's innovations included transporting characters into the past as well as into the future. Scholes and Rabkin remark that

> in the sense of travelling backward, into the past, the closest approxima-
> tions before Wells involve the interrogation of spirits of the dead about
> their lives (as in Homer's Hades or in Book III of *Gulliver's Travels*). Martin
> Gardner has suggested that the Outlandish Clock in Lewis Carroll's *Sylvie
> and Bruno* (1889), which sets back events when its hands are set back and
> which makes time run backwards when it runs backwards, anticipates
> Wells. However, "The Chronic Argonauts," the first—though quite differ-
> ent—version of *The Time Machine* (1895) appeared serially in 1888. Hence,
> we must either grant primacy to Wells or at least suggest that in the ninth
> decade of the nineteenth century, time travel was a motif whose time had
> come.[41]

As a motif whose time came in the late nineteenth century, the literary device of time travel embodied an imagination of being able to be "in"
the past, to witness and participate in a former time. Science fiction is
sometimes defined as the construction of alternative universes. But at a
formal, compositional level, there need be little to differentiate future
settings of a science fiction tale from the past settings of a historical fiction, once the science fiction is submitted to practices of literary verisimilitude or probabilities. And if science fiction can serve as the basis for
constructing utopic or dystopic universes, as well as metaphoric or even
allegorical parallels to the present, so can constructions of the past, as in
the museum village. The crucial point is that both propose a narrational
or epistemological stance that transcends its own "real" temporal location
in the present.

The science-fictional character who can travel in time is a figure for
imagining this transcendence, but it also exists in the narration of historical fiction: a transcendence of the divisions of past, present, and future,
a transcendence of temporal location and determinations. H. G. Wells
himself sometimes assumed a double cultural role, as "inventor" of modern science fiction and also as master of all human history. Not only was

one of Wells's most successful books the nonfiction *An Outline of History* (1920); *The Time Machine* itself has a strongly "historiographic" sub-text, for its journey to the future is structured as a Darwinian history of terrestrial species in reverse, wherein the future is plotted as a paradoxical regression to the biological past of life on Earth.

Such examples suggest that the trope of time travel in the contemporary rhetoric surrounding museum villages does not necessarily register a radical break. The imagination of time travel is rooted in the same period as the preservation movement, with its scientific sheen feeding a need for versimilitudinous detail that recalls restorationist exactitude. It does not in itself obviate the fascination of Viollet-le-Duc or Ruskin and Morris with coming to terms with the absence of the past and conceiving of ways to make it present. On the contrary, the two may well be inter-connected. In 1890 William Morris himself published a time-travel novel, *News from Nowhere*, which he conceived as a historically realistic response to Bellamy's limited utopic vision. If "time travel was a motif whose time had come," that time was also centrally concerned with historicity.[42]

Let us jump to another era and another medium that also involves the device of journeying to pasts and futures. The construction of imagined futures inseparable from imaginaries of pastness has also made its way into built environments of a different yet closely related type. In their fabrications of mythic historicities, "theme parks" merge the ethos of the amusement park with historiographic components that are overtly restorationist to the point of explicit stylization. The breakthrough model from the mid- to late-twentieth century was undoubtedly Disneyland, another achievement of the post–World War II era. Over the years, Disneyland has invited tourists to enter various periods of the past with a kind of imaginative playfulness and marketing atmosphere that at first seems far from the quasi-religious solemnity of a Ruskin: the heroic American iconographies of "Frontierland," for example, the Western colonialist expansionism of "Adventureland," and the everyday tranquillities of a turn-of-the-century "Main Street, U.S.A." While the playfulness is rein-forced both by the family-vacation ethos and the references to Disney car-toon worlds, there is nevertheless a subterranean admixture of reverence that occasionally surfaces in sometime attractions like the Hall of Presidents, where robotic effigies of the dead move and speak. These were certainly not Lenin-like mummies (everyone knows the corpses of the presidents are elsewhere and long since decayed), and yet they were mummy-like, high-tech likenesses that pedagogically revivified spirits of the past through the quasi-sacred words they repeated. The restorationism was thus explicit, for the exhibit reveled in its own capacity to substitute likeness for identity, as does all of Disneyland.

For many years Disneyland has also used "Tomorrowland" to reveal a "future" to the spectator's playful but educable witness and participation. (The future has required periodic updating; it always seems to look different now than it did a few years ago.) This impulse was extended in Epcot Center (which opened in 1982), a Disney theme park descended from the World's Fairs. Epcot Center was initiated with the explicit purpose of presenting the technological wonders of the twenty-first century as foreseen by such participating multinational corporations as General Electric and American Telephone and Telegraph. But while Disneyland itself involves historical pasts as well as futures, Epcot Center mixed the two, addressing the spectators with the now standard trope of time travel. Wallace remarks,

> An amazing amount of the World of Tomorrow is devoted to the world of yesterday. Virtually all the rides are time travels. Passengers settle themselves into moving vehicles which carry them from the dim past to an imagined future.[43]

Clearly an ideology of progress promoted by large capitalist corporations might find validation in such spectacles of the past, if only by showing that the future will be better. But the progressive directionality of this historical passage is not simply from primitive to advanced. As with Rockefeller's and Ford's museum villages, the past can continue to provide ideal models, and thus remain a source of timeless authority, with values that cannot be allowed to die but must continually be brought to life. The Masters of Ceremonies in the American Adventure were high-tech effigies, a robotic Mark Twain and Ben Franklin. Other dead eminences included Thomas Edison (one of Ford's American heroes) and Frederick Douglass. The past is to be both surpassed and the locus of wisdom, the authorizer of truth. The future refers to the past and the past to the future as we experience both in the present.

But all the paradoxes that might follow are smothered by another imagination or fantasy, that of being completely free in time. The touristic play of Epcot thus repeats a basic, overriding principle that persists through all the artifacts and media discussed in this chapter: that of a fantastic temporal transcendence. This principle may be figured as the capacity to go back and forth in time, or even to be in the past, present, and future simultaneously. The ideal of such temporal transcendence may occur in a number of emotional and cultural contexts, from the reverentiality of the nineteenth-century preservationist to the scholarly soberness of the restorationist, the serious historiographic missionizing of the mid-twentieth-century museum village, and the touristic playfulness of the twentieth-century theme park. Yet, these seemingly different attitudes commingle. Even the preservationist must admit that a minimal level of imagination informs the experience of authentic pastness, despite the serious spirituality involved; and even the touristic party ethos of Disneyland retains a substratum of reverence in its stylized constructions of pastness. Furthermore, it is not a matter of one kind of enterprise of pastness replacing another in a smooth historical line. Just as the preservationist-restorationist debates provided an ideological module capable of reinvocation and adjustment in later years, museum villages continue in the era of Disney theme parks.

Of course it would be possible to examine specific differences between, say, the theme park experience and time travel narratives, between earlier and recent time travel fictions, and so forth. But perhaps this is enough to point to something that they share. To different degrees and in different ways, they all manifest a founding assertion or obsession with overcoming the breaks between the present and past. Preserving remains, reviving vanished lifeways, replicating old artifacts—these share the ambition to have something of the past available to perception in the present and thereby to freeze time at the service of a beholder or spectator. The narrative device of time travel crystallizes this ambition.

Conclusion: Toward a Historical Time

Disneyland, of course, is unthinkable without the movies, a central concern of this book. The kinds of discourses and cultural practices discussed above are coincident with the era of photography and cinema. Many connections could be made. For example, H. G. Wells, mythical father-figure of modern science fiction, was a contemporary of D. W. Griffith, mythical father-figure of mainstream film. Not only did the most emblematic moments of Griffith's career involve staging the historical past (*Birth of a Nation*, 1915), but in his most famous experiment, *Intolerance* (1916), Griffith hyperbolized the implicit temporal transcendence of the spectator of the historical film by intercutting four spectacular stories set in different historical periods. Viewing this film is comparable to the notion of time traveling. But all this does is foreground something implicit in his other, and for that matter any, "historical films," namely a construction of film spectatorship as a transhistorical viewpoint on a historical past.[44]

Bazin argued that cinema is based on a preservative obsession grounded in a defensive subjective stance, even though he argued for the value of cases where those defenses are sublated through an investment in the real and its temporality. Bazin's linkage of preservation and subjective defenses is an insight that might be taken in different directions than he often took it. The idea that time is a threat that must be transcended could itself be treated as "historical," as embedded in social conflict, social disavowals, and so forth. This would include his emphasis on the indexical basis of normalized cinema, but with an awareness that indexicality and the drive to value the preservation of artifacts from the past goes well beyond cinema and has its own history. This history is tied into "a continuum of forms of historical representation," as Bann puts it, which blossomed in the nineteenth century.

Any form of historical representation is inevitably intricated with the construction of a temporality, and this is true of the preservationist-restorationist polarity, which may also serve to define the range of conceptions available for the indexical trace in modernity. As we have seen, the extreme preservationist depends on one of the classic conceptions of time, as an irreversibly linear, directional stream, any instant of which is unstoppable and unrepeatable. Irreversibility is constant loss, always threatening decay, death, disappearance. In compensation, the preservationist fastens on objective historical remains and survivals from the past as an index of that past. He or she becomes a seeker after unending connection and identity; hence the high evidentiary and spiritual value placed on the authenticated artifact and the ruin. Recall once more a point about Ruskin's preservationism. Certain elements of his argument could suggest that all remains of past cultures are worthy of preservation, regardless of style or period—and this despite his sympathy for the medieval. For if the work of time can be found in any object, then an extreme preservationism has no grounds for privileging any period. This is because it assumes the corrosiveness of time as a foundational, universal force. That is, the unlimited temporal breadth of significant authenticity ultimately follows from a thesis asserting the universal force of temporality. In fact, preservationism highlights the inevitability of the passage of time and the losses it entails (figured as death), while it seeks to fend off those losses. Disputes around the authenticity of preserved objects and the uses to which they should be put are therefore disputes about the best ways to deal with temporality, always associated with change (the difference between past and present) and therefore evanescence in time.

The extreme restorationist, more functionalist and pragmatic, takes another classic conception of time, as a sequence of points. Since this makes time segmentable, it may appear to better acknowledge the break between present and past. Further, since any instant of the past is such a point or separable segment, it is possible to conceive of a single point as being susceptible to more or less successful miming.

The restorationist is therefore willing to deal with a present substitution that claims to resemble that which is lost, as opposed to the thing itself. Yet, restorationism does share its most fundamental tenet about temporality with preservationism. To resort to a substitution is an even more submissive response to the gap between past and present produced by the irreversible directionality of time. It gives up the idea that fragments from the past can be the basis for genuine contact with the past. Such a substitution therefore depends on likeness rather than identity, and it can therefore claim some degree of authority only by appealing to disciplined historical research. (As we will see in the next chapter, however, this still means dealing in authenticated traces from the past, the historical source document.) In the face of an admittedly necessary failure, then, the restorationist may be more open to replications and ideal-typical reproductions, but, like the preservationist, holds a basic premise: the corrosiveness of time.

So when values treated as timeless are sought through the various admixtures of preservation and restoration, the substructure of the problem is that a corrosive temporality has become inescapable and profoundly problematic in the present. For the original museum villages, of course, spiritual virtues were located not in the medieval as opposed to the modern, as with the original preservationists, but in an immediately preindustrial social order instead of that associated with a fully industrial, corporate capitalism. But the crucial antinomy grounding the relation of present to past is between change and stasis, the time-filled and the timeless. At issue is the configuration that awareness of time itself takes. The museum village illustrates how this awareness resolves into configurations of the impossible desire to be in the presence of the past. This generates various aesthetics of totality linked to an investment, an indexicality focused (positively or negatively) on objects that have survived from past to present, constructing a positionality that might well be described as a defensive subjectivity. The defense is against time.

It might seem that the distinction between preservation and restoration could be likened to that between indexicality and iconicity, between identity and mimesis, and between continuity and segmentation.[45] But, once again, these are dialectical polarities rather than absolute contraries, for they admit of significantly different admixtures and resolutions. This is because the presence of the past is always impossible to realize literally. In this problematic, then, the terrain of pastness will always be realized as impure. Likeness and being, present and past, lie and truth, death and life, restoration and preservation can never be completely disjoined or completely unified. A referential pastness is the epistemologically central premise, but constructions of pastness always occur as answers to a fundamental inadequacy, which may or may not be acknowledged as such; and they are produced for specific kinds of reasons and purposes that may usefully be called "historical." For, as we will see in the next chapter, this historicity necessarily produces accounts of the past that are themselves always subject to revision or "historical" change. No wonder historicity can become so prominent a discursive terrain for social disavowals.

It could follow that no modern historicity—not even the most careful and scholarly—ever quite rids itself of at least some residue of the fantastic, the desire for temporal transcendence, the mummification of change. But this leaves open the question of whether imaginary and fantastic components always must necessarily be excluded from claims to knowledge, such as those proposed in historiography. In Philip K. Dick's *The Man in the High Castle*, the obnoxious Wyndam-Matson points out, "A gun goes through a famous battle and it's the same as if it hadn't, unless you know," explaining, "It's in here ... In the mind, not the gun." Yet, even if the effectivity of historicity and historical authenticity were only in the mind, and this made authoritative historical knowledge a matter of persuasion, psychic investment, positioning to disavow and believe, there are different modes of persuasion, desire, and belief. More important, their mere presence entails nothing one way or the other about the knowledge claims of any historiography—unless one actually presupposed that any "valid" knowledge consists in its separation from desire, persuasion, and belief.

A better route to understanding claims to historical knowledge is to historicize not only the preservative obsession, but modern historicity itself. This will require consideration of disciplined, professional historiography, which is now the most institutionally and epistemologically prestigious recovery of a real past. But the emergence of this discipline to high epistemological and cultural status was coincident with preservationism and other practices discussed in this chapter. So it will be necessary to keep in mind something noted by Paul Ricoeur—no enemy of historiography—when he theorizes historical referentiality. "Everything takes place," he writes 140 years after Ruskin, "as though the historians knew themselves to be bound by a debt to people from earlier times, a debt to the dead."[46]

CHAPTER 3

Once upon a Time
in the West

Change, mutation, becoming in general were formerly taken as
proof of appearance, as a sign of the presence of something which
led us astray. Today, on the contrary, we see ourselves as it were
entangled in error, necessitated to error, to precisely the extent that
our prejudice in favor of reason compels us to posit unity, identity,
duration, substance, cause, materiality, being. . . .

—Friedrich Nietzsche, *Twilight of the Idols* (1889)

Trace and aura. The trace is the appearance of a nearness, however
far removed the thing that left it behind may be. The aura is the
appearance of a distance, however close the thing that calls it forth.
In the trace, we gain possession of the thing; in the aura, it takes
possession of us.

—Walter Benjamin, *The Arcades Project* [M16a,3]

Gaining Time

As is typical in such attractions, tourists exit Old Sturbridge Village through
a gift and souvenir shop, in this case including a bookstore. One of the
items recently available there was an edition—a facsimile edition, a kind
of replication or restoration—of a book copublished by Old Sturbridge
Village and said to have been popular among nineteenth-century American homemakers: Lydia Maria Child's *The American Frugal Housewife:
Dedicated to Those Who Are Not Ashamed of Economy*. A volume of recipes,
home remedies, and tips on household procedures and management, it
begins as follows:

The true economy of housekeeping is simply the art of gathering up all the fragments, so that nothing be lost. I mean fragments of time, as well as materials. Nothing should be thrown away so long as it is possible to make any use of it, however trifling that use may be; and whatever the size of a family, every member should be employed either in earning or saving money. "Time is money."[1]

In the emergent capitalist ethos of the early nineteenth century, here is another kind of preservative obsession, one congruent with entrepreneurial and industrial enterprise. It was common sense to conceive of time as an economically valuable resource, something that could be fragmented, counted, organized, and, like Ben Franklin's pennies, saved. It is thus not far-fetched if the organization of time into useful segments at the level of the individual household seems reminiscent of the organization of the factory working day. That is, the shaping of that kind of day, which had already been occurring for some time when Child's book was first published, was implicated with the diffusion of novel attitudes toward time and novel experiences in the temporal arrangements of everyday life. The appearance of a monetary conception of time in a model of ideal domesticity attests to the general strength of those attitudes and experiences.

Historians have sometimes noted that a major issue during the industrial revolution was the manufacturer's need to impose new kinds of discipline on workers. Temporality was central to this discipline. In previous, nonfactory (farm, home manufacture) kinds of production, workers were often able to determine their own daily work schedules to a significant extent. Or rather, constraints on the use of time had tended to revolve around the completion of whole tasks, such as the fashioning of a garment or the plowing of a field. Furthermore, such labor tended to be scheduled in relatively vague and sometimes variable periodicities associated with categories of natural temporalities, such as those heavenly cycles that cultures had marked with calendars from time immemorial. So many garments had to be woven in so many days, for example, or planting and harvesting followed deadlines imposed by the seasons. Even if daily work was subject to more detailed time constraints, some of these could still be associated with categories of naturalized and seemingly cyclical needs, such as food and sleep. Such "natural" periodicities were also intimately intricated with a range of activities, from everyday tasks to the cultural rituals of festivals and carnivals.

The gradual increase in wage-manufacturing factory labor that began in England in the seventeenth century, along with a steady accretion of technological shifts implemented especially in the second half of the next century, entailed a concomitant intensification of divisions of labor. Stimulated by the interacting growth of productivity and commerce, the steadily increasing emphasis on detailed coordination between different subtasks in the production process eroded the importance of the unity of the whole task or product for the worker, as well as the use of natural cycles as temporal markers for labor. In the interest of the economic efficiency of a rationalized industrial capitalism, manufacturers found it desirable to regularize the timing of labor by other standards, namely quantifiable units of temporality that could be compared to quantities of currency. By the nineteenth century, these newer forms of temporal regularization had become quite normalized in many Western regions, but not before laboring classes experienced their development as the subjection of a naturalized temporal freedom to the requirements of the centralized factory and the manufacturer.

This distinction between task-oriented and time-oriented labor was emphasized in seminal work by the historian E. P. Thompson. For Thompson, major worker-manufacturer battles during industrialization concerned time, and in these, "the conflict is over two cultural modes or ways of life."[2] In efforts to regulate something that had not previously been regulated on this scale—the day-by-day, hour-by-hour, and even minute-by-minute activities of employees—employers quickly developed a number of procedures that became widespread. These included close surveillance of the labor process, fines and financial incentives, propaganda about work (often class-based and written by ideologists such as ministers), schooling of working-class children, and the repression or control of popular cultural forms, including seasonal festivals and sports, that could interrupt the regularization of labor time. The combination of clocks with time-based signals such as bells had been generally instituted in the late medieval city. It now became a typical element of the work environment, although factories used horns as well as bells.

The employers had a material interest in reconceiving time, at the level of the daily schedule, as segmentable and measurable according to exchange value. They were successful at normalizing this perspective for laborers. As Thompson puts it:

> The first generation of factory workers were taught by their masters the importance of time; the second generation formed their short-time committees in the ten-hour movement; the third generation struck for overtime or time-and-a-half. They had accepted the categories of their employers and learned to fight back within them. They had learned their lesson, that time is money, only too well.

Even the increasing ubiquity of new timekeeping technology may be related to such struggles. There developed a market for inexpensive watches, one segment of which was workers, because they often did not trust the employers' timekeeping. However, the interests of the manufacturers are indicated by the fact that a favorite reward for good employees who adhered to schedule, as well as honored retirees, was often, already, a clock.[3]

But the economic rationalization of time cannot be separated from its societal institutionalization, a transformation in daily life and activities that extended beyond the workplace. Of course, as the example of the medieval city indicates, the idea that time had value and the consequent need for techniques to organize it predated the spread of wage labor. For example, Michel Foucault, surely the most prominent recent theorist of disciplinary techniques, agrees with many scholars that the timetable or work schedule had long been an aspect of religious life, especially in monastic orders. According to Foucault, such devices for organizing bodies and their activities then spread to qualitatively different spheres, appearing in new organizational and training methods in seventeenth-century armies and schools. Institutions such as these provided models for the gradual saturation of practices and discourses with techniques of discipline. This makes emergent eighteenth-century factory methods appear as just one such form. Yet, even Foucault's "micro-physics of power" must admit that the societal spread of unprecedentedly subtle methods for regulatively ordering human bodies is imbricated with the development of industrial capitalism: "the two processes—the accumulation of men and the accumulation of capital—cannot be separated; it would not have been possible to solve the problem of the accumulation of men without the growth of an apparatus of production capable of both sustaining them and using them; conversely the techniques that made the cumulative multiplicity of men useful accelerated the accumulation of capital."[4]

For present purposes, a point of special interest is that by the end of the nineteenth century, temporal rationalization had massively proliferated in Western capitalist societies as an ongoing aspect not only of industry, but also scientific progress. The merger of economic efficiency and modern rationality exudes one of the great ideological strengths of rationalization techniques, in an operation that Horkheimer and Adorno called the dialectic of Enlightenment: even as they organize and control humans and delimit human subjectivity, such techniques are associated with an advance of human knowledge and thus an advance of free human subjectivity. The time-motion studies of Taylorism remain the most striking example, bringing together the motifs of time discipline and rationalized economic efficiency with the sheen of scientific method. But Taylorism itself presupposed prior technological advances in the measurement of time, which gives a good idea of the stake of social practices and knowledges in measuring and thereby exerting control over time.

Increasing exactitude in timekeeping had been stimulated in part by the needs of such practical sciences as astronomy and navigation. These sciences were often associated with economic activities ranging from fishing to imperialist exploration and expansion, but they also provided new tools, evidence, and conceptual inspirations for less immediately pragmatic natural sciences, such as theoretical physics. In the middle of the seventeenth century, the best mechanical clocks accumulated errors of more than five hundred seconds per day; by 1700, this figure had dropped below ten seconds, and around 1900, when Taylor was "scientifically" timing labor with stopwatches, the best clocks were accurate to within .01 second per day. Still, time-discipline for labor should not be regarded as a straightforward consequence of available technology; rather, it was intricated in the socioeconomic constitution of production. For example, as early as the seventeenth century, long before the accurate stopwatch, the largest ironworks in Europe already had a detailed written scheme for regulation of office work time that was impossible to implement, since it required workers to record their labor time according to a single authoritative office clock with a "minute dial"—something that did not yet exist. The conception of absolute temporal control over labor preceded any possible implementation; it was another one of those ideas whose time had come, a project seeking a technical solution rather than an available technology seeking a project.[5]

Nevertheless, by the beginning of the twentieth century, one can discern two extremes of time-discipline that were associated with technical developments in timekeeping and that included workplaces but extended beyond them. The first can be called planetary. Temporal rationalization expanded its reach to nations, continents, and the world as such, as the political and commercial organization of planetary space was solidified by the geographical regularization of time. It took three-quarters of a century to finalize. In the early nineteenth century, individual regions or locales still generally had their own temporal identities, in Wolfgang Schivelbusch's term. In all countries, every town kept its own "sun time," that is, it determined the time by local solar observations. Consequently, even within a single country such as Britain, there were five, seven, even fourteen minutes difference between the times adhered to among various cities. Improved roads and speedier carriage technology had already made this a problem for commerce and coordination in Europe in the eighteenth century. By the nineteenth century, railway scheduling, combined with the synchronizing opportunities afforded by the telegraph, made it seem intolerable. In the culmination of a process that began in the 1840s, a standardized railroad time replaced all such "natural" local times in 1880 for Britain, in 1891 for France, and in 1893 for Germany. In the United States, four time zones were established in 1889, though they were not given national legal force until 1918. However, it was in Washington, D.C., in 1884 that an international conference on time standards divided the world into time zones based on a scheme devised by the chief engineer of the Canadian Pacific Railway.

From a planetary perspective, there was always a difference, a gap, between natural time and abstract time, sun time and clock time, body time and commercial time. In the eighteenth century, for example, tables were developed to relate "solar true time" (based on when the sun actually crossed the meridian at a given locality, which is seasonably variable) to "solar mean time" (an invariable periodicity based on averages for the locality). In fact, Henry Ford began his business life as a watch repairman and was one of many who devised a two-dial watch that kept both local time and standard railway time. Such solutions were not uncommon, and only slowly disappeared. As late as 1941, when an elderly H. G. Wells summarized his late worldview, he started from these disjunctions in modern temporality. Deducing the likelihood of what is now called jet lag from the possibilities of intercontinental flying, Wells still proposed a double time scale solution, suggesting that all individuals might henceforth have to live in both "a local time in relation to the sun" (though since Wells probably assumed "solar mean time," this is already an abstraction) and a common, "world time" (a term derived in the late nineteenth century).[6]

From an early twenty-first century perspective, it appears that, as commerce, transport, and communications increased volume and speed and clocks had to be increasingly precise, temporal coordination across such splits became crucial. In retrospect this appears unavoidable because modern time awareness was inseparable from capitalism. Time awareness in capitalist modernity envisioned the scheduling of activities and practices covering entire continents, even the planet as such. The 1884 Meridian Conference resolved the problem for international commerce and communications by establishing stable and calculable solar mean times for any given point in the world. But there was another dimension to the time awareness of capitalist modernity. In addition to this macroscopic optic, it also encompassed a relatively microscopic side, affecting the daily and yearly schedules of singular workers. Collected in a specific factory, their activities might be planned to the hour and sometimes the minute, but the impetus to schedule went beyond the workplace.[7]

This brings us to the other extreme of time-discipline clearly associated with developments of timekeeping. For lack of a better term, this extreme can be called that of the individual. I have so far emphasized the timing and scheduling of the individual body as a matter of labor practices within the framework of industrial capitalism. But it is also true that activities in spheres of life outside the work environment were often to be timed and scheduled in detail. These included both activities explicitly conceived as individualized and those thought to relate individuals to one another in social and cultural life.

One indication of this is the increased availability and reliability of the personal timepiece. Miniaturized, portable clocks had long been available, first as unique items for the aristocracy and the wealthy, and later as bourgeois accoutrements. In the nineteenth century, they made their way to mass populations. Technical problems in the factory production of watches were solved in the 1860s, and according to one 1875 report, worldwide watch production was 2.5 million per year as opposed to 350,000–400,000 around 1800.[8] In 1902 the personal timepiece was so common that Georg Simmel illustrated the interdependent nature of modern existence by imagining the effects if every pocket watch in Berlin suddenly went wrong: "[A]ll economic life and communication of the city would be disrupted.... [T]he technique of metropolitan life is unimaginable without the most punctual integration of all activities and mutual relations into a stable and impersonal time schedule."[9] By the end of the nineteenth century, the wide dissemination of temporal rationalization and its connection to economics and modern social order was a cultural theme, taken up not only by social theorists, but by literary narrativists. The way was well prepared in 1904–1905, when Max Weber published his classic book on the mentality of capitalism and typified the capitalist ethos through the same quotations from Benjamin Franklin that had served as the starting point of Lydia Maria Child: "Remember, that time is money."[10]

So in 1934, when Lewis Mumford asserted, "The clock, not the steam-engine, is the key machine of the modern industrial age," he was writing in a well-established line of social thought. During the Enlightenment, the idea of the clock as the symbol of a perfect mechanism was already a well-established trope. But Mumford treats the clock as a machine with a product—hours and minutes—that is distributed throughout society and culture to impose order through the quantification of time. "Let the reader examine for himself the part played by mechanical routine and mechanical apparatus in his day, from the alarm clock that wakes him to the radio program that puts him to sleep," wrote Mumford to his Depression-era public:

> The first characteristic of modern machine civilization is its temporal regularity. From the moment of waking the rhythm of the day is punctuated by the clock. Irrespective of strain or fatigue, despite reluctance or apathy, the household rises close to its set hour. Tardiness in rising is penalized by extra haste in eating breakfast or in walking to catch the train: in the long run, it may even mean the loss of a job or of advancement in business. Breakfast, lunch, dinner, occur at regular hours and are of definitely limited duration: a million people perform these functions within a very narrow band of time, and only minor provisions are made for those who would have food outside this regular schedule. As the scale of industrial organization grows, the punctuality and regularity of the mechanical regime tend to increase with it: the time-clock enters automatically to regulate the entrance and exit of the worker, while an irregular worker—tempted by the trout in spring streams or ducks on salt meadows—finds that these impulses are as unfavorably treated as habitual drunkenness: if he would retain them, he must remain attached to the less routinized provinces of agriculture. 'The refractory tempers of work-people accustomed to irregular paroxysms of diligence,' of which Ure wrote a century ago with such pious horror, have indeed been tamed.[11]

It is characteristic that the "irregular worker" is here depicted in a kind of return to Nature. The abstraction of human life from organic duration is a constant theme in this line of social thought, which figures modern industry and modernity as the recession of the natural from everyday life. Elements of this line penetrated the anti-industrial handicraft movement even in the work of politicized artists like William Morris. It is only a short step to idealizing agriculture or the rural as being a kind of life most resistant to economic rationalization (an idea that often appears as cliché since the nineteenth century). There may be a residue of such idealization even in E. P. Thompson, despite the fact that he was writing at a time when agricultural production was clearly becoming subject to the exigencies of international commerce, as corporate agri-business. As a Marxist, however, Thompson does evince at least some awareness of the dangers of unmediated appeals to nature. His distinction is between task-oriented and time-oriented *labor*. He clearly hopes to highlight the attraction of naturalized categories of temporality in pre-industrial popular cultural and economic life to agricultural and factory workers, and he is interested in the resistances such categories might motivate. Thompson is therefore aware of the contradictions they entailed, and tries (perhaps not always with complete success) to avoid invoking them in any explanatory or nostalgic sense.[12]

At any rate, this modern time-consciousness involved the more or less successful pervasion of clock time, in different ways and to different degrees, throughout the sociocultural formation. During the nineteenth century, an unprecedented awareness of the temporal precisions of clock time increasingly penetrated everyday life and labor. By the early twentieth century, this was commonly discussed by many kinds of intellectuals, and was a central concern for those analyzing and conceptualizing modern society. Modern clock time had, in fact, become a kind of ideological and cultural "dominant." Awareness of it impinged on all social sectors and strata, from "white collar" classes to factory laborers and factory owners, in the home as well as in the workplace. Now, one of the elements of preindustrial lifeways associated with natural time cycles was recreations, such as festivals, holidays, and sports. In its function of differentially organizing masses of people across many class fractions, the temporality associated with capitalist modernity brings us to film as mass entertainment.

Cinema appeared during the later nineteenth century, with its intensified time awareness. It can be argued that the institutionalization of the movies as a leading mass entertainment medium was intertwined with the pervasiveness of time-based organization, because the remarkable success that the new medium achieved by the end of World War I was dependent on temporal ordering at the level of the day symbolized by the diffusion of the watch. In the first instance, as the *production* of narratives in indexical images for mass audiences, mainstream cinema required a large degree of rationalization procedures. By World War I, the film industry was able to borrow loosely and selectively from assembly line and large business methods to construct relatively predictable regularities with respect to labor, production, and marketing schedules. (In a mediated way, these were also dependent on planetary regularization of time associated with any national and international commerce; but they also interacted with residues of "natural time," which of course did not completely disappear, for example, insofar as market fluctuations were correlated with traditional holiday and vacation periods.) On the *distribution* and *consumption* side, this meant that the film industry required unprecedentedly large numbers of steady customers to supply the liquid capital necessary to support the production plant and provide a profit margin. These customers had to possess not only what came to be called "leisure time," but leisure time that was regularized enough to make a large volume of film viewing reasonably constant and calculable by the production, distribution, and exhibition companies.

Consequently, the kinds of cinema that became economically and culturally dominant could only exist in societies where powerful, large-scale forces sought to organize and regulate the week and the day, such that, as a relief from or reward for work, there were a certain number of hours regularly allotted to leisure among large segments of the population. As Ford famously recognized with respect to autoworkers, this also assumes that the consuming population has access to a certain minimum of "disposable income." The latter is dependent on labor time, the immediate basis of wages. Two pillars of a consumer economy, leisure time and disposable income derived from labor time, provided the film industry with the potential for a mass audience that could fuel the production of mass entertainment with capital and profit. This whole structure was unthinkable without a line of temporal organization running from wage labor to the standardization of the workday and workweek. As E. P. Thompson notes of an earlier moment, labor movements could not help working within the very terms of the business interests they opposed. They often sought to impose their own temporal counterregulations. These rapidly came to include a minimum of leisure time, as in the struggles for the ten-hour and then the eight-hour working day.

Film theorists have sometimes been interested in arguing for a special relationship of the film medium to temporality. In Bazin's case, this argument produced an emphasis on what might be called cinema's documentary aspects, whereby cinematic specificity resides in the indexically based representation of events from the past. But a social theorist or historian could well see cinema's relationship to temporality in a different light: cinema manifests a special relation to modern time awareness first as a matter of distribution through its status as a mass medium, and only second as a matter of representation. By World War I, the production of mass-entertainment films was organized with an understanding of the benefits of bureaucratized planning and scheduling, and in a sense, so was filmic textuality and consumption itself. For example, one constraint on the duration of films and film programs was the need to coordinate and distinguish offerings and admissions according to society-wide norms of available leisure time (matinee versus evening screenings, weekday versus weekend, and so forth).[13]

It is therefore possible to conceive of cinema as a kind of juncture of indexicality and rationalization, a crossroads within the emphasis on temporality that developed throughout industrializing culture. This is not necessarily an ontological specificity, but it may still suggest some historically crucial specificities of its innovation and development as a representational medium. As a juncture of indexicality and rationalization, cinema can be compared to another set of discourses and another variant of rational order in time that manifest their own special relationship to indexicality: those implicated in modern historical studies concurrent with the proliferation of automatically produced media. For historical consciousness became part and parcel of the dominant scientific epistemologies of the West in the nineteenth century, and for a time claimed the status of a master discipline.

In this light, the burgeoning time consciousness of capitalist modernity was the setting for those aspects of nineteenth-century epistemologies that have caused some to call it "the age of history." Historiography engages in the study of changes and stases in time. It is necessarily involved in the construction and reconstruction of temporalities. The prestigious, professionalized study of authenticated pasts became a "discipline," a "human science," one of whose grounding assumptions was the universal force of temporality. But this discipline revolved around a central paradox or contradiction. One major aspect of the new constructions of temporality was a general consensus on the value of understanding the past, and of instituting systematic, minimally ordered procedures for investigating and explaining it. Yet, it turned out that serious concern with the past could be *dis*ordering.

Losing Time

Part of the art of writing history is making a selection from the mass of information available from the past to be displayed in a historiographic account, one that orders the information synthetically. My sketchy exposition from Lydia Maria Child to Lewis Mumford and the emergence of cinema as a mass medium has taken us through such a selection of illustrative and summative details designed to introduce the idea that the reorganization and reconceptualization of temporality was a nodal project of nineteenth-century Western economic and social life. Since they affected everything from the details of everyday life to international relations, it is not surprising that issues of temporality also asserted themselves throughout Western cultural and intellectual spheres.

The multigenerational ambit of pervasive revisions in experiences and relations of humans to temporality included rethinking its status with respect to knowledge claims. Like the large-scale economic and social developments from which they cannot be separated, this rethinking did not completely originate and certainly did not end in the nineteenth century; however, to a large extent its terms were solidified, normalized, and institutionalized then. Some of the contemporaneous reconsiderations of time that took place in science, philosophy, and cultural production undoubtedly drew on tendencies toward rationalization associated with industrialization, the diffusion of new technologies and the prestige of science. But rationalizing, positivist confidence notwithstanding, it is also clear that by the end of the century the epistemological and cultural ramifications of a radical concentration on temporality could be radically unsettling.

An efficient way to broach this last point is to mention some aspects of one of the most famous and consequential achievements of nineteenth-century thought: establishing the premise of the gigantic expanse of time in comparison to, say, human life spans as lived or as biblically based temporal projections ("generations"). The best-known instance here is Darwinian theory, which is often described as decisively revising dominant conceptions of time scale in the natural and the human sciences. Of course, Darwin did not invent the idea of a vast, nonbiblical chronology. What he did accomplish, with a rarely equaled combination of scientific and cultural success, was, first, to place humanity within the "deep time" already proposed by Enlightenment thinkers such as Diderot and Kant, as well as pioneering geological formalizers such as Hutton and Lyell. Second, on the basis of fossil research made possible by recent developments in geology, he established that, through the concept of natural selection, humanity is potentially changeable and developing. One was unthinkable without the other, since a plausible account of evolutionary change through natural selection required operations on a time scale in the millions of years. In effect, geological deep time enabled Darwinism to assert the mutability of the human species, which called into question notions of human essence, identity, and/or stable subjectivity. Henceforth these might be submitted to the unending work of natural selection and hence the possibility of unending transformation. This is why Darwinism could seem a radically threatening challenge to some established conceptions of humanity and human reason.[14]

What is crucial for present purposes is that this challenge was therefore associated with a qualitative expansion of the past itself. This was not only a matter of a tremendous temporal enlargement of fields of research.

It also made the very concept of pastness central to questions of episte-mology and knowledge. By the late nineteenth century, Darwinism was only one of many approaches and disciplines of knowledge, as well as cul-tural practices, built on the dynamics of temporality. Like Darwinism, many of these had a special stake in the interrogation of pastness.

One need only list some of the chief kinds of disciplines formed, refurbished, and/or institutionalized between the French Revolution and World War I.[15] As part of the new considerations of time and its powers, the breakthrough conceptualization of the sheer "quantity" of pastness opened up by geology and evolutionary biology affected a range of theo-retical fields, including cosmology, philosophy, and social theory (the low point of which was surely the hypertrophy of "social Darwinism," a view that political conservativism has often taken the opportunity to refurbish, right up through the present). In addition, examination of pastness was a basic theme for other new disciplines such as archaeology and, of course, the emergent professionalized discipline of academic historical studies or "History." Psychoanalysis, the development of which culminated at the end of the century, is an excellent example of a particularly unsettling con-cern with reading the effectivity of the past on the present. Freud's sys-tematic emphases on such ideas as infantile sexuality, the formation of the Oedipus complex, repression, and the return of the repressed utilized procedures stemming from Enlightenment rationality to decenter reason; the consciousness of a subject is submitted to and inextricable from that subject's past, but the availability of that past to the subject is inseparable from the unconscious, and so must emerge in distorted form. The psy-choanalyst is a specialist in the etiology of such distortions of pastness, much as the evolutionary biologist is a specialist reader of fossils. It is both appropriate and telling that Freud had an interest in archaeology and early civilizations, and in books such as *Moses and Monotheism* and *Totem and Taboo*, he theorized the distant history of the collective or species, as well as the histories of contemporary individual subjects.[16]

This is comparable to the epistemological circularity of evolutionary biology. Darwinism is founded on the premise that species characteristics, including those of Homo sapiens, are mutable. Scientific examination of the past in evolutionary biology brings the unstoppable processes of mutability in time within the prospect of human reason, submitting particular instances to generalizing categories or at least universally applicable mechanisms (e.g., natural selection). In a certain way, it is a rational response to Ruskin's problem, that the present must deal with the past, but the power of time entails the constant disappearance of the past. Yet, for Darwinism to be consistent, human reason itself would have to be temporalized, because of the unavoidability of biological change, which evolutionary theory foregrounded.

Thus, in a period when socioeconomic structures as well as practical sciences were heavily concerned with temporal order, some of the theoretical sciences and means of understanding even socioeconomic structures suggested that there may be something epistemologically disordering about modern temporality. If the dynamics of temporality and pastness had become a fundamental element of advanced knowledge, perhaps the radically problematic potential of these emphases revealed by Darwinism and its cousins might have greater or lesser parallels in other disciplines. This would especially be the case for the one that makes the human past within written and recorded recall its defining object—the study of history.

The Time of History: Koselleck's Account

In a series of important studies of temporality and historiography in the West, Reinhart Koselleck emphasizes a conceptual shift that occurred during the Enlightenment and soon after, which generated protocols and procedures still affecting the historical profession today. According to Koselleck, these innovations implanted into historiography a new understanding of time, a historical temporality that displaced previously normalized ones. His account of this transformation is nuanced and careful. It goes back to the sixteenth century, insists that historicity is generally experienced in mixed forms of temporality, and elaborates on some of those mixtures during the period of transformation, especially in the eighteenth century. Nevertheless, he identifies dominant modes, and for purposes of my own exposition, I will sharpen certain of his distinctions.[17]

Koselleck argues that modern Western historiography invented itself by displacing, supplanting, and then rejecting historicities whose genealogy was in a long-lasting assumption: that the future can be known as a metaphysical certainty. That certain future had been guaranteed by Christian eschatology, which determined that the future would bring a single key "historical" occurrence, namely the end of the world. All events in human history anticipate the same Event and are to be read against it and through it. Note, incidentally, that this Event would also be the end of time, which means that history—as events in time—was to be understood through the prism of the emergence of timelessness. There was something methodologically and rhetorically timeless about historiography.

Indeed, on this basis, there could never be anything completely unique in human history, for everything of interest to the historian had to be positioned and evaluated according to a common denominator, the same eternal standard. Conversely, if all historical occurrences anticipate the identical end, they must have fundamentally common traits. Any superficial intimations of qualitative distinctions among different historical periods were ultimately to be canceled out. Therefore, a key goal of historiography became the demonstration of an essential repetition in history. As a matter of historiographic form, this implies a rhetoric of comparison and parallelisms. Any historical action or agent could be compared to those of different times, and equating them across many years, even centuries, was common. This affected varied representational genres. For example, historical painting included unmistakable (at least to modern eyes) anachronism of detail, as when biblical figures were depicted in contemporary costume to assert parallels across time. It also included influential variations that were applicable in more secularized historiographies. A crucial example was history conceived as the repetitive occurrence of exemplary situations and the repository of reapplicable experiences (*historia magistra vitae*), which Koselleck believes was the dominant function of history from the ancients until the middle of the eighteenth century. In summary, pre-Enlightenment historical temporality was not exclusively directional, but reversible, recursive, or better, the medium of something like a universal simultaneity.

In the second half of the eighteenth century, according to Koselleck, changes in historicity crossed a threshold, into a qualitatively distinct mode. The new historicity rested on a different temporality, one that no longer presumes that all historical sequences necessarily refer to the same future and/or have fundamental common denominators. One radical consequence was that historical sequences could henceforth be conceived as unrepeatable, hence unique. Thus, for example, it becomes possible to discover fundamental differences among various historical periods, and the old distinctions among Antiquity, Medieval, and Modern would develop into a historiographic tool with unprecedented distinguishing power in modern historiographic periodization. More generally, it becomes conceivable that a historical sequence can produce something genuinely novel. The opposition between old and new became central for historical thinking.

This is inseparable from another radical consequence of the new temporality. To say that a sequence is unrepeatable is to say that it is unified in itself. Formally and rhetorically, the old historiography had referred historical occurrences and agents to something *exterior* to their own particular situation or period, whether that was the end of history or occurrences and agents from other times. Henceforth historiography would seek *internal* unifying principles to explain successions of past events and actions. The combination of the unrepeatable and internally unified sequence entailed a productive temporality; that is, a temporality of pluralized outcomes that, consequently, destabilized the future. As Koselleck puts it, "Time becomes a dynamic and historical force in its own right."[18]

This is not only a distinctively modern conception of historical temporality; it opened the way for social commentators to define modernity itself. Life becomes a process of unending transition to a different future, for the present is the perpetual change of old into new. Every generation may experience its own new time, such that humanity exists in an unending *neue Zeit* (Koselleck plays on the fact that the German term for modernity, coined in the later nineteenth century, is *Neuzeit*). This was not simply a theoretical or methodological point. According to Koselleck, it was a response "to the challenge of a society changing itself technolog-ically and industrially."[19] Politically, the possibility of different futures, hence radical novelty and differential temporalities, was abetted by the European system of the Absolute State, whose balance-of-power projec-tions rested on the idea of a directional temporality whose outcome could be affected; by the French Revolution, which placed the notion of radical social change at the center of politics; and by European colonializing con-quests of "New Worlds." Socioeconomically, the idea of the need to get a grasp on an unending movement of time, and to abstract from it, has its own correspondences with the problems of controlling time by quantify-ing it in wage labor and other social factors discussed above as the devel-opment of modern Western time consciousness.

For the sake of clarity, it is worth pausing to remark that the shift away from the reversible, recursive, universally simultaneous temporality of pre-Enlightenment historiography to a directional modern temporal-ity should not be directly equated with two standard oppositions. First, this was not exactly a change from cyclic to linear conceptions of time, even though Koselleck himself sometimes writes as if it were.[20] The older forms of temporality included an element of simultaneity of past, present, and future; this implies something even more static than the cycle, as opposed to the dynamism of modern historical temporality that is crucial to Koselleck's account. Second, this transformation was not from a con-tinuous and linear to a ruptural historical time, an opposition fashionable in more recent cultural criticism. Both historical continuity and rupture involve sequence and direction, and they are therefore both subsumed under post-Enlightenment historical temporality. However, it is also true that by comparison to what it replaced in Koselleck's account, it can be useful to discuss the temporality of modern historicity as linear or direc-tional, for it defines history as a set of unique sequences, each leading to delimitable and potentially distinct futures.

The modern belief that there are principles of change internal to distinctive historical sequences is what Koselleck calls the temporaliza-tion of history. It became a fundamental assumption even for opposing approaches. For example, the linked postulates of a directional temporality and historical reality as an internally related sequence could be joined to Enlightenment notions of progress and, after 1789, revolution. But as an a priori ideology, the idea of progress could soon be challenged without disturbing underlying notions of historical time. What ultimately marked the new turn in this regard was not any specific principle of the sequence, but the very idea that a sequence is internally unified, by whatever principle or principles. Divinity, secularized natural law, positivist laws of history, or empathetically inferred causal connections, to mention a few, could oppose one another and/or overlap in the development of historiographic approaches and schools. But, from this point on, disputes over such unifying (hence explanatory) principles were properly and centrally historiographic.

In fact, for Koselleck, the temporalization of history was an enabling condition for the "discovery" of the specific object History. History per se could not exist when the past always referred to the present (as moral lesson) and the future (as eschatology), but it could when temporality possesses its own productivity, as it does in modern historiography. This kind of temporality was therefore an intellectual precondition for both disciplinary historical studies and its putative opponent, speculative philosophy of history. Furthermore, the concept of a sequence that can produce something distinctive and new—a premise of modern historicity and, increasingly, an experience identified with modernity—also gave great intellectual import and social prestige to the vocation of the historian. By the early twentieth century, it was well established that the rigorous historian as academic professional was a specialist in the study of particular, real, temporalized segments, or sequences.[21]

However, this historicity does generate its own questions and difficulties for historiography in its practice of disciplined research and its philosophy. In what follows, I will focus on two issues. First, if the internally unified sequence is a definitive element of modern historicity, on what grounds would historians argue and settle disputes over the principles and extent of the unified sequence and, for that matter, the constitution of a historical sequence? Second, the new conception of historical time might lead to a peculiarly modern difficulty. If the destabilization of the future means that there can be sharp distinctions among different historical periods, then the past under study might be radically different from the present in which the historian is writing—hence the widespread assumption of a radical gap between past and present, including the concerns of thinkers discussed in earlier chapters, such as Ruskin and Bazin. This difference or otherness of the past raises questions about how secure any knowledge of the past can be. It became central to discussions of historiographic methodology and epistemology.

Indexing History

Let us agree with Koselleck that the internally unified sequence, and the temporality it implies, is one definitive element of modern historicity. When we ask for the grounds on which historians would argue and settle disputes about the constitution of historical sequences, we come to a second definitive element: primary source materials. Modern historiographies appeal for evidence to critically authenticated survivals from the past. As the historian's profession emerged in the nineteenth century, these were usually but not necessarily written documents. An emphasis on critically examined primary source materials in the training and work of the historian has been extraordinarily functional in justifying the establishment of and claims to professional disciplinarity. In fact, if it were possible to reduce the appearance of historical studies as a modern scholarly profession to a single distinguishing feature, this might be it.

A figure who usually serves to typify this element is the prolific, influential, and professionally powerful Leopold von Ranke. The preface to his first book in 1824 provided a famous formula that has often been said to epitomize the new "scientific" consciousness of the modern historian:

> To history has been assigned the office of judging the past, of instructing the present for the benefit of future ages. To such high offices this work does not aspire: It wants only to show what actually happened (*wie es eigentlich gewesen*).

(The last four words may be the most cited phrase ever written by a historian about historiography, but it has been translated in several subtly different ways.)[22]

This is often taken as a definition and an affirmation of the vocation of modern, professionalized historicity; it would be materially referential or, if one prefers, it would adhere to some form of a realist aesthetic. Ranke states his methodological strictures in the very next paragraph:

> But whence the sources for such a new investigation? The basis of the present work, the sources of its material, are memoirs, diaries, letters, diplomatic reports, and original narratives of eyewitnesses; other writings were used only if they were immediately derived from the above mentioned or seemed to equal them because of some original information. These sources will be identified on every page; a second volume, to be published concurrently, will present the method of investigation and the critical conclusions.[23]

Ranke here formulates a hierarchy of types of evidence that, roughly speaking, would govern the historical profession; artifacts generated in the processes of the historical occurrences being studied, then eyewitness accounts, and only then "other writings." Consequently, reliable authentication of sources must be a fundamental tool of the professional historian. In that second volume, Ranke registered the impact of philology and textual criticism in this emerging ethos. Painstakingly examining the accounts that composed the historiography of the Renaissance period, he exposed contradictions, inventions, second- and thirdhand repetitions, distortions, plagiarisms, and unacknowledged sources. This critique of sources and historiographic predecessors established his reputation. It became a key model of the standards and attitudes of the new historical scholarship, which he also implanted in his noted seminar. The relatively early integration of History as a distinctive discipline into the modern German university curriculum was a factor in making that country a leader in historiography, and the long-lived Ranke became one of its most powerful academics.[24]

The privilege of critically evaluated sources in arguments for the constitution of a specific internally unified sequence also became a professional standard in other Western countries, where there was almost always awareness of the German model. This is not to imply an internationally unified school, for there were varied and changing conceptions on everything from what constituted proper explanatory or unifying principles to what constituted properly historical objects of study. As far as direct influence goes, for example, in the German context Ranke was clearly a philosophical idealist and an essentially religious seeker after universal history; even his famous 1824 preface concluded with the need to search for ideal unity behind source-derived factuality, a unity he explicitly associated with God. Yet, in English-speaking countries he was commonly invoked as the originating methodologist for scientific and/or positivistic historiography.

Fritz Stern has collected statements by major historians involved in consolidating the status of historiography as a specialized intellectual and professional field in the later nineteenth and early twentieth centuries. The dual problematic of internally unified sequence and critical examination of sources is repeatedly asserted as definitive, although there is sometimes an undercurrent of concern that the two could come into conflict. For example, in an 1874 rectorial address at the University of Berlin, Theodor Mommsen declared the historical discipline "the distinct knowledge of actual happenings, consisting on the one hand of the discovery and examination of the available testimony, and on the other of the weaving of this testimony into a narrative," and was already complaining about an overemphasis on critical method in the training of historians.[25] In its inaugural issue in 1876, the *Revue historique* (edited by Gabriel Monod) announced it would accept "only original contributions, based on original sources, which will enrich science either with their basic research or with the results of their conclusions; but while we demand from our contributors strictly scientific methods of exposition, with each assertion accompanied by proof, by source references and quotations, while we severely exclude vague generalities and rhetoric, we shall preserve in the *Revue historique* that literary quality which scholars as well as French readers justly value so highly."[26] On assuming the Regius Professorship in Modern History at Cambridge, J. B. Bury delivered an inaugural lecture entitled "The Science of History," promoting historical studies as a specific science— neither social science nor literature—and the emergent master discipline. In Bury's view, this science had appeared in Germany when Barthold Niebuhr and Ranke approached the study of the past through scientific procedures, which consisted in "the critical method" of dealing with sources and the systematic postulate of "the principle of unity and continuity" and "the doctrine of development."[27]

While insisting on critically evaluated and deployed sources as the basis for modern historiography, Bury's remarkable lecture (which, descriptively if not theoretically, condenses many themes stressed by Koselleck sixty years later) is typical in reserving fullest discussion for the idea of unified development. In general, modern theorists and historians of historiography have paid the most attention to principles for unifying sequences, whether they accept the claims of historiography to epistemological legitimacy as science or discipline or they contest such claims. Without in any way diminishing the importance of the thesis of internally unified development and debates over the principles of unification for the emergence of modern historiography, I would reemphasize the other side of the problematic, which has remained relatively unquestioned to this day among working historians: the historical account must be constructed with reference to critically authenticated sources.[28]

This is important in the present context, because these sources can be understood as a species of indexical signs: they signify the actuality of the past to the historian (and by relay to his or her reader) because they are produced by the actuality of the past, which is the historian's object of study. Consider the following from an 1891 essay by another major figure in the professionalization of historical studies, the American Frederick Jackson Turner:

> *History is all the remains that have come down to us from the past, studied with all the critical and interpretive power that the present can bring to the task.* ... To the historian the materials for his work are found in all that remains from the ages gone by—in papers, roads, mounds, customs, languages; in monuments, coins, medals, names, titles, inscriptions, charters; in contemporary annals and chronicles; and finally, in the secondary sources, or histories in the common acceptance of the term. Wherever there remains a chipped flint, a spearhead, a piece of pottery, a pyramid, a picture, a poem, a coliseum or a coin, there is history.

Says Taine: "What is your first remark on turning over the great still leaves of a folio, the yellow sheets of a manuscript, a poem, a code of laws, a declaration of faith? This, you say, was not created alone. It is but a mold, like a fossil shell, an imprint like one of those shapes embossed in stone by an animal which lived and perished. Under the shell there was an animal, and behind the document there was a man. Why do you study the shell except to represent to yourself the animal? So do you study the document only in order to know the man. The shell and the document are lifeless wrecks, valuable only as a clue to the entire and living existence. We must reach back to this existence, endeavor to recreate it."[29]

There are several things to say about this passage. First it demonstrates that the professional historian's sources are definable not only as indexical signs, but more specifically as indexical traces. This means that, as the material remains of an otherwise no longer perceivable, constantly receding past, historical sources are implicated in a modern temporality. The historian's problem is that as the new appears, the old disappears. But preserved by design or accident, historical sources can be handled, perused, analyzed. They are what is left from the products of humans and cultures that are objects of historical study. Like Ruskin's ruins, they both manifest the break between present and past and provide a bridge over that gap for the right kind of subject.

This will require further discussion, but here let us go on to a second element of this passage, Turner's triumphalist tone. This tone expresses a certain imperialization of human pastness by historiography, perhaps as a function of the then current ambitions of historiography to be the new master discipline of the human. Writing at the end of the nineteenth century, Turner foresees widening the range of the disciplinary historian's field from the purview of narrowly political and constitutional questions, which had dominated its earlier stages. Consequently, the compass of the critically authenticated sources must be extended far beyond the recently opened government archives that had been key stockpiles of historical raw materials for Ranke and others of his generation. A historiographic account can now be about a whole way of life. Any and all remains of societies and cultures become potential means of contact with the past. The only requirement is continuous existence from past to present. We might say that historiography here expands its evidentiary basis, from the written document to the more inclusive realm of the documentary in general, in the sense that any artifacts, written or not, could be used as historical evidence.[30]

Another point worth highlighting is how Turner is able to liken the historian's sources—all the way from written documents to everyday cultural remains—to fossils, that category of indexical trace that brings even deep time into the reach of human knowledge. As I noted earlier, it is common to posit the widespread impact of the idea of evolution in the imaginative, intellectual, and scientific life of the later nineteenth century; however, Turner here points us toward the inverse. Darwinism itself is a kind of historiography, one whose project is the historicization of life forms. Like the historian, Darwin studied indexical remains of the period he was investigating (fossils), and from them inferred a continuous development or sequencing (evolution in deep time) according to its own internal principles (natural selection). Despite its extraordinary cultural and intellectual prestige by the early twentieth century, then, Darwinism cannot be treated as a disciplinary origin or "influence" on historiography in any simple sense. Rather, evolutionary biology may be understood as an instance of the underlying problematic of the new post-Enlightenment historiography.

This can be illustrated by brief reference to the place of early nineteenth century geology in relation to both historiography and evolutionary biology. The study of fossil remains is closely connected to stratigraphy, whereby rock strata are read and dated to establish a chronology of the actions of the earth in deep time. Stratigraphy was a key geological procedure before Darwin, and Charles Lyell's *Principles of Geology* (first edition 1830–33) was the central geological text for Darwin's generation. For Lyell, geology was the reconstruction of unique sequences whose outcome is open to chance and therefore not predictable. Any similarities to Koselleck's new historical temporality may be taken seriously, for Lyell explicitly conceived of geology as a historical science, "the empirical study of preserved records" in Stephen Jay Gould's words, Lyell even cites "a great historian of our times," Barthold Niebuhr, on the joys of historical research as a model for geologists: "[H]e who calls what has vanished back again into being, enjoys a bliss like that of creating."[31]

This connection is telling, first because Niebuhr was a pioneer in the use of philological methods for critical evaluation of written historical sources and a model for Ranke; second because it is yet another appeal to the trope of re-creating or restoring life to describe a historiographic project (the fossil is particularly germane here); and relatedly, because of the remarkable, exuberant emotionality of the phrasing, to which I will return shortly. Drawing on Lyell to date fossil remains, Darwin could use them as evidence to infer or reconstruct a continuous developmental sequence unified by the principle of natural selection. This clearly partakes of the modern problematic of historicity, but that problematic just as clearly precedes Darwin, as Lyell's reference to "scientific" source criticism illustrates.

If the fossil seems particularly germane in relation to the trope that historiography restores bygone life, this stands for another, more abstract commonality with the historical source, namely that they are both readable as the only extant physical, material links to the objects of study. This makes them both the best grounds for any reliable reconstruction of the past. Documents, remains, survivals, ruins and edifices, fossils—in short, indexical traces that attest to a past by emerging into the present from it— achieved a kind of epistemological prestige in an era of intensifying time consciousness. This privilege surely contributed to the credibility of historians, who thought they were formulating a master discipline, and they in turn fortified that privilege. However, the great evidentiary value placed on preserved remains of the past and the temporality underlying its great utility and appeal also led to certain logical and epistemological difficulties.

Past Present

Let me review two such difficulties, which are implicit in modern historicity, and then return to the functioning of the indexical trace. The first difficulty has to do with the logical relation between source documents and the historical sequence in a historiographic argument. According to professional practices and conventions established in the nineteenth century, historiography should present the reality of the past in the form of an internally unified sequence. Among other things, this means that a rigorous telling, construction, or reconstruction of the past must constitute a synthesis: the elements or parts of the past invoked in the historical account should cohere into a whole. The internally unified sequence is the likely form of such a synthesizing reconstruction because professional historians have generally accepted the directional temporality grounding post-Enlightenment historicity. Furthermore, indexical traces, conceived as primary sources attesting to the actuality of elements of the past because they are themselves elements of the past, are considered the best evidence in an argument for the reality of such a synthesis.

Can this kind of reasoning ever achieve satisfying logical coherence? This is one kind of question that follows from this fundamental problematic of modern historicity. It was of special interest to post–World War II analytic philosophers, some of whom tried to hold up absolute logical necessity as the standard of argument to which historiography should aspire. Perhaps the most widely debated example of this position was formulated by Carl Hempel. He asserted that any valid historical explanation manifests the same type of syllogistic or deductive logical structure that (in his view) underpins the strongest form of scientific explanation. In this type of structure, particular instances are connected to one another by explicit or implicit appeal to an applicable general law or set of such laws. The general laws effectively serve as the major premise of a syllogism. For historiography, they would thereby logically warrant the connection of conditions in the past (the minor premise) and explain a given event or state of affairs (the conclusion). In effect, Hempel wishes to define an ideal form of historiographic reasoning, for the deductive syllogism constituted for him a kind of airtight, irrefutable logical structure.[32]

I am not interested in pursuing Hempel's view of explanation or the definition of science that he was concerned to defend; rather I cite it as just one famous illustration, a reminder of the pursuit of a model of security in a theory of history. And as such, it also illustrates a consequence of the fundamental problematic of modern historicity. It seems that even if there were grounds for believing in the desirability of absolutely secure forms of historiographic reasoning (scientific or otherwise), it can never be achieved within the conventional procedures of modern historiography. This is because of the evidentiary authority of primary sources, which is inextricable from its post-Enlightenment temporality. As we have seen, this temporality entails the perpetual recession of the past, which has regularly been figured as death. One reason this figure is so attractive (to the point of operating as a cultural cliché in some instances) is simply that it connotes a material disappearance; all possible physical elements of even a single instant of the past do not and cannot persist into the present. Leaving aside the fact that they would have to include the humans that lived in the past (resurrection again), if they did the situation would be analogous to Borges's famous map only more so: there would be no room for our own world of the present. Furthermore, they would be unnecessary as evidence to reconstruct the past, for the past would be present. I previously made this point in relation to preservationism, and I compared it to Bazin's myth of total cinema. Now consider it in relation to historiography.

One characteristic of indexical survivals that makes them so valuable to the professional historian and the preservationist alike is that survival is *selective*. Furthermore, from the perspective of the concerns of the historian's present, this selectivity may also seem random.[33] This selectivity has a major consequence for the historical synthesis: to reason from indexical traces to a historical sequence is, in effect, to infer a synthesis from some of its parts, namely those elements of pastness that have survived (whether by chance or by planning) into the present. Now, as a general point a synthetic whole can never be strictly and perfectly demonstrated from the existence of some of its parts; there must always be some extrapolation to fill in the missing parts. In historiography, given that the best evidence for the synthetic whole—the internally unified sequence—is supposed to be material survivals from the past in the present, then the very disjunction between parts and wholes defines the enterprise. The perpetual recession of the past, which apparently motivates historiography in the first place, entails the material absence of parts of pastness; hence the need to reconstruct the past hypothetically and in a sequential form that reconfirms that temporality even as it makes a whole.

To put it differently, even if we went to an extreme and assumed (against experience and practice) that critically authenticated sources were reliably transparent indicators of past existents and states of affairs, one cannot reason with logical security from them to an internally unified historical sequence. The integral form of a complete historical whole does not follow from a citation of some of its elements, *which is the best a historian can do;* therefore, a logical gap between source and conclusion is constitutive of the argumentative field of the modern historian. The historical account must always include not just logically warranted inferences, but inferential jumps—from fragmentary remains of a segment of the past serving as pieces of indexical evidence to assertions about a complete segment of past reality.

This is why a convincing or powerful historical account can never be based exclusively on primary sources, but must draw on a miscellany of additional resources. These may include sources less authoritative than primary sources, such as secondhand accounts or previous historiography ("secondary sources"). They also include conceptual assumptions and frameworks (which are sometimes openly debated by historians)—for example, contentions about the proper form of a synthetic sequence, which mandates estimates as to the probable composition of missing fragments and the relative pertinences of various surviving fragments; general notions, theories, and ideologies about human or societal causation, and so forth. This suggests that, in making a case for a certain internally unified sequence, the historian must have not only a set of pertinent sources, but also a conceptual or discursive tool kit ready to hand prior to his or her research. Yet, the specifics of the sequence are not supposed to be known in advance of the research, for the temporality is one of change and potentiality for the new, and the final or best court is referential discovery and verification by means of primary sources. Thus, the problem of relating historical parts to a specifically historiographic whole explains why many have found that historiographic reason inevitably leads to some version of the hermeneutic circle: knowledge of the whole depends on certain kinds of piecemeal evidence, but taking that evidence into account requires prior knowledge of the form and contents of the whole.

"For the historian, everything begins and ends with time," remarks Fernand Braudel, a post–World War II innovator in conceptions of historiographic temporality. Yet, even Braudel continues to refer to "historical time, so imperious because it is irreversible."[34] The fundamental priority given to both the omnipresence and the directionality of time, and consequently the continual production of significant differences between pasts and presents, necessarily makes the historian's logic a slippery or fuzzy one. This has been implicitly recognized by historians, who generally reject logical standards of absolute security such as that formulated by Hempel. It is also closely related to the second difficulty implicit in the problematic of modern historicity, one that has been foregrounded in discussions among historians.

This second difficulty may be understood as the problem of historiographic positionality. It has to do with the status of the epistemological subject of historiography. By the late nineteenth century, modern disciplinary historiography often claimed a position from which to produce a kind of authoritative referentiality. Authority and position are, of course, social, political, and institutional; hence, for example, the importance of professional academic status in the emergence of disciplinary historiography. Authority and position are also "linguistic" and discursive constructions. Structuralist, poststructuralist, and rhetorical accounts of historiography and its theory have been especially effective at unpacking the conventionalized textual "voice" of modern historiography as a voice authorizing a writing subject who knows the real in time. However, the problem of positionality was recognized by historians themselves, virtually from the inception of modern historicity, and by the early twentieth century it was a familiar topic among them. Both the early appearance of this problem and the theoretical attention it drew from historians suggest that the authoritative positionality claimed by its avatars is precarious for reasons internal to modern historicity.[35]

The basic problem can be put briefly. For modern historicity, temporality always entails the possibility of change. Furthermore, the force of time is so extensive as to be a universal (something crystallized in the scientific and general cultural recognition of deep time in the nineteenth century). But in that case historiographic knowledge itself cannot be exempted from the postulate of constant changeability. For if the study of history aspired to be a master discipline because all humans are shaped and may change in time, this tenet could apply to their ideas; therefore, the same could be said of the study and representation of history. This threatened a pure relativism, an evanescence of all historiographic truth claims in the stream of time.

Considerations of this issue by historians may often seem typically modernist in their self-reflexivity and in their attention to subjectivity, because the problem is precisely the historical positioning of the subject of historical knowledge. A center of discussion was, once again, the influential historiographic culture of Germany, where the so-called crisis of historicism pushed these issues very far indeed. Whatever its vicissitudes and internal debates, German historicism tended to understand the priority of primary source materials from a presumption of the differentiating power of time. The critical method itself was intricated with the premise that the historical sequence can produce the new: each era must be understood as much as possible through its own products (primary source materials) and in its own terms. In fact, a classic distinction in German thought that was taken up by philosophers treated individuality and uniqueness as attributes that distinguished objects of historical-cultural sciences from those of the law-seeking natural sciences.[36]

For example, in 1902, the year of Simmel's comment about the dependence of the urban socioeconomic order on the personal timepiece, the neo-Kantian Heinrich Rickert put it as follows:

> [T]he temporality of everything that is real results in a distinctive quality of unique and individual realities.... [I]n the scientific investigation of the uniqueness and individuality of real objects, they are never conceived as present. They are always situated in the past, and their existence in the past always occupies a certain period of time.... Every account of reality itself, every account that ... concerns the unique individual event that takes place at a specific point in space and time, we call history.[37]

This passage concisely states the crucial constellation: the real is indissolubly welded to the radically differentiating properties of time, and therefore so is historiography. For Rickert, the consequence of the ongoing state of change of the real is that proper historiographic understanding deals with unique, individualized states of affairs; it is predicated on pluralizing the real into temporalized strings of unique realities. For Rickert, the danger was that so temporalized a reality is anarchically individualized, and therefore irrational; that is, not graspable by historical rationality because it may escape the rule of any generality. A further implication is that historiography itself might be subject to the same pluralization, breaking down into a set of disparate assertions without any connection. Rickert's solution is a theory of cognitive values that enables the historian to supercede those of historical agents. He wishes to define historical "objectivity" as a strict but explicit and self-aware adherence to the value norms of his or her culture by the historian (as opposed to individualized, therefore nonrational whims). That is, historical particularity would be overcome by consciousness of its own general presumptions, even though they themselves may be historical and therefore unique.[38]

Thus, some of the most radical issues relating to historiographic subjectivity were formulated by asking about the consequences of an unrestricted historicization of historiography. It seemed inescapable that the historian's own historical locus could affect both the choices from available source evidence and principles of sequencing. This placed in question what, in many discussions, was called historical objectivity, but which is more clearly conceived as a problem of maintaining the referential authority of the historiographic subject, since it is a matter of epistemological security. By 1900 terms such as *standpoint, point of view*, and *historical perspective* had already been in play for over a century in conceptions and interrogations of modern historicity. They were widely understood as marking a profoundly troublesome theoretical and philosophical issue for historiography, despite the sometime triumphalism of the historical profession.[39]

While German historiographic culture was an arena for some of the sharpest formulations of the problem among disciplinary historians, awareness of the theoretical tangle that could result cropped up everywhere.

A revealing instance is in yet another 1902 text, Bury's Inaugural Lecture at Cambridge, where he proclaims that professional historiography is a specific science that constitutes a master discipline. Yet, at one point Bury implicates history in a decentering of the subject of historiographic knowledge, based on his own definition of the science of history. According to Bury, a precept of continuous development is fundamental to modern historicity. Combined with knowledge of the great scale of temporality (again the currency of Darwinism), this leads to the conclusion that future historians will always be able to discover new consequences of past events. This causes him to scoff at the notion that even his own age of professionalized historiography can aspire to absolute knowledge of the past. Since history is perpetually in development, sequenciation must be perpetually renovated. Here again is the problem that historiography must submit itself to its own temporal postulate of perpetual novelty. Bury reasons from this that no historical account can be finally secured against future revisions, for it is necessarily caught in the very process of unending change that makes for modern historiography. Yet, if historiography is to maintain the status Bury claims for it, he must find a way to characterize a secure positionality that would validate the knowledge historians produce, one from which historians can assume a reliable ground. His solution is a rule: Historians must take into account the very fact that historical development occurs not only in the past, but also extends into the future: "We must see our petty periods *sub specie perennitatis.*"

Bury's lecture is admirably comprehensive and sophisticated, but the depth of the problem of positionality is indicated by the oddity of his solution. Historiography is supposed to find a stable standpoint in the superior (historical) knowledge that it is always already incomplete with respect to its object, the historical sequence. In one way this seems appealingly modest and anti-teleological. It means that historians are to recognize that history does not culminate in their own period, and, consequently, that it is not centered on the position of the historian in the present. Therefore, according to Bury, all periods—including both the historian's own and even those that have not yet occurred—are of equal importance in the study of the past. On the other hand, this seeming modesty intersects with the rhetoric of the master discipline, and the implications for the practice of historiography seem nearly megalomaniac. For if a historian cannot assume a stable framework, standpoint, or "perspective" in the present for reliable comprehension of the *past*, then it is difficult to understand the grounds on which she or he might take the *future* into account. After all, short of the fiction of time travel, there are no artifacts from the future susceptible to critical authentication. So what at first seems a becoming modesty is actually a transcendent turn. The ultimate implication is made explicit when Bury recommends that the education of a historian should involve "the training of the mind to look at experience objectively, without immediate relation to one's own time and place." This amounts to deciding that the most valuable outcome of a proper historical education is the capacity to establish a position for oneself outside history.[40]

This manifests an internal contradiction fundamental to modern historicity. To secure historical knowledge, historiographic positionality had to somehow exit history, to limit the impact of time itself on the historian's work. But the authority of historiography is predicated on the universal force of temporality. This contradiction is well illustrated by Bury's lecture, and the nature of his solution was on a path widely taken by those grappling with the problem (one could tease it out of Rickert, for example). In fact, the issue of historiographic "standpoint" has troubled not only historiography itself, but various kinds of modern thought and social theory grounded on consciousness of history, even when they rejected German historicism. Here I will review two landmark examples that involve new conceptualizations of ideology, chosen to illustrate how these issues persist in a concept I continue to use in this study.

The term ideology had been famously appropriated by Marx and Engels, who were part of a rigorous but nonacademic radical tendency in nineteenth-century conceptualizations of modern historicity.[41] They introduced it as a place-marker for the historical determination of ideas. This raises a version of the problem of positionality inherent in modern historicity: If all socioeconomic formations generate particular systems of ideas to sustain themselves over time, then must the analyst of ideology, who is presumably within a historical socioeconomic formation, claim to be enough "outside" ideology to reliably analyze it? Marx and Engels only elaborated on this dialectic in fragmentary ways, but it brings us to my first example in social theory.

Eighty years after Marx and Engels and an intellectual generation after Bury's lecture, Karl Mannheim's "sociology of knowledge" reconfigured the concept of ideology for non-Marxist social theory. He agrees that all positions of knowledge are restricted by their attachment to historically determined social groupings: "man," he writes, is "bound ... in his knowledge by his position in time and society," so "the sociology of knowledge seeks to comprehend thought in the concrete setting of a historical-social situation." But, as did Bury, Mannheim envisages an agency that can escape from this temporal binding and progress toward a secure, objective, comprehensive positionality for the production of knowledge. This agency appears in the historical emergence of a peculiar kind of sociological grouping, a free-floating intelligentsia, whose members increasingly identify their interest with the production of valid, general knowledge. This interest detaches this single group from the class-bound socioeconomic interests that define all other social groupings and restrict their knowledges. Such specialists of the intellect are therefore defined by a historically generated standpoint capable of evading historically determined partiality.[42]

It is as if Mannheim set out to produce a bourgeois revision of the Hegelian Marxist solution of his old acquaintance, Georg Lukács, whose slightly earlier *History and Class Consciousness* provides the second example. Lukács was intimately familiar with the German discussions of temporality and historicity (he takes historicism as one of his theoretical opponents but mentions Rickert with respect).[43] Whereas Mannheim believed that secure social knowledge would have to be associated with the socio-historic position of professional specialists in knowledge production, Lukács found it in the position of the revolutionary proletariat. He followed Marx in arguing that, as the only class in history exploited to such a degree, its overriding material interest was in an unprecedentedly total transformation of society, which would end all exploitation. But he further emphasized that this proletariat would consequently be the first social class compelled to develop a general epistemological standpoint based on the need to understand the totality of society. Paradoxically, its particular class situatedness drives it beyond the ideological positionality of particular class situatedness, characteristic of all previous social classes. As for historians and other intellectuals, the solution to the problem of positional security in history would be to affiliate with the implied or imputed class standpoint of the proletariat. This would mean becoming dialecticians (something possible only on the basis of their own contradictory social, political, and ideological situations). The undialectical historian, on the other hand, would continually run up against the antinomies of modern historicity. For that historian, Lukács remarks, "every true change must be incomprehensible ... a catastrophe."[44] This catastrophe would be not only social and political, but ideological and epistemological, since it brings such intellectuals face to face with the instability of their own positionality.

The association of change with anxiety or fear is a theme we have encountered repeatedly. This suggests to me the acuity of Lukács's insight in 1922. But if Lukács's solution is that the historical position of the proletariat and Marxism is the only basis for a secure standpoint to comprehend change, he himself achieved his insights by finding an unacknowledged outlet from history. In a way, his auto-critique, written many years later, acknowledged this.[45] In it, Lukács rejects his earlier understanding of the revolution as an epistemological telos that resolves all conceptual antinomies. He now attributes this view to a residual Hegelianism, which led to his contention that a proletarian position of knowledge could escape the determinations of all previous history foreshadowing freedom of the human subject. For our purposes, this amounts to yet another example of a claim to historiographic security resting on an ahistorical element. But it is interesting to note that, despite this auto-critique, the problem of establishing a secure standpoint on history remained central to Lukács's work throughout his long life, as did his conviction that such a standpoint is ultimately limited or enabled by a combination of class and the conceptual-ideological tools provided by history. His writings on literature, culture, and ideology continued to be framed by such metaphors as that of historical perspective, derived from the old debates over historicism.[46]

The force of time impinges on everything; and yet in order to bring this understanding into the realm of knowledge, it is necessary somehow to sidestep the force of time. As in Bury and Mannheim, historical consciousness in Lukács found it necessary to construct an escape hatch from radical historical temporality in order to deal with it in any measure of epistemological security. The examples from social theory illustrate that assuming a positionality from which to claim secure knowledge of history was not only a fundamental problem of epistemological conceptions for modernity, but also a political one. Such a positionality has often been imagined as a stable standpoint or subject-position from which to deal with the instabilities defining modern historicity. For historians, this could be figured as a positionality that supercedes the breach between the historian's own temporally defined reality (a historically determined present) and other realities (the past). Bury's suggestion that the historian can equalize a standpoint among past, present, and future is a utopian one in this regard. If Bury's solution is on directly temporal grounds, Mannheim and Lukács understand history through sociological and social categories and identify one social grouping—the free-floating intelligentsia, the revolutionary proletariat—which, like Bury's historian, is produced in history but whose knowledge or consciousness evades its force. Leaving aside the specific definitions of such social groupings, it is not at all clear that a better type of solution to the problem as posed has ever been suggested.[47]

When Foucault proposed that there was a vast rearrangement of Western disciplines and knowledges—an epistemic break—in progress by the beginning of the nineteenth century, he found that it established historical investigation as a master discipline. He summarized the specificity of this shift as a period when philosophy "will necessarily lead thought back to the question of knowing what it means for thought to have a history."[48] In fact, more traditional intellectual history has long treated the nineteenth century as an "age of history." As Foucault might insist, this is not a matter of an interpretation in depth. Both the idea of historiography as a master discipline and the difficulties raised by the fact that historiography must therefore historicize itself were explicitly confronted by members of the emergent discipline themselves. The disciplinary professional Bury, the bourgeois social theorist Mannheim, and the radical revolutionary theorist Lukács are just three of many examples of attempts to overcome the basic instability inherent in modern historicity and the influential protocols of professional historiography. If historiography is itself historical, how can it claim validity in the selection and interrogation of sources, much less the construction of an internally unified, developmental sequence or any form of synthesis?

The Appeal of the Index

There can be little doubt that the professionalization of historiography remade historical studies according to more rigorous standards of accuracy, even as they participated in a culturally widespread attention to pastness. But the disciplinary protocols of the critical method also fended off or, perhaps better, disavowed a basic uncertainty implicit in modern historicity. This uncertainty is about the very possibility of making secure referential truth claims in historiography. I have been summarizing two related kinds of conceptual or theoretical difficulties that always trouble the authority of modern historiography to assert the truth of a time-filled real world. One is the logical inevitability of an inferential gap between indexical fragments serving as evidence, and the form of a unified sequence that serves as a result. The other is the instability of historiographic positionality. Since the inception of modern historicity, these have been repeatedly addressed by historians as well as social theorists and philosophers. This suggests that arguing for the reality of a purported historical sequence and assuming a stable standpoint require operations that are not always explicit in disciplinary protocols.

A major part of the work of historiography would have to consist in filling in the inevitable gaps between sources and synthesis; and relatedly in establishing some kind of positionality that can maintain the authority of the historiography against the threat posed to stable position by temporality. Historical discourse is therefore necessarily rhetorical in at least two senses. The first is the common-sense meaning of the term, for the historian's job must be to make an account convincing in the face of the gaps and instabilities of historiography. Historical discourse may also be analyzed as rhetoric in a second, more technical sense stemming from the classical categorizations of tropes. This has been important to post-Hempel Anglo-American theory of history, the shift to which was definitively marked by the publication of Hayden White's *Metahistory*. This book announced a displacement from a theoretical focus on historiography as explanatory logic to a focus on historiography as narrative figuration. White proposed that four classic tropes (metaphor, metonymy, synecdoche, irony) underlie modern Western historiography and prefigure the field of historical reference. They are established in historiography in a configuration of modes of emplotment (sequencing), modes of argument, and modes of ideological implication. As with Hempel, I mention White not to engage in a detailed reading of his work, but rather as a central, much discussed illustration of a major attitude in the theory of history. The importance of White's kind of argument as an account of modern historicity can be indicated by two quick points. First, in effect, White defines tropes as varieties of part-whole relationships, and, as we have seen, part-whole relationships are one of the key difficulties in the logic of modern historicity. Second, according to White, tropes and modes of emplotment, argument, and ideological implication are interwoven to achieve a historical work's "explanatory affect." Tropes do not work by logical coherence, but are affective forms that provide persuasive constructs of coherence between part and whole.[49]

In fact, mechanisms by which historians can achieve persuasive force have commonly been of concern in the theory of history, and this concern has included accounting for the historian's explicit and implicit predispositions. These may be conceived as ideological, political, interpretive, discursive, philosophical, theoretical, and/or something else. From my perspective they are descriptions of the conceptual and discursive tendencies on which historians draw (sometimes self-consciously, sometimes not) to fill in the inevitable gap between sources and synthesis, and relatedly to establish positions in ways that maintain the authority of their historiographies. But note that this kind of theorization is not "anti-historical"; on the contrary, it participates in a kind of historicization of historiography, and therefore shares the presumptions of modern historicity. White himself introduces his *Metahistory* not just as a theory of history, but as "a *history* of historical consciousness in nineteenth-century Europe."[50]

So this attitude does not imply that there has never been any modern historiography that is "valid" or at least necessary in some significant sense of the term, for the old problem of "what it means for [historiographic] thought to have a history" remains basic. Nor, in that case, could it be to say that historiography is exclusively illogical, irrational, or something of the sort. But it is to suggest that the referential coherence and the social and institutional authority claimed by modern historiography is implicated in an *appeal:* an appeal to take it as serious knowledge, an invitation to take the referential claims of the historical account seriously.

This brings us back to the primary source as indexical trace, which was implanted in the historical profession during the nineteenth century. The discourse of newly professionalized rigor and sometime adoption of scientific self-labeling in connection with source criticism—which went along with the intimations of historiography as a master discipline in an era of extensive time consciousness—was surely part of this appeal. Modern disciplinary historiography was established with a claim to evidentiary procedures that would provide an unprecedentedly reliable account of the real past. As we have seen, this kind of evidence was implicated in a temporality that instituted a fundamental gap between past and present, along with irreplaceable losses entailed in the passage of time. Surviving fragments of previous occurrences and lives were understood to help counter that loss for disciplined knowledge.

But from the beginning, a different kind of explanation coexisted with that of rigor. Enthusiastic, even emotive evocation of the power of contact with authentic pastness intruded into the writings of some of the most sober and influential representatives of the new historiography. In 1831, shortly before his death, Niebuhr already provides a paradigmatic example when discussing the resurgence of philology, which informed his own seminal promotion of the critical method at the turn of the nineteenth century: "[Philology] had recognized its calling, to be the transmitter of eternity, thus affording us the enjoyment of unbroken identity, across thousands of years, with the noblest and greatest peoples of antiquity; to make us as familiar with their spiritual creations and their history as if no gulf separated us."[51] It is typical that Lyell cites Niebuhr on the "bliss" of recreating the past, and decades later Turner cites Taine's reference to the re-creation of life. A striking example is Ranke himself, who personalizes this experience while recalling his continent-wide search for primary sources for a book:

> Let no one pity the man who devotes himself to studies apparently so dry, and neglects for them the delights of many a joyous day. It is true that the companions of his solitary hours are but lifeless papers, but they are the remnants of the life of past ages, which gradually assume form and substance to the eye occupied in the study of them.[52]

Such passages figure the standpoint of the historian, and their exuberance is telling. The historian begins from remains and remnants that, because of their continuous existence through time, can be converted from death and lifelessness to life; nonbeing is called back into being. The gulf separating the dead past from the living present is overcome, as the passage of time is countered by a timelessness ("eternity") available through and as Niebuhr's "unbroken identity." Christian eschatology might no longer be respectable as an explicit basis for conceptions of historical temporality, but, it turns out, elements of timelessness not only infiltrate the logic of historiographic argument; they also arise in language that imagined historiography's transcendence of time against its own consciousness of time—the basic contradiction at the heart of modern historicity. The figurative language is ultimately an intimation of an ideal positionality for the historian, perfect contact with the past. It is motivated by encounters with the primary source, the indexical trace, and yet its tone is decidedly unempirical and subjective. As such it is undoubtedly applicable in other nineteenth-century disciplines of the indexical trace, such as geology, evolutionary biology, archaeology, and so forth. Thus, Lyell provides one example and the fossil trace was a powerful cultural icon of the indexical trace.

At the same time, however, this language had a wider cultural ambit. Of particular interest here is that it links up with the kind of discursive universe exemplified by preservationism, with its own privileged icon of the indexical trace, the ancient ruin. In chapter 2 I suggested that the polarity or dialectic of preservationism and restorationism encapsulates vicissitudes of the indexical trace, which in turn motivate various aesthetics of reconstructed totalities. A similar dialectic might be mapped onto the uses of the indexical trace as evidence in historiography, which must also assert an unavoidably hypothetical synthesis, the internally unified sequence. Now, preservationism also formulated the experience of pastness as resurrection of the dead. Perhaps in Ruskin such language could serve as valid description of subjective experience in the contemplation of an old building. But how could it be conceivable within disciplined historiography, with its founding ethos of empirically warranted inference from documents authenticated through the critical method? It seems more akin to religion or magic than to science. And yet, as with the contemporaneous preservationist movement, it may be a bit more than a "mere" figure, for its status can become somewhat more literal at the nonmaterial, spiritual, or mental level. It is notable, for instance, that the idea of mental concord with the past has been admitted to the realm of rigorous theory of history stemming from German historicism and disciplined historiography, as in the concepts of *verstehen* and mental reenactment.[53]

This suggests something about the appeal of history and the standpoint of the historian. While claims, protocols, and institutions of rigorous, disciplined scholarship undoubtedly helped establish the persuasive force of modern historiography, that strength was also inextricable from a certain imagination or imaginary. In saying this, I am not particularly interested in the debates, constant since the nineteenth century, over whether historiography is a science or a poetics, not least because there are too many cases in various disciplines (including physical sciences) for which that opposition is difficult to sustain or at least highly complex.

I am interested in the intersection of a cognitive ideal of a rigorous, disciplined, authoritative historiography with an imaginative ideal in which the past can be present to the subject. The authority of indexical traces authenticated by proper, critical research procedures is not in itself simply an irrationality, but it is drawn to a dream, an irrationality, having to do with historiographic positionality.

A version of this dream was articulated at the outset of disciplinary historiography in descriptions of the subjective experience of the modern historian. It is almost explicitly a dream of transcendence, manifested in the personage of the all-powerful historical researcher who can re-create a full, coherent, and true past and then transmit it for the benefit of society and culture. This kind of dream might be better conceived as a desire, for it is pegged to an impossible object. Insofar as the express object of this desire is a perfect historiography, the latter is defined by a subject able to fully communicate, or commune, with the past in the present. This entails the co-presence of old and new in the face of temporal assumptions that insist on their absolute separation. The "bliss" of the historians who envision this object is the bliss of a subject that can envision itself as full and stable because it is the point of such a co-presence.

It is clear why the indexical trace could serve as a medium (in several senses) for conceiving of this state. Produced in the absent "then," but actually present in the "now," the indexical trace offers a type of object enabling the subject's connection over this break. The logically requisite inferential jump between fragments of the past attested indexically and integral sequence is, in effect, a jump between the activities of the historian in an ongoing present and the unified, explained past, between presence and absence. The material, perceivable reality of the indexical trace makes it appropriate as disciplinary evidence of the absent past, but this overlaps with an imaginative transcendence of temporal distance and epistemological security.

In their actual work, of course, most professional historians usually avoid claims of such perfection. They carefully demarcate the most certain assertions from probabilities and from speculation. They often indicate where the primary evidence is insufficient and stage debates among alternative interpretations or selections of the evidence. When such care and even reflexive modesty is found in the work of professional historians, it is an acknowledgment of the basic gaps that define the field of modern historicity and its productivity. However, from another angle, it only amounts to acknowledging limitations with respect to a certain ideal, which is thereby reconfirmed since it remains the implicit standard. This suggests that modern historiography is built on the consistent presumption of the ideal on the one hand *and* unavoidable limitations in realizing it on the other. On the one hand, the disciplined historian is so through specialized knowledge and the experience of the authenticity of indexical traces, as well as through the rigorous inference of unified sequences from such traces. On the other hand, this disciplinary specialization is tied to a literal impossiblity, the kind of subject-position that could secure knowledge of the past, as if it could supercede the divisions between past and present.

Beginning from the postulate of a time-filled universe of unending change, the ambition of the historian is to be able to discover and authoritatively transmit the actuality of the past. The claims of historiography are therefore always under pressure. A perfect historian would have to be out of time, able to be in at least two different times simultaneously—past and present, old and new; within the constructions of modern historical temporality, this is to be time-less. The imaginary position of the ideal historian would have to involve something like the position of the spectator (or better, the narrator) of Griffith's *Intolerance*, but also, for that matter, of more conventional historical films: capable of a bi- or multitemporal capacity, simultaneously in past and present, able to pinpoint and include any time and any place necessary to compose the integral sequence. The antinomy between this ideal and the gaps that provide the conceptual working space of historiography is only resolvable as an imaginative construct. Among other things, the indexical trace is a prop for figuring or imagining this ideal.

Conclusion: From Historicity to Cinema and Back

About one hundred years after Ranke defined the object of modern historiography as *"wie es eigentlich gewesen,"* Siegfried Kracauer made the following comment in an essay on photography:

Photography presents a spatial continuum; historicism seeks to provide the temporal continuum. According to historicism the complete mirroring of an intratemporal sequence simultaneously contains the meaning of all that occurred within that time.... Historicism is concerned with the photography of time. The equivalent of its temporal photography would be a giant film depicting the temporally interconnected events from every vantage point.[54]

When cinema was just over thirty years old, this young German observer of modern culture could already suggest correspondences between historiography and the mass-distributed media of indexical imaging. Kracauer's familiarity with the crisis of historicism is evident from the position he assigns cinema in this comparison. On the one hand, he implies that cinema provides a better parallel to historiography than does photography, because cinema's fuller temporalization admits of a fuller internally unified sequence. On the other, Kracauer was unsympathetic to academic historicism, and he may also be hinting at another point: that cinema could compensate for the limitations of modern historicity, including the impossibility of a proper, secure historiographic "perspective" in modern temporality. That is, in the face of the disordering and subjectively alienating aspects of that temporality, he attributes to cinema the potential for constructing more appropriate subject-positions.

If modern historiography involves the simultaneity of a cognitive ideal with an imaginative ideal, theories of disciplined historiography that emphasize the former often come up against the latter. Kracauer, on the other hand, begins with purportedly imaginative forms—photography and film as components of modern mass culture. But can this then lead back to historical knowledge in some sense? What is the relation between historical representation and filmic representation? Throughout film history, journalists, critics, and scholars have intermittently written about the deployment of historical narratives in films; however, the related but more fundamental question broached by Kracauer is that of overlaps, intersections, and parallels between the conceptual architecture of modern historicity and the modern, mass-disseminated indexical media of photography and film. This question has rarely if ever been a focus of film theory proper. Probably because of the referential ambitions of historiography, the most suggestive lines of approach may be found in the work of classical film theorists who argued for the realist vocation of cinema, including the older Kracauer. Indexicality, whether identified as such or not, is a crucial element in such interrogations. It is, for example, the unnamed quality shared by photography and cinema that allows Kracauer to yoke them together.[55]

This brings us back to my starting point, for Bazin remains the most significant theorist of cinematic indexicality. About two decades after Kracauer's article, Bazin independently described the specificity of automatically produced, indexical images as a special kind of appeal to the spectator. To review, he proposed that photography appropriates standards of recognizability associated with dominant uses of perspectival imagery, but that it adds indexicality. The addition of identity over time to likeness is such that the real pregivenness, or referentiality, of imaged objects seems guaranteed. From this he extrapolated a postulate that served him as a starting point for any consideration of cinema: the specific contribution of cinema was to complete the photographic claim to referentiality by expanding its tracing of space to time itself. Bazin regarded this cinematic temporalization of indexicality as a qualitative leap rather than a mere supplement to photography, precisely because it affords the possibility of (aesthetically) structuring actual duration. This understanding of cinematic representation is tied to a postulate about subjectivity. Within his history of imaging media, cinema is an unprecedentedly effective response—albeit a potentially variegated one—to a constitutive anxiety. For the Bazinian subject's ultimate stake in indexical images derives from the threat of loss, decay, and fatality inherent in the passage of time.

Bazin's emphasis on temporality suggests a certain kinship with Kracauer's likening of film and historiography. True, in many respects Bazin was a very different kind of thinker. He draws on a different theoretical heritage than Kracauer with regard to modernity and temporality—to put it emblematically, let's say Bergson and Teilhard rather than Marx and Simmel. Bazin's considerations of cinema do not begin with its mass qualities, but with the figure of an individual subject's life and death. Furthermore, they contain only a few direct analogies or comparisons between cinema and historiography. Yet, Bazin's writings are shot through with implicit and terminological references to historicity and nineteenth-century disciplines of the indexical trace, such as geology and evolutionary biology. And his entire film theory is built on the problem of objectifications of pastness against the flow of time.

Thus his figurative characterization of cinema as "change mummified" encapsulates the idea that the specific appeal and import of cinema stems from two mutually defining elements. The first is a subject that is defensive in relation to temporality, caught between a time-filled objectivity and a desire for the timeless, between materiality (the real) and a transcendence (psychology, aesthetics). The second is its character as a representational mode that offers that subject degrees of amelioration in its relations to a time-filled material reality. Bazin's subject of cinema—which is, in the end, the human itself—is therefore obsessed with preservation, with the remains of pastness that can bring it into perception in the present. This is the basis for the privilege of the indexical trace in his film theory.

At the end of chapter 1, I asked whether Bazin's preservative obsession might itself be historicized. Throughout chapters 2 and 3, I have been attempting to sketch reasons to believe that the Bazinian preservative obsession is a variant on a broad range of Western cultural, intellectual, and social practices founded on the centrality of time and that coalesced during the nineteenth century. From the social and representational disavowals of architectural preservationism and the museum village to the underlying (and sometimes self-conscious) epistemological precariousness of positionality in disciplined historiography, the modern present is compelled to engage with pastness. Its very self-definition in the recession of the old and the advent of the new depends on postulating the force of temporality. In considering examples of this engagement, we have repeatedly encountered variations on defining elements of the preservative obsession: the antinomy between the time-filled and the timeless, an anxious subject seeking security with respect to time and change, negotiations of with pastness through some form of or relation to indexicality.

My "historicization" therefore places Bazin's thought squarely within the epistemology and culture of modern historicity, and the formulation "change mummified" appears to be its product. Inversely, it is a trope that may be used to describe not only cinema, but modern historicity itself. This connection allows us to conclude by settling accounts with Bazin, but in order to move in a somewhat different direction from him.

Bazin's film theory is an explicitly phenomenological one, and phenomenology is intimately implicated in the theoretical centrality of temporality in modern Western thought. In fact, it and its construction of the subject have often been treated as a response to the epistemological crises of Western theory so well established by the beginning of the twentieth century.[56] There are some suggestive formulations in this regard in a 1930s critique of German phenomenological philosophy by Adorno. Adorno finds that a central problem in the constitution of the phenomenological subject is the disjunction between the stream of time of actual existence and the search for a kind of epistemological security—a positionality that entails the timelessness of a transcendence. Treating Husserl as its most admirable representative, Adorno thus characterizes phenomenology as seeking a way to formulate (onto)logical security in the face of its own postulate that the real is definitionally temporalized. He argues that it only overcomes the contradiction between the universal effectivity of temporality in existence and a timeless consciousness (hence essence) through logical sleight of hand. At points Adorno explicitly connects this disturbance to historical consciousness. He complains, for example, about "Heidegger's tendency to camouflage irresolvable contradictions, like those between timeless ontology and history, by ontologizing history itself as historicality and turning the contradiction as such into a 'structure of being.'"[57]

Adorno therefore argues that the immediate motivation of such errors is exemplified by the urgency of Husserl's quest for logical security, in the face of a temporalization of the real. But for Adorno, the susceptibility of even such master thinkers as Husserl to such contradictory moves is an indication that these difficulties may be treated as sociohistoric symptoms:

Dread [*angst*] stamps the ideal of Husserlian philosophy as one of absolute security, on the model of private property. Its reductions aim at the secure: viz. the immanence to consciousness of lived experiences whose title deeds the philosophical self-consciousness to which they "belong" should possess securely from the grasp of any force; and essences which, free from all factical existence, defy vexation from factical existence.

The two postulates contradict each other. The world of lived experiences is, according to Husserl, changeable and nothing but a 'stream'. But the transcendence of essences can itself never become lived experience. Husserl's development may be understood in the tendency to unite the two postulates of security in a final one which identifies essence and stream of consciousness.

His [Husserl's] drive to security is so great that he mistakes with the beguiled naiveté of all propertied belief (*Besitzglauben*): how compulsively the ideal of absolute security drives to its own destruction; how the reduction of essences to the world of consciousness makes them dependent on the factical and the past; how, on the other hand, the essentiality of consciousness robs it of all specific content and sacrifices to chance everything that should be secured.

Security is left as an ultimate and lonely fetish like the number, one million, on a long deflated bank note.[58]

Whatever one thinks of Adorno's inimitable combination of logical critique, social analysis, and acid humor, his view of phenomenology is grounded in the notion that it is not just a Western modernity, but a *capitalist* modernity that produces both a certain conception of a time-filled universe and the consequent anxiety about finding secure positionality for a subject confronting the real. Like Bazin's cinematic subject, the subject produced by phenomenological philosophy is understood by Adorno as defensive in the face of temporality. But that temporality is itself sociohistorically determined. This suggests two concluding points not only about Bazin, but through him, about historicity and cinema. The first involves the status of Bazin's theory of film. The second has to do with situating cinema as an indexical medium in the "historical context" of capitalist modernity, which determines the junctures between historicity and cinema.

As to the first: If the trope "change mummified" can be appropriated to characterize modern historicity, the preservative obsession with its defensive subject might be treated as the historical self-consciousness of Bazin's phenomenology, even if it is a paradoxically implicit self-consciousness. Like the subject Adorno reads in Husserl, Bazin's ever-anxious subject always needs an impossible reassurance of its own stability and always threatens to slip into the error of a logically illegitimate transcendence. But Bazin evinces awareness of the difficulties discussed by such critics of phenomenology as Adorno. He is concerned about the danger of falsifying transcendence—that is, the danger of claiming security by dissolving the postulate of a time-filled universe into time-lessness—in his discussion of Stalinist cinema as well as certain other movements in the history of film style. Bazin's sophistication is thus indicated by the fact that he thematizes the threats to secure human subjectivity posed by a radical time awareness. Yet, over and against this awareness, at the level of theory he tries to provide means to counter the existentialist angst, the dread described by Adorno, first by identifying, internalizing, and essentializing it as the mummy complex; and second, by making the indexical image the basis of a valid response to the insecurities of subjectivity without eliminating them. As I argued in chapter 1, however, he negates their historicity by attributing ahistorical stability to the preservative obsession and the mummy complex.

On the one hand, then, Bazin's phenomenology seems to sensitize him to the antinomy between the time-filled and the timeless; on the other hand, his film theory, with its axiom of an unchanging preservative obsession, manifests the flight from history that Adorno derides. Bazin's logic can therefore be understood within the constellations of temporal disavowal we have repeatedly encountered: from the concerns about architectural and cultural loss in the preservation debates or the class-based anxieties associated with the loss of mythical socioeconomic hierarchies of the museum village, to the conundrums of modern historicity wherein the historian can only provide a secure account of history by writing it from outside history. This is the symptomatic side of the mummification of change.

But this does not make Bazin's theoretical approach valueless. In the spirit of Adorno's way of reading philosophy, it seems to me that Bazin's work simultaneously designates and explores (however partially) a configuration historically crucial for cinema, even while it participates in that configuration and registers it symptomatically. There is a certain line of French film theory, including not only Bazin but also Merleau-Ponty and Metz, which suggests that there are special affinities between phenomenology and cinema. Those affinities are said to circulate around definitions and experiences of subjectivity.[59] My view is that this is a productive idea, but its productivity does not rest in a secured (atemporal) fit between phenomenological metalanguage and its cinematic object. Instead, these affinities should themselves be considered floating, "historical."

It then still remains possible to share with Bazin the project of reading subjective constructions, relations, and positionalities off the history of representations, which involves the presumption that the two are inseparable. It is also possible to agree on the central importance of the indexical trace to the history of filmic representation and therefore film theory. But it is not permissible to share with him the unification of the time-filled with the timeless in a victory over time, so that "the" fundamental subjective relation to cinema "as such" is the same now as it was in, say, 1895. Instead, the contradiction between the time-filled and the timeless requires its own understanding in a peculiar balancing act whereby the very terms that compel conceiving of cultural formations in a radically "historical" way are themselves under that kind of interrogation.[60]

This leads to my second concluding comment. It should be clear by now that, in my view, the Bazinian trope "change mummified" is so widely applicable because it partakes of a socially and culturally powerful aspect of modern time-awareness, and therefore modern historicity. In that sense it follows from nineteenth-century socioeconomic forces and associated representational conceptions that bear on cinema indirectly and directly. From this very general, sweeping "perspective," what unites cinema and historiography as practices drawing on indexicality to organize temporality is nothing less than the capitalist nature of modernity, and the time-consciousness it generates. This is the broadest underpinning of any consideration of overlaps between cinema and historicity.

Thus, I began this chapter with generalizations about social and economic processes of rationalization related to industry, technology, and economy, which required a secure regularization and control of time. Only then did I move to the suggestion that the quantum increase in time awareness thereby promoted also had unsettling cultural and intellectual consequences, and that the problem of historiographic perspective was a privileged example. This is what made "the nineteenth century" an innovative, even foundational period for Western thought with respect to the significance of time.[61]

In this regard, modern temporality may be pictured as a kind of battle terrain. On this terrain the disordering force of time struggles with the need and desire to order or control time, to subsume it under a rationality. This struggle manifests itself not only on an epistemological-representational level, but also on the socioeconomic level. Here, that rationality is aligned with economic processes complicit with social hierarchies, something clear to social thinkers at least since Marx. As we have seen, the notion of a battle over time has often been literalized with respect to working conditions. Furthermore, the temporal coordination of labor and everyday life in conjunction with commerce and transport had a fundamental impact. On this plane, the opposition between the time-filled and the timeless might be expressed from the standpoint of political economy as another polarity with an infinity of mediate mixtures: between a shapeless or at least irregular, hence less efficient temporality, and a rationally comprehensible, therefore more manageable, hence more efficient temporality. But note that to formulate it thus is already to assume the premises of capitalist efficiency as the standard.

In epistemology and representation, this battle was implicated in models and imaginaries of ideal representation, human knowledge, but also in corrosive critiques of those possibilities. The problem of defining and justifying positionality was central to this terrain, which could not help but be political and imaginative as well as a matter of cognition and reason. The authority that could be attributed to the logic of disciplinary historiography shades into an imagination of perfect knowledge of the real in time, even when it is a matter of acknowledging that a given account falls short of that ideal. A crucial element in this logic was the critically authenticated primary source. Determining definitions understood it as specific to disciplinary historiography, but it was also a variant on a culturally widespread fascination with the indexical trace.

Cinema was innovated as a commercial technology in the late nineteenth century, and for a large part of the twentieth century it was arguably a socioculturally dominant technology of the imaged indexical trace. If the battle between temporal ordering and time as disordering occurs on both epistemological-representational and socioeconomic planes, the latter comes to the forefront in especially direct ways in film as a representational medium. Film history is intimately and explicitly intertwined with the history of late nineteenth- and twentieth-century societal institutions and ideologies unthinkable outside capitalism. The dominant textual norms of filmmaking were established roughly between 1905 and 1920, when the mainstream cinematic institution succeeded in adjusting its range of manipulations of images and sound to the necessities of sustaining national and global mass markets. The notion of mass market here applies not only in a sectoral sense, involving the specific economics of the film industry, but also includes the association of mainstream cinema with the development of twentieth-century consumerist capitalism, something often noted by scholars. As I have already remarked, the fact that mainstream film was and is conceived as the production of a leisure-time activity aligns commercial cinema with the socioeconomic rationalization of time on many levels. These include production and exhibition, filmmaking standards and spectatorship, the coordination of the workplace and the everyday domestic, "private" spheres of life. To put it as broadly as possible, the establishment of mainstream U.S. cinema in the early twentieth century was one of the key developments of later capitalist modernity. The intrication between cinema and modern historicity with which this book is concerned is not limited to mainstream cinema. But as suggested above, the history of cinematic textuality must be treated not only within the history of indexicality, but as existing in the intersection of indexicality and rationalization. On the one hand, it developed in the domain of enterprises and media of the indexical trace, those many "effects of resurrection" Stephen Bann finds to be such a great concern of nineteenth-century Western culture. It implicitly partakes of the ethos and conundrums of modern historicity, including questions of subjective positionality. On the other hand, a wide range of cinematic practices were more or less immediately dependent on temporal rationalization and the capitalist socioeconomic foundations that were crucial mediating factors for the epistemological conceptions associated with modern historicity.

Ranke's landmark 1824 definition of disciplinary historiography was almost contemporaneous with the invention of photography, for Nièpce achieved the hazy likenesses that now count as the earliest photographs just the year before. Some seventy years later, at the 1893 Chicago World Columbian Exposition, exhibits included Eadweard Muybridge's proto-cinematic Zoopraxiscope, as well as one of the first public demonstrations of Thomas Edison's new breakthrough movie machine, the kinetoscope. Among the other spectacles embodying the progress of modern civilization available at this same event was a meeting of the relatively new American Historical Association. (In fact, this was the meeting where Frederick Jackson Turner presented "The Significance of the Frontier in American History," for decades the most famous single scholarly paper in all of U.S. professional historiography.) Perhaps it is not completely surprising that cinema was advertised as the "*historiographe*" in some of its earliest commercial manifestations.[62]

As the nineteenth century unrolled into the twentieth and the twentieth proceeded to its end, such coincidences were increasingly likely to occur. Historical discourse, based on rigorous documentation, was an increasingly familiar as well as prestigious form of knowledge, while indexical media of photography, cinema, and (later) video became ubiquitous markers of modernity. Automatically produced indexical images and historiography: these were two regimes of the indexical trace, two masteries of time and pastness, two experiences of knowledge, two kinds of spectacle, both of which achieved contemporaneous and long-lasting cultural success, as well as controversy.[63]

As early as the 1920s, Kracauer suggested that considering overlaps and the interplay of historicity and cinema can reveal something about the history and theory of modern historicity, and also about the history and theory of film. The rest of this book is concerned with the latter in light of the former. We will begin from a consideration of the nature and import of indexicality and historical representation in mainstream film, which established more or less "global" expectations for cinematic representation.

Part II. From Historicity to Film: Case Studies

CHAPTER 4

Detail, Document, and Diegesis in Mainstream Film

If the film were to give itself up to the blind representation of everyday life, following the precepts of, say, Zola, as would indeed be practicable with moving photography and sound recording, the result would be a construction alien to the visual habits of the audience, diffuse, unarticulated outwards. Radical naturalism, to which the technology of film lends itself, would dissolve all surface coherence of meaning and finish up as the antithesis of familiar realism.

—Theodor Adorno, *Minimia Moralia: Reflections from Damaged Life*

Motion picture producers have sometimes been criticized for spending so much money on research—in the case of *The Ten Commandments* more than ever before. I do not agree with the criticism. I consider it money well spent to bring to the screen the results of the work of so many patient and selfless scholars whose labors, with spade and with pen, have helped us make the days of Moses live again. Research does not sell tickets at the box office, I may be told. But research does help bring out the majesty of the Lawgiver and the eternal verity of the Law.

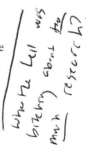

—Cecil B. DeMille

The Rationalization of the Detail

- In ancient Egypt, men plucked or shaved—but did not cut—both hair and beards, and wore false beards and wigs. Among ancient Hebrews, on the other hand, the men did cut it from time to time unless they were Nazarites, but only shaved it when in mourning

147

(though this was against the law); and women only cut their hair for mourning. The hair of Hebrews was usually black, though one can find references to an occasional blond. Assyrian men wore their hair in braids, and this may be related to the biblical Samson's wearing his hair in braids.

- The phrase "Finger of God" appears in the book of Exodus several times with respect to the actions of God. An Egyptian instrument called a *sacrum*—a wood carving of a finger springing from the head of a falcon that stood for the gods Ra and Horus—was a common symbol for divine action in ancient Egypt.

- The Emperor of Mexico, Maximilian von Hapsburg, never used a blotter and did not allow his secretary to use one; consequently, his secretary often spread letters around the floor for the ink to dry. The father of his wife addressed her in letters as "My dear Charlotte," or "My dear Daughter" and not as Carlotta, the name by which she is more usually known.

- Gummed labels on bottles did not come into general use until after 1903.

What might such a list of diverse details from the past have in common? One can imagine a giant comparative social history that might include them all. Actually, each was found in written research materials compiled during the production process of major Hollywood historical films and "true stories" made between 1938 and 1956.[1]

Studio companies kept systematic records of research activities for films. A good example is provided by Warner Brothers during the high studio period. There was a corporate form called "General Research Record" filled in for each production. This was a tabular form with five columns: the date of the query to the research department, the name of the inquirer, a summary of the request, the initials of the researcher, and the disposition of the request, including the source of the answer or materials provided by the research department (see Figure 4.1). Research departments and researchers were consulted throughout the filmmaking process by almost every "creative" specialization in the studio division of labor, including screenwriters and art directors, about what kinds of objects and details could be included in the film. Especially in historical films, the research "bible"—a compendium of written and visual materials —was circulated and excerpted as a basis for the work of the various creative departments. Research departments were relied upon for exclusionary as well as inclusionary purposes, as when it was believed legally necessary to avoid using the names of real people in "true stories."[2]

Warner Brothers is legendary for some of the most efficient accounting methods among the major companies of the high studio period. But it is thought-provoking to find that details had to be accounted for. In one of the few extensive scholarly considerations of studio-era research departments, George F. Custen correctly emphasizes that the publicity around research departments served as a marketing device to differentiate the biographical film, his object of study, as a special product. But for our purposes here, the biopic is one subtype of the historical film, which was and is associated with similar kinds of publicity, and also of historical representation more generally in mainstream cinema. Even though generic considerations made research activities in certain kinds of filmmaking more prominent than in others, as Custen notes, research departments worked on *all* kinds of films, even musicals.[3]

Research has been a constant in film history, for claims to accurate knowledge and authenticity of the filmed detail have traversed cinema history at least since Méliès. Hollywood studio–era research departments provide especially fertile ground for scholars, not only because of the overwhelming historical significance of Hollywood filmmaking, but because, like all studio departments, they generated a mass of documents that display their own procedures and protocols. But research was becoming normalized well before the introduction of the studio system, at least as far back as 1910, and it continues to be a standard practice in the present, although the forms of institutional organization have changed. Given the constant recourse to research and researched detail throughout the history of mainstream film, this seemingly routine aspect of film production may reveal something fundamental about the kinds of cinema it supports.[4]

Within the studio system, research was standardized labor conducted under the aegis of a bureaucratically defined, paper-generating

GENERAL RESEARCH RECORD

DR. EHRLICH
NAME OF PICTURE

DATE	BY	REQUEST	ASSIGN	DISPOSITION
11.14.39	Goldie	Did laboratory workers use rubber gloves in 1910?	C.M.	No. Pictures of labs in Ehrlich's Institute in "bible" collection
11.14.39	Tyler	German type lettering for stencil in shipping crate	C.M.	Various types in Illus. Zeitung, 1918
11.14.39	Goldie	1. What did shipping crates look like in 1910? 2. Were gummed labels used on bottles in 1910? 3. Was gummed tape used to seal packages in 1910?	C.M.	1. Ill Lon News, Feb. 12, 1910 2. Gummed labels were used generally after 1903 Inf. - Dennison's 3. No Inf. - Dennison's
11.16.39	Levy	German lettering	G.B.	1 clip - Lettering-German
11.17.39	Stark	Attitude of the churches with regard to dissemination of knowledge on venereal diseases	H.G.	Catholic Church would object; others not. Matter to be referred to Dr. Lissauer who will call Stark Inf. - Personal Knowledge
11.17.39	Moss	German telephones	G.B.	3 clips--Germany-Tel.
11.18.39	Joseph	Spelling of Leewenhoek's name	J.B.	As is
11.18.39	Goff	Shape of ampules in which 606 was shipped	C.M.	Showed him picture in "bible" and advised him of sequence of changes in shape; suggested he consult Bob Martin as to shape they actually will use
11.18.39	Goff	Chemists scale, Germany, 1910	C.M.	"Das Jahrhundet un Wert und Bild", Vol. 3 P. 277
11.20.39	Cox	Picture of a bunsen burner	C.M.	O.K. Western Surgical Supply Catalogue
11.20.39	Cox	Pictures of hands	G.B.	2 clips - Anatomy-Hands

Figure 4.1. Sample pages of General Research Record for (a) *Dr. Ehrlich's Magic Bullet* and (b) *Juarez*. Courtesy of Warner Bros.

GENERAL RESEARCH RECORD

(b)

JUAREZ
NAME OF PICTURE

DATE	BY	REQUEST	ASSIGN	DISPOSITION
10.22.38	Patterson	Coat of Arms that would appear on letter paper from Count Metternich to Maximilian	H.G.	This would be the Austri Coat of Arms on the letterhead of the Austrian Embassy Inf. from Mr. MacKenzie
10.22.38	Patterson	Detail of saddle blankets Maximilian's and other officers of the French and Mexican army	H.G.	1. Max. saddle blankets and horse trapping from "Mexico a Traver de l's Siglos" and "bible"
10.22.38	Patterson	Juarez writing	W.D.	Van de Velde's book "Porfirio Diaz and his Work"
10.22.38	Patterson	Carlotta's monogram	H.G.	"Charlotte of Belgium" b Foussemagne
10.24.38	Patterson	Names of European regiments that fought in Mexico and their insignia	H.G.	Belgian body guard Foreign Legion 3rd Division of Infantry of Army of Paris
10.24.38	MacKenzie	What uniform did Maximilian wear when he landed at Vera Cruz or entered Mexico City	H.G.	Simple traveling clothes which very macy disappointed the Mexicans Inf.--P. 423, Corti
10.24.38	MacKenzie	Name of the rows of black points on the five mantles worn at coronations	E.H.	Miniver, which is a fur
10.24.38	Patterson	Style of documents used in Mexico in the 1860's	J.R.	Mexico, Its Social Revolution, Vol. 1
10.24.38	Levy	Map of Mexico to find town called Solidad		
10.25.38	Blanke	Speech by young Masaryk broadcast to U.S. from London recently	C.M.	Program Dept. CBS, N. Y. City H. B. Kiltenborne Paul White, Director of Special Events
10.25.38	Patterson	Letterhead that would be used by Lincoln writing to Juarez	E.H.	Copies from clipping fil and Century for 1888

office. The systematization of research procedures by a research department was part of an overall tendency to seek standardization and economic efficiencies of scale in film production. Publicity and other writing about Hollywood filmmaking, especially during the "golden age" of studio production, has sometimes emphasized a certain irrationality and unpredictability of its production processes, often in the name of personality (of star, of director, even of producer). But "Hollywood" is a concatenation of institutional and textual practices making up a large industry that required large amounts of capital to seek large amounts of profit. This kind of bureaucratized division of labor in film production was linked to a particular, and particularly influential, film-historical development.

It is a truism among film historians that during "Hollywood's Golden Age" the handful of largest and most powerful American filmmaking corporations vertically integrated the three branches of production, distribution, and exhibition that were taken to compose the industry. The tendency toward large-scale vertical integration was the result of drives for industry-wide control present in film history at least since Thomas Edison's patent suits against competitors in the 1890s. In this model, profitability was associated with significant centralization of production and marketing decisions, which were in turn associated with strategies for restricting competition. The consequence was less monopoly than oligopoly. Both centralization and restraints on competition were instrumental in forming and maintaining access to a mass market for films, and for making that market more predictable. Inversely, the combination of vertical integration and oligopoly required a relatively stable and predictable supply of film product to the distribution and exhibition branches; hence, the strong impetus to amass capital resources in the production branch and to rationalize its means and practices in the name of regularized production efficiencies.

The development of this rationalization of production was one significant determinant of mainstream film textuality as we know it today, and therefore a major development in the history of modern culture generally. This is not to deny subsequent changes, in both the organization of film production and aspects of its financial underpinnings. For example, it is arguable that, for various reasons, by the late 1970s and 1980s major distribution companies tended to seek profits through shorter-term bonanzas rather than the long-term stability of income that classical studio companies achieved through producing a large quantity of films for a relatively secure market; hence the emergence, or reemergence, of the blockbuster film as a key product at this time. Nevertheless, even this strategy became associated in part with such developments as the dissemination of the videocassette and the benefits for marketing projections of preselling a film, so if broadcast and pay television along with videocassette sales and rentals are taken into account as exhibition venues, longer-term calculations may have been more important than is superficially evident. And in the more recent round of concentration and integration involving cinema, video, television, and multimedia products—abetted by government deregulation—the drive toward vertical integration lives on, albeit in new forms having to do in part with the acceleration of the post–World War II expansion of the exhibition sector into "new media."[5]

But have shifts in organizational and economic context made a difference for principles and goals of filmic *textuality?* Some scholars and critics argue this is indeed the case, ultimately linking textual differences to shifts in society and culture as well as industrial and economic structures.[6] Yet, many normalized textual procedures, especially with respect to narrativization and narrative-image/sound relations, seem close "descendants" of those associated with production goals and practices that were instituted and fixed by the early 1920s. This certainly is true of research protocols in mainstream film, my concern here. The breakup of the model of centralized mass production of films only means that producers may now "outsource" research, employing individuals or separate companies to provide research. In the 1980s, for example, deForest Research Inc. provided services to a number of theatrical film productions, from *Platoon* to *Porky's,* as well as to several television series, including *Cagney and Lacey, The Golden Girls, Moonlighting, The Cosby Show, Matlock,* and *Cheers.* One might expect this with *Platoon,* which was marketed as the first film to transmit the authentic experience of the U.S. Vietnam combat soldier.

But *Porky's* was a raunchy adolescent/frat house comedy, *Cagney and Lacey* was a cop drama using some location settings with liberal social realist and feminist overtones, and *Golden Girls* a situation comedy. This range of production types and genres indicates again the degree to which "research" has been a constant presence in mainstream screen production.[7]

Researched detail, with an accounting of sources as grounds for making referential claims, is also an aspect of disciplined historical scholarship. In that sense, Hollywood research departments are, in their own way, another kind of professionalization of historical thinking, one that both assumes and may stand for a certain general cultural penetration of its ideals (if not all of its practices). But what is implied when a mass medium whose dominant product is fictional narrative makes this element of referentiality a necessary component of its production processes? On the other hand, what is implied when a medium that is supposedly indexical requires such labor to secure its referentiality? How may we describe the chief relations of mainstream cinema to historical referentiality? Such questions mandate attention to intersections of the constraints of historicity and the constraints of mainstream filmic textuality, keeping in mind that the latter has been a particularly dominant and determinant practice within film history. I will propose that this attention must extend along a continuum from authenticated detail to historical spectacle. I will also suggest that such questions can make the historical film an important instance for film theory, as well as for the historiography of mainstream cinema. Because I will be paying attention to the status of the detail, I will not argue by reference to complete narratives, but to a very few exemplary fragments of mainstream films.

One can begin by focusing the question of the place of historicity in mainstream cinema as follows. During the high studio period, research seems to have been submitted most clearly to forms of bureaucratic-industrial organization as the systematic accounting of objects, that is, as a certain rationalization of the detail. By this I mean the application of methods of modern industrial organization, even and especially in the protocols that determine the types of objects and actions that may or may not be filmed in a specific narrative. This implanted a relatively constant recourse to research and researched detail throughout the history of much of mainstream film, inflecting not only explicit historical representation, but also other genres and modes.

The Knowing Game

The fact that researching detail has been such a normalized procedure in mainstream cinema raises an issue that has not been of intensive film-theoretical concern. In every narrative-representational film, specific choices must be made about what constructed or found objects to put in front of the camera to be filmed—about the content of what film theorists call the profilmic field. Precisely what is to be seen in the frame, planned for in the preproduction stages, which for mainstream narrative film includes dialogue and script writing. It might seem reasonable to suppose that the more physically dense the diegetic world, the more some sorts of criteria of accuracy and/or plausibility must impinge on the mise-en-scène, but note that this already presupposes accuracy and plausibility as desirable. Research departments systematically manifest this desirability.

Yet, since the 1960s much of the most enlightening film-theoretical work has subjected such criteria to antirealist critiques, emphasizing the conventionality of the construction of space and time through filmic means, as well as the unavoidable mediations of profilmic artifice. One result of this attitude has been a strong tendency to elide a fundamental aspect of the history of photographic cinema, namely the problem of just what things are to be filmed and depicted in the final product. Or more precisely, there has, of course, been acknowledgment of components of narrative film production that dovetail with these areas, such as costume, set design, and so forth. And one type of profilmic object, the human body, has received and continues to receive a great deal of scholarly attention. But the choice of the object per se—a question that has to be faced for every shot and indeed, every frame—deserves theoretically informed attention in itself, at the very least because of the photographic/cinematic impression of accurate reproduction associated not just with codes of spatial verisimilitude, but with indexicality.[8]

Of course a very wide range of social and cultural constraints and pertinences bears on the seeming necessity of choosing which objects are to be included in a shot. A complete account, if such were possible, would have to interrelate a large number of determinants indeed, ranging from generic considerations to cultural practices and ideological processes often thought to originate "outside" the cinematic institution strictly speaking. No wonder so much film theory and analysis has designated this terrain by bracketing it with terms like cultural coding. However, even a cursory look at production records from the studio period will strongly suggest that one significant nodal point for all these constraints and determinations in mainstream narrative film was and is research.

One way to get at the import of research is to consider the expectations it generated during the studio period, when it was systematically implemented. Studio files indicate there was a game at work, a game of accuracy and knowledge. At least some in the audience were quite willing to call the studios to account according to the rules of that game. For example, in a 1938 letter to Warner Brothers, Charles Everett of Hingham, Massachusetts, politely raises an objection about the accuracy of the profilmic field, in this case in relation to language. In the film *The Life of Emile Zola*, when Zola and his wife buy *langoustes* at the Paris fish market, they are given lobsters, he writes, while *langouste* actually denotes

> the ordinary craw-fish or Spanish 'langousta.' If I am wrong I should much like to know it, but I am still convinced that those were lobsters and not craw-fish as advertised by the fish-wife. I have lived in France and I know that one can usually obtain either of the above-mentioned at almost any season.[9]

This is a standard move in what I will call Everett's Game. This game has to do with knowledge of the detail, and it is an implicit aspect of the experience of mainstream historical films. Mr. Everett is invoking its basic rule, namely that every detail of the film be gotten "right" or else he can assert a victory, consisting in a claim of knowledge of the detail superior to that of the film. Of course, were he not familiar with the availability of different kinds of shellfish in a foreign land and foreign terminologies denoting them, the film would remain superior, inaccuracies and all. In that case, the film would succeed in *its* claim to knowledge of the detail. Note, however, that it would still be transmitting the profilmic for his comprehension, thereby treating him as a beneficiary of research and appearing to give him (in his hypothetical ignorance) perception of the past "as it was." Thus, on the one hand, Everett's Game can entail a jockeying between spectator and film for superiority; on the other hand, the spectator achieves a knowledge of the detail no matter what. It is a rather pleasing game, where knowledge claims are the goal and the spectator cannot lose.[10]

Everett's Game had been promoted in the U.S. film industry at least since the 1910s, and was embraced by the production/marketing apparatus of the vertically integrated corporations that were soon established. Publicity material for many kinds of narrative films systematically included the idea that the film should get the details right, and of course this impulse was especially pronounced for "historical films." Here is Warner Brothers with an example of the work of its research department:

> For "The Adventures of Mark Twain" [released 1944] the department perused over 1,750 books, assembled 2,345 photographs, and interviewed 448 individuals. Research for "The Adventures of Don Juan" has already involved over six years in the never-ending quest for *authenticity* in every production.[11]

The same kind of publicity persisted after the demise of the classical studio apparatus. For example, in a book promoting *Barabbas* (1962), the article signed by the production designer includes the following:

> On top of the many sets and costumes we designed, was the dressing of the sets: the glassware, the pottery, the plates and cutlery; the wagons, chariots, water jars, camel and donkey packs and saddles, armor for the soldiers, and a thousand and one other items, all of which had to be painstakingly researched, sketched and then drawn to scale so that our craftsmen could make these items *accurately*.[12]

Such publicity rhetoric, which buttresses expectations of correctness by quantifying research activities, is typical. But it also indicates there is something excessive, something being defensively insisted upon in the researched production of detail as accurate. For one thing, research efforts in production were excessive to any reasonable presumption of the amount of detailed knowledge on the part of most audience members. How many would know in advance what cutlery or donkey packs from the first century C.E. looked like, or how ancient Egyptians of a certain period groomed their hair, or about the Emperor Maximilian's relations to ink? Second, it seems clear that much of the information provided by the research department for a given historical film might never appear in the film itself. And third, it is also the case that *deliberate* deviations from literal accuracy might sometimes be allowable for dramatic and narrative purposes. For example (to stay with hair) star codes and conventions of glamour have almost always mandated that hairstyles—especially those of female characters—be inflected by current tendencies in hair fashion, no matter what the period setting of the film.[13] In the classical historical film, such deviations could sometimes be more overt. They might extend to the level of the narrative itself, and might be acknowledged rather than concealed by the Hollywood studio apparatus.

The ways that deviations from researched accuracy could be justified by discourses of the Hollywood institution and in the understanding of practitioners of mainstream film production are suggestive. For one thing, they could be explained as exceptions necessary to produce different levels of knowledge. A good example is in an educational publication promoted by the film industry, which did not repress but foregrounded some major plot inaccuracies of *The Charge of the Light Brigade* (1936). It presents students with a supposed controversy in screenwriting, suggesting a mixture of narrative and authenticating criteria by which such inaccuracies could be justified, all with their own level of appeal to knowledge of reality: "Are the characters alive? Would they really act in the way shown? Is the plot plausible? ... Is the conflict represented a genuine or an artificial one?"[14] Note that this is, in effect, to retain criteria of plausibility and accuracy, but simply to move them to another level.

A second approach to understanding conscious deviation from literal accuracy had to do with addressing contemporary audiences. Discussing research into fifteenth-century painting as a source for authentic costume design in a historical film, Edward Maeder puts it precisely: "To translate a painting into an exact replica of period dress, a designer must transcend the contemporary aesthetic standard, an impossible task because the design must also create a wardrobe that will address the contemporary audience in a fashion language that they understand and that is consistent with the movie's tone."[15] This particular example draws on the discourse of fashion, but in doing so it depends on a certain conjunction between notions of fashion, linked to consumerism, and a certain kind of historical temporality. For in its invocation of the power of the era to change meanings for the audience, it presupposes the split between past and present that, as is emphasized in earlier chapters, is foundational for modern historicity.

It is unsurprising that in a mass entertainment cinema, a crucial standard for measuring the suitability of profilmic objects is understandability, but the issue goes beyond mass marketing to the question of the value of the past in the present. If value is connected with address to a present-day audience, this suggests a third, related kind of rationale for deviation from literal accuracy. Maeder's consistency of tone is something like an aesthetic criterion. As the art designer of *Barrabas* puts it after trumpeting the accuracy of his settings and props: "The entire production was designed in a certain style and manner that runs through the entire film."[16] Given the presupposition of a separation between past and present, it is not farfetched to point out that this impulse is reminiscent of Viollet-le-Duc's *l'unité de style*.

Readable in such justifications for designed deviation from literal accuracy, then, is a polarity of attitudes between resorting to a notion of accuracy or authenticity with respect to pastness at one extreme, and use value for the present at the other extreme. This polarity may be described as historiographic, and it resonates with the dialectic of preservationism and restorationism discussed in chapter 2. Note that certain limitations on the standard of literal accuracy invoked by some of the research departments in their publicity are materially absolute. They include factors such as the unavailability of authentic period building materials or textiles for sets and costumes. That is, an actual preservationism is impossible in narrative cinema, much as it is for the museum village. Analogously, historiography in mainstream cinema excessively insists on a standard of researched accuracy for its cinematic "restorationism," but may—like Viollet-le-Duc—limit implementation of that standard in the name of current practicalities as well as aesthetics. Of course, these practicalities and aesthetics also have to do with things that were not always acknowledged in industry discourses, such as naturalized textual conventions and normalized production practices, contemporary cultural and ideological formations, and related marketing considerations.

Most generally, the fact that conscious anachronism and designed deviation from literally correct detail were and remain common components of mainstream cinema indicates that mainstream historical films have always to be regarded as compromise formations with respect to the standard of referential accuracy held up by the fact of research and publicity around it. But this is a conception that participates in historiographic constructions in other cultural practices. And despite that, research departments in the studio system commonly afforded creative personnel working on a historical film some potential "maximum" of accuracy. It is as if it were necessary to establish a baseline of historical authenticity of the detail, a fund of researched knowledge, upon which the creative personnel could draw, even while submitting to an intersection of constraints on accuracy.

All of this makes things complex with respect to expected audiences and audience expectations, and we can return to Everett's Game with these complexities in mind. If the work of setting up the game is in excess of the needs of the film itself, then there is something obsessive about it. Such excesses indicate the peculiar and high stake this cinema has in the assumption of knowledge and meaning from the level of the detail, even when this assumption can operate in compromise or contradiction with some of its own actual practices. But it is crucial to note that, even at the pole of researched accuracy, there is more at work than a simple effort to dupe the audience into assuming the image provides unquestionable knowledge.

Historical films appear not as monolithic instances of some "ideology of vision" as truth, for even what is given in the film image is not necessarily a source of knowledge beyond criticism. Everett's Game presumes a play of demands and standards, whereby at certain points a justification of accuracy becomes its move. This enables audience members such as Mr. Everett to mount a critique at the level of the detail. In a historical film as opposed to a documentary—but also to different degrees in different kinds of fictional genres—the game seeks something like an *impression* of witness to the details of a past age. The fact of difference between present and past, inevitable in modernity, means that the actual objects and actions of that age cannot be placed in the profilmic, so instead the film must at least include a minimum of convincing, researched reconstruction. Failing that, it can at least add to our comprehension of the period. Ideally, however, given to the spectator's perception should be visual and sonic objects that *would* have been there.

The Rationalization of the Detail and the Rationalization of Narrative

Can we infer from the excessive impulses of research practices that mainstream cinema cares about getting details "right" or at least getting them to look right? The common image of a Hollywood film on such matters is often one of careless spectacle. Indeed, there have always been those who have complained that mainstream films are filled with historical inaccuracies, that they put entertainment before fact, allowing industrial considerations and/or narrative conventions to overbalance documentary evidence. Professors of history are sometimes consulted to demonstrate this. Such complaints find their inverse complement among film and cultural theorists who dismiss as mistaken or even naive conceptions of literal accuracy unmediated by techniques of representation and criteria of selection and transformation.[17] I will eventually come to historical spectacle, but before proceeding I want to sketch some reasons for believing that the rationalization of the detail reveals something more profound

about the relation between structures of historical presentation and narrative cinema *tout court,* or at least its mainstream forms as they have
developed historically.

Some concept of mainstream cinema has become central to the theoretical and historical understandings of cinema in Film Studies. The
notion of a classical cinema, usually identified with Hollywood studio cinema from the teens to the 1950s, retains scholarly currency because it is
not only a periodizing concept, but also because it blends into a broader
and more vague notion of a long-lasting mainstream cinema whose most
economically powerful model remains Hollywood film. The importance
of conceptualizing mainstream cinema flows in part from an extraordinary fact of film history, the economic, cultural, and aesthetic power of
the flexible yet delimiting paradigmatics of narrative cinema, most influentially developed and promulgated in the U.S. film industry. It is important to be suspicious of making either mainstream cinema or that which
falls outside it (such as avant-garde cinema, art cinema, third cinema, and
so forth) into monolithic entities with unitary and globalized historical
roles, as does some 1970s film theory. Nevertheless, the fact remains that
the study of film seems to need a term that designates a sense of the range
of textual practices that have constituted and constitute filmic "normalcy,"
with normalcy conceived as a set of textual regularities and regulations.
But that said, even the most formalistically defined attributes of classical
or mainstream cinema implicitly bear a certain historiographic weight,
for such accounts usually come back to the consistencies and changes in
Hollywood filmmaking.[18]

Now, one of the most striking things about cinema is the way that
dominant, naturalized versions of it have been channeled into explicit
forms of narrative.[19] Yet, the long-term power of U.S. narrative-industrial
cinema in film history makes it easy to forget that neither classical stylistic and formal parameters, nor even explicit narrative itself were always
definitionally necessary for commercial cinema, even in the United States.
There was a time when the founding premise of classical cinema, narrative per se, was not an absolute given of popular filmmaking. For some years
before the normalization of the feature-length fictional film, commercial

cinema was dominated by the documentary impulse of the actuality film and variants on it. For example, in Robert Allen's count of the most marketable major genres during much of the pre-nickelodeon period of vaudeville film exhibition (1894–95 to 1903–4), two of them—trick films and comic vignettes—are fictional, but three of them—local actualities, kinesthetic films, and, most important, visual newspapers ("topicals")— are of a documentary rather than an acted nature. And noncomic fiction—dramatic narrative—is notable for its absence.[20]

If we take 1908 to 1917 as the period that saw the development and normalization of the feature-length classical film, with the formal and stylistic procedures as well as the emergence of the industrial configurations that implies, then it is clear that a prior transition in textuality must have occurred. This prior transition was to deliberate, explicit narrative itself. This raises an exemplary and fundamental issue in film historiography: How and why did explicitly fictional narrative become dominant in popular cinema?

Several historians of this transition emphasize its importance in the development of the fledgling film business, but there has been disagreement even as to precisely when it took place. One dispute has to do with the nickelodeon boom, the explosive expansion of storefront outlets for film exhibition between 1905 and 1908. Such an expansion was a crucial precondition for the development of the stabilized, massive U.S. film industry. It established the possibility of a consistent, secure, and truly national market for films, which was the basis for the development of concentrated production facilities during the studio period and the international economic power associated with U.S. mainstream film through most of its history. In sheer numbers of film types produced, some scholars found that various kinds of actuality films were dominant components of U.S. film production from its beginnings in 1894–96 until at least 1906. But it appears that by 1908, a point around the end of the nickelodeon boom, actuality production had virtually ceased.[21]

These numbers seem to suggest that the transition to narrative was somehow based on the nickelodeon boom. But Charles Musser turned to records of comparative profitability—that is, income versus costs—of specific film types in order to mount a strong argument against this expla-nation. Fictional films were lengthier and more expensive at a time when films were sold on a per-foot basis. After reviewing records of print lengths and income figures of key production companies, Musser con-cludes that narrative films became economically dominant for production companies a little before, rather than after, the beginning of the nick-elodeon years. In his account, narrative may well have been a precondi-tion for the nickelodeon boom, rather than the reverse.[22]

This modifies the chronology of the transition from an actuality-dominated cinema to a narrative-dominated cinema. But even in this optic, actualities and subtypes of actualities such as visual newspapers, were preponderant in U.S. film production through at least 1903–4, and were still commonly seen on commercial film programs until a point during the nickelodeon boom. This suggests that the commercial heyday of the actuality in various forms was 1896–1903. Preclassical narratives emerged as one of the leading products during 1903–4, but actualities remained a common component of the film viewing experience until around 1908. Once narrative genres had displaced actuality genres as the predominant impulse in commercialized film, another transition, to what we now treat as classical narrative cinema, occurred after 1908. It was capped by the normalization of the feature-length film, fully completed by 1916 or so.

Since the late 1970s, the status of preclassical cinema as a mode of representation, and therefore the textual aspects of these transitions, have generated productive scholarly reconceptualizations, discussions, and disputes.[23] Here, I want to emphasize that a major determinant of the denormalization of preclassical documentary genres was probably eco-nomic, namely the need for a regularized supply of new product. As Allen points out, this supply was not reliably available when visual newspapers were a leading product. Events that drew large crowds to see movies in vaudeville, such as the Spanish-American War, a hurricane, or a presi-dential funeral, didn't happen every day. But new fictional stories could be conceived every day, enabling a consistent production output to meet any foreseeable demand. This amounts to saying that given a certain level of actual or potential demand, there was economic motivation from the side of production for the transition to narrative, because the narrative cinema was more favorable than actuality cinema to industrial rationalization. An expanding market, a desideratum of all wings of the film business, could only be exploited through increased levels of consistent, predictable production that could be adjusted to meet any foreseeable demand. Thus, the extent to which the shift to narrative was driven purely by popular demand for film stories remains undecided. From articles and editorials in trade papers, along with a 1908 boomlet in travelogue magic lantern shows between reels of film, Allen once inferred that at least some segments of the audience looked on the passing of actualities with regret. Narrative may have been imposed more from the supply end of the industry than as a response to audience preferences.[24]

It is worth pausing over this point. For even though narrative was of economic benefit to the producer, and even if (as Musser argues against Allen) there was a generalized audience desire for narrative, constructing a cinema institution dominated by narrative would still have had to deal with a preexisting audience acquaintance with actuality from films that presumed an audience interest in it. From its earliest successes to some point during the nickelodeon boom, filmic textuality made the vision of actuality per se one of its primary selling points. Not only their easy availability, but the breadth of actuality views regularly seen by early film audiences must be appreciated. A local actuality could give spectators a refreshed view of their own city, or they could see such an exotic sight as a mandarin bowing in front of the Forbidden City in Peking. Films presented current events, such as the political solemnities of President McKinley's funeral, natural disasters, such as the aftermath of the Galveston flood, or the grotesque novelty of the electrocution of a dangerous elephant. In addition to deadly and grotesque events, street scenes, processions, and ceremonies from world capitals were common subject matter, as were quasi-scientific sights. As late as 1913, *Moving Picture World* included an advertisement for *Circulation of the Blood*, which displayed a pumping human heart, exposed by means of micro- and X-ray cinematography. By then, however, exhibition practices had changed radically: the fictional film was now the key product, the still lengthening "feature-length" film was becoming standardized, and major production companies had undertaken weekly newsreels, something that Allen argues was a response to popular demand for now absent topicals.[25]

The sheer range of actuality subjects and locales makes it tempting to label much of the era of preclassical cinema a time of the expanded travelogue, when commercial cinema made available documentary views of anything or anywhere it could imprint on film. A fundamental presumption of this cinema was thus a mass desire for sights of the real. *It made money by bringing into vision what had never before been seen by such numbers of people.* It seemed to make visible what had heretofore been unseeable by the many.

It is difficult to assume that this established fascination simply disappeared with the onset of a rationalized, economically prescribed, and institutionally regularized narrativity. It is more likely that the new emphasis in commercial filmmaking on fictional narrative had somehow to negotiate the desire to see actuality through the moving indexical image, to presuppose it and compromise with it. Consequently, it would also be likely that the transition to fictional narrative as a dominant of commercial cinema partook of broader cultural tendencies with respect to capturing reality. At any rate, a case can be made not only that this fascination remained evident during the transition to narrative as the dominant product of the nascent film industry, but also that it was implanted in the textual practices regularized by the development of what came to be called classical studio cinema. Given the historical impact of classical cinema, its worldwide influence on cinematic narration and filmmaking procedures, it may even be that derivations of such presumptions can still be read in elements of narrative filmmaking to the present day. This returns us to Everett's Game. Assumptions about the spectator are embedded in arrangements of the profilmic, from the rationalization of the detail to the spectacle of history on film, but routed through the rationalization of narrative.

Detail and Historicity in Mainstream Cinema:
Reality and Indexicality from Bazin to Barthes

Let us suppose that the image as visual document was one of the chief principles underlying uses of film during the preclassical period, and that some aspects of this ambition were taken up and implanted in mainstream cinema. As already noted, there is much theoretical literature that would treat this as naive spectatorship, but a countervailing point can be made. Whether or not the image of something in photography and photographic cinema "looks like" the actual object, the latter is supposed to have been in range of the camera viewfinder at the time the camera was operating. Among other things, every photographic and film image that counts as culturally normal solicits a basic apprehension as an indexical sign, for which at some time in the past, the depicted objects existed within range of the camera's lens. Thus, whatever else is implicit in the film actuality, there is something rational and correct about the spectatorial "naïveté" on which it is allegedly based. For it is founded in a knowledge, even if partial, about how such images have most often been produced.

Emphases other than Bazin's are possible in this regard. So different a thinker as Walter Benjamin also made much of this with respect to cinema, but he connected indexicality to mass distribution as well. From a perspective emphasizing the modernity of the society and culture that innovated and normalized media of technical reproduction, Benjamin's most famous essay remarks on "the desire of the contemporary masses to bring things 'closer' spatially and humanly, which is just as ardent as their bent toward overcoming the uniqueness of every reality by accepting its reproduction." This aligns the visual media of technical reproduction not only with modes of apprehension and representation, but simultaneously with modes of mass dissemination—precisely the combination that is exploited by mainstream cinema. Note that both can be conceived as functions of indexicality, for if an indexical image attests to the reality of the profilmic, the mass distribution of such images is also made possible by indexicality: the print of a film projected to an audience is, in principle, the film of a film. Thus, Benjamin's key modern exemplars were the two most prominent indexical media, photography and cinema. "To ask for the 'authentic' print [made from a photographic negative] makes no sense," he writes; yet, the camera offers "the thoroughgoing permeation of *reality* with mechanical equipment" [my emphasis]. Benjamin thus yokes together in productive tension two seemingly opposed functions of indexicality: its pluralization of imaged objects in mass distribution over and above any imputed authentic origin, and yet their culturally reliable trans-mission of a real object that serves as an origin.[26]

Bazin's ontological biases lead him to stake everything on the latter, sometimes at the expense of the former. But this allows him to highlight a point also present in Benjamin: that objects in indexical imaging appeal to us not only from another space, but from a particular past existence, that is, from a specific time that is no longer available. If asked why this past is no longer available, Bazin could refer us to the phenomenology of time, in which the present is a divide between an ever-receding past and a con-stantly renewing future; however, Benjamin evinces more awareness that this is a particularly modern construction of temporality. Defined by the perpetual possibility of the new, hence the continuous recession of the old, modern temporality opens up a radical separation or gap between present and past. As noted in earlier chapters, modern historiography characteristically establishes knowledge of the past from a standpoint in time by privileging a certain form of evidence that bridges the gap between past and present; namely, the critically authenticated primary source document. It is indicative that a certain regime of nonfiction film-making soon came to be known as documentary, and preclassical actuality cinema was centered on what we now conceive as a documentary appeal.[27] Both Benjamin and Bazin posit a spectatorial demand: for recovery of the distant, in time at least as much as space. From very different viewpoints and to different theoretical ends, they both suggest that the film image is sought as a document in vision, but a document achieved in relation to time, as preservation from a past, as widespread availability and exhibition of sights of past existents.

But how might this fascination persist after the transition to classi-cal cinema? Consider a somewhat random example from a relatively later ("postclassical"?), well-respected, non-Hollywood historical film, which nevertheless deviates little from most of the stylistic canons of main-stream cinema. One reason for choosing it is because it is such a well-respected historical film, with serious referential ambitions. The purpose of this example is not to embark on a full-fledged "reading" of the film, but rather to interrogate a brief fragment as an illustration.

In the story of *The Return of Martin Guerre* (directed by Daniel Vigné, 1982), there is a point when the villagers travel to Toulouse to get a second decision from Coras and the parliamentary officials regarding challenges to the identity of the individual claiming to be Martin Guerre. The approach of the villagers into the town is depicted through a succession of transitional shots. There is plentiful visual detail in this sequence, during which nothing absolutely necessary to the progress of the narrative occurs.

It is possible to become attracted by or curious about one or more of these details. Take the smoke from varying sources in these shots (see, for example, Figure 4.2). Perhaps its presence in the profilmic could be explained through a narrational analogy, as a kind of literalism: the intrigue is becoming dark, smoky; the identity of the stranger claiming to be Martin Guerre has been reaffirmed, but now there are new doubts. However, it may be more convincing to adduce a compositional rationale, having to do with the repetition of the smoke in shot to shot, as well as its placement in the left of the frames. This would also accord with a painterly impulse detectable in the mise-en-scène elsewhere in the film. But both an expressivist and a formal reading of these shots miss

Figure 4.2

something else, namely the plausibilistic aspects of the mise-en-scène, the film's recurrent insistence on peripheral props, backgrounds, and activities that compose a physical, cultural, and economic context for the major narrative agents and events. More directly, then, we must add historiographically denotative considerations of the setting: at this time of the year the weather is cool, and inhabitants of this world of sixteenth-century France have smoke-making mechanisms, such as the stove on the boat, to keep them warm. Indeed, given that the formidable historian Natalie Zemon Davis worked on the film, should we not expect a certain authenticity as to these smoke-making implements? We are in the realm of the Warner Brothers research department and Everett's Game: details are accounted for, this is what it might have looked like.[28]

But as a formulation of the relation of the detail to narrative, it is also reminiscent of Roland Barthes's notion of the unsignifying detail, the "reality effect." In his much-cited 1968 essay, with illustrations from Flaubert and Michelet, Barthes defines the exemplary mechanism of the literary reality-effect as the "concrete detail." In literary narrative, he asserts, descriptions of concrete details can be relatively unnecessary to the chain of story events, but their presence in the narration has a double function: first, they provide occasions for a certain linguistic performance or beauty in the very act of description, and second, they serve as indicators of referentiality. In the nineteenth century, according to Barthes, an appeal to the real as motivation for signification became theorized as a move to bypass the form of the signified—that is, to convince the reader of a direct link between signifier and referent by means of an impression of precise accuracy, often figured as visualized or pictorial. In Barthes's distinctive terminology, the nineteenth century is thus the period that develops a "realism" rather than a rhetoric of codified "verisimilitude."

Furthermore, Barthes emphasizes the saturation of that discursive ambition called realism by and within large-scale nineteenth-century cultural configurations. He proposes that nineteenth-century historiography provided the model for the literary, novelistic signifying procedures he is exploring. (Not only does he use Michelet as an example, but an immediate predecessor and companion piece to "The Reality Effect" was an essay called "The Discourse of History.") And he associates the new sociocultural dominance of the historical-novelistic impulse with the rise of photography. Indeed, what better example of a signifier that appears to bypass the form of the signified by means of a direct connection with the referent than a photograph, constituted as it is by indexicality?[29]

So Barthes proposes a tripartite configuration of discursive aspirations for direct signification of the real established in the nineteenth century: (1) literary narrative structure, which at this time comes under ever-increasing pressures to process a greater quantity of descriptive detail, something it does by having the details embody "beauty" or connote "reality"; (2) the photographic image, as a brute testimony to the existence of the objects included in the frame, seeming "always already" to present the spectating subject with something akin to the narratively unpredictable "concrete detail"—so that photography can be a medium par excellence of a referential impression; and (3) between and behind these two, mediating and processing them, the operations of "the discourse of history," whose procedures also encourage the reading subject to relate to a "real" past by eliding the form of the signified. This confluence is highly suggestive for a consideration of cinema, for mainstream film is often treated as something like moving photography plus the novelistic (or, in some variants, the short story).[30]

But Barthes's tripartite constellation also makes it possible to ask about distinctions as well as similarities among literature, photography, and cinema with respect to their referential or "realist" aspirations. I want to pursue this through a very different Barthes, the ironic, melancholy, "post-post-structuralist" of *Camera Lucida*. In this, his last book, an awareness of semiology, poststructuralist theory, and Lacanian psychoanalysis—all overtly antiphenomenological—feed into an interrogation of photographic indexicality cast as a first-person, phenomenological investigation.

In *Camera Lucida*, Barthes's stated purpose is to explore the subjective intentionality or positionality of the spectator desiring and faced with the real, specifically in photographs. At one point, his insistence on the specificity of the photography leads to an emphasis on the difference between literature and photography for such a subject. As he explains it, literature cannot match photography's assertion of the past existence of the object depicted because it is grounded in an arbitrary signifier (written verbal language). In order to assert reference, therefore, literature requires an arsenal of persuasive, rhetorical devices. This makes the reality-effect an exemplary mechanism within that arsenal, which comprises a larger linguistic rhetoric straining toward referentiality. The grounding of photography, on the other hand, is an indexicality that gives it an automatically referential character for the spectator—a referentiality whose impact is not dependent on, but is rather diminished by a rhetoric: "[T]he attempt to render language unfictional requires an enormous apparatus of measurements: we convoke logic, or, lacking that, sworn oath; but the Photograph is indifferent to all intermediaries: it does not invent; it is authentication itself." In this phenomenology of the photograph, "consciousness [posits] the object encountered outside any analogy."[31]

So far, this account of the photographic image coalesces with Bazin's emphasis on indexicality and the preservative obsession in cinema. It centers on the relation of subjectivity to prior existents, and Barthes therefore insists that what is new in photography stems not from its optics (perspective, mapping space), but from its chemistry (indexical imprinting, capturing time). Thus, at a certain time in the early 1980s, a boat on a river did indeed have an apparatus that made smoke, and the camera was in a conjoining space with it. No matter what the narrative significance or diegetic placement of that smoke in the film *The Return of Martin Guerre*, as photographic cinema there is a certain documentary force at work in these images. Indeed, to have narrative import, the film must convert its image from document to diegesis. This is a conversion from one time to another, from the past time of the camera's operation to the temporal setting of a different past, that of the narrative; and both of these are addressed to the spectator in his or her own present. The conversion from document to diegesis is thus a process involving the temporality not just of the image, but of organizing the subject's relation to an image that represents not one but two past times.

But on this point, Barthes draws a distinction not only between literature and photography, but between photography and film, one that goes beyond the common idea (found in Bazin) that film simply adds the recording of duration to still photography. For the late Barthes, photography grants the opportunity for a radically private scansion of the image. Our gaze at the photograph, as projection of the self toward experience of the real, is so private that we may contemplate the depicted object(s) in our own time. A film, on the other hand, necessarily delimits the duration that the spectator is permitted to gaze at the object(s). The time any given perspective may be held on a filmed object is circumscribed by factors such as motion of the camera, movements within the profilmic field, and of course editing, a primary function of which is to determine the amount of time spectators are permitted to regard a given shot.[32] Any configuration of detail on screen is available for a restricted period of time, determined by something other than the existence of the object for the subject.

In an immediate sense, we can say that the determining "something other" is the formal principles by which the film organizes its fields of imaging and its fields of interest; in mainstream film this means its relation (whether it is full or partial) to a narrative construction. In a less immediate sense, this "something other" is social order itself. The photograph can be experienced as belonging to an unshared temporality, one that is therefore radically asocial or antisocial. But a film, with its kinetic and durational limitations on the spectatorial gaze, diminishes the privatization of the purely photographic spectator.

This has a peculiar, un-Bazinian consequence for Barthes. It means that cinema has a *lesser* capacity to indulge the kind of spectatorial fantasms that can result in a subjectively intensive, even absolute and hence disruptive, experience of realism. For Barthes, any photograph is more likely to become a kind of "zero degree" of imagery, which can release the subject into a double movement: inward toward originary fantasies (hence the obsession in *Camera Lucida* with an image, never shown, of Barthes's mother, to whose essence he seeks a return); and therefore back outward toward objects, via a powerful psychic investment that finds its goal "outside of any analogy," in the object itself.[33] Whatever else such a movement is for Barthes, it can constitute a kind of social resistance in and through the movement of subjective investment. The fantasmatic experience of an absolute realism existing "outside of any analogy" is an experience subjectively freed from comprehension through regularized sociocultural protocols of art, compositional clarity, or even articulable ideas. "The incapacity to name is a good symptom of disturbance," he remarks.[34] The subject finds itself in a direct encounter with a pure particularity available for an absolutely free contemplation. The irreducible particularity of the depicted object manifests itself in a fascination with concrete details that serve neither a rhetoric of beauty, nor that of a diegeticizing reality-effect. This is, of course, the kind of detail he famously labels the *punctum*, as opposed to the tamed *studium*, which is the detail apprehended according to socially disseminated protocols of information, art, and historiography.

In this account, any realism that cinema asserts must begin from a more socialized stance than that of photography. This is to characterize cinema as more socializing than photography, going back to what has sometimes been taken as a definitional characteristic of the medium: because it includes movement within and of the image, always progresses toward the next viewpoint and finally the blank screen at the film's termination, the appearance of cinema as a new medium can be conceived as the appearance of unprecedented means for managing the spectatorial investment in the indexical image and, through it, configurations of the real. Insofar as cinema submits the gaze of the subject to a more shared, public time, a more collective temporality, then to that extent cinema becomes a participant in the defanging of the antisocial potential represented by a certain experience of the detail in photographic indexicality. From the claim that there exist instances of approach to the real that, for the subject at least, seem radically asocial, *Camera Lucida* finds cinema massively implicated in the process of socially sublimating the fantasmatically absolute particularity that the photograph threatens to release for the subject.

Film History as Managing the Real

To tame the social threat represented by Barthes's ideal photograph, to regularize and regulate any subjective claim to an absolute, particularized realism—is this where a consideration of cinematic temporality might lead us? At first glance, this does not seem a particularly attractive premise for conceptualizing or studying cinema, since it seems to indict it definitionally as a regulative medium. Nevertheless, there are ways that it might be profitable to take the Barthes of *Camera Lucida* into account, beginning from its restatement of the problem of realism and cinema.

In the 1970s, major tendencies in film theory veered strongly toward treating any cinematic aspiration for the real as an ideological category. This was based in part on a problematic of film spectatorship that generated a series of subsequent discussions and debates. Antirealist assumptions have since persisted in other kinds of accounts of film and types of film theory, and have perhaps too often become unspoken and unexamined. But indexicality and temporality were always the blind spots of 1970s film theory, whatever its strengths (and in my view they were many). In *Camera Lucida*, Barthes—whose earlier work was one of the key reference points for 1970s film theory—initiated a reconsideration of indexicality and pastness, beginning from the relation of subjective desire to the configurations of representational technologies.

So it may be worth finding ways to make *Camera Lucida* a bit less constricting for the consideration of cinema. First, consider some of the grounds for the distinctions made in *Camera Lucida*: the notion of a direct encounter with the real outside signification; an absolute distinction between the private and the public; the book's privileged photograph evincing nostalgia for direct, unmediated access to his mother as the exemplary privatized and particularized experience. Whatever these are in the immediate experience of Barthes's subject, they are themselves all socially mediated, ideologically produced configurations, as Barthes is also aware. Against the experience of the ideal subject that it designates, then, his phenomenology of disruptive particularity still defines that subject within socially given terms.

In that case, Barthes's stance is, precisely, utopian; it can exist in no place except the fantasies of a hypothetical subject. On the one hand, such fantasies paradoxically call into question the very nonideological outside they are supposed to manifest, just because, in the end, a nonideological outside can only be constructed as subjective fantasy. On the other hand, these same fantasies do provide ideals, standards for significant social critique and grounds for resistance; they become a junction of desire and politics. For present purposes, we can go further and treat this utopia as providing a critical standpoint on the history of filmic textuality. But any such critique and any such history would therefore be one routed through the status of the normalized processes of indexical imaging configurations and alternatives to them—both of which engage with fantasy life.[35]

Second, despite its ego-centered phenomenological mode of expression, *Camera Lucida* locates "realism" as a contested mode of sociality. This means that it is not an automatic effect of a specific medium or technology. According to Barthes, the history of photography is replete with compositional and artistic devices that work to reign in socially dispersive subjectivity. He complains that the mass of photographs are commonly aestheticized, conventionalized, "informationalized" and/or disseminated so as to sublimate the fantasmatically absolute particularity that photography may engender. Presumably, any social formation requires such operations, which bring to bear on image-production a set of economic, institutional, educational, class, cultural, and/or even legal constraints, regulating the network of available contacts with any postulated real.[36]

But this means that the opposition between heavily socialized and radically dispersive significations of the real exists even *within* the medium that exemplifies Barthes's ideal. It would follow that the converse is possible in his contrary indexical medium, cinema. It becomes thinkable that cinema may retain elements of the threat and problematicity offered by indexicality to the socialized norms for subjectivity. And *Camera Lucida* is driven by its logic to some piecemeal indications that the neutralizing aspects it attributes to cinema are not necessarily universal to the medium, even including occasional claims for disruptive moments in individual films. For present purposes, the most suggestive of such indications is Barthes's remark that when he treats cinema as other to the radically privatized potential of photography, he is referring to narrative cinema: "The cinema participates in this domestication of Photography—*at least the fictional cinema,* precisely the one said to be the seventh art" [my emphasis].[37]

Suppose we speculate on how this might serve as a heuristics or an optic—a standpoint—for conceiving of the history of film. To begin with, cinema would be treated within a history of indexical representation, as a complex regime circulating around the social management of subjective constructions of the real and accesses to it. This does imply a more flexible attitude toward cinema than one might expect from some of the ontologizing language Barthes uses in characterizing indexical media, for management is not mere suppression. It assumes that there is at least a potential for conflict, for departure from socializing norms. Even mainstream film would also appeal to and moreover provoke such aspirations, if only (in the most restrictive conception) to channel them. Incidentally, there is plenty of historical evidence in institutional and public discourses for the idea that indexical media in general and filmic textuality in particular present potential or actualized sociocultural danger. Direct examples are provided by the often class-bound censorship debates during the first decades of its existence as a mass medium, and film history has remained dotted with such instances right up to more recent and incessant debates over violence in film, children's television, pornography, and so forth.[38]

Of course, this focus on indexicality also leads back to the idea that film draws on and participates in the kinds of aspirations for the real through indexicality that are rooted in the nineteenth century. And with specific reference to cinema, this approach makes the transition from preclassical to classical cinema, which suppressed actuality filmmaking in favor of explicit narrative, a crucial conjuncture in the social history of representation. Fundamental textual practices standardized in the development of classical cinema, tied to the impulse to rationalize production, can be treated as participating in processes of managing and regulating indexicality and the desires associated with it.

Connected to this is a theoretical point having to do with distinctions between media and bearing on textual procedures. Within the Barthesian problematic, mainstream cinema would meet subjective desire for the real and truth more like literature and less like the photograph

than one might expect. The submission of foreground-background relations to a narrational rhetoric including the deployment of the reality-
effect; the use of preexisting models of visual composition to present a
well-organized, harmonious collection of details; the regularization of offscreen space; the very imposition of the parameters of a certain range of
familiar types of narrative form on cinematic space (which is qualitatively
different from the individualized narration of photographic space by
subjective fantasy)—all these and other givens of most mainstream film
narratives are, among other things, social processes seeking to exploit the
opportunities offered by the cinematic medium to tame the indexical
image as document. In rationalizing the detail, they align it with certain
regimes of social rationality.

History in Film

Let us return to the broad textual and spectatorial relations between
document and diegesis postulated by the normalized fiction film, with
attention to the vicissitudes of indexicality. A profilmic field—from the
standpoint of the spectator, a visual field of objects that was indexically
imprinted as they existed at some point in the past—is staged or performed as another (fictional) time. The spectator processes this staging
in his or her present time. This is already historiographic in a sense, for
it locates the film-spectator relation as a point where pastnesses and presentness confront one another. To this extent, then, the chief or dominant
lines in the development of mainstream cinema necessarily and already
participate in a cultural terrain of historicity. (This is not to say it is the
only kind of fabrication of the image ever at work, even in mainstream
films.)

But what of explicitly historical representation in film? The "historical film" can be defined here as a certain conjunction of regimes of narrative and profilmic: in its purest form, it consists of a "true story" (or
elements of a "true story") plus enough profilmic detail to designate a
period recognizable as significantly "historical," that is, as signifying a
generally accepted minimum of referential pastness.[39] As a definition this
may seem slippery, but only because so many of its terms themselves

designate discursive and ideological arenas subject to historical change ("regimes," "enough," "recognizable," "generally accepted").

The historical film throws the passages between document and diegesis in the mainstream narrative film into a special kind of relief. In any conventional fiction film, insofar as we apprehend depicted objects as having actually existed in front of the camera, to that extent there is a documentary (or actuality) component to our apprehension. But since a conventional fiction film is not supposed to be understood as a documentary, such details are to be apprehended as in some sense constructed, diegetic. In that case, this indexically imprinted profilmic is organized according to the narrative hierarchies of a "virtual" time, that of the fictional world. The extra twist of the historical film is that this "virtual" time also claims to have its own previously documentable "reality," that of a researchable historiography. There is a second referential preexistent.

Nevertheless, the sense of explicit historiography is conveyed not as a genuine document, but as diegesis, as in my example of *The Return of Martin Guerre* (taken as a historical film in its "pure form"). As a narrative film, *The Return of Martin Guerre* must employ textual mechanisms associated with fiction, something unavoidable in any historical reenactment (for example, there must be actors). Yet, precisely as a "historical film," it must simultaneously propose some extra supplement of referential truth, but one that can only be signified as diegesis. Consequently, this supplement comes through as a reconstruction, as a restoration rather than a preservation. If I can employ architectural terminology, it is because (as always with the restorationism-preservationism spectrum), the quest for referentiality is an underlying premise for both ends; this means it is generally realized as a simultaneity or oscillation of differing registers of referentiality. What 1970s film theory hypostasized as the cinematic impression of reality is a processing or play of shifting or simultaneous degrees and levels of differentiated spectatorial investment. Everett's Game is an indicator of that play.

But it is worth noting that at least one concept invoked in 1970s film theory can be used to address this play in the historical film, namely the psychoanalytic concept of fetishism. I mention it because it recalls the defensive, disavowing aspects of modern historicity discussed in earlier chapters. In a remarkable 1977 article, Jean-Louis Comolli attempts a description of the representational structure of the narrative historical film. It is on the more or less implicit model of the fetishistic splitting of knowledge and belief (the fetishistic subject unconsciously believes the woman had a penis, but knows she does not—is castrated—and in order to achieve sexual pleasure reinstates that belief in the present via the fetish object). But while Comolli's key example is the body of an actor (Pierre Renoir playing Louis XVI in *La Marseillaise*), his tacit invocation of fetishistic positioning has less to do with corporeal fragmentation than with assumptions about spectatorial investment. Comolli emphasizes that the film image as such documents that Pierre Renoir was actually present during the filming, but this means that the historical personage he plays cannot have been present. In an ordinary fiction film the actor portrays a character who he or she is not, but that character never existed; in a historical film, the actor portrays a *referential* figure who he or she is not. Therefore, although the historical film may claim to deal with real events, it is actually more artificial with respect to a spectator's desire to believe in the reality of the image. According to Comolli, Pierre Renoir highlights this gap through an eccentric performance rather than attempting to suppress it by a naturalistic performance.

On the one hand, then, Comolli infers that a historical film must draw a greater quotient of irrational investment from a spectator to sustain his or her investment in its reality. This is comparable to the belief pole in a fetishistic position, and it resonates with the emphasis on subjective investment in both Bazinian and Barthesian realisms. On the other hand, pleasure is also available from a certain range of artifice and stylization manifesting distance from authenticity. The latter, in effect, acknowledges and addresses the spectator's awareness that the historical film is not "really" history but a performance. This awareness corresponds to the knowledge pole in a fetishistic position. Any film or part of a film is a play on differing combinations of knowledge and belief, neither of which can be completely eliminated. Textually and institutionally, then, to downplay the knowledge pole in favor of the belief pole is a "realist" tendency. (Perhaps paradoxically, this means that the belief pole may be aligned with—or propped onto—a rhetoric of disciplined accuracy, research department publicity, and so forth.) At the other end, an option for text and spectator involves highlighting the knowledge pole to include some degree of acknowledgment of the inevitable artificiality of the historical reconstruction. Comolli goes on to argue that pleasure and position may be abetted by setting up a game with the spectator and taking the risk of stretching out the gap between knowledge and belief, something exemplified for him in Pierre Renoir's enactment of Louis.

As a moment in 1970s film theory, Comolli's account of the historical film illustrates something about the range of possibilities in psychoanalytic film theory, which is wider than is sometimes recognized. He postulates spectatorship as a kind of dialectic between a "realist" quest for the referential, and a certain simultaneous spectatorial awareness of and pleasure in the artifice of the film. One might even say that the latter leaves openings for a degree of critical activity on the part of the spectator, and the spectatorial positioning Comolli describes is consonant with Everett's Game. So it should be added that while Comolli emphasizes the actor, this approach is in principle applicable to all profilmic objects in a historical film. But like most 1970s film theory, Comolli does not theorize indexicality, and as a consequence is vague on the roots of the documentary force of the image (the basis for the presumption of the reality of Pierre Renoir's body), and therefore does not fully develop what I call the distinction between documentary and diegetic levels of spectatorial engagement.[40]

For now, I would put it most simply as follows. There is a complex play in the spectatorial apprehension of every image of a historical film like *The Return of Martin Guerre*, among a documentary "substructure" (smoke was indexically imprinted in 1981–82); the conversion of document into narrationally positioned diegetic detail (details such as the smoke must be situated as narratively significant and/or insignificant as in any fiction film); and then—if we understand the pictured objects as appropriately or reasonably "authentic" reconstructions of sixteenth-century French life—a conversion back from the diegetic to a quasi-document, which results in a spectatorial comprehension that might be summed up as follows: "Oh, that's what it looked like, I see how people kept themselves warm in 1560." What we see, then, is not what actually *was*, but what it would have looked *like* in 1560.

This means that the diegeticized profilmic, as historical representation, inevitably falls short of the kind of documentary authority claimed by the the image as an indexical trace of the profilmic. As with Ranke's "*wie es eigentlich gewesen*," the apprehension of history confronts the gap between likeness and being. The Rankean historians understand this as the break between the discourse produced by the historian and the dream of a hypothetically complete, rigorous documentation that would completely secure the truth of that historiography. In the historical film, it is the disjunction between the image as authenticating document, beginning from the camera's relation to the profilmic during the making of the film, and the imaged as diegesis. All of these divisions are ultimately between a past and a present, which for modern Western historicity is the site of the very necessity for historical representation in the first place.

However, it is also true that my definition of the historical film as the conjunction of a certain regime of story and of mise-en-scène makes it difficult to absolutize a distinction between the historical film and other kinds of mainstream films. On this point, the problematic character of the notion of a "true story" has been discussed often enough with respect to historiography, but here I would highlight the level of the detail per se. Even though the historical film gives relations between document and diegesis an extra referential twist, there are important similarities and parallels to the organization of document-diegesis relationships throughout classical and mainstream cinema, including films that do not claim to convey a "true story." There are even degrees of the historical film; for example, a "period" romance, adventure film, or literary adaptation usually does not have any pretense to the referential truth of its story or characters, yet its mise-en-scène might be heavily researched and detailed (or, alternatively, researched to include some historical indicators, but stylized, which is still a play on historical referentiality). But even for films with contemporary settings, a nodal point of the underlying principles bearing on the profilmic is "research."

A certain intrication of ideals of indexicality and of constructed resemblance is pervasive in mainstream film history. One indication of this intrication is the extensive use of photographs of distant locales and objects in classical studio research "bibles" to provide models for the constructed profilmic of the studio; indexical documentation counts as a suitable source for conceiving of the form of a diegesis. This intrication meshes with other standard practices such as location shooting, sets coded as verisimilitudinous (often constructed not only on the basis of research, but to blend acceptably with locations), and a conventional minimum of plausible props and actions, whether they have to do with making coffee in a made-for-television romance movie or the settings and locations in a thriller.[41]

This fluidity of boundaries between historiographic appeals and fictional genres on the level of the profilmic field suggests both the inevitability of film as documented and documenting, but also, always, its insufficiency as document. Because they are always hybridized with some degree of narrativized diegesis, details are also to be understood as components of a diegetic construction. The work of studio research departments participated in this overall process of converting document to diegesis in the narrative registers of mainstream film. This has made them a good emblem for the amount of effort and regulatory labor it requires.

A link between studio research departments, the normalization of narrative in the classical film as a film-historical development of signification, and broad expectations about spectatorship in mainstream cinema may be glossed by an analogy. It is as if the ontogeny of viewing an individual film recapitulates the historical phylogeny of classical cinema. Phylogenetically, commercial cinema passed through a brief period when its status as document was dominant, and then stabilized enough to make the status of the image as explicit diegesis the mark of dominant filmmaking. Ontogenetically, there is also a kind of passage or play between document and diegesis, but with a kind of residue, as if the diegeticized film attempts to retain something of the factual convincingness of the document. (It is here that some of the work and publicity around studio research departments makes its contribution.) The historical film is only that which pushes this passage to an extreme. In so doing, it can serve as one privileged site for understanding the stakes of the transition to classical cinema, as rationalization not only of production and exhibition, but of filmic textuality.

The Spectacle of History

At this point it may still be objected that my account of the profilmic in mainstream textuality in relation to a postulated desire to apprehend the real underplays the artifices of mainstream cinema. The discussion of document and diegesis has been pegged to the disposition of a documentary or quasi-documentary force, which can be aligned with concerns proper to modern historiography. What about the range of stylizations one can find throughout the history of mainstream film? What of such seeming departures from indexicality as overt special effects, composite imagery, and the like? What about the effects on the profilmic of kinds of narrative worlds other than the doubly referential ones proper to the historical film, which include fantasy and the fantastic? In short, there is much more to deployments of the profilmic in mainstream cinema than reality effects.

Let me address this kind of objection through another filmic example, but one that belongs to one of the most stylized and artificial of classical genres, the studio musical. In the justly well known climactic title ballet from *An American in Paris* (1951), settings and costumes are modeled on Parisian scenes from famous impressionist paintings. The main character, Jerry (Gene Kelly), is at the center of an elaborate, heavily populated choreography, whose tone ranges from the comic to the ethereal to the sentimental. There is a deliberately "unrealistic" use of Technicolor, and the particular stylization of mise-en-scène varies depending on the painting and particular dance format at that moment.

During this segment, spectatorial understanding is obviously not supposed to be that these are indexical registrations of Paris, nor that actual paintings are being used as backdrop. Nor is there supposed to be an understanding of the diegesis to the effect of "That's what it [Paris] looks like." It is rather that set and art designers created a showily artificial

Paris as a background environment for a lengthy dance sequence. But if the sequence does not document Paris, nor provide an exacting reconstruction of what Paris looks like, it implicates spectatorial investment in a documentary fascination nevertheless—a document of Hollywood skills, of a show that is put on for the spectator. The preeminent objects in this document are probably the dance skills of Gene Kelly, Leslie Caron, and the troupe, but also include the artificial backgrounds and costumes. These actually existed for the making of this film and are themselves part of its display of virtuoso achievement.[42]

This suggests that spectatorial investment in the show does presume a certain documentary substructure based on assumptions circulating around the appeal of indexicality. This appeal is intertwined with other characteristics often attributed to the classical Hollywood musical. These include its emphasis on performance and performativity, which is associated with a certain foregrounding of artifice. In its turn, this is sometimes said to include the possibility of attenuating the saturation of narrative orderliness in the normalized feature-length film in favor of the insertion of musical performances.

Yet, one can still argue that a pretext framing all this indexically imprinted virtuosity with its documentary appeal is ultimately narrative order. In my example, the ballet itself has a general direction, which is to express and summarize the traumatic emotional progression that Jerry has experienced in the overall story that encloses the dance. Furthermore, within that story, this concluding ballet sequence serves as the culmination of Jerry's defeat before the quick dramatic reversal and happy ending that immediately follows it. During the ballet, the film may present itself as a document of performed virtuosity, but that virtuosity is still alibied by a certain administration of sense governed by narrative emplacement, which provides its rationale, or perhaps rationalization, depending on your viewpoint.

Furthermore, this documented performativity does not obviate an appeal to researched preexistents. Much as research for historical films commonly uses paintings originating in the depicted period as sources to model set and costume design, so does this classic musical sequence;

however, it does textually foreground this genre of sources in a spectacular way, as part of its effects of virtuosity and "style." A spectator knowledgeable in the high (or commodity) culture of art history can have that knowledge confirmed by recognizing the virtuoso transformations involved in enacting those paintings. So if the performativity of the ballet sequence includes an overt invitation to exercise spectatorial knowledge, it is in ways akin to Everett's Game.[43]

In fact, research and appealing to a sense of the preexistent could be as common in the musical as in any other classical studio genre, though its intensity varied at different periods and among individual films; however, there is something suggestive about their mobilization in *An American in Paris*. A common thematic of classical studio musicals is an opposition between values attributed to subjectivity, such as lyrical freedom of expression, the realization of fantasy or desire, and interpersonal harmony on the one hand, and exigencies that obstruct their realization on the other. In show business musicals, for example, this could be narrativized as an opposition between performance itself and the blockage of performance. *An American in Paris* is representative of a type that narrativizes it as a division between subjectivity expressing itself through dream or daydream and a resistant everyday reality that is not subject to dream. (The ballet is not the only fantasy/dream sequence in the film.) The activation of a dream-reality dialectic requires, precisely, a "reality" against which the lyricism of the dream can be defined. That "reality" must be constructed as a profilmic field constituting a diegesis, and this usually involves the restoration of culturally recognizable preexistents; hence Parisian settings for non-oneiric scenes were fully "authentic," based (as usual) on research, including thousands of photographs of Paris. But the film uses the researched fantastic, painterly mises-en-scène of the ballet near the end of *An American in Paris* as a polar counterpart to the researched relative accuracy of Jerry's Paris apartment and neighborhood side street at the film's beginning. The representing of fantasy and free subjectivity as well as "reality" is channeled through an order of knowledge, even at the level of the profilmic detail.

In general terms, this example is emblematic of some ways the musical—a classical genre one might reasonably postulate as significantly different in ambition from the historical film—shares some assumptions with the latter about the profilmic. The passage between preexistent detail and reality-effect must be negotiated even in the classical musical, which is to say that it even here remains necessary to organize and put in to play relations between document and diegesis. This is not to argue for an absolute equivalence; the emphasis on overt performance characteristic of so many musicals certainly makes for distinctions with respect to mise-en-scène. My point is that, whatever the range of options, these constructions partake of a broad textual rationality common within mainstream cinema. Reconfirming the ubiquity of appeals to an origin in the real as both documentable profilmic and/or researchable pre-text, the musical also takes us back to the regularizing sociocultural drive evident in the rationalization of the detail. This is the arena of the management of indexicality that, I have suggested through Barthes, has been a primary cultural assignment for cinema. And such constructions of indexicality, reference, and pastness in the present of the spectator connect mainstream cinema to historicity.

But an inverse point can be made. The direct appeal of the documented performance for the spectator that I have associated with the musical can also be activated in the mainstream historical film. Comolli suggests there is always some element of such overt, performed artifice in the historical film. There are cases where this element goes to an extreme. One such extreme is often called historical spectacle. In historical spectacle, a proliferation of detail seems to exceed the reality-effect, and in so doing becomes something like a virtuoso performance of the profilmic. From the perspective of the "serious" historical film, historical spectacle unbalances the interplay between a "true story" and a recognizably "historical" mise-en-scène by emphasizing the underlying ambivalences of the latter with respect to referentiality. As we will see, it illustrates that the organization of socialized security—the management of indexicality—has more at its disposal than the construction of the profilmic as narrativized reality-effect, even if it never completely evades this level of significance.

Consider one more filmic fragment, the Tarsus sequence of DeMille's *Cleopatra* (1934). Made during the heyday of the classical studio period, this film draws on culturally prominent narrative-historical raw material. (It was neither the first nor the last film version of that material; it could draw on a long-standing iconographic tradition of representing it, as well as such illustrious theatrical predecessors as Shakespeare, Dryden, and Shaw.) The story events covered in the whole Tarsus sequence comprise the confrontation between a heretofore misogynist Antony, attempting to bring Egypt and Cleopatra under Rome's political and masculine discipline, and Cleopatra, who counters with a calculated, politically motivated, successful seduction of Antony. The Tarsus sequence as a whole manifests great narrative attenuation, taking approximately one-fifth of the film's running time (about eighteen minutes). As filmic performance and profilmic display, it is arguably the most sustained spectacular construction in a film that constitutes itself as historical spectacle.

There are a variety of narrative and spectacular elements in the sequence that could draw pertinent commentary. Since my concern is the detail, I will simply emphasize that the performativity of the sequence is itself thematized in the mise-en-scène. Cleopatra's throne is on a kind of quasi-proscenium, onto which she invites Antony. In addition to making a show of herself, Cleopatra positions Antony as spectator to the "show after show" (her words) she organizes to titillate him, and some of these involve stylized sadomaschistic dances/performances.

The final shot of the sequence can serve as an example of the organization of the detail as historical spectacle. It is preceded by a calm, intimately filmed interlude. As Antony embraces Cleopatra, there is an analytically edited relay of looks whereby she signals her minister Appolodorus, who in turn signals to others. Nondiegetic music wells up as the full orchestra repeats the love theme, which is geopolitically coded since it is in an "oriental minor" musical mode. From the analytic editing of facial close-ups, we cut back to a squared, fuller view of the room, with the proscenium in the background and the triumphantly attendant audience of Egyptian retainers in the foreground, and a curtain is drawn hiding Antony and Cleopatra from us and the retainers. This is the beginning of the last shot inside the barge, a long, slow track straight back away from the proscenium where Antony and Cleopatra will make love.

This shot takes in the most pictorially excessive detail, provoking and stimulating the importance of seeing the image. But now hidden by the drawn curtain, Antony and Cleopatra can no longer see the spectacle as they had the previous "shows." (In fact, it can be argued that their invisible lovemaking is the epitome of visual spectacle and pleasure that is then displaced to the rest of the mise-en-scène.) And the new, onscreen audience of anonymous extras-retainers are part of the spectacle, so it is invisible to them also. Presented as if it were a diegetic occurrence, the excessive detail has no diegetic addressee. It is for the film spectator alone. If the characters do not play overtly and directly to the camera, the mise-en-scène does. The film *Cleopatra* is putting on a show.

The excessive nature of this climactic shot consists in a proliferation of carefully arranged detail, and it can only be suggested verbally by attempting a partial list of profilmic components (see Figures 4.3–4.7). In an ever-growing inflation of pictorially organized detail, the backward-traveling frame becomes increasingly filled with carefully organized actions involving dozens of extras. This is when the concealing drapes are drawn by handmaidens across the proscenium on which Cleopatra and Antony are hidden. Two strings of flowers cross diagonally in front of this stage, echoing the centered crossing pattern of drapes now raised from the outside corners. Innumerable flower petals drop from the ceiling, and continue to fill the frame for the rest of the shot. A muscular Black sentinel holding a large sword walks onscreen and faces the camera frame center, forbiddingly guarding the stage. In front of him, more women enter and sit in a semicircle facing away from the camera, toward the proscenium, ceremonially holding raised lamps. Through all this, the camera continues its slow, steady track back, maintaining a compositional symmetry centered on the receding proscenium, while still holding all this action within the shot. As the track continues, there enter on both sides of the frame two constantly extending rows of oar handles, carved as giant birds' heads matching the figurehead on the barge's prow (seen earlier in the sequence). On a signal from Appolodorus, the two lines of oars, which symmetrically recede into the distance, now begin moving in unison to a deep drum beat, which seems part of the continually swelling symphonic love theme. When the tracking movement reaches the end of

Figure 4.3

Figure 4.4

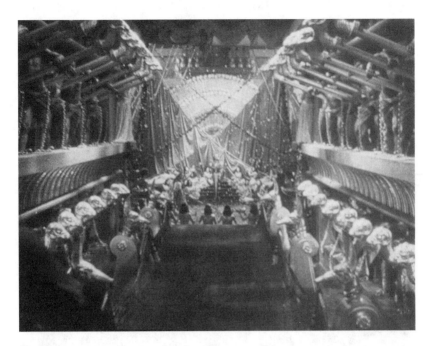

Figure 4.5

Figure 4.6

Figure 4.7

the receding lines of oars, it brings into foreground the silhouette of the beater, seen from behind, as diegetic musical elements coordinate with non-diegetic. The shot finally terminates with the camera, apparently having backed into the interior bow of the barge, minutely craning up. By now the proscenium and curtains behind which Antony and Cleopatra are making love are in extreme long shot, framed in the geometrical center of all this symmetrically organized detail. Finally, we dissolve to exterior long shot of the barge leaving the harbor, in an exact reversal of the first shot of the entire Tarsus action. The barge sequence has ended. Antony is on his way to Egypt with Cleopatra, where he will eventually regain his political manhood in war, so that she will truly fall in love with him, and both will die.

This fragment demonstrates how concern with the detail in a historical film can go well beyond the goals of the reality-effect, and become transformed into a virtuosity of spectacle comparable to that of the musical.[44] Departing from the claims of accuracy, the detail has been liberated from background reality-effect to foregrounded, masterful address to the present that invites the spectatorial eye to exult in its apotheosis. This address to the present entails a certain release from referential claims, which is enacted throughout the film; for example, there are anachronistic patterns of design and costuming that go well beyond the usual compromise formations between past and present by appealing overwhelmingly to contemporary styles (e.g., the Art Deco inspirations obvious at many points), as well as indulgences in narrative and dialogue overtly addressed to the present (references to lines from Shakespeare, invented events, and so forth).

With respect to the detail, this liberation is so overwhelming, so extravagant, so playful, so performative as opposed to referential, that we call it spectacle. For what is spectacle in this sense other than the virtuosic textual organization of an impossibly large quantity of details, in a way that draws the spectator's attention to them as a construction for the spectator? Thus, Vivian Sobchak concludes that "the phenomenological significance and discursive power of the Hollywood historical epic is not to be found in the specificity and accuracy of its historical detail." Hence Steve Neale's remark that spectacle is concerned with "the processes of rendering visible and of looking themselves."[45]

And yet, perhaps astonishingly, none of this excludes a supporting discourse of research and the reality-effect. Whatever its excesses in this regard, *Cleopatra* does remain a species of the historical film, invoking actual historical personages, events, and settings, and this seems to provide an opening for a certain salesmanship of the detail in the usual terms. Here is Gordon Jennings, head of Paramount's Special Effects Department in 1934, discussing one element of the Tarsus sequence, Cleopatra's barge:

> This barge was painstakingly constructed from historical records of the ancient queen's actual barge: built to the scale of 100 feet to the foot, it was over twelve feet long and weighed several tons. The actual barge was propelled by 300 oars arranged in five banks, 150 to the side; this was not practical for our purposes, so the miniature was propelled by ropes attached

below the water-line, and pulled by stagehands outside of the picture area. None the less, the oars must function, and this was achieved by . . . [46]

The conventional rationales of research are recognizable here. It is made clear that this is not the actual barge (it requires special effects to make images of it), but exactitude of reconstruction is said to be the rule and is confirmed quantitatively. We are again in the realm of "what it [actually] looked like."

How is it that such a rhetoric of referentiality can be applied to the profilmic elements of a film like *Cleopatra*? Conjunctural answers are conceivable (marketing rhetorics need not be logically coherent, research actually did occur in preproduction as it always does, and so forth), but this also points back toward a definitional principle: if spectacle is a form of excessive profilmic detail, excessiveness does not in itself radically separate it from the kind of reality-effect usually associated with more sober representations of history. Recall that Barthes's definition of the reality-effect as narrative rhetoric is the concrete detail elaborated over and above the necessities of any story functions. In that case, excessive detail is the common arena of both spectacle and the reality-effect. Of course, the transitional shots from *The Return of Martin Guerre* do seem significantly different than the finale of the Tarsus sequence in *Cleopatra*, but this only indicates that there are distinctive registers in the deployment and the regulation of excessive detail. From this perspective, such differences may be conceived as differences in degree rather than kind.

Note that the passage attributed to Gordon Jennings counters the impossibility of filming Cleopatra's actual barge with the miraculous exactitude enabled by special effects fakery, *which is being sold as such*. The construction of a scale-model barge based on research converges with a notion of Hollywood virtuosity. A virtuosity of the profilmic object is one of the attractions of the historical film as such. Consequently, this type of conflation underlies any film performance of the past for the present in the mainstream tradition. It amounts to a kind of hide-and-seek between referentiality with respect to the past and performance for the present, with both predicated on indexicality.

As a general proposition concerning mainstream cinema, it may be that neither reality-effect nor spectacle is ever completely absent; there are only different degrees of their import and intensities in relation to one another. That is, the opposition of reality-effect and spectacle, which superficially seems to be a division, is better treated as yet another dialectical polarity. As such, it is inseparable from other such polarities I inferred earlier: image as document and image as diegesis, spectatorial belief and spectatorial knowledge, preservation and restoration in Western cultural practices. It is conceivable that, at certain points in historical spectacle, the gap between document and diegesis may open so wide that it no longer makes sense to ask, for example, whether the interior of Cleopatra's barge actually looked like that, whether that is an authentic Egyptian dance, and so forth. But Everett's Game still remains a condition for the liberations of spectacle, simply because one must recognize when that point has been reached.

Such gaps do not evince failures of textual rationality, but rather regimes of spectatorial knowledges. Mainstream narrative cinema has postulated spectatorship not in relation to an illusion of brute reality, but, precisely, to an *effect* of the real, which is best considered to be part and parcel of an effect of knowledgeability. Beginning from Barthes's conception of a large-scale sociocultural operation needed to regularize spectatorial investment in an indexical image as document from a real past, we can say that such regularization is a matter of the play of such knowledges, textually assumed, prompted, organized. These are knowledges about how the image is supposedly formed, in relation to socially and narrationally provoked kinds of knowledges and knowledge-protocols. They have afforded a privileged (if often implicit) place to kinds of knowledge we can call historiographic.

To this extent, at least, the identification of mainstream cinematic textuality with a monolithic "impression of reality" in some early 1970s theoretical polemics was at best a partial insight, but it was not completely wrongheaded. The rationalization of the detail, textualized as the passage from brute detail to reality-effect, does evince a stabilizing sociocultural drive with respect to indexicality. This is what Adorno calls "familiar realism," and I have opposed it to the utopian, disruptive experience of the indexical imagined by Barthes. But this drive is not limited to the reality-effect, even in the mainstream historical film and even on the level of diegetic detail. I have extended its scope with suggestions about the explicit artifice of historical spectacle. Standing for the processing of excessive detail, such spectacle is not a break with the impulses of the reality-effect, much less the antithesis of "familiar realism." However, it is an indication that the relations of document and diegesis are a process, constituting the grounds for a textual and spectatorial play, which must take into account spectatorial knowledgeability. It may be possible from the broadest scope to conceive of them as a relatively stable paradigm, but they must simultaneously be understood in terms of variations and vicissitudes, contradictions and fluidities. And in the end, these themselves can productively be called "historical."

The Spectacular Idea

Finally, however, regularization of the detail need not and does not stop on this level. Consider again the sensuous visual display of the Tarsus sequence in *Cleopatra*, which so seems to exceed research, historical knowledges, and narrative enchainment in its direct performance for the spectator in the present. It nevertheless remains an apotheosis of unmistakable meaning. This is signaled by the overwhelming visual impression of purposiveness in the tracking shot I have evoked. Spatially, all that superfluous detail is compositionally centered and thereby clearly targeted at the spectator; temporally, the movement has a beginning, middle, and end. Narratively, the profilmic excesses of the shot signify themselves as a climactic coda for a crucial plot transition, whose telling has lasted one-fifth of the film's running time.

An auteur analysis of DeMille would reveal that the construction of this kind of diegetic spectacle in this kind of fictional setting is not limited to *Cleopatra*. From Araku's chamber in *The Cheat* (1915) to Dathan's tent in the second *Ten Commandments* (1956), analogous environments appear as places of seduction. They are hyperbolically designed reserves of the East, the Oriental. And they are most often places where foreign, Eastern men attempt to rape or seduce Western women, or places where (as in *Cleopatra*) Eastern women use Western men. The detail has indeed become spectacularized and performative. But that spectacle and performance is instantly understandable as a sensuous figuration of ideologically central otherness, a knotting of sexual and racial difference so typical that it can be called a cliché, although one that bears filmic elaboration far beyond the automatism that the term connotes.[47]

In one sense, the spectacle thus returns to narrative meaning after all. This spectacular apotheosis is in part an apotheosis of oppositions and hierarchies evoked in dialogue throughout the film: female/male, East/West, passivity/activity, private/public. It is surely not too surprising to find that such virtuosity of design in the display of historical knowledge of the detail can be described as conveying a threat and mastery of the Western male spectator. But of special interest here is that, as with the early film actualities, the distant in time and space is being brought to the vision of the spectator. But now, having been diegeticized, it is more efficiently tagged, identified (via gender and orientalism) with an ideological security informing and informed by narrative elements. The investment of the spectator in the indexical image has here been socially secured against the kind of privatized, radically disruptive fantasmatic diversion imagined by Barthes, and turned instead toward the socially requisite fantasies that ground DeMille's virtuosity. This socialized understanding of the other, of the distant in time and space, has been built in the very conversions between document and diegesis.

My argument is not that such ideological or ideational configurations are mechanically effective or untroubled "messages." (A more extensive analysis of *Cleopatra* could elaborate on contradictions, instabilities, and perversions of hierarchy around the conjunction of femininity, the East, and histories, as the character of Cleopatra, along with the term *love*, becomes a problematic confusion of public and private, male and female, West and East; this helps explain the perversions of the spectacle the film constructs.) But I am interested in them as clusters of associations and/or articulable descriptions or arguments that preexist the film and in which the film may participate in various explicit and implicit ways.

One characteristic of these representational-ideational configurations, considered as processes driving to secure socialized understandings, is their notional generality. As with logically formulated abstract ideas, concepts, and generalizations, they claim a wide applicability for themselves, one broader than any particular instance of the idea or the particular events being represented. That is, a generality is such because it can be reemployed in many particular cases and objects, regardless of referential or nonreferential context. This wide applicability with respect to referents and knowledge claims makes for repeatability, which helps a generality take on, as the classic accounts of ideology would have it, the appearance of the natural and/or the universal. To take an obvious example, it seems nearly impossible to avoid resolving mainstream narrative without coming to a conclusion about the status of a heterosexual couple, as evidenced by such different films as *The Return of Martin Guerre, An American in Paris,* and *Cleopatra.* This is not to deny differences in the status and treatment of the heterosexual couple. In these films alone, it is variously intricated with property and identity, romantic convention, love-death. It is simply to make the obvious point that the sheer repetition to which the routing of narrative problems through heterosexual coupling is subject bestows on the latter an ethos of the general. Not only narratives but spectacles, in order to remain within the bounds of social meanings, may call on such generalities. Performance as well as reference evinces the pull to *make sense.* Ideological generality thus provides an overdetermining justification or alibi for the detail.

In the present context, I would add that the temporal aspects of such generalities are responsive to, or at least reminiscent of, key elements of Western historicity. Once more one can find hints in some of the rhetoric surrounding research for the historical film. The statement of DeMille himself, cited as an epigraph to this chapter, moves from the promotion of research in the historical film to "the eternal verity of the Law." The very generality asserted by such ideational configurations suggests that they tend to assert a force valid in other times than the present, outside of time; the strongest in this regard would be, precisely, "eternal." I have argued many times that the appeal of indexicality, including filmic indexicality, has been intertwined with the division between past and present characteristic of modern historical temporality. But such generalities serve precisely as a bridge over the gulf between past and present. They help the past "live" because they apply then as now. More formally, to the extent that they are generalities, propositions and concepts known to be applicable in the present can also be applied to the past. The logic of employing currently acceptable general "truths" to bridge the gap between past and present is also an aspect of disciplined historiography and is recognized as a necessity in many kinds of theories of history. The submission of the time-filled, researched particularities of the past to time-less truths provides a standpoint, a stability of positionality, on history and change. The reliance and/or evocation of such general "truths" in mainstream film is one more indication of the importance of historical representation for mainstream cinematic textuality.

In this chapter, I have moved from a rationalization detail to a textual rationality, a practice evincing social order as human control with respect to time; that is, control against the flood of disordering, temporally unique particulars that is such a conundrum for the epistemology of modern Western historiography, and which reappears in hallucinatory form in Barthes's utopian account of the photographic spectator. In cinema, these threats are embodied in the image as details. But mainstream cinema has ways to place, order, and judge even disorder and perversion, on an axis that includes pictorial design and narrative function but also ideation, whether implicit or explicit.

Since the normalization of narrative cinema, yoking such disorder with order in a pleasurable, skillful way has been a task of the mainstream filmmaker, as artist, as professional, as expert, as social agent. From this perspective, filmic textuality becomes a construction of standpoints in time, against time. The transition from preclassical to classical cinema—during which historical spectacle was an important and prominent genre—was, among other things, the institutionalization of the means for addressing this social task.

CHAPTER 5

Disjunction and Ideology in a Preclassical Film: *A Policeman's Tour of the World*

In *Notorious* (1946), Alicia and Devlin could be placed "in" the scenic actuality of Rio de Janeiro without Ingrid Bergman and Cary Grant ever leaving Hollywood. It was simple to send a crew to Rio to shoot locations for establishing and transitional shots, and for backgrounds to be used in process work. Thus, if we play the game once beloved of scholars and ask which mechanisms in Edwin Porter films hit on protoclassical means, it strikes me that the exterior shots matted into studio sets in two scenes of *The Great Train Robbery* could be considered more "forward looking" than his often-discussed editing. For in preclassical cinema there was a general distinction between interior and exterior shooting. In the studio, the norm for mise-en-scène was a background flat placed perpendicular to the lens, usually cutting off great depth of field, though diegetic depth could be painted onto the flat. Exteriors tended to be shot with great depth of field, often emphasized by receding diagonals and sometimes by movement between foreground and background to dynamize relations among depth planes. Since virtually all actualities were shot outdoors, this style of exterior shooting takes on generic connotations and can be called actuality composition.[1]

The drive in classical studio cinema to override such distinctions among types of shots—a drive evinced in later (postclassical?) mainstream and many other kinds of narrative cinema—reminds us that even classical cinema can include something of the documentary spectatorial interest presumed by the preclassical actuality. But mainstream narrative cinema normally flattens out compositional differences between studio and actuality, interior and exterior, so that stylistic distinctions between the two are minimized. The document takes on some stylistic characteristics of the fictional diegesis; the diegetic borrows characteristics of the document; the document is integrated "into" the fiction to serve the latter. This stylistic unification of shot constructions encourages a spectatorial apprehension that coalesces readings of different shots with respect to their origins, and hence their "reality-status." It is fundamental to continuity editing as well as to the internal relations of the mise-en-scène, the construction of which can be more piecemeal in classical cinema than is often acknowledged. Thus, the matte shots of *The Great Train Robbery* exist in a historically important, transitional arena: the sublimation of actuality into narrative.[2]

This is the background for the following consideration of a late preclassical film, the 1906 *Tour du monde d'un policier* (*A Policeman's Tour of the World*). It is perhaps the most elaborate of a number of Pathé releases that mix actuality footage and fictional narrative. Textual procedures and modes of production in preclassical cinema went through a rapid series of transitions and innovations, but a "final" shift that stabilized parameters of commercial filmmaking pertinent here can be located in the years 1908–1916. Pathé was a dominant force during the U.S. nickelodeon period and therefore in the early models of mass production and consumption of cinema.[3] *A Policeman's Tour of the World* is a remarkable example of certain textual pressures on preclassical cinema just a couple of years before the definitive transition to classicism.

The major characters are a French banker who embezzles funds and a detective who chases him around the world. The film is structured as a repetitive discovery-escape-chase pattern that progresses eastward from Europe. Most scenes are set in areas inhabited by non-Caucasian or at least non-European civilizations: Egypt, India, China, Japan, an election in the United States, the American Wild West with Indians. The only real narrative development occurs toward the beginning, which establishes the theft and chase situation, and toward the end, when the embezzler saves the detective from American Indians and the two men return to Atlantic civilization in New York City. Here the detective accepts the erstwhile crook's offer of a partnership, established after the latter had made enough money on investments of stolen funds to repay that original theft and establish his own bank.

A norm of camera setups in *A Policeman's Tour of the World* is a norm of preclassical cinema in general: what is sometimes called the tableau shot, the often discussed fixed, frontal, medium-long to long shot of a scene. This is usually opposed to the classical cinematic norm of unobtrusive editing "into" the scene. Yet, though *A Policeman's Tour of the World* retains preclassical premises with respect to camera placement, the majority of its shots do function as elements of edited sequences. The film opens with a tableau shot, and maintains camera fixity and frontality in nonactuality shots, but of twenty-eight shots in the film, only six of them—1, 3, 7, 9, 10, and 12 (see the shot table and still, pages 213–24)— might be considered true one-scene/one-shot tableaux, with no relation of fictional action and situation to any adjoining shots. This illustrates the film's historical position as it appears from a current hard-and-fast categorization of classical cinema as opposed to other cinemas, namely interestingly transitional and contradictory.[4]

Given this first division between shots that function as tableaux versus those that function as elements of edited sequences, the editing can in turn be subdivided into two overarching functions with respect to diegetic time and space. The first is cutting to continue an action in a completely different background representing a relatively contiguous diegetic space (e.g., scenes 2, 6, 11). This kind of editing had already been developed in preclassical chase films, a genre to which *A Policeman's Tour of the World* responds, although in most of this film's exteriors, the more lateralized arrangement of action and consequently flatter sense of space may be untypical of the chase film.

The second category of editing is cutting into the scene, as in scenes 13 and, most elaborately, 4. These instances seem to embody the most definite breakdown of the notorious "exteriority" of the preclassical tableau. Just a few years later the wholesale rapid evolution toward continuity cutting into scenes would begin, permitting variations of shot scale, camera angles, and incidence of camera to action, for informational dramatic and characterological purpose. In *A Policeman's Tour of the World*, there is only one motivation for "continuity editing" within the scene: optical point of view.

The cut to shot 13B, which is an inserted close-up of a letter as it is read by the detective, is a special case of this. It transmits information sealing narrative closure.[5] But the most elaborately edited sequence in *A Policeman's Tour of the World* is scene 4. It is composed of eight shots—over one-fourth the number of shots in the whole film. The first and fourth shots of the scene (4A and 4D) show the embezzler looking through binoculars from a set representing a ship's deck. These envelop 4B and 4C, actuality views of the banks of the Suez Canal and shipping activity therein. These two shots contain unmistakable cues denoting the embezzler's optical point of view. The first is a lateral traveling shot, as taken from a boat moving through the Canal, and both are masked to appear as if viewed through binoculars. Actuality is thus pulled "into" the diegesis, and the audience's orientation toward screen and diegesis is articulated through the character's viewpoint. This is followed by three successive actuality shots (4E–4G), all masked, and the sequence concludes with a return to the embezzler on the ship, reconfirming the accord between views of spectators and character (4H).

It is worth pausing over ways this scene confounds a simple distinction between the classical and the preclassical. Its editing may appear to be a proto-classical development of analytical editing. But we never get closer views of objects *within* the tableau (4A), which in classical editing would be the establishing shot. In a way, the cut-ins are not to objects within this "establishing shot," but to optical *positions* inside it that are nevertheless directed *outside*. That is, the cut-ins consist of perspectives that are presented as originating within the diegetic space of the tableau shot; but they are perspectives on objects actually outside the orienting tableau itself. On the one hand, this construction activates offscreen space in an operation of creative geography and eyeline matching. But on the other hand, it bears at least as close a kinship to the preclassical chase film, with its cuts to different but contiguous spaces where the chase is continued. (This kind of chase editing is used in *A Policeman's Tour of the World*, for example, in scenes 2 and 6.) Classical establishing shot/cut-in analysis proposes overlapping spaces that form an integral whole, not an additive set of continuous spaces. Thus, the major difference between the chase film editing of scenes 2 and 6 and the point-of-view editing of scene 4 is that the contiguity of spaces is signified by the character's look rather than the movement of identical bodies or objects from shot to shot.[6]

Point-of-view editing per se was not innovative in the cinema of 1906. Furthermore, scholars have often emphasized motifs of overt voyeurism and dirty jokes and their dramatization in preclassical cinema.[7] Yet ideals of looking in *A Policeman's Tour of the World* cannot quite be described by the privatized sexuality of voyeurism. The film certainly does include woman as spectacle. Females dance for onscreen audiences in all locations between Egypt and Japan, and the embezzler's dream in the opium den (7)—the closest the film comes to depicting internal subjectivity—involves posed women. But what is interesting here is that these scenes do not utilize point-of-view editing, but maintain the tableau. In fact, given that the dancing scenes include a large number of onlookers as well as dancers in the same tableau, the pleasurable look at women is represented as collective spectacle as much as private fantasy. So spectators observe characters observing female dancers—but the diegetic act of observation is not differentiated from the spectacle by a play of onscreen and offscreen space in editing. If we compare the Suez sequence in scene 4, it becomes possible to propose another division, wherein the point-of-view construction that aligns the viewer's visual mastery with that of a private look by a character is associated not with the look at the woman, but rather the look at a non-Western space by the tourist.

In the Suez point-of-view sequence, we are shown two disjunctively edited actualities of the landscape, interrupted just once (4D) by a confirming return to the diegetic source of our perspective. By the criteria of classical cinema and its mainstream successors, this might seem to be a slight loosening of the characterological anchor for our perspective. But by preclassical criteria, this probably registers the film's penetration by yet another well-known genre: a set of actuality views strung together, the travel film. Although the actuality views first seem elaborately aligned with the fiction, the objects we see are then intermittently edited as non-fictional footage.[8]

Keeping this vacillation between a travelogue offering distant reality directly to the spectator and the strong yet partial operation in this scene to vector the spectator's view through that of a fictional character, the following can be proposed. Given the film's overwhelming emphasis on non-European locations and its resort to travelogue actuality in this and other scenes, ideal looking in *A Policeman's Tour of the World* brings the exotic to the masterful vision of the Western spectator. The vacillation is between the spectator's perspective on a document of reality and that document's mediation through a diegetic master tourist. For the narrative and chase leave little doubt as to the mastery of the embezzler/trickster. He is always a little more clever than the detective, always a little richer, always leading the way; and he is the one concerned with the landscape and the exotic, while the detective is only concerned with apprehending him.

Walter Benjamin's insight that the mass diffusion of mechanically produced images is linked to a desire to make the distant closer seems as pertinent here as Metz's occasionally literalistic discussion of voyeurism and the sense of sight as operating in a distance from its object.[9] But the issue arising from this organization of spectacle is that of the means and functions of implementing hierarchies in the organization of distance and closeness in the historical development of textual practices. In *A Policeman's Tour of the World*, sexually hierarchized looking is implanted within a pervasive set of further dichotomies. These include Western versus Eastern; dynamic, geographically mobile travelers versus static natives; served versus servant; advanced, technologically progressive societies versus regressive, historically static societies; and of course Caucasian versus non-Caucasian peoples. (The tour of the world leaves out the entire Mediterranean world west of Egypt as well as the rest of Africa, so it concentrates on non-Black but darker-skinned civilizations to the East.)

Thus, the touristic hierarchies of this voyeurism are colonialist.

This reading makes the Suez point-of-view sequence crucial, for as the first appearance of actuality footage, it is a strategy not only to establish the crook as master tourist, but also to define spectatorial position as possession of distant landscape. The freedom of the diegetic spectator/tourist to travel, to be served by foreign nationalities, to encounter foreign lands and female inhabitants as objects of spectacle is to be read as emblem and evidence of a historical Western mastery that is inclusive of the spectator. This definition of vision is an ideological specification for the film as a whole, which helps explain the ideological ramifications of introducing a fictional world and characters into the actuality context.

Yet, if this ideological generality informs *A Policeman's Tour of the World*, it is not a stylistically unifying generality. In fact, to viewers now the film's "primitive" disruptions of stylistic unity will seem obvious and striking. Retaining the norm of the tableau, it contains several multishot scenes; as a fiction film, it includes clearly discernible actuality footage—and this in turn is just one component of its multigeneric character. This inclusion of actuality footage as such shifts the status of the camera in relation to the profilmic. Throughout the film, then, unpredictable inconsistencies appear as a certain plurality of origins in mises-en-scène and the "reality-status" of the profilmic. This makes it worth pursuing a question in more detail: if a chief organizing principle of the film is to bring the non-West to Western vision, what are the requirements and benefits at the ideological level of exhibiting something more than a travelogue actuality? How does the interplay between actuality and narrative operate?

It is easy enough to divide the mise-en-scène generically, between actuality and fictional shots. But then the backgrounds for fictional sets can be subdivided between *sets* with painted flats and *locations* (see table). The Suez sequence attempts to integrate actuality as subject to the gaze of the master tourist. But after the Suez sequence, transitions among these three types—actuality, sets, locations—are unmediated by point-of-view editing or any other smoothing technique. On this level, the film is marked as "primitive" by the fluidity of this shifting, combined with the fact that the differences don't make much difference; they signify little narratively, so we can now experience them as stylistic disruption. For example, we are introduced to India with actuality footage of a religious procession; then, fictional action occurs in sets representing the interior and exterior of a pagoda; finally, our views of India conclude with a location background for the continuing chase.

But although these distinctions do not signify, it is possible to argue that *A Policeman's Tour of the World* does manifest awareness of them as a stylistic problem. There is evidence of this in the Pathé catalog, which lists as an attraction of the film "curious scenes taken from life, notably a festival in Calcutta, the interior of an opium den, merry-making in Yokohama, etc. etc."[10] In fact, the first of these (scene 5) is actuality footage; but the second (7), which includes dream superimpositions, is completely studio-shot; and the Yokohama sequence opens with an actuality shot (8), but the merry-making and subsequent narrative action is against a studio set painted to mimic composition of the actuality shot (9). This need to unify origins of mise-en-scène and attractions by reference to the real is a familiar one, but seems quite striking in a preclassical film with such a diversity of mise-en-scènes.[11]

In addition, it is possible to argue from spatial arrangements of shots that the tendency to counter the obvious and generic differentiations among origins of mise-en-scène is evinced in the film text itself. Briefly, preclassical location filming often partook of actuality composition, but *A Policeman's Tour of the World* seems to be seeking ways to treat set and location shooting similarly. On the one hand, except for the Paris train station (2A–B) location mise-en-scène does not have the great depth that is associated with location and actuality composition. Instead, extremely deep space is cut off by natural background terrain functioning like the background flat on a set. This has such consequences as in 6D, where some of the chase action occurs parallel to the picture plane as it would on a set, instead of diagonally as was common in the location shots of chase films.

Conversely, studio settings appear to be conceived in more depth than would have been likely even a few years earlier. As noted above, great distances can be represented on perspectivally painted sets, some of which clearly mimic actuality composition. But more subtly, studio-shot action can be staged to exploit a multi-planed area. This is evident in the play of entrances and exits by major characters, which occur with equal probability from the back or the wings of the set. For example, in shot 6A the embezzler exits the frame by walking into the pagoda entrance, screen right, as the detective enters background right; in shot 6C, the embezzler comes into frame from the pagoda and exits background right, followed by the detective. In fact, location settings seem chosen to permit a similar functioning. Within a mise-en-scène that occludes the extreme depth of actuality composition, there occurs the same kind of play of entrances and exits that the studio sets were built to accommodate, as in the setup of the "redskin" attack and rescue (11A–B).

Against the nonsignifying differences between actuality and fiction footage, then, this play of entrances and exits suggests the presence of certain goals familiar since the onset of classical cinema: hierarchization of mise-en-scène into narratively foregrounded and backgrounded actions— often the literal foreground and background, sometimes not. For example, on the set of the Suez dock, the detective is arrested in the foreground as the embezzler waves good-bye to him from a deck high in the background, and action between them is by extras; the extra action is narratively less pertinent and compositionally less differentiated (scene 3). Of course *A Policeman's Tour of the World* cannot be described as exemplifying a classical system in which lighting, pictorial composition, set design, blocking, and other means are consistently and overwhelmingly configured to make key narrative information exclusively central to the act of seeing the image. In its studio-shot scenes, the sense of space tends to be flatter than the classical norm (backgrounds painted in perspective are less melded to foreground space); the stability of the tableau's shot frontal, head-on camera position along with the lateralized movement and horizontal composition of sets sometimes militates against a strongly diagonal pictorial design; and characters regularly mime reactions toward the camera, which also contradicts tendencies toward a voluminous, naturalistically illusionary space. It is therefore unsurprising that there are still occasional manifestations of the famous "acentricity" of the preclassical scene, as in the U.S. election scene (10), when it is difficult to pick the embezzler out of the crowd. Nevertheless, there remains a contradictory impulse to diminish at least some differences between location and studio filming. This impulse includes an effort to hierarchize an increasingly complex mise-en-scène that is itself plural in its origins, and involves attempts at stylistic unification in such a way as to figure narrative pertinence in the construction of that unity.

So, is the film an early participant in the transition to narrative dominance and classicism? Perhaps, but it is more immediately a participant in the transition to fictional cinema itself. This is a period when the actuality film as a genre was rapidly disappearing as one of the dominant products of commercial cinema. The subordination of actuality genres to narrative genres meant that commercial cinema was becoming less preservationist, in the sense of distributing sights supposed to be taken as preserved instances of a practically unmediated reality. It is as if, in a kind of compensation, the reality-effects of studio settings would have to take on some aspects of actuality. And this in turn meant that location shooting would provide an environment framed and narratively hierarchized in ways consistent with shots made in the studio. In this 1906 film, tension between cinema as preserved document of actuality and as narrativized diegesis was apparently felt, but not as a problem important enough to destroy comprehension. The inclusion of evident disjunctions in mise-en-scène in *A Policeman's Tour of the World* represents one option in managing the tension, an option that appears in other, less elaborate films.[12] What is at stake ideologically in the tendencies toward leveling out distinctions among origins in mise-en-scène can be indicated by another example from the film.

We have now been trained by decades of mainstream cinema to expect either narrative pertinence or quick orientation from shots that introduce new locales. To us, then, the shot of the festival in Calcutta (scene 5) preceding the fictional action in India may seem simply to go on and on. No action related to the narrative situation occurs, and its temporal length exceeds any narratively functional significance. We are presented with Indian after Indian, in native dress and sometimes with elephants, parading by the camera from background to foreground and out of the screen. Combined with the fact that this is actuality footage that includes none of the characters, the temporal excess over any narrative positioning invites a spectatorial shifting of gears. This shot provides a moment of leisure, apart from the work of decoding narrative events, if not narrative progress, on which many other shots of the film insist. Pleasure and interest here would have to be in contemplation of filmed details, not in relation to the chase around the world, but as aspects of the real collected for our view independent of the characters' situation. In a way, the preservation of an actual Indian festival is loosened from the reconstructions of other parts of the world in shots filmed on location or sets. This is precisely why we may now experience this actuality footage as odd, slow, frustrating, or as exhilarating disjunction.

This is not to say that this shot escapes any colonialist ideology carried in the opposed, unifying pressures of the narrative. It is to say that if the shot can be pinned down to such an ideological configuration, this is not assured by the narrative. It may well be, for example, that a 1906 French or American spectator experiences it as a component of the Western appropriation of the world—perhaps, for example, brought to his or her vision by modern Western technology—a reading encouraged by other discourses such as journalism, schools, advertising, and so forth.[13] (And *this* is not to say that in later mainstream film such external discourses do not exist to support ideological configurations in the film.) But this does indicate that fictional procedures for displacing or dominating actuality might supply means *within* the film text for an especially effective specification of ideological direction.

In this respect, the last shot (14) of *A Policeman's Tour of the World* is at the opposite pole from the Indian actuality footage. A spectacular, stencil-colored allegorical scene without relation to narrative space and time, it is an instance of the preclassical practice of providing a thematic apotheosis following a narrative ending. Trios of extras, each trio dressed in costumes associated with a different national culture, are symmetrically arranged in the frame. The background is dominated by a large world globe. The two major characters move to either side of the globe and, at a gesture from the crook, additional groups of three in yet more national costumes enter and take carefully arranged positions in the frame. Finally, the embezzler and detective move to frame center in the foreground and shake hands; then the film ends as the embezzler guides the detective to extreme foreground and offscreen left, followed by these trios of national types.

This apotheosis might be treated as a conclusion that seeks to counter fragmentation, inconsistencies, and textual indeterminacies such as the Calcutta festival. That is, it attempts to enforce specific meanings of all the previous views around ideologies of Western leadership. The embezzler shows the detective the nations of the world, appearing at his bidding and following them offscreen. In this respect, it is a supplement to, or even a contestant for, the place of the preclassical lecturer, whose commentary on travel films seems to have included such ideological formulations.[14] It is as if the film wishes to present actuality, but only to the extent that actuality can be pinned within the film text itself by an interpretation prior to that of the spectator or the travelogue lecturer.

This would require the textual fabrication of an authoritative positionality, the textualization of a standpoint from which indexical images as documents of a reality are ordered. It would be comparable in certain ways to the historian's authoritative positionality, from which the shape and meanings of pastness can be inferred from the invocation and ordering of source documents. But the apotheosis is a somewhat weak solution, because it can lock in ideological meanings only after the shots have already been projected, instead of during their actual viewing. A stronger, *pre*-interpretative organization of the views around narrativized ideological themes would permit the spectator to be properly cued during the view itself. This would require a unifying consciousness manifested in every shot throughout the film. The ideological complicity of the apotheosis only highlights what was at stake in the preclassical film-historical arena wherein the integration of actuality and fictional elements was being worked through. The clear mastery of the embezzler and the elaboration of point-of-view editing to orient the spectator through his perspective point the way toward displacing the lecturer and the apotheosis, with integrating relations among shots that are thus pre-interpreted by means internal to the text as narrative.

But finally, it is necessary to note that the supreme Western tourist, that guide and delegate of our masterful views of the non-Western world, is an embezzling banker. This makes the reading almost too easy, too appropriate as an emblem of the ideological configuration the film assumes. The debt of this film to Jules Verne's *Around the World in Eighty Days* can only reinforce this reading.[15] Yet, the fact remains that in the logic of narrative motivation, our master tourist–banker–allegorical representative of Western worldwide control is a crook. And he restores his respectability by profiting from investments of stolen money. Of course, the logic of narrative motivation is pertinent only in the opening and closing of the film, for the rest of the story occurs as variations on the chase situation that moves the film to new settings, new attractions. But how should we now read the colonialist tourist as crook? Unconscious slippage into a subtextual, figurative truth? Joke? Ideological contradiction? An antibourgeois, populist, or even working-class consciousness? Deliberate or subliminal irony? Perhaps a double-voiced moment, where both seriousness and parody are at play? Perhaps all of these and more. But we can conclude with the film's conclusion by proposing that the film lacks the means, and perhaps the will, to decide even this narrational ambivalence textually. This is a fundamental issue in what we now experience as inconsistency and disjunction, the lack of constant centering and unity, the contradictory, historically transitional status of so much preclassical cinema— here registered on the ideological plane.

SCENE/SHOT LIST FOR
A POLICEMAN'S TOUR OF THE WORLD

Notations: Numbers are for scenes, a narrative unit defined by continuity of action in diegetic time and space. When a scene is composed of more than one shot, letters are appended to the scene number for each shot (e.g., 2A, 2B). All shots are labeled as one of the following: SET (studio shooting, painted flats, etc.); ACTUALITY (exterior documentary filming, no fictional action); LOCATION (exterior shooting with fictional action). The following is based on a Museum of Modern Art rental print.

TITLE: "FRAUDULENT BANKRUPTCY"

1. SET, interior of bank office. Narrative premises established, as embezzler signs for money brought by messenger, shaves to disguise himself, starts to leave via door at back of set, but returns and exits screen right. Police enter first door with authority figure (bank president?). They confirm theft, and a plainclothes detective is sent after crook.

2A. LOCATION, front of railroad station, actuality type of composition in depth. Various anonymous pedestrians appear in background during this shot. Embezzler asks detective to light his cigarette, then enters station screen right. Detective receives last instructions and enters station.

2B. LOCATION, loading platform of railroad station, actuality composition. Embezzler changes to conspicuous broad-brimmed hat, boards train, waves as train pulls out. Detective enters frame, briefly mimes disgust to camera, finds items left by embezzler, and exits.

TITLE: "SUEZ CANAL"

3. SET, outdoor café with tourists at boat loading area on canal, the deck of a docked ship in background, with sky and other ships in canal painted on backdrop. Woman in sailor pantaloons dances for sailors on boat and tourists. Boat loading. Embezzler enters, refuses service by Egyptian adults but has shoes shined by child. He sits at table in left foreground as detective enters and eventually sits with him. (All this time, background action among extras.) Embezzler slips something in detective's drink, detective passes out. Embezzler takes warrant from detective and has the detective arrested as crowd forms to watch. The protesting detective is taken off by police in

foreground as embezzler, laughing, waves good-bye from boat, high in background.

4A. SET, embezzler on ship in *plan americain,* looking screen left, lifts binoculars to eyes.

4B. ACTUALITY, traveling shot right to left of banks of Suez Canal (house, boat, dock, etc.), masked as though seen through binoculars.

4C. ACTUALITY, a ship passing through canal with banks of canal in background, masked for binoculars.

4D. SET, embezzler on ship (as 4A) now looking through binoculars toward foreground left, puts down binoculars and gestures at camera, then looks through binoculars again toward foreground right.

4E. ACTUALITY of other bank; traveling shot right to left, desert horizon, telegraph wires, etc., masked for binoculars.

4F. ACTUALITY traveling right to left of palatial buildings, masked for binoculars.

4G. ACTUALITY, pan left to large ship coming from left background toward foreground, masked for binoculars.

4H. SET, embezzler looking through binoculars toward foreground right. Puts down binoculars, gestures in delight (briefly at camera).

TITLE: "A FESTIVAL IN CALCUTTA"

5. ACTUALITY of procession of Indians passing through screen from left background toward right foreground, including elephants, religious emblems, and so forth. Print viewed includes a cut within this scene to the same camera setup and similar action.

TITLE: "BOMBAY PAGODA"

6A. SET, plaza with exterior of pagoda on screen right. British officer enters from right background on horse, followed by embezzler walking, who tips hat. Native takes horse. Others offer services and are rebuffed by embezzler. Westerners to background as eight native women bearing baskets come out. Other Indians bow to them and they dance in unison including some ballet steps, then exit background right. Officer and embezzler return to foreground, officer exits left. Detective enters background right and embezzler runs into temple right. Detective talks to Indians who point into temple, and he follows embezzler into temple, followed by two natives, one of whom falls comically.

6B. SET, interior of pagoda. Three women enter and kowtow to idol foreground left. Embezzler enters, looks around, is grabbed by two Indians. He escapes and leaves as they kowtow with women. Detective runs in, mimes respect to idols (but does not kneel) and gets information about embezzler. Detective gestures to camera with clenched fist, then exits as natives continue to worship.

6C. SET, exterior pagoda (as 6A). Embezzler runs out of pagoda from right to native holding horse, exits on horse led by native as other Indian in foreground right takes rubber snake out of basket. Detective enters from temple just as embezzler on horse disappears, talks to snake handler, looks at camera and pounds fist, and gives chase after embezzler.

6D. LOCATION, road parallel to picture plane, with background rise in terrain cutting off great depth. Embezzler enters on horse, from right, briefly talks to Indian screen center, exits foreground left. Indians go up hill. Detective enters midground left, talks to Indian. Detective looks right, elephant enters from right. He pays mahout, mounts elephant, and they exit toward foreground left.

TITLE: "OPIUM SMOKERS"

7. SET, relatively shallow interior Chinese opium den. Three Chinese in mandarin costume sitting on centered platform. Embezzler enters, gestures incomprehension at camera, talks to them. They hand him pipe and leave, he smokes and falls asleep, head on platform. Three classically dressed women fade into same shot, standing on platform. One pours water out of pitcher for other two; they hold a pose, then fade out. Embezzler awakens from his dream, smiling and gesturing. Detective enters, embezzler quickly exits. At invitation, detective also smokes, then falls back on platform. Two police fade into same shot, holding embezzler between them as the latter gestures resignation at camera. Dream fades out, detective awakens, arises, gestures determination at camera.

TITLE: "YOKOHAMA"

8. ACTUALITY, Japanese city street composed on left foreground to right background diagonal. People cross street, seem sensitive to being in frame—look at camera and retreat.

9. SET, different Japanese street painted on background flat in perspective, with some details and composition in depth similar to those of 8. A few people dressed variously on street (including coolie hats, which did not appear in 8). Six women in kimonos plus one child in coolie dress dance as passersby watch. Embezzler enters and walks through crowd to foreground center, takes off hat, gestures to others. Mutual bowing. Detective enters, moves along right edge of frame to foreground, looks at paper, comes up to embezzler. Embezzler knocks him down and flees toward background. Detective arises, paces laterally back and forth, turns to camera and gestures determination, clenched fist, and so forth, departs following crook as crowd makes way for him.

TITLE: "AN AMERICAN ELECTION"

10. SET, exterior U.S. street (San Francisco?) painted in detailed perspective. Political procession from background to foreground left, includes embezzler, led by man passing out materials as onlookers cheer. Detective in foreground right. They see each other, embezzler runs to background, detective held back by crowd. Another parade group comes to foreground. Detective sees embezzler but is held back by police guarding parade route, and must stay and cheer after parade passes through frame. General cheering and waving of U.S. flags.

TITLE: "THE RED SKINS"

11A. LOCATION, wilderness with foliage. Eight American Indians and chief are standing, then one points down incline off right and they hide. Detective comes up the hill, is captured and tied up in midground as chief stands in foreground left. Detective is shot but not killed by chief. As chief prepares to shoot again, embezzler enters up the incline and shoots chief. Other Whites follow and chase the Indians away. Embezzler recognizes detective at tree, puts gun to detective's head but does not shoot, then throws gun down. Embezzler calls his companions back, gestures orders, and they carry the unconscious detective off toward center background.

11B. LOCATION, exterior with pot over fire in midground right. Group enters through notch in background, led by embezzler. They put detective down midground left. Detective arises, grabs embezzler, tears up warrant. Detective and embezzler shake hands.

TITLE: "LEAVING NEW YORK"

12. SET, exterior, dockside, with Statue of Liberty visible right background. Several figures of both sexes walking. Enter horse-drawn

carriage, from which embezzler and detective disembark. Embezzler gets directions from passerby. Detective mimes lack of money. Detective and embezzler shake hands and walk off, with embezzler's hand over detective's shoulder.

TITLE: "UNEXPECTED PARTNERSHIP"

13A. SET, interior office, embezzler seated at desk. Detective enters, the two embrace, and embezzler hands detective a letter.

13B. NO SETTING. Inserted closeup of handwritten letter, indicating that embezzler's stock speculations have been successful, he has paid off his debts, and he is opening a new bank. The letter offers a partnership to the detective, whom the embezzler has come to admire during their "tour through the world."

13C. SET, as 13A. Detective signs paper. Uniformed office staff enter from rear. Embezzler introduces detective. Erstwhile embezzler and detective shake hands, others bow. They start to leave and embezzler starts to sit.

14. SET, for allegorical apotheosis (stencil-colored in print viewed) with large globe of world high in background. Trios of figures dressed in various national costumes arranged around sides of set. (Trios are composed mostly of one man and two women, some of three women.) Embezzler and detective walk to opposite sides of globe. Embezzler gestures to sides of frame, directing in additional national trios, who arrange themselves around frame. Embezzler and detective move to foreground in front of globe and shake hands. Embezzler puts arm over detective's shoulder and they walk toward extreme foreground and off with embezzler still talking and gesturing, followed by procession of national trios as film ends.

1

2A

2B

3

4A

4B

4C

4D

4E

4F

4G

4H

5

6A

6B

6C

6D

7

8

9

10

11A

11B

12

13A

13B

13C

14

CHAPTER 6

Document and Documentary: On the Persistence of Historical Concepts

As Murphy pointed out to you there, that was unscreened, which means he saw it for the very first time as you saw it, unedited films of, uh, what happened—some of what happened—in the motorcade. If I might explain to you that blurry and confusing scene: obviously what happened, when the shots were fired, the cameraman, who was riding in one of the cars behind the President, very wisely kept his camera running, even as he jumped from the car and ran towards the President's car, and then over towards the people who were shielding themselves, ducking down, trying to avoid what was going on. It was the only way the cameraman could have gotten you a picture of what went on. He very wisely took no time to try to wind the spring on the camera or anything else—just keep it rolling, get as much picture as possible, and get as close as possible to the scene of action. That is what the cameraman did, that is why it looked somewhat unorthodox in terms of what you are used to seeing, and that is why it's such a precious piece of film, because the cameraman *thought*.

—Bill Ryan, NBC anchorperson during John F. Kennedy assassination coverage

This Is Not a Documentary

At about 1:45 P.M. U.S. eastern time on November 22, 1963, the NBC television network broke into its broadcast day with the bulletin that the president had been shot in Dallas. This began several hours of instantaneous coverage of a classically traumatic event in recent U.S. cultural

and political history. It is now possible to watch this coverage as a significant historical document—I use this word advisedly—in the early shaping
of that event in public discourse. It is also a document in the history of
television news coverage. Ex post facto, in comparison to the current
practices and conventions of U.S. television news, this 1963 coverage
undoubtedly appears primitive. Just on the level of sheer "thematic" content, it is striking to observe the adjustment of the newsmen to the shock
of political assassination in the United States. Nowadays we know that
this kind of event would become a widely generalized cultural sign over
the next seven years. We now always know more than they did then. The
gap between this "we" and this "they" is, as we have seen, a basic condition
for modern historiography. My chief concern in this chapter is how fundamental elements of modern historiography encompass documentary
film as it has been defined in its founding conceptualizations, along with
some implications for more recent debates that bear on the history of
film and media.

We may begin from the question of what counts as a desirable
account of the real in this example, for the practices of both historiography and documentary cinema constantly manifest this issue. On a parallel but distinctive plane, "primitiveness" also appears in the modes of
staging the marathon bulletin. Take the studio mise-en-scène; three white
males (Frank Magee, Chet Huntley, and Bill Ryan) sit at a table, appearing cramped against a blank background flat, perhaps hastily put up to
obscure other uses of that studio space. They face cameras that accentu-
ate the cramped quality by holding them in medium close-up, with cuts
and sometimes pans from one to the other or to photographs that they
hold up to the camera. This is a far cry from the spaciousness of our contemporary network newsrooms, which are always at some point (usually
openings and closings) shown in a long shot that emphasizes the resources
the network has committed to the news department—not just in the number of subsidiary personnel supporting the anchor and reporters, but in
its technologies of news recording, gathering, and transmission. A major
element of the "primitive" appearance of this assassination coverage is the

lack of any of the now conventional signs of massive technological apparatuses for news gathering.[1]

Yet, consciousness of a technological lack seems to be not just ours, but theirs. It is overtly manifested in the assassination coverage itself. Its pressure point is the unavailability of any firsthand, indexical depictions of the events in Dallas. The insufficiency of the television medium is manifest as coverage begins, for the anchorpersons can only read *newspaper* wire service reports and speculate on the situation among themselves. Their commentaries are speculation because they are on camera, "live," in New York as the pertinent events are happening in Dallas, but the problems evinced in the broadcast tell us something about the expectations the medium represents itself as fulfilling.

The possibility of liveness is, of course, a distinguishing possibility of broadcast technologies, with television adding moving perspectival images to radio's sound. These media embody a potential for temporal simultaneity between a reality and its electronic encoding and transmission to a spectator in a distant place.[2] To indexical media in which liveness is a possibility, we can oppose these media of indexical traces, such as photography, phonography, and cinema, in which liveness is not possible. In media of the indexical trace, the availability of the representations of a reality to spectators is subject to noticeable delay because of the time necessary to process, manufacture, and/or distribute the representations. As a result, this latter class of media generally presupposes a temporal disjunction between the referential events producing them and audience apprehension of them, so that their representations become fixed as preservations from a past. (The later advent of videotaping of live events for repetition was a significant overlapping of these two modes, which are now always mixed on newscasts.)

This already suggests that documentary cinema, whose reality is necessarily from a past, may embody different, more "historical" expectations than those possible in a newscast. At any rate, news programming is a television mode that typically, if only partially, utilizes liveness, and the emergency bulletin is the epitome of that utilization. Here is a problem for the NBC assassination coverage. In it the price paid for instantaneity is a technological insufficiency linked to the spatial disjunction between broadcasting site and the referential events being depicted. In an era when portable video/television cameras were not available, there could be no live images from such crucial locations in Dallas as the assassination site and the hospital where Kennedy was treated. The president dies, Lee Harvey Oswald is arrested, and politicians and the populace react, but far into the story NBC's reporters are always a little behind. In particular, they seem constantly aware that their broadcast lacks images from the scene.

The technological surplus of television constructions of reality over that of radio—its sibling medium with "live" potential—is clearly the addition of the visual register. On November 22, 1963, NBC newsmen in a New York studio verbally narrate an overt and suspenseful story of the condition of the president "as it happens," with most of the image track being the bodies of narrating anchorpersons and the site of narration as the newsroom. One could argue that, as dramatic situation, this story is resolved within fifty minutes by the announcement of the president's death, and the several hours of coverage that follow only narrate anti-climactic consequences (world reaction, a new president, shock and continuity, and so forth). But alongside such narrations, there is a subtextual drama of the medium's struggle to depict itself: where are the sights not just of the narrating, but of the narrated? Can NBC get pictures from Dallas onto the air? This other drama is foregrounded by the fact that the live NBC coverage from the scene in Dallas comes to Frank Magee on camera over the telephone from Robert MacNeil, and that there are technical problems in getting MacNeil's telephone transmission audible on air; for a time, direct, simultaneous reports from Dallas (off camera) must be relayed, spoken line by spoken line, by Magee. The camera can only hold on him, listening to the phone and then repeating the news.

But, as part of this subtextual drama, ways are found to insert admittedly insufficient live images other than those of the narration itself: interviews from outside the constricted mise-en-scène of NBC's New York studio, switches to newsmen in Washington, and so forth. However, as if in compensation for the insufficiency of live indexical images from the scene, a series of indexically traced representations is gradually integrated into the coverage. This series begins less than thirty minutes after going on the air, when one of the anchorpersons holds up to the camera a *photograph* taken in Texas of Kennedy in a convertible limousine. Then there is a switch (emphasized by some technical difficulties) to local anchorperson Charles Murphy in a similarly plain desk at the NBC Fort Worth affiliate WBAP. Murphy, too, can only read—in this case local reports—but at least he is in the geographical area of the story; spatial separation is being broken down. After a switch for comments to David Brinkley in a Washington studio, it is back to WBAP, which finally gets indexical representations from the assassination site: not yet images from the instant and the place of the shooting, but *sound recordings* of interviews with eyewitnesses who recount what they had seen. (The lack of images is oddly accentuated, for as the witnesses are heard, the camera holds on a fidgety Murphy.) Back to New York, where the anchorpersons manifest the problem, with an on-air discussion of the fact that they now have a still photograph of the Kennedys and of how best to show it to the camera. Soon after come the reports of Kennedy's death, which is first read from an Associated Press (i.e., print journalism) teletype report, and only then reported by Murphy, and (on the telephone) Robert MacNeil. Yet, the groping for indexical images from outside the New York studio continues: more still photographs, live shots from Fort Worth and Washington newsrooms conveying newsmen's commentaries as well as interviews with witnesses, and live exterior setups where cameras are readily available—outside the White House, outside the New York studios for reaction interviews with passersby.

This subtextual drama of the medium's aspirations, which progresses through the security of newspaper reports to telephones, photographs, and narration on television from Dallas, circulates around a kind of black hole, the structuring absence of images from the key scenes of the motivating action. Finally, about 3:00 P.M., the anchors in New York are able to show a photograph (presumably a wirephoto) of bystanders lying flat on the ground at the scene of the assassination. Over this image, MacNeil and Magee provide a verbal narration of the moment of the shooting. At 3:40, Murphy announces late film is in. But this first motion picture film from Dallas at the time of the assassination turns out to be of an announcement of the shooting at a locale where Kennedy was due to speak. Then at about 4:00, NBC switches once more to WBAP in Fort Worth and Charles Murphy announces "late and unscreened film," taken from a reporter's car in the presidential motorcade. Murphy narrates the location of silent traveling shots from the car of cheering crowds on the curbsides, and then comes the moment of the assassination. Neither shooter nor target are visible, of course. Suddenly the camera seems to vault from the car, in a long take composed of violent, short pans back and forth as the cameraman runs toward the action, finding people taking cover. The result is shaky, blurry, Brakhage-like footage of earth and background buildings that sometimes holds briefly on human figures. A couple of more quick pans and cuts, and the clip runs out after some shots taken from the procession heading toward the hospital and from outside the hospital. Immediately identified by the anchors as important footage, this will be shown again.

At this point NBC switches back to New York, and Bill Ryan makes the comments I quote to begin this chapter. Those comments nicely summarize the stakes of the self-presentation of television coverage. Throughout NBC's narration of the crisis, the overt desire for hard information about the events has been crisscrossed by a (usually) less overt desire for images of the real of the actual scene, a presence of the news apparatus at the moment of the shooting. This moment is already becoming part of a past, for all participants know it will be an event drafted into official History. Yet, when that presence and that moment are indexically represented—when that representation is explicitly said to be valuable because of the presence of the apparatus, the indexicality of the image— the image emerges as insufficient in itself. It must immediately be explained, sense must be made, the very shape of the image requires verbal explication and pinpointing. Ryan's commentary takes up that task, "naturally" and in the interests of clarity, by explaining the effects of such an event on the camera, whose presence is certified and personalized as the skill of an individual. It looks "unorthodox," but it is "precious" thanks to the wisdom of the cameraman. In a kind of climax to the subtextual drama of the medium's aspirations, a micronarrative is constructed around the figure of a skilled filmmaker, the NBC professional who has done his job well and filled in some of the missing images.

Looking back as we must from the age of MTV and a seemingly incessant display of the film and television apparatus, this might appear to be a rather quaint, "pre-postmodern" consciousness, seeking to hold representation in place. Again, there is the felt gap between what we know and what they could know; this gap situates us with historians and them as historical agents. But it is instructive to compare this to *JFK: A Time Remembered* (Mark Oberhaus, 1988), a documentary film made after the event was firmly placed in the past of instituted History. This film depicts the assassination and the national reaction through a combination of found news footage (images of the past) and the filmmakers' interviews with participants in the events and journalists who covered them (the perspective of the present). *JFK: A Time Remembered* includes that NBC footage of the moment of the assassination, but cuts it up, slightly rearranging its order and interspersing it with both other found footage and interviewees recounting the event. Thus, as the sudden, jerky motion of the camera begins, a voice on the sound track says "Suddenly . . . ," and we cut to the interview with Larry O'Brien, where he continues, "shots were fired." Additional segments of the NBC long take are also shown, but intercut with other shots of the scene from a less determined time, such as a policeman staring up at the Texas Book Depository. In fact, the blurriest seconds of the NBC camerawork are excised. Thus, on the one hand, the unusual jerkiness of the image is given immediate semantic firmness—suddenness, a break in the ordinary, a shift in History. Here is the thematic of temporality and change, organized as an awareness of key determining instants of momentous transition. On the other hand, some of it still counts as excessive, perhaps unreadable, within the purposes of this recollective documentary and so is omitted. This suggests something to which I will return; a degree of pastness that exceeds historical sense.

With the notion of film as providing indexical traces of a real past, but one that may be potentially troubling to sense, we approach the arena not only of history, but of documentary, or the convergence of historiography and documentary cinema. No one would argue, I think, that *JFK: A Time Remembered* is not a documentary. In our standard expectations and modes of apprehension, it is recognizable as such both in its use of footage from the actuality of the events being depicted, and also because they are arranged in careful sequence and thus presented in a form that places and makes sense of that actuality. Such a "well-formed" sequence is justified precisely as History; sense can be made because the event is over. From this perspective, Bill Ryan's commentary is only a halting start to the ongoing project of converting a relatively unbridled visual indexicality into sense; the closer the image comes to being reduced to pure presence, the more it threatens to become unreadable and requires explication. In the NBC coverage, the event is just past, barely in the process of becoming history, and a sure, meaning-determining sequence is not yet formed; there has not been time. *JFK: A Time Remembered* has had both production time and cultural time to know its history and so is a proper documentary. The NBC coverage, caught between past and present, is not a "real" documentary, because it is not "real" historiography.

The measure of this difference is rooted in film history (note how difficult it remains to avoid this last word). Classical proponents of the documentary tradition in cinema repeatedly define documentary against what it is not. Thus, when appropriating the term in his "First Principles of Documentary" (1932–34), John Grierson goes on to distinguish its "lower," less valuable forms from its "higher" forms. His preferred category of filmmaking excludes such "films made from natural materials" as travelogues, newsreels, "magazine items," and other short "interests" or "lecture films," as well as scientific and educational films. Beyond such nonfiction film types, "one begins to wander into the world of documentary proper, into the only world in which documentary can hope to achieve the ordinary virtues of an art. Here we pass from the plain (or fancy) descriptions of natural material, to arrangements, rearrangements, and creative shapings of it." Or, as he put it in a 1937 discussion that connects the preclassical actuality film and the cinema programming of his day, "The newsreel has gone dithering on, mistaking the phenomenon for the thing in itself, and ignoring everything that gave it the trouble of conscience and penetration and thought." Grierson's sometime use of Kantian slogans sketches an epistemology of actuality through film. He rejects neither a concern with the surface of reality nor its aestheticization, but seeks to demonstrate (as he still could say in 1943) that "even so complex a world as ours could be patterned for all to appreciate if only we got away from the servile accumulation of fact and struck for the story which held the facts in living organic relationship together."[3]

Such passages were published during years when the term *documentary* was elevated to a major presence in film practices, the discourses surrounding them, and their inscription in film histories. In the English-speaking world this occurred very much, though not exclusively, in relation to the work and polemicizing of Grierson, his coworkers, and his allies. Here we see the documentary tradition—that spoken of by Grierson as the "higher form" of filming actuality—self-consciously inventing itself. In this invention, there is rarely if ever unvarnished faith in the possibility or, more tellingly, the utility of a complete record of the surface of reality. While some would argue more strongly for the check that "reality" might place on the filmmaking, it was from the beginning a lasting truism of the documentary tradition that patterning, rhetoric, artistry, or something had to be added to the indexical capacity of the medium. This is why Grierson could use concepts of story, drama, and the organic to indicate a prerequisite of genuine, "higher" documentary. Whatever the critic's or practitioner's proclivities with respect to filmmaking, a number of texts and discourses from these years emphasize the importance for documentary of preplanning, of aesthetics, of dramatizing, and even of scripting the reality to be filmed. A consistent formula in the main line of this tradition is that documentary is neither newsreel nor travelogue, but something more profound and certainly something with a more important social mission.[4]

It is precisely the distinction between actuality and meaning, document and documentary, that we see enacted in the recycling of the NBC footage in *JFK: A Time Remembered*. Of course, that footage relates a very privileged kind of historical actuality. But as I have argued in earlier chapters, there is a sense in which every "normal" film image is supposed to be apprehended as a preservation from the past, and this is so even if what is preserved is an overt fiction. When I apprehend a certain body diegetically named as Walter in *His Girl Friday*, at a basic factual level I am seeing an indexical depiction of the actual body of the now-deceased individual born Archibald Leitch, which, as the Hollywood institution requires, I know as Cary Grant. My examples here suggest that part of the stake in making documentaries is controlling documents, indexical traces of the presence of a real past, but this is a grounding issue for the cultural history of cinema in toto. This is to say, first, that the scope of such questions is not limited to documentary as a specific "mode" or "genre" of cinema. But furthermore, it also suggests another path of understanding that cultural history. The control of pastness in the register of meanings achieves its most culturally prestigious, disciplined versions in the practice of historiography. The concept of documentary, as a mode of understanding the nature, potential, and functions of cinema and indexical representations, is in intimate ways intricated with the concept of *historical* meaning.

What Is a Document/ary?

Notions of documentary have a genealogy that could be sketched with reference to historical consciousness. According to the 1933 edition of the *Oxford English Dictionary*, the noun *document* entered the English language by the mid-fifteenth century with two chief derivations from its Latin and Old French roots, now obsolete. One of these interrelated semantic clusters has to do with teaching and/or warning, and the other with evidence or proof. A seemingly subsidiary association arose in the eighteenth century, when the term *document* developed an association with evidence that is written, such as manuscripts and deeds, but could also encompass such artifacts as tombstones and coins as well as official legal and commercial artifacts such as bills of lading, insurance policies, and so forth.

As for the noun *documentary*, it seems to have entered the language only in the nineteenth century, when *documentation* was also increasingly common. The OED indicates *documentary* was first used as an adjective straightforwardly indicating reference to documentation, as in "They were in possession of documentary evidence which would confound the guilty" (Macauley, 1855). But, significantly, this usage now included historiographic extensions of a Rankean sort, such as "Going back beyond annalists to original and documentary authorities" (Pattison, 1861). The 1933 OED does not mention film. However, Griersonianism is fully registered in the 1989 revised edition, which adds a new definition: "Factual, realistic; applied esp. to a film or literary work, etc., based on real events or circumstances, and intended primarily for instruction or record purposes." This is followed by a relatively lengthy group of sample uses, the earliest of which is from John Grierson's 1926 review of *Moana*, and six of which are from the 1930s. Such usages expand beyond cinema in the last three examples, dating from 1957 to 1962. These extend the notion of documentary as an effect of factual reality to film makeup, to a book, and finally (in a way Freud might have appreciated) to its putative contrary, as in the seemingly oxymoronic phrase "documentary fiction." This revised OED also adds the new subsidiary term *documentarist*, meaning documentary filmmaker, as being in use by the 1950s. All in all, then, Grierson's phraseology appears to have become current almost as soon as he proposed it. This suggests less his individual importance than a cultural conjuncture *requiring* some designation of the field he named: an arena of meaning centering on the authority of the real founded in the indexical trace, various forms of which were being rapidly disseminated at all levels of industrial and now post-industrial culture.

This cultural conjuncture is undoubtedly connected to the semantic development around concepts of document and documentary stemming from the nineteenth century and lasting into the twentieth, whereby the terms enlarge their compass to embrace written evidence and historical artifacts, then the factual film, and then simply factuality. This was, in effect, an overall shift in semantic emphasis from education to authentication in an expansion from the written that took in, characterized, and was characterized by the filmic. One could consider that shift as a process of lexical adaptation partly in response to technological changes, or perhaps as a conceptual slide that provides some "historical" basis for a theoretically convenient analogy between writing and film. But it is also the case that such changes were situated in a sociocultural matrix bestowing authority on purported conveyances of a real. The written legal document embodies a real of the intentionality of legal subjects, the original or historical document a real of dated authentication, and (photographic) cinema a real of perceivable concrete past existents in movement. In the evolution of the idea of document, the connection of authenticity and authority goes beyond etymological kinship. The authority of documenting was first drawn from the power implicit in its denotations, i.e., warning, admonishing, or teaching; it then became an evidentiary element in an argument or rhetoric; and, within a semantic history that seems linked to film, this authority can exceed even its modes of inscription, as a claim that achieves the authority of the real itself.

The period that gave rise to these semantic expansions in concepts of documentary and document was crucial for the organization of pastness and indexicality as general cultural concerns. It saw the invention of photography and cinema (the indexical media on which NBC drew to fill in its lacks while covering the John Kennedy assassination), as well as the professionalization of historiography, with its concomitant sociocultural aspirations as a master Western discipline offering the most prestigious knowledge of a real past. The instituted disciplinary requirement that has been most influentially discussed by recent theorists of history has been for an account of the real as coherent sequence; hence the supposed omnipresence in this historiography of a narrativity of closure. One of the most influential thinkers in this regard is Hayden White, who finds it as epistemologically suspect as it is rhetorically powerful. But there was also the striking fact that this supposedly supreme process of Western knowledge dealt with an object not susceptible to direct observation, much less (for the scientifically minded) experimental manipulation, for both of these depend on the presence of an observer, and for modern temporality the past is by definition absent to any observer. As I have emphasized in earlier chapters, the response of disciplined historiography lay in its other central epistemological component: the systematically critical study of historical documents, that is, traces left by the past. The reality of an internally unified sequence was thus to be claimed on the strength of inferences from critically authenticated source documents, and the accurate placement of written historical documents was often held up as the specific mark of modern historiography by historians. As we have also seen, by the end of the nineteenth century, partly under the impact of other disciplines of the indexical trace, and partly under the impact of modernity and the growing discursive centrality of new mass populations, historiography was expanding the notion of the historical document beyond the written.[5]

The OED outlines an extension of the semantics of the document past the limit of written language, eventually to encompass technologies of indexicality. But, depending on one's position on the purview of historiography, an expansion of the realm of historical evidence beyond the written was always a theoretical possibility for modern historicity. At a certain point, instead of being sui generis, the written document could therefore come to stand synecdochically for all survivals, all traces in continuous existence from a past. This coalesces with a vision of historiography as taking in all sectors and practices of society and culture. Any materials left to the present from any aspect of past human activity are potential evidence for the historian, connecting past and present. Implicitly, then, any human activities must be subject to the historian's inspection, insofar as they are documentable in the broadest sense of the term.[6] Taking this to a logical extreme, it might seem that the utopia of modern disciplinary historiography is a complete surveillance, in the sense of the availability of all conceivable historical documents, with documents conceived in the broadest possible way. In this utopia, all artifacts produced by the past reality being studied would have to be accessible, to have some form of continuous existence from the past to the present. For various reasons, this is impossible, and apprentice historians learn to confront this impossibility by shaping investigations according to kinds of documentary evidence that are actually available, by seeking new, previously unused sources, by critiquing the use by others of available sources, and so forth. But even leaving aside the unavoidable incompleteness of the documentary record, there are other difficulties. The most central one here relates to the disciplinary requirements that an internally unified sequence should be inferred from the source documents.

In his important study of the logic of modern professionalized historiography, Arthur Danto succinctly explores the conjunction of these two ambitions of coherent sequenciation and complete "documentation." To conceptualize a historian with perfect documentation of the past, he hypothesizes an imaginary Ideal Chronicler who "knows whatever happens the moment it happens" and instantaneously transcribes "everything that happens across the whole forward rim of the past ... as it happens, the way it happens." Yet, the full, running description of the past that constitutes an Ideal Chronicle would not in itself be historiography as the professional historian conceives it. For the historian's account is always produced from a point in time after the sequence is completed; otherwise the end of the sequence could not be securely identified and its integrity would therefore be in doubt. This historiography therefore assumes a disjunction in knowledge between actual historical agents and historians, and the possibility of a convincingly secure narrative ending is the site of this disjunction. The historian always locates a beginning and an ending that anchor the sequence as a sequence, but the historical agent would have to know his or her future with absolute certainty in order to construct a correct integral sequence. Without such certainty, what seems to be an ending might be followed by even more conclusive consequences. For Danto this explains why there can be no history of the present, but only of the past, why all aspects of history are constructed ex post facto. That we, now, always know more than they did, then, is a premise of modern historical knowledge and part of its justification.

A necessary condition for sequenciation of the real, this premise also contaminates the status of survivals from the past, the putative documentary basis for inferring the reality of the sequence. Danto points out that in practice it seems impossible to regard a preserved survival of the past simply as an index of elements of an ongoing Ideal Chronicle. This is because, as with any historical document in the broad sense, we already have some idea of its possible significances within sets of putatively closed sequences prior to encountering them. At least this is suggested by Danto's example of Newton's house. A seventeenth-century artifact preserved to look much as it did in the seventeenth century, it would seem serviceable as a piece of historical evidence in continuous existence up to the present; however, according to Danto, in the twentieth century we cannot help but see it as an element of an accomplished historical narrative, as "the place where Newton made those great discoveries in the Plague Year of 1665." This point bears comparison to the projects of living museums such as Old Sturbridge and Greenfield Village, with their dialectic of preservationism and restorationism. Danto attributes the conundrum to the structure of historical knowledge itself. Modern historicity constructs meaningful, unified temporal sequences, and whatever the rhetorical and disciplinary importance of documentary evidence in asserting their factuality, the pertinence of documents is intricated a priori with the ex post facto significance of the historical sequence.[7]

My intent here is not to plow again over hoary ground involving the necessary selectivity of sources, nor the even hoarier ground of distinctions between evidence and interpretation, fact and value, and so forth. It is to highlight something about cinema by comparison to the underlying structure of modern historicity. The perfect Ideal Chronicle would be the perfect historical source document, since (a) it is the unquestionable eyewitness account (allowed by Ranke as a primary source), impartially apprehending everything in the past and leaving a record; and (b) like any indexical trace, it derives its current authenticity from the fact that it was present in the past yet survives to the present. "Perhaps the work of the Ideal Chronicler could be given over to a machine," remarks Danto. This machine would be the perfect, omniscient producer of absolutely reliable, complete indexical representations of everything in the past, including, as Danto reminds us, minds. So the prospect seems far off.

But as cultural fantasm, epistemological ideal, or combination of the two, such a machine of universal surveillance may seem to be suggested in some of the discourses around modern indexical media, especially since the late nineteenth century. Today the mise-en-scène of contemporary television news, with CNN and its imitators as the epitome, seems to signify a technology aiming precisely at this, one that mobilizes all mechanical and electronic capacities yet invented for the purpose of tracking and storing information from all conceivable sectors of human activity. And yet, in its presentness, its ongoing, *unending* succession, news can only guess at, project, speculate about sequence and therefore what counts as proper knowledge of the real as history. Pure presence and pure (unfinishable) chronicle, which would imply a historicity without meaning secured by stable sequencing, is unacceptable; hence, perhaps, the currency of the anchorperson adapted by television from the newsreader of radio. Bill Ryan can at least attempt to position even the most extreme, unstable indications of presence to suggest ways of foreseeing its transformation from pure chronicle to history.

In the discourse of the original documentary film movement, the newsreel is not a documentary; and neither is television news a documentary in this sense, much less emergency bulletins. But NBC's 1963 assassination coverage provides an extreme example that indicates tendencies driving even the latter toward documentary. This is a coverage that tries to counter the effects of its own need for simultaneity or "liveness," its own dream of immediate presence at the real. The problem is not just technological insufficiencies with respect to such instantaneity, but the concurrent and contradictory need for meaning. Thus, regularly scheduled television news includes such momentary positionings by announcers, with the anchorperson as the apex of a pyramid of knowledge, and characteristically provides retrospective summaries and accounts, sometimes called "perspective" or "context," for the most recent and contemporary news events. This edges it toward documentary film/video. If shots as indexical traces of past reality may be treated as documents in the broad sense, documentary can be treated as a conversion from the document. This conversion involves a synthesizing knowledge claim, by virtue of a sequence that sublates an undoubtable referential field of pastness into meaning. Documentary as it comes to us from this tradition is not just ex post facto, but historical in the modern sense.

Documentary Is Not Actuality

There is something odd about a comparison of documentary cinema and historiography that leads to differentiating documentary from less coherently sequenced constructions of the real. For it does not differentiate documentary from another of its "others," the mainstream narrative film. Instead, it suggests a certain kinship between the two, because mainstream cinema also works through the sublation of document into sequence. The "document" here is the shot comprehended as an indexically traced record of a preexistent, profilmic field. Such preexistents include actors' bodies (in certain ways we really do see "Cary Grant"), performances, and studio or location settings. In this kind of cinema, some two hours of such "documents" are sequentially ordered as a less or (most often) more conventionalized narrative form.

This sweeping characterization is open to kinds of objections that I would not completely resist, although full elaboration is not possible here. A most pertinent one might emphasize the play of technical artifice and style in mainstream cinema, asking whether its spectator is not invited to go beyond comprehending the shot as document. In this regard, it is useful to remember that when special effects, process shots, and so forth are foregrounded, as in the construction of alternative universes, fantasies, imagined futures, magic, and so forth, much of the point is how such manipulations of the image mesh, through composite imagery or editing, with a general photographic effect. That is, the product is a kind of imaging hybridity that to this point in film history still asserts the prior indisputable existence of elements of profilmic actuality, such as (or perhaps especially) actors' bodies. This is the case even when special effects are foregrounded as performance or spectacle (see chapter 3), as opposed to being utilized as illusionistic complement to indexicality. A relatively recent Hollywood example was the heavily techno-hyped *Tron* (Steven Lisberger, 1982), but the best emblem for contemporary Hollywood in this respect may be the climactic scene of *Total Recall* (Paul Verhoeven, 1990), a film whose selling points included its spectacular special effects: Arnold Schwarzenegger's face is morphed into impossible contortions (representing the effects of a diegetic vacuum), only to be returned to photographic normalcy to seal the story resolution. Another common usage for explicit special effects is the classical cinematic practice of fore-grounding optical effects as "punctuation," as in dissolves or wipes. If these do not place individual shots or scenes in terms of narrative orientation (e.g., dissolve to dream), they demarcate individual scenes as members of a set composing a coherent, whole string of fictional events; that is, they accent and delineate sequential organization. At a fundamental level, then, such intrusions of the technical artifice are subordinated to the assump-tion that the composition of the mainstream film includes shots that are traces of a past real incorporated into an overall sequencing process. And again, this echoes the basic structure of modern historiography.

Within film history, one can adduce additional quick indications of a generally undiscussed kinship between mainstream cinema and the original documentary tradition. Recall that the classical fiction film and the industrialization of entertainment filmmaking that developed in tan-dem roughly between 1908 and 1917 ejected the actuality film as a lead-ing commercial product. In general, after that the mainstream ethos strongly tended to denigrate the preclassical era as a primitive time that, whatever its charms, was soon left behind for real "film art." This posi-tion was rapidly taken up by influential film historians. Primitiveness and lack of artistry was evidenced by narrational and visual strategies that were described as simplistic and inflexible. These included setting the camera in front of an unprepared chunk of reality, turning it on for a few minutes, and then presenting the result to audiences. Such historio-graphic attitudes have quite properly been criticized in the new wave of film scholarship on early cinematic modes of representation, as teleologi-cally naturalizing mainstream practices.

But furthermore, there seems little doubt that the appeal of many actualities was in the relatively extreme rawness of the real they pre-sent, which is ultimately to say that they do not seem overtly planned or reorganized to fit into an intratextual sequence. This is so not just in com-parison to later kinds of filmmaking, but also in comparison to various accounts of the real available in other contemporary forms such as jour-nalism, narrative prose, and historiography. In the register of the last, actuality shots may indeed appear as relatively pure instances of documents. The move to classical cinema, with its normalization of the fictional feature film as sole leading product, appears now to have been one of a set of industrial decisions, enabling regularization of production for a rapidly expanding market. However, it simultaneously constituted an epistemological insistence on integrating the shot into larger narrative structures whereby its meanings could be better controlled and regulated.[8]

In its own originary self-definitions, the documentary tradition shares the denigration of preclassical cinema as primitive with its putative other, mainstream fictional filmmaking. If proponents of documentary banished the newsreels that became a secondary mainstream product from their realm, it is all the more clear that actualities could not be admitted. In the 1930s Grierson himself associated actuality films with an outgrown childhood—his own as well as the medium's.[9] While the term *documentary* as applied to cinema did not begin gaining currency until the late 1920s, textbooks have often followed Grierson in dating documentary filmmaking proper a bit earlier; *Nanook of the North* (Robert Flaherty, 1922), released just a few years after the economic and cultural success of the fictional feature was assured, is a standard originary monument. The fashioning of such chronologies by textbook writers and the originating documentary polemicists led by Grierson may be critiqued symptomatically. But they do point to a correlation between the institutionalization of the mainstream feature film and the conceptualization of documentary, in which the latter appears as a relatively immediate aftermath of the normalization of the former. Of course, it is not surprising if the documentary ethos appears as a reaction to industrialized entertainment filmmaking, but it is interesting if it simultaneously incorporates some attitudes shared by promoters of the classical feature film.

Evidently the actuality film lacked elements implicitly or explicitly claimed by both the documentary and the mainstream ethos. Basic to these is the value placed on sequenciation. This value lies in the great assistance sequenciation provides in centralizing and restricting meanings derived from the points at which actual contact with the real is asserted—the realm of the document. This is what makes the actuality such an important component in denigrating the preclassical as constituted in both traditions. Consider that almost all aspects of the visible world theoretically lay within the purview of actuality filmmaking: the smallest or largest event, the most ordinary or extraordinary spatiotemporal fragment was potentially subject to cinematic surveillance and re-presentation as an indexical trace of the real. But although such traces appeared precisely as fragments more or less extracted from the continuum of reality, they may be related to the activity of Danto's Ideal Chronicler. Like the product of this hypothetical agency, actualities in themselves provided fewer means for the filmmaker to attribute significance to the real. This is certainly not to say that there was a complete absence of order, meaning, or even convention in the making and viewing of actualities, nor that, for example, topicals did not represent occurrences that fit into larger, generally understood metanarratives. But, as I argued in earlier chapters, such films possessed much less of the textually saturating directionality of meanings based on internal sequenciation and elaboration to which we are so accustomed after ninety-odd years of narrative dominance. Like mainstream narrative, then, the later documentary impulse insists on the elementary structure of modern historicity by rejecting a specter raised by—though not necessarily realized in—the preclassical actuality genre: that of comprehension of the real through a decentralized, potentially free-floating spectatorship.

On the level of theoretical conceptualization one could here go back to similarities and differences with the Barthes of *Camera Lucida;* however, I just want to emphasize that I say decentralized rather than decentered as a matter of emphasis. For centralization of meaning-production was one of the stakes in the series of transitions away from preclassical practices. Classical narrative form seeks to organize the shots composing it with more or less explicit, often conventionalized principles of sequence that delimit a range of intended meanings, *determinable by the filmmakers within a film text itself.* In early preclassical cinema, as Charles Musser has emphasized, meanings could often be structured by exhibitors, for example through lecturers who imposed ideological order on films with their spoken commentaries, or by cutting together shorter actualities to form elementary sequences. Such exhibition practices indicate, first of all, that some sense of the utility of sequence was felt very early, but second, that in much preclassical practice constructions aiming at such significance were often a result of activities that were dispersed and localized rather than centralized. The normalization of longer, multishot films, narrative dominance, and the regularized sequencing associated with them sought to identify the determination of textual meanings with the production as opposed to exhibition companies. As classical narrative form, common sequencing principles are both culturally widespread and repeatable (important for the industrial organization of entertainment that resulted in the Hollywood mode of production).[10]

While the documentary tradition is not locked into highly conventionalized narrative forms, it does share a commitment to the centralization of meaning through internal sequenciation; hence its own rejection of the preclassical. Thus, just as Danto's Ideal Chronicle is not in itself good disciplinary history, even an omnipresent actuality would not be good documentary filmmaking. The problem posed by actualities for documentary as well as fiction filmmaking is that they are too pure as document; machines of indexical representation, even when used by the most amateurish, can indeed produce a seeming infinity of such documents. The home video camcorder is the latest realization of this sociotechnological dream, and it is not surprising if, like its predecessor the home movie camera, it is sometimes invaded by discourses of skill and craft education.

This brings us to a sociological point. A medium that finds its value in relatively unelaborated documents might seem to leave little function for the professional, threatening to individualize sequence and meaning as activities of the spectator. The actuality was a peculiarity. It was a kind of commercialized, hence professional manifestation of the possibility of representation of the real, but one that did not necessarily claim to impose sense from the site of textual production, where many of the professionals performed their work. From this perspective, both Hollywood film and the documentary tradition, in their insistence on craft, skill, and sequence—in short on aesthetics and meaning—provide a function for a specialized elite in the imposition of significance for the spectator by means of the configuration and organization of documents. We will return to the idea of the filmmakers as a professional-intellectual elite. More narrowly, mainstream and documentary film share an underlying logic of the document that helps explain why the normalization of "film art" as narrative cinema was important for the original documentary movement, and why for the Grierson school, documentary has to be more than actuality, travelogue, or newsreel.

Of course in the history of the two modes there are also fundamental differences in assumptions about textual form and epistemology. But these stem from differing conceptions of the sequence or of shot-sequence relations rather than from differing definitions of the basic goals for spectatorship of the shot or disputes over the need for sequence. For both these traditions, as for modern historiography, sequences organize temporality, providing endings that confer retrospective significance on shots. While it need not utilize an overtly narrative form, documentary film must minimally share this assumption with mainstream fictional cinema; hence, the ambivalent relation of documentary to narrative. If there have been tendencies within the documentary tradition to avoid classical narrative form, this has not been true for all its sectors and, more important, has rarely committed documentarians to a definitional rejection of narrative per se. Given the relation of the ambitions of documentary cinema to modern historicity, this is not surprising; many theorists of history have argued that narrative is the most powerful and perhaps only means for achieving coherent temporal sequenciation. Thus, Grierson and other of its proponents in the 1930s already emphasized documentary as the dramatization of reality, and they often articulated aims on the level of representational forms. Documentary is the "creative treatment" of "natural materials," he tells us; it was the need for a dramatic apprehension of life that led to the EMB film unit. In this problematic, representational indexicality in itself never results in a strong form of knowledge, and hence is only a precondition for documentary. This is why his higher type of documentary cinema is necessarily an *aesthetic* of the document.

On this level, at least, there may be another kind of objection to drawing industrial entertainment cinema and the documentary tradition too closely together. For it is also clear that certain strands of documentary filmmaking have a long and honorable commitment to alternative and oppositional constructions, with practitioners and supporters conceiving or justifying them on the basis of social and political goals. It is worth remarking that politicized documentarians might have the greatest stake in the inadequacy of the isolated document. Consider again the preclassical actuality. After the more complex, often conventionalized and institutionalized types of sequenciation that were to come in film history, they seem to give the filmmaker radically fewer textual means to direct the spectator's comprehension of the real being transmitted. To continue the comparison, it is as if a historian simply presented the reader with fragmentary source documents from a given period, without overt thesis, narrative, or contextualization. Once, however, the document is placed in a context that makes it part of an assertion of meaning from the real, the reader is defined as the rhetorical aim of that significance. Similarly, for politically committed filmmakers, work in documentary implies that the spectator can be defined as a terrain to be organized, a terrain of struggle over such meanings and hence of social struggles. Of course there are many different kinds of spectators and filmmaking impulses that can answer to such a description. But this may well be a kind of generalizable definition inherent in most claims to specifically politicized filmmaking.

What Does a Documentary Do? From Grierson to Baudrillard

If Griersonian concepts are significant in film history, it is not so much because of his supposed paternity over the term *documentary film* or even his energetic promotion of it as a slogan. But beginning from these, it is useful to say that he was the English-language polemicist who had the perspicacity to articulate a concept that conjoined aesthetic and concrete situational concerns of nonmainstream filmmakers around the indexical characteristics of cinema. Aesthetically, from the point in film history when the Hollywood narrative film became a leading model of economic and mass cultural success, variants of the documentary film have often offered a battle standard for alternative constructions of the medium.

These constructions involve a range of documenting and sequencing strategies that claim to be based in the presence of the apparatus at past events; hence, to an extremely variable degree, these events are represented as being preserved in their actuality. Situationally, documentary film has always offered, in Paul Willemen's words, the possibility of "an artisanal, relatively low-cost cinema working with a mixture of public and private funds, enabling directors to work in a different way and on a different economic scale from that required by Hollywood and its various national-industrial rivals." This helps Willemen explain the interest of at least some Griersonian models for at least some third cinema filmmakers.[11]

But what is the relation for the classical documentary tradition between the situation of documentary cinema per se and the overall social functioning of the filmmaker? This seemingly abstract question was fundamental for Griersonianism. His answers bear in surprising ways on the recent debates, such as those over cultural studies and postmodern theories of signification. The concluding section of this chapter is, in part, an attempt to begin positioning the persistence of documentary and historicity in contemporary culture.

The crucial sector in the conceptual site staked out by Grierson for cinema was the sociopolitical. It is not coincidental that, as noted earlier, U.S. publications from the 1930s and 1940s forwarding the idea of documentary tended strongly toward politically committed leftist stances. This should not imply that Grierson himself, with his famous promotion of government sponsorship, was radical. It is well known that Grierson often insisted that his rationales for the British documentary movement originated not among film aestheticians or theorists, but in the political science department of the University of Chicago. In particular, he recalled discussions of Walter Lippmann's argument that the ideal of successful democracy requires informed, rational decision makers as subject-citizens, but that modern mass society provides insufficiently generalized access to the kinds of specific knowledges necessary to produce such beings on a mass scale. As Grierson informally encapsulated it in 1937:

If I am to be counted as the founder and leader of the movement, its origins certainly lay in sociological rather than aesthetic aims. Many of us after 1918 (and particularly in the United States) were impressed by the pessimism that had settled on Liberal theory. We noted the conclusion of such men as Walter Lippmann, that because the citizen, under modern conditions, could not know everything about everything all the time, democratic citizenship was therefore impossible. We set to thinking how a dramatic apprehension of the modern scene might solve the problem, and we turned to the new wide-reaching instruments of radio and cinema as necessary instruments in both the practice of government and the enjoyment of citizenship. It was no wonder, looking back on it, that we found our first sponsorship outside the trade and in a Government department, for the Empire Marketing Board had, from a governmental point of view, come to realize the same issue. Set to bring the Empire alive in contemporary terms, as a commonwealth of nations and as an international combine of industrial, commercial, and scientific forces, it, too, was finding a need for dramatic methods. For the imaginative mind of Sir Stephen Tallents, head of that department, it was a quick step to the documentary cinema.[12]

This move from the democratic citizen-subject to support of Britain's colonial structures may now seem breathtaking in its unselfconscious contradictoriness. But in addition to the effectivity of colonialist ideologies, there were specific conjunctural overdeterminations of such contradictions, such as the EMB's giving relatively free aesthetic reign to the documentarians who gathered under Grierson's management. Still, such a passage does reveal certain implications of the vision forwarded by Grierson's early formulations, of a liberal social harmony based on the diffusion of social knowledge. The ultimate issue addressed by Grierson's discourse on the documentary film is nothing less than the fate of individual civic rationality in the face of the differentiated socioeconomic complexity of modern mass life; that is, making modernity work from his version of a liberal, Enlightenment standpoint. The operative difficulty is establishing a mutually effective, overall knowledge among a public that is subject to (and the subject of?) divisions—economic, social, regional, and so forth—that are determinants on an unprecedented scale. That is, commonality of knowledge is conceived against such divisions, as a universally harmonizing force. One can see, after all, how this fundamental Griersonian impulse may lend itself to the EMB's goal of unifying the Empire under an ideology of general human (i.e., Western) progress.

In his self-presentation, the epistemological consequences of social division motivate Grierson's turn to another aspect of modern social life, the mass media, with film conceived as its most powerful version. In this view, the value of film stems "in the last instance" not just from any purportedly unique representational capabilities—for example to show the real—but precisely from its mass character. Recall that mass distributability as well as representational characteristics are attached to indexicality. In historiography, an original document preserved from the actual past is unique, "auratic"; the critical historian must go to it, and most readers of history can at best see only facsimiles of it. But in film a negative image of a shot that documents a fragment of reality can be processed into a relatively countless number of positive images. The release print seen by audiences is a film of a film. In his seminal thoughts on mass distributability of images, this was a point of importance to Benjamin, who argues that "to ask for the 'authentic' print of a film makes no sense."[13] But if indexicality is basic to the mass production and distributability of photographic and cinematic representation, this simultaneously means that all positives might retain their ethos of contact with a real past, unlike the printed facsimile of a written historical document. For there is a relay of indexical reproduction, from actual time and space to negative, and then from negative to positive prints viewed by the audience. Thus all positives also have equal representational value or "reality status" as documents for the spectator. The mechanism underlying mass distributability of cinema has been inseparable from the possibility of documentation.

But, as the Lippmann reference indicates, Griersonianism is most basically concerned with the social utility as well as the pedagogical direction of such massively distributed documentations. This returns us to the idea of a certain artistry, craft, or professionalism as inherent in the very concept of documentary cinema. The crucial utility of film is supposed to begin from its wide distribution potential across socioeconomic and geographical lines that otherwise disrupt flows of mutual knowledge. However, the argument goes, this distributability is socially useful only when it can be appropriated in an innovative way by the right kind of sociocultural agency. This agency is a grouping with which Grierson clearly identifies, namely a knowledgeable elite motivated by the polis rather than the dollar. Grierson seems to believe that an overriding social and civic virtue can be grasped and manifested by an educated, liberal elite seeking the social good. Implicitly, such an elite must first of all have access to an encompassing knowledge usually obstructed by specific class and socioeconomic position.

In this respect, Grierson's responsible documentary filmmaker looks much like the "relatively unattached intellectual" associated with the "free-floating intelligentsia" as conceived by Karl Mannheim at about the same time Grierson was formalizing his concept of documentary. As I already noted in chapter 3, for Mannheim this kind of intellectual represents an ideal of secure historiographic positionality. Here we see possible political implications. Bearer of generalized knowledge and hence the secret of harmonious social rationality, the intellectual must find social and institutional means to make that knowledge effective. In Grierson the virtuous filmmaker fulfills a duty to educate, to transmit such knowledge to the modern, divided mass, for whom it is otherwise inaccessible. In the end, the Griersonian conceptualization of documentary film is a theory about the function and duties of elites with respect to the mass of the population, not just as political leaders but as "educators" who, among other things, are urged to work as productive agents of the media. We have returned to one of the semantic origins of documentary, teaching or warning.[14]

The references to contemporaries such as Benjamin, Lippmann, and Mannheim indicate that even in his own time, Grierson's social concerns were not unique. Rather, he can be treated as part of a wave of major intellectuals, non-Marxist as well as Marxist, in the first half of the twentieth

century who sought to register the emergence of the masses on conceptions of society, culture, and politics. For this wave, issues often turn on
specifying the possible political and cultural relations between intellectuals and masses as separate social strata (often separated by the very capacity to theorize the masses). Just in the West, in addition to Benjamin,
Mannheim, and Lippmann, such diverse names as Max Weber, Lukács,
Adorno, and Gramsci begin to indicate the centrality of this problem and
the range of approaches to it. Indicatively, most of these theorists were
concerned with conceptualizing history, which since the mid-nineteenth
century had designated a privileged mode of knowing and by the early
twentieth was a key site of epistemological problematization. But furthermore, their work remains an important touchstone in current debates,
though the implications of that continuity around issues of historicity are
sometimes obscured by the various theoretical rhetorics of rupture that
have culminated in some widespread notions of the postmodern.

For example, it would be interesting to compare certain of
Grierson's views to those of Antonio Gramsci, a thinker roughly contemporary with him who had formative impact for discussions in cultural
studies and in postcolonial theory. Gramsci was also concerned with conceiving of intellectual as well as technical elites in relation to modern
social divisions. In certain respects, the Griersonian educator fills a
slot analogous to that of the intellectual in Gramsci's writings. But in
Gramsci's view of modern history, the activities of intellectuals respond to
and stand for the interests of specific social groupings struggling to maintain or attain hegemonic status. For Griersonian liberalism, the formulations of his favored types of intellectuals stand, in classic ideological
manner, for the ultimate coherence of the social system and the interest of
the universal. Documentary cinema appears as a conscious response to
modernized mass society, one of whose defining components is, of course,
what are now simply called "the media." Grierson fastens on the idea that
the appearance of such a society has engendered the reorganization of
modes of hierarchizing and distributing knowledge to the extent that key
sociopolitical forms or aspirations, such as "democracy," are endangered
unless they find previously unforeseen kinds of reinforcement.

More oppositional conceptions could align the intellectual with more particular sociopolitical groupings. Within cultural theory, a view of social division and contradictions not predicated on the goal of an over-all harmony—such as a Gramscian approach promoted by members of the Birmingham wing of the cultural studies movement—would involve revision of the trickle-down theory of social knowledge implicit in Grierson, Lippmann, and Mannheim. Within media production, this would enable appropriation of aspects of Griersonianism by filmmakers committed to other kinds of politics. For Willemen is correct in pointing out that one major tendency in the historical appropriation of the term *documentary film* has been by oppositional filmmakers and even resistance groups. And in general, all of this indicates how the constellation Grierson designated after 1926 with the term *documentary film*—encompassing not only mechanically indexical signification and constructions of the real, but also mass distributability and the relationships of social strata who produce such representations to social order and the general population—pertains directly to questions central to late twentieth-century debates.[15]

Theories of the postmodern may in fact seem even more critically pertinent to Griersonian concerns, in that they often focus on mass-mediated culture and also emphasize a general breakup of Enlightenment-oriented modes of organizing, producing, and distributing knowledge. In such arguments, the concept of postmodernity declares not just the failure, but the misapprehension that is necessarily at work in the Griersonian project, however modified. Perhaps the most extreme and therefore clarifying of the initiating arguments in this respect are those of Jean Baudrillard. I will move toward a conclusion by a somewhat more sustained consideration of where the documentary seems to fit in Baudrillard's account of contemporary culture. This will be to ask about the state of the concepts of document and documentary today, for Baudrillard seems to address the central conceptual nodes of the classical documentary tradition in all of its Griersonian tenets: the indexical nature of media representation, the consequences of mass distributability, and the relation of intellectuals and the masses.

Baudrillard leads a wing of postmodern theory that announces the contemporary dissolution of representation into simulation. Simulation implicates the reading of signs of reality with an inevitable knowledge of both their arbitrariness and the impossibility of experiencing the real outside of the constructedness of the sign-model. With references to Benjamin, Baudrillard seems to attribute this to a quantum increase in the mass distribution of signification generated by mass society, based both in the presence of the new reproductive media initiated in later modernity and the postmodern spread of the universal duplicability of signs through development of worldwide media communications. In a universe of constructed simulations, where all representations are only copies of other signs, there is no imposable standard for judging the epistemological adequacy of sign to object, so Baudrillard declares the end of epistemology based on a subject-object relation, even as mediated through signification.

By the early 1980s Baudrillard had linked the mass distributability of representations of the real to the functioning of elites, a concern that, as we have seen, was well known in earlier twentieth-century sociocultural theory. But Baudrillard focuses on the self-serving nature of intellectuals' conceptions of contact between themselves and the mass. Intellectuals are said to construct the mass in order to have something to direct information toward, as an addressee that can be moved to the end of promoting the good (liberal or revolutionary) society. Any such version of the mass, whether as the potential site of social harmony or revolution, becomes a fantasmatic social unity and directionality, because it now stands revealed as a product of the delusory self-identifications of the intellectuals. This critique can justifiably be applied to the Griersonian educator, who appropriates the distributability of cinema in order to reach the masses with his or her own enlightened perspective, which surpasses the limitations of social division.

Whatever one's reading of Baudrillard, he is suggestive in treating "the masses" in modernity as an object of desire for the intellectuals, with the latter conceived as a sociocultural stratum that produces formalized social, political, and theoretical conceptions. For Baudrillard, this is most clearly revealed in the postmodern period, when the mass is explicitly manifested as simulation, as in demographic statistical models, but is not referentially representable. Notoriously, Baudrillard sketches a picture of a general population that absorbs and recycles "information" aimed at it and/or about it, but that has no consequent determinable direction and effect except in the models and dreams of intellectuals. Any "truths" of the mass are now manifested only in the modes of enunciating it. Hence, the postmodern end of epistemology is also "the end of the social," according to Baudrillard. Or more precisely, it is the end of the relation between the political and the social as conceived by intellectuals since the Renaissance. As the proliferation of mass-distributed signs normalize simulation, significations of the real become excessive to the ambitions of the deluded elites and intellectuals seeking to constitute and thus direct the mass via constructions of the real. So in this situation, perhaps the best thing that can be said is that the gigantic distribution of mass mediated signs that characterizes the postmodern finds a directionless mass as brute resistance to the unity of social and political, including the purport of such elites.[16]

Baudrillard's claims about the status of representation are thus intimately connected to his critique of ideas that knowledge, as a possession of intellectuals, can interrogate power and direct history. Signification is now encountered as a "massive" universe of reality-effects that can always already be known as such; they are comprehended less like separable representations of the real and more like explicit models that are inextricable from any experience of the real. They never come from or fully find their subjects, for determining origins, goals, or referents can never be fully attached to them, and they therefore convince and move none. Nevertheless, according to Baudrillard, social order requires the real to provide grounds for truth, falsity, rational distinction, and equivalence on which power depends. In an ironic inversion, power must compulsively derive its reality from the simulated model but still continue to claim the model is only secondary to the real, in order to establish at least some possibility of their correspondence that demonstrates the sign can possess a referentiality and so be judged as true or false. As a result, social order, from its need for real outside signification, compulsively propagates simulation, a hyperreal.[17]

What does this view imply for the contemporary status of document and documentary, whose course has been so intertwined with that of historiography? In a universe of simulation, there can be no place for the kinds of relations of intellectuals and politics envisioned even by a Gramsci, much less a Grierson, for there can be no history in the modern sense. Modern historicity demands reference to a real outside signification, a preexistent spatiotemporal ("historical") specificity; but in postmodernity the unending duplicability of any one of the many signs of the real, which enables the mass distribution of that sign, undercuts its claims to a unique representability. By extension, the document, which had been understood since the eighteenth century as binding and often auratic, must lose its force. It is therefore no surprise if the implication of this position is that the claims of media documentary are definitively wrongheaded in the age of simulation.

There is a point in *Simulations* where Baudrillard, who often argues by example, embarks on a discussion of *An American Family* (Craig Gilbert, 1973). This film, which was shown on television in twelve parts, was arguably an attempt at an "ultimate" cinema verité documentary. In fact, it might be treated as aspiring to the status of Danto's Ideal Chronicle. With its use of the lightweight equipment associated with cinema verité, the film was planned as an unprecedented documentary observation of the everyday life of one family over an extended period of time. Instead, the equipment witnessed the dissolution of a family unit, and includes a famous scene where the wife, Pat Loud, tells her husband, Bill, on camera that she wants a divorce.

Baudrillard recalls the ensuing public debate over whether the breakup of the Louds' marriage was a result of the seemingly incessant presence of a working crew and camera over several months of their lives. Remarking on the impossibility of arguing that the film is simply a record of a preexisting real, Baudrillard aligns it with the hyperreal, since it embodies a referentiality whose truth is unimaginable without its means of sign-production. Within his argument the film becomes a stick with which to beat a series of theories that allegedly propose the experience of an organizing gaze as exterior to its objects, including psychoanalysis and even Foucault (the panopticon in *Discipline and Punish*). Such theories are said to postulate an implicated and/or empowered subject of vision seeking truth exterior to itself, so all fall to the postmodern confusion of the medium with the real it depicts exemplified by the case of *An American Family*. As the sign-referent distinction is supposedly collapsed by cinema verité, so is that between the filmmaker as subject and the Louds as object. Thus, the fate of the documentary in the postmodern world becomes to unveil the irrelevancy of the pretensions of intellectuals, as exemplified by the filmmakers. This irrelevance is demonstrated by the collapse of key distinctions that define them and their work. I would add that this also applies to the pretensions of modern historiography to represent the past, which also depends on the work of the historian as skilled, professional subject. Not only are subject and object of knowledge conflated, but cause and effect, hence meaningful sequence as a property of the referent.

However, before throwing out the pretensions of the classical documentary tradition—and historiography—*tout court*, a closer inspection of this example is in order. Having admitted the utility of Baudrillard's critical attitude for understanding Grierson, I would also argue that Baudrillard rhetorically disavows the close relationship of his problematic with those of somewhat earlier thinkers. (Several of them, such as Gramsci, embody a leftism he wishes to attack.) For the paradox of this extreme postmodern rhetoric of rupture is that it must be mobilized to explain a certain continuity. To put it simply, it would appear that contemporary culture has not fewer but more significations claiming to attach to referentiality. Our concern here is the prominent persistence of documentation in media, beginning from news and informational television programming, and the documentary impulse. Baudrillard's clever resolution is to subsume all of this under the sign of the hyperreal, as he does with *An American Family*.

Yet, it is striking that the terms in which he discusses the hyperreal of documentary are themselves not new. In fact, they embody a theoretical persistence that parallels the cultural persistence of the documentary and the historical. In some ways, the discussions of the film he cites are akin to two centuries' worth of often tortured discussions in the theory of history, for they return once more to the question of historiographic perspective, standpoint, the position of the historian in history: to what extent does the writing historian's own subjectivity—conceived as social, cultural, textual, personal, or (most crucially) historical—affect the construction of the past as object? The difference is that in historiography, issues flow from the subject's absence from a past reality, and in documentary cinema from its presence. But this is only an inversion, something that may be masked by displacing agency from a personalized entity (the historian) to a technological apparatus; however, the whole problematic of the film equipment's presence as distorting, shaping, and even exploiting profilmic entities rests on a subject-object opposition that Baudrillard, with much ruptural postmodern theory, believes himself to be collapsing. This is what enables him to dismiss theories of visual representation that treat the gaze as external to its object. At best, then, he is engaged in a deconstructive erasure in which the marks of the erased persist. Nevertheless, this entire move does require the very opposition and separation he is supposedly rejecting. And more specifically, the problem in documentary cinema of the effect of the presence of the camera on the profilmic is familiar not only with respect to cinema verité, but also such variants as anthropological filmmaking. In fact, as we have seen, the idea of a shaping consciousness is well known in the aesthetic of the classical documentary tradition from its beginnings, and integrated into it. Baudrillard might well object to importing the concept of an aesthetic consciousness, but the notion of pure access to the object had never been paramount for documentary filmmaking. It appears that the public discussions of *An American Family* he invokes as revelatory occurred because it was rooted in terms that were culturally familiar rather than disturbing.

My digression on Baudrillard and the contemporary situation of the concept of documentary therefore reflects back on several points already made in this chapter. It is true that for media of mechanical and electronic reproduction, the question of the presence and effects of the apparatus cannot be disentangled from the indexical quality of a medium. In cinema, indexicality designates the presence of camera and sound recording machinery at the profilmic event, which in turn guarantees that the profilmic really did exist in the past. Now reconsider Baudrillard's account of the general debate over *An American Family*, which supposedly illustrates the contemporary confusion of traditional epistemological and representational categories. Even in his own account, this debate was never about the reality status of the filmic images and sounds. Instead it was about causality, of all things, and a very commonsensical, two-term, cause-effect relationship at that: Did the camera cause a divorce that wouldn't have happened except for the filming? That is, was the presence of the cinema apparatus and filmmakers a necessary and sufficient cause for the ensuing divorce? This is the nub not only of this particular case, but of many discourses that propose that we are now in a postmodern media environment, where experiences are always mediatized. But note that Baudrillard's problem can also be rewritten in terms of subject and object: Was the cinema apparatus/crew the subject of the object depicted, or were the Louds their own subject, which the image then properly reflects? Baudrillard has his answers—the filmmaking was the cause/subject, and this is a scandal for representation. But my view is that this answer makes little difference for his case. In fact, no matter what the answer, the status of the shot as document of a real that preexists the spectators' viewing remains in force, for otherwise the film could be received as a conventional fiction and there would have been nothing to debate. What is at stake in the debate remains, precisely, a referent.

If so, we are edging back toward familiar territory. Whether or not the truth of the question is decidable, the very terms in which Baudrillard's exemplary debate over a documentary occurs continues to hinge on the truth of the real—that is, representation rather than simulation, a historical referentiality at least as much as awareness of a constructed model. And in this regard, it is most striking that Baudrillard makes the debate center precisely on an ending: "The Louds went their separate ways, etc. Whence that insoluble controversy...."[18] This suggests that sequence—

a historiographic sequence, a succession of events in a modern, directional temporality—is the grounds on which disputes over the presence of the apparatus arise, and where the meaning of a past reality becomes susceptible to discussion. In short, the effects of a confusion of apparatus and profilmic do not necessarily inhibit faith in the preexistence of a real that can be indexed—hence documented—and also be made meaningful. For this debate turns not on the possibility of an exteriorized gaze at the real (almost always a problematic notion in the documentary film tradition), but rather explaining the sequence of such gazes.

To put it differently, a claim of historical representation does not depend on the existence of an imaginary Ideal Chronicler, but is instead implicated in the inseparability of the chronicling activity and sequenciation. Even if the work of the cinema verité apparatus is to aspire toward being something like an Ideal Chronicler, that work is sublimated into a conclusion around which spectators can organize understandings of a reality preexisting their own viewing. The debate Baudrillard invokes is about explanations and meanings that can appropriately be attributed to a past. It is about history, understood for more than 150 years as the construction of sequence whose basis is documents and that is articulated from a standpoint that seeks to claim secure positionality but may well encounter difficulties in making that claim. This is revealed in Baudrillard's own use of this example to invert expectations about causality and the location of subjects of actions, which are typical concerns of historians. Both documentary cinema and its kin, modern historiography, persist, even in Baudrillard's own discourse.

Baudrillard's extension of Benjamin does allow him to refocus the special potential of indexicality with respect to mass distributability and the relationship of elites and intellectuals to the mass. But this means he is contributing to a discussion that has been ongoing since intellectuals identified the emergence of the masses as a key component of modernity. Documentary cinema is one of the twentieth century's conceptual nodes for engaging this constellation. But this is precisely why a cinema verité film such as *An American Family* can be treated as one culminating variant on an older dream as much as a radical novelty. When Baudrillard fastens on the self-definitive stake that specialized intellectual and professional strata have in the construction of the masses and the real, one can understand his gleeful desire to argue for the increasing irrelevance of that activity. But what he consequently misses is that a film's status as a cultural object rests in great part on what makes it documentary, rather than a document.

Not only is the unending profusion of indexical significations of the real a constant fact of contemporary life (the Benjaminian point), but so also is the constant scrabbling for sequence in the face of that profusion. This can be observed even in the daily and (on CNN and its imitators) continuous television news, and even, as we have seen, in catastrophic occurrences such as the Kennedy assassination. Here we may locate a crucial sociocultural task of professional intellectuals and elites with respect to the real and the masses, one that cannot be willed away with an extremist theory of postmodern, mediatized simulation. The explanatory narrativizing of journalism, the coordinating authority of the broadcast reporter, and especially the figure of the anchorperson, testify to the continuing sociocultural importance of this task.

There is another way of putting it, in relation to the documentary cinema tradition. Film historians and theorists have sometimes written as if the main pretense of documentary cinema has been the rather naive one providing unmediated access to an ongoing profilmic event, as if the main line of the documentary cinema tradition consists in a constant attempt to convince the spectator he or she is watching the unfolding of the real, as if actuality could be reproduced through cinema. This has often allowed theorists to apply prevalent critiques of cinematic illusionism.[19] But for the generation of Griersonians who established the concept of documentary cinema as well as their successors, even including a number of cinema vérité practitioners, this is just not true. We must keep reminding ourselves that the documentary tradition has rarely supposed that the photographic/ cinematic "impression of reality" is in itself sufficient for knowledge. Knowledge is supposed to take place on the grounds of the synthetic and generalizing, thus the sequence. Grierson's "higher forms" of documentary do not flow simply from the raw presence of the film apparatus at an event, which is in itself always inadequate. Hence, his appeal to an intellectual elite, as a special kind of subject, for something more must be done than setting up chronicling machines. This elite becomes a social group with the capacity and the will to synthesize across difference, in the senses both of differing fragments of the real in the shot/document and different social sectors reachable by means of the mass distributability of the cinema.

Documentarians have rarely if ever believed in "total cinema," as perfect gaze or Ideal Chronicler; and even those who have treated it as an ideal goal probably assumed its adequacy no more than does the professional historian. From the beginning, Grierson himself invoked aesthetics, and discourses associated with the classic documentary movements of the 1930s often articulated aims on the level of manipulating representational forms. Such attention to "aesthetics" designates a specific area of interest for sociopolitically informed and concerned media specialists. Indeed, that area could just as well serve the general processes of social order that Baudrillard (often wrongly) believes embarrassed by the profusion of indexical images. They need not be embarrassing since they can occupy it as a place wherein the sequence counters dispersive threats from the massive distributability of indexicalized "realities." On the other hand, there is no epistemological reason that more divisive knowledges, self-defined as oppositional, could not emanate from that same area, and they often have.

The original negative of a shot of John F. Kennedy in a motorcade is a document of the preexistence of a certain kind of car, a certain location, a certain event. Positive prints made from this negative became indexical documents of that first document, and by this relay stand as documents of this past event for spectators of *JFK: A Time Remembered.* This same element of indexical sign production—that which gives film its force as document—is the technological basis for the mass distributability of film prized or puzzled over by so many social theorists. The two poles of reproduction of a preexistent real and distributability are thus difficult to disentangle from one another. But as such different thinkers as Grierson and Baudrillard recognize, these two poles are intricated with a third factor, the cultural and political functioning of elites. Members of such elites may be conceived as a social stratum, whether intellectual or professional, and as sociopolitically oppositional, complicit, and/or even neutral, as can be seen in social theorists such as Gramsci and Mannheim, to name only two. But the task of such social strata with respect to the poles of media reproduction is not just re-presenting the real in ways that might be culturally guaranteed by an indexical technology, but with constructing and organizing it. In film and television, this is inseparable from general meanings grounding the temporal organizing of shots as sequence.

So when Bill Ryan explained the suddenly deconventionalized jerkiness of the camera in the real at the moment of the Kennedy assassination, he was only doing his job, restoring meaning to an extreme form of document. He began the process of converting document into documentary. In doing so, he asserted his social position as synthesizer of reality against the unmediated, unorganized index. Baudrillard's polemic, considered simply as a description of contemporary culture, misses the pervasiveness, the pull of the documentary and, implicitly but consistently, avoids the sociocultural persistence of modern historiography in relation to power. Histories are still being written, and historiographic consciousness continues to appeal toward meaning in the real from the document. Postmodernist theory, analysis, and artistic practice remind us that there have been significant changes in the balance between document and sequence. But however much the fragmentary and often ephemeral experience of representation in contemporary culture is emphasized, it is not at all clear that a shift in the norm of the sequence so radical as to disrupt the fundamental structure of ordering the real on general and synthetic principles has been achieved.

The conclusion, then, is not a defense of Griersonianism, but rather a contextualization of its intellectual terrain and a recognition of the arena it marked out with the term *documentary cinema*. With a number of important differences, this arena now extends to television and video. Bill Ryan's position, function, and task remain central to conceiving of the documentary mode, its history, and its import. And the profusion of indexical signs may make the documentary mode and the historicity it embodies not less but more pertinent to understanding contemporary culture and politics.

CHAPTER 7

Toward a Radical Historicity: Making a Nation in Sembene's *Ceddo*

"It would be a dangerous step backwards, to revert to our traditions ... "

"That's not what I'm saying, *Joom Galle*," she interrupted. "We must achieve a synthesis ... Yes, a synthesis ... I don't mean a step backwards ... A new type of society."

There followed a brief silence.

Kad was observing them. This elderly couple amazed him. He was full of admiration for them.

"You've a most interesting theme there, Kad. You must work it out well," said the old man, his masculine vanity slightly wounded by his wife's forceful points.

—Sembene Ousmane, *The Last of the Empire*

For the Third World filmmaker, it is not a question of coming to overwhelm the people, because technical prowess is very easy, and after all, cinema, when you know it, is a very simple thing. It is a question of allowing the people to summon up their own history, to identify themselves with it. People must listen to what is in the film, and they must talk about it.

—Ousmane Sembene

Sembene, the Nation, and Historiography

Nations are made, not born. Or rather, to exist they must be made and remade, figured and refigured, constantly defining and perpetuating themselves. Classic distinctions in political and social theory differentiate nation and state. Nations are cultural, discursive fields. They are imaginary, ideal collective unities that, especially since the nineteenth-century era of nationalism, aspire to define the state. The state is an institutional site constructed as overt repository and manager of legitimated power. Nation is on the side of culture, ideological formations, civil society; state is on the side of political institutions, repressive apparatuses, political society.

Conceiving of cinema in relation to the nation is familiar enough. In the West, the notion of a national cinema has a range of uses, from delineating institutionalized subfields for scholars and teachers to providing an advertising rationale for such organizations as the American Film Institute. In third world countries, however, the question of national cinemas partakes of the ambiguities of postcolonial national identities and cultural practices. Intellectuals and artists have often not had the luxury of opting out of this issue, which so obviously exceeds merely methodological debates. Especially strong examples are provided by sub-Saharan Africa, where postcolonial states were often defined as a result of colonial histories and political configurations, with less relation to cultural and linguistic groupings and indigenous histories than other colonized areas, such as southeast Asia.

Historiography can thus become a primary concern, for the very concept of a nation presupposes a past, and both nation and state are concepts emphasized in the effective heritage of modern historical representation as it developed in the nineteenth-century West. Rooted in very different cultural contexts as well as ideological and political purposes, a number of crucial discussions and figurations of African culture and identity have been intricately tied up with reconsidering the hegemonic categories of Western historiography. The broad implication is that even a consideration of Western historiography (including, more modestly, film historiography) would do well to take into account perspectives from regions such as sub-Saharan Africa. The problem of constructing postcolonial cinemas and making films specific to African experiences and needs provides one of the best nodal points for exploring resulting issues. This chapter approaches these issues through *Ceddo* (1976), a film that deliberately sets out to reconfigure a key moment in West African history, realized by a leading narrative artist from that region, Ousmane Sembene.

Sembene's Senegal has experienced many of the ambivalences and difficulties involved in the making of postcolonial nations and states. For example, at least six indigenous languages are used within state borders. Yet, the area gained independence as Senegal, formally speaking a centralized nation-state on the colonizer's model. Sembene's film *Xala* (1974) finds it ironically appropriate that the language of official business remains French. Economics as well as the structure of international power relations have made this kind of dialectic of colonialism and liberation a central fact in the existence of such states. Hence the gravity of issues of identity and self-definition for those working in culture and ideology, as inevitable sites of contradiction, ambiguity, and struggle. Sembene's career as a self-educated, distinguished West African novelist who turned to cinema as a medium that could address a mass African audience has consistently centered on issues deriving from the heritage of colonialism and liberation, on African identity, and consequently on history. Since 1968 all his films have employed Senegalese dialects and languages, usually Wolof (the most widely used). Thus, in *Ceddo* the issue of the nation and its representation is located as a problem of history and its representation. Only in the constructions of its histories will a nation be defined. All of this also applies to the question of making a national cinema. For, after all, one of the founding facts of African film history is that cinema is a machine that, like the French language, was imported from the West.

It is worth digressing briefly to stress the situatedness and the consequent positionality of Sembene's cinematic historiography. He is one of a generation of African intellectuals, artists, and politicians who experienced—and sometimes led—the liberation of Africa from European colonial occupation and governance. Much of Africa eventually became what is now called postcolonial, and this is what we must call almost all of Sembene's work. The formation of many African states such as Senegal in the early 1960s occurred very much as the outcome of the politics of national liberation struggles. This partly explains the underlying importance of issues of collectivity framed through nationness in many of

Sembene's films. But a central issue in theories and practices of national liberation was the relationships that might be sustained between the tiny proportion of indigenous persons that, in effect, constituted an educated political and cultural elite in comparison to the large number of people constituting, in effect, indigenous masses. Whether it was a matter of rallying support for armed revolution, political mobilization, or cultural practices, on what grounds could such elites address and claim unity or partnership with large masses of Africans not so privileged? This question opens onto a terrain generated by the history of colonialism, which meant that, at least within the terms of anticolonial liberation, such elites would conceive of themselves differently from those in noncolonized regions. This self-conception would certainly not be as the kind of professional specialist we have encountered elsewhere in this book: the professional disciplinary historian, the professional entertainer/artist of a rationalized mainstream cinema, or even the Griersonian sociological expert aesthetically conveying sense and knowledge to the general population, much less Baudrillard's modern intellectual, who self-servingly pretends to speak for a definitionally unresponsive mass (which knows all is simulation anyway). Perhaps, some postcolonial theorists have suggested, it is the terrain of Gramsci's organic intellectual. At the very least, the problem of the anticolonial and postcolonial intellectual strata was one of signifying for and to masses, establishing some kind of unity with them.[1]

This chapter, an analysis and commentary on *Ceddo*, is therefore a case study of a different kind of positionality with respect to functions and configurations of historicity and cinema, and it is tied to a problem of address. *Ceddo* is exemplary in its relation of modes of representation to a historical—and historiographic—situatedness, one that is interrogating modes of knowing the past in ways that may be engaged with Western historicity, while simultaneously claiming a certain political and cultural specificity. In its construction of historiographic sequence and positionality, it makes up something I will call a radical historicity.

Ceddo as Filmic Historiography

There are two aspects of *Ceddo* that can serve as useful starting points.

First, the clarity of the film's visual style is inseparable from the directness of its editing. This is to assert that the shot-to-shot succession of camera positions and mises-en-scène generally provide immediate access to the most pertinent narrative events, but of course this is not an exhaustive description of their functioning. For example, it would be possible to analyze a rather consistent, though not exclusive, horizontal organization of movement, both within the frame and of the frame (pans). Along with the exterior location shooting and choices of shot scales and camera positions, this helps emphasize both the flatness of the ground and the spaciousness of mise-en-scène. All of these contribute to the strong sense of rural, elemental background environment that is a constant element of the film. These in turn also compose a kind of referential indicator; whatever its diegetic significance, the film indexically documents something of the Senegalese landscape.

Similarly, it would not be correct simply to say *Ceddo* diminishes the effects of cutting in its concern for narrative clarity. Aside from certain strategically surprising jumps in time and space discussed below, the film's visual organization of conversational scenes (but not only these) most often depends on a spatially analytic impulse, in which cuts into scenic space provide immediate visual delineation of speakers and interlocutors.[2] This clear access to the central narrative agents of a scene can be alternated with cutaways to peripheral spaces, as in shots of listeners not participating in central conversations, that can also serve as coverage for changes in camera position with respect to the main action.

Sometimes it seems possible to describe this with reference to mainstream practices. Indeed, principles of scene construction recognizable as virtually classical are established in the very first dialogue sequence, between Princess Dior and her Ceddo kidnapper. Their brief, angry exchange is presented in a shot/reverse shot construction, setting up an axis of action and adhering to the 180-degree rule. In a classical kind of nicety, all shots keep Dior's head in frame, but not her kidnapper's, to underline her position as the ultimately privileged political object and narrative agent. (See Figures 7.1–7.2.) Although this description will shortly be modified, so far it seems that the dialectic of colonialism and liberation

Figure 7.1

Figure 7.2

holds for Sembene's film, for at least in this scene, cinema is being used in Western ways by this African filmmaker.

A second starting point for analyzing *Ceddo* is its emphasis on collectivities. As a Senegalese filmmaker dealing with Senegalese history and nationhood in a film whose general issues are familiar in many African states, Sembene is concerned in the first instance to address spectators as members of collectives (whether African or specific Senegalese nationalities). But relatedly, as a historical film *Ceddo* embodies an attitude toward history and its representation. For Sembene, history is to be comprehended as the interplay of collective groups and forces. The film, set in an unidentified Wolof Kingdom at some indefinite time perhaps in the eighteenth or early nineteenth centuries, abstracts itself from absolute chronological precision in order to function as a microcosm of the pre-twentieth century political and cultural forces and contradictions that were the crucible of the modern Senegalese nation. Four of the most important are

1. *Black African power versus foreign power and influence.* The decision-making powers of the king and his aristocracy are at stake in the game being played by the European slave trader, the European Catholic priest, and the Arab imam. Most of the common people are Ceddo. They resist the imported influences in a traditional way, which is to kidnap a hostage—Princess Dior—against their demands to the king to restore their rights to be heard and their traditional freedom of choice.[3] The imam's goal is achieved late in the film, when he takes the position of king and puts his own disciples in positions of aristocratic power.

2. *Religious divisions within the foreigners and within the Wolof.* At the beginning of the film, the Muslim import has already defeated the Christian import among the Wolof aristocracy led by the family of the king; however, the bulk of the population is Ceddo, and the most explicit narrative issue is whether or not the entire nation will accede to Islam. In the precolonial period, the word *ceddo* designated crown slaves of special distinction whose support might be

necessary to the power of the king, but it has since taken on a range of meanings. Sembene himself emphasizes that the term, which is used in several Senegalese languages, signifies those who cling to the old ways and resist the onslaught of the foreign, especially Islam. In the film, the Ceddo are the common people, who remain true to the traditional fetish religion against the increasingly successful converting zeal of the Muslims. The recession of the traditional religion upsets the self-determining balance of indigenous African political structures, leading to a loss of institutional continuity. This is exemplified by the shift from traditional, ritualistically circum-scribed uses of violence to settle disputes by individual combat to the more pragmatic, anything-goes uses of violence ordered by the imam and justified by militant Islam. Sembene's representation of Islam as a historically foreign force and the imam as a short, dis-tinctively lighter-skinned Arab who uses tactics reminiscent of the trickster figure of African narrative should be read in relation to contemporary Senegal's being the most overwhelmingly Muslim state in Black Africa. It may have contributed to the film's being banned there.[4]

3. *Political divisions within the Wolof.* The Ceddo, having lost their old political rights and under pressure to convert, formally announce their opposition to the court and the consequent hostage-taking by planting the traditional challenge stick (the *samp*), which gives them the opportunity to articulate their grievances. Later, treasonous nobles among the Islamic Wolof desert the king. Furthermore, the anti-Islamic forces, divided by caste distinctions, cannot unite: Princess Dior holds the Ceddo in contempt as slaves until the final scenes; the fearsome warrior Saxewar is anti-Muslim but never even imagines allying with the lower-caste Ceddo; and after recanting Islam to maintain his own right of succession to the throne, Prince Madior does not seek to join the Ceddo, but instead becomes a commenting character marginal to the determining actions. Such divisions are conditions for the shift away from traditional social and cultural forms.

4. *Matrilateral succession versus patrilineal succession.* Not just the nature of power, but how it is transferred is a site where religious and political issues conjoin. This conjoining implicitly demonstrates that, as Sembene has put it, African religion is not mere animism, but "a creed which has its foundations, its laws, and its theory."[5] Patrilineal succession is foreign, imported to the court through Islam and inextricable from its own vision of power. When the king accepts it, he undermines the basis of his authority, which is Senegalese in origin and matrilateral in its rationale in that it passed to him from his mother's brother. In this sense, this change stands for the social, political, and cultural subordination of women in the colonization of Africa. But, as we will see, the film's interrogation of the symbolic and political significance of women exceeds this narrow equation. The narrative importance of the conflict between these two modes is part of a network of other elements having to do with women, ranging from the carved female figure at the head of the *samp* to the fact that the story concludes when Princess Dior shoots the imam in the genitals. Sembene has suggested that, considering the position of women in Islam, for a female to kill the imam is "more than sacrilege." He also once said that the only reason the film was banned in Senegal was the symbolic significance of the princess.[6]

The clear narrative representation of such a dynamic historical complex (not exhausted by these four levels) is itself an achievement worthy of notice. However, let us proceed here by considering a possible contradictoriness in Sembene's use of analytic editing in a film that represents history as an interplay of collective groups and forces. This issue can be understood within the history of narrative film style, so a brief digression is required.

Western cinema has its own historiographic practices, which most often depend on focalizing narrative and hence historical knowledge through the experiences and knowledge of privileged individualized characters. This is the case even when a film emphasizes supra-individual determinations, and not only in routine mainstream productions. For example, *The End of St. Petersburg* (Pudovkin, 1927) conceives of history from a class perspective, but its famous finale emotively solicits empathy with the new comprehension of a single working class woman walking through the Winter Palace and grounds that now belong to the people. At another extreme, the narrative of *The Leopard* (Visconti, 1962) proceeds with an emphasis on Prince Salina's exceptional perceptions and consciousness, so that a scene in which he expresses his reflections on why Sicily, by its very nature, necessarily resists modernization is privileged as historical explanation. Throughout film history, one finds a wide range of such strategies for aligning narrative authority with individual characters. In a historical film, whether routed through emotive empathy or analytic discourse or varying combinations of the two, the drama of attaining historiographic comprehension is then commonly anchored for the spectator in such individualized authority. This authority, this identification (if that is the best term), becomes associated in different ways with a plane of secure knowledge of history—its outcomes, its causes, its historical explanation.

This ties even such distinctive historical films to the mainstream development of analytic editing. Textually, the film-historical innovation and standardization of analytic editing in the transition from preclassical to classical cinema instituted a double move inward: enlarged shot scale signified movement into a scene, naturalized as physical closeness to objects of the mise-en-scène for such purposes as better viewpoint and hence more reliable or interesting information. But also, such spatial closeness can undergo a second transformation, or rather it has a central special case: "closeness" to characters is translated into access to psychological and moral interiority of individualized characters. The counterexample of Eisenstein indicates that analytic editing need not necessarily be tied to a concern with interior character depth or even individualized character goals. But the narrative priorities of mainstream cinema have massively instituted the link between scene analysis and individual interiority; the facial close-up becomes the signifier of motivation and/or psychology, and speech becomes allied with the face as a locus from which interior truth can come. One of the common techniques of this tendency often isolated among Western scholars is the shot/reverse shot dialogue sequence. But this binary spatial alternation, so useful in pinning editorial analysis of a scene to character face and voice, is not determining in itself; rather, it is exemplary as one standardized pattern within a larger project that makes decoding of an interiorized character goal, knowledge, psychology, and/or soul basic to the task of reading the scene. The impact of this general impulse is indicated by the fact that even the example from *The End of St. Petersburg* depends on eyeline matching, and the one from *The Leopard* depends on a more complex combination of narrative presence, eyeline matching, and authoritative speech throughout the film.

Ceddo is particularly interesting in this regard. Sembene presents its complex mix of collective historical forces using analytical editing, yet resists the institutionalized models of narrative authority and the ideologies of individualism with which this practice is historically allied. We can undoubtedly assume the filmmaker's acquaintance with such generally instituted practices. But beyond biography (the imported films he's likely to have seen in Senegal, the facts that when a young man he was a worker in France and that he studied filmmaking in the Soviet Union), as one of the first leading and self-consciously African narrative filmmakers, Sembene confronted the stylistic options instituted by film history from a fresh and distinctive position. By the time he took up filmmaking, several of his novels had already situated Sembene as an *auteur*, but of a particular type: the anticolonialist African intellectual, familiar with certain Western techniques of knowledge and/or culture, who experienced the transition to independence. Thus, the place of his work within a comparative history of cinema could only be established on the basis of his African context, within which he is also inventing something distinctive, but from his understanding of African traditions, needs, and modes of apprehension.

More specifically, we can begin examining certain unobtrusive complexities in the editing of *Ceddo* by considering them in relation to the stylized speech of individual characters, who appear as functions of historical groups and supra-individual forces. As already noted, a standard shot/reverse shot construction is employed in the first dialogue sequence of the film, thus seeming to invite the viewer to a film employing standard spatial articulations. Yet, it is not quite correct to call this a dialogue, for there is a third present, whose name is Fara (see Figure 7.1). Though for long periods Fara does not speak, the princess and the kidnapper usually address one another through Fara as intermediary, with locutions such as "Fara, tell her that. . . ." This form of address is clearly courtly and ceremonial. Mbye Baboucar Cham has carefully explained it as adhering to the Wolof communicative concept of *jottali*, or formally passing on an utterance.[7] The pervasiveness of *jottali* in *Ceddo* is one of the major instances of several traditional Senegalese social and cultural practices that the film employs or to which it makes reference. But of special interest in this early dialogue is that its utilization runs counter to the potential intimacy of the situation and the power of conventional shot/reverse shot editing to reinforce the impression of a binary relation between two interiorized individuals, for it opposes the dual space of the shot/reverse shot to the presence of a third.

Jottali is a central aspect of the very lengthy scene that follows, a meeting of the Wolof nation called by the king to investigate and decide on responses to the kidnapping of the princess. In it, the complex of forces and contradictions are laid out by spokespersons for the various groups and viewpoints, and its construction is worthy of extended analysis. Narratively, the scene proceeds as a series of debates, seemingly taking shape as a series of binary confrontations: the Ceddo elder Diogomay against the king, Prince Biram against Diogomay, Diogomay against the imam, the warrior Saxewar against Prince Madior, Madior against Biram, and so forth. This binarism of character divisions reveals a fragmentation of national interests and forces, but by the end of the scene there has emerged a unifying logic that does not, however, drive the divided representative characters to unify: the growing power of Islam and the consequently far-reaching changes occurring in indigenous culture and politics. At the level of narration, there are also factors that can be said to counter the binarism in the presentation of these conflicts. The most striking of these is, again, a third participating in the successive debates that make up the public discussion, a court noble Jaraaf. In fact, throughout the scene, he is the most constant visual and verbal presence. Jaraaf is a more active intermediary than Fara, introducing speakers, often commenting on their words, and even taking sides—all with rhetorical flourish and verbal imagery.

Jaraaf's verbal flamboyance and the fact that Fara has a *xalam* (a stringed musical instrument) makes the cultural reference for this third evident: the noted West African figure of the griot. The griot can be public storyteller, rhetorician, musician, hired praise-singer, poet. Despite an often lower-caste aura, griots traditionally function at all social levels, including noble families, and after national independence could even work for politicians and their parties. The griot is possessor of verbal and narrative expertise, a repository of the power of the word and of social memory. After moving into filmmaking, Sembene often compared himself to the griot, and indicated his desire to use the Western machine, cinema, in this traditional sociocultural function.[8]

A number of commentators have pointed to the forceful presence of the griot in *Ceddo* and emphasized that this is an overt reference to the centrality of African oral tradition, conceived as one of the most important sources of the specificity of postcolonial African film in general. Oral culture is often considered to be a most significant determinant of many aspects of Sembene's filmmaking, from character typology to narrative structure and the pictorial organization of space and especially time. Indeed, in *Ceddo*, speech is generally ceremonial and/or declamatory, and proverbs are skillfully used to punctuate already conventionalized conversations. In addition, acting and gesture are stylized and some objects are overtly symbolic, all of which underlines the fact of the diegetically immediate performance of word and sign. These and other procedures are evidence of the film's self-conscious connection with oral tradition. The imam's first official act after the victory of Islam is linguistic: in an elaborate public ceremony, he inaugurates the Ceddo into what he had previously called "the beautiful language of the Koran" by renaming each one individually after figures in the Islamic Holy Books. When Islam is victorious, then, one aspect of its triumph is the advent of the authority of the book—the imam always carries and claims authority from the Koran—over performed speech.[9]

I would add that the presence of the griot can also be read as overdetermining a historiographic project. It is not only that the griot is sometimes treated as a kind of oral alternative to the writing of the Western specialist historian. More specific to *Ceddo* is the following. If the griot, as representative of African cultural tradition, is an intermediary witness to, as well as a conveyor of, dialogue, then the appearance of the griot marks the interest of the collective in all individual speech and the definition of the individual through the collective. With respect to establishing agencies of narrative authority, the apparently standard shot/reverse shot sequence of the first dialogue scene does not isolate individuals as such because the presence of the third—*a recognizable sociocultural function*—is manifest. The practice of *jottali* announces the emphasis of the film as a whole. Even in scenes without griots, all conversations are to and for a group, sometimes implicitly and usually explicitly. In short, even during the most binary spatial articulations, there is no discussion between a pure *two* in the film. From another perspective, this necessarily requires a theatricalization of action and speech, for there is always an audience beyond the immediate speech situation. This theater has two publics: the diegetic audience within the film, which is the Wolof nation defining itself through all the speech it witnesses, and the film-going public, which, if African, is constructed as a collective in some way continuous with the first through national traditions, histories, and politics.

The breakup of individualized intimacy and interiority, signaled in the film's first dialogue by the presence of a third, is related to the film's analytic editing, which can be described in some ways as deviating from standard Western analytic *découpage* but which, from a different perspective, manifests Sembene's solution to the problem of clearly articulating spaces while maintaining the collectivization of discourses, associated by the film with African tradition. The most complex and significant scene in this respect is the general convocation of the nation just mentioned, which exemplifies some of the stylistic means by which the film sustains the presence of the collective. The succession of binary conflicts takes place in a spacious, somewhat circular enclosure delimited by the placement around a large open area of the various national factions—king and court, imam and disciples, the European slave trader and priest, and, most numerous yet directly across and thus most distant from the court, the Ceddo. Those who speak through Jaraaf to the king or who argue with each other step into the enclosure, which thus becomes a kind of arena or stage for national politics (Figure 7.3).[10]

The editing of this scene intermittently incorporates various cutaways from the binary conflicts, including brief close-ups of Ceddo and especially non-Ceddo individuals. The most significant of these might be described as reverse shots away from the arguing speakers to the king listening; these close-ups spatially isolate the king as a decisive aristocratic presence who remains silent unless announcing a question or a decisive order. (Their slight strangeness is heightened by the fact that they are a bit "off-line" according to the 180-degree logic conventionalized for much of world cinema by Hollywood dominance, but despite the early dialogue between Dior and her kidnapper, the 180-degree rule is not a consistent factor in this film.) These shots of the king thus establish something like a "reverse field" superior to whatever discourses are in play in the center of the enclosure. But when the binary conflicts occur

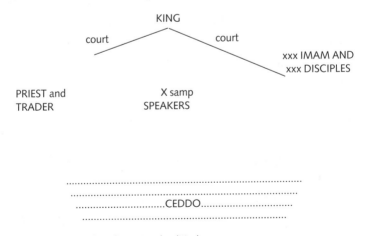

Figure 7.3 The geography of a national political arena.

in the center of the enclosure, there are no shot/reverse shots between the debaters who share center stage with Jaraaf anyway. Rather, whatever sense of dual spatial alternation exists is between the inside of the enclosure and certain positions on its border.

Throughout the scene, then, what might count as reverse shots are of the rim of the enclosure. If at first these are cuts to the king and court, as the growing power of Islam is revealed by the progression of disputes, debates become addressed to the imam, and some of the reverse shots are established between the participants in the center of the enclosure and a different point on the rim, the Islamic group. The difference is that the imam, unlike the king, engages in spoken debate with opponents inside the circle and, unlike the king, is not spatially isolated with big facial close-ups. But it turns out that it is the imam's declaration that the Koran mandates patrilineal inheritance that determines the king's ruling. The cutaway shots to Ceddo or Europeans on the rim never function like reverse shots, either through verbal address or eyelines toward them from the enclosure. Shots of the Europeans especially possess a certain ambiguity; mute, they seem powerless in this highly verbalized world. But the patient, ever-ready presence of the slave trader turns out to be a significant plot element. In sum, the spatial construction of the scene emphasizes the play of power among addressers, addressees, and bystanding witnesses to the verbal and symbolic actions inside the enclosure. As they reflect relations of diegetic authority, strengths, and weaknesses, the shifting constructions that result not only reflect relations of diegetic authority and strengths, but also mark the area of the reverse shot and audiences as a place of potential national power or exploitation.

Thus, as an exercise in avoiding reverse shot constructions within the enclosure, the scene reserves the potential power of reverse fields for a diegetic audience.[11] A review of some of the spatial articulations in successive segments of this scene illustrates the theatricalizing strategy, already emphasized by the stylized language and acting, that the editorial analysis of scenic space augments. For example the debate between Saxewar and Madior is theatricalized through the camera's being positioned in the reverse field of the court, which motivates the debaters'

Figure 7.4

sometimes playing directly to the camera (Figure 7.4). Then, when the next and key debate between Biram and Madior introduces the linkages between political power, religion, and matrilateral succession, the two disputants and the griot Jaraaf are triangularly blocked in the center of the circle. The 180-degree rule becomes irrelevant as the film cuts to all sides of the triangle, generally centering frontally whichever of the three is speaking, to theatricalize the scene further (Figures 7.5–7.7). This motivates the next binary debate witnessed by the nation, between Madior and the imam. Spatially, this discussion is presented in part by setups that do reverse fields, though not in the repetitive binary alternation from one side of an axis of action so familiar from mainstream Western cinema, not without interruption from a cutaway, and with variation in the shot scale of Madior. In another binary setup, Madior appeals to the king, who breaks his silence to decide in favor of the imam. Next, when Saxewar and the imam exchange threats, there is a brief alternation of setups, which does look very much like a standard shot/reverse shot, since camera placement remains on one side of an axis of action; however, this mechanism is by now just one option among many for filming such confrontations.

Figure 7.5

Figure 7.6

The import of this stylistic analysis might be claims for a denormalization of historically dominant Western editing patterns. Given the international experience and sophistication of Sembene (typical of the strata of postcolonial African writers and filmmakers) such an approach might seem reasonable. But the denormalization revealed here is not just defamiliarizing in a purely formalistic sense, nor is it "deconstructive" à la Godard, whereby a dominant aspect of reading the film would at some point be an explicit awareness of stylistic self-reflection and critique as such. What deserves special emphasis about *Ceddo* is how functional Sembene's strategies are in narrative and historiographic terms. The editing of this scene, for example, causes no problems in the viewer's spatial orientation or access to story events. Rather, it operates in concert with a narrative and historical logic that does not induce concern with the interiority of individual narrative agents, but insists on their collectivization. This collectivization is established by a theatricalization of discourse that is associated with strong markers of African tradition and that insists on the importance of address to the nation as African. That is, it is inseparable from a positionality on history.

Figure 7.7

Presenting the Past

In the film as a whole, such limits on individualized interiorization have their most important payoff for historiographic positionality precisely at moments when the film seems, finally, to cue us most unavoidably to read the image as the subjectivity of individual characters. At one point, when the European priest sees Prince Madior observing his church, the priest approaches Madior, looks up apparently to the heavens, and in a heavily marked false eyeline match, we dissolve to a shot straight up at the interior of a cathedral dome painted in a Christian iconography of angelic ascent in which all the figures are Blacks. Along with the music (part of a choral mass sung in African harmonies and to African percussion and rhythm), this announces the extended sequence that follows. It is an outdoor, twentieth-century African Christian communion service, presented in part by means of some seemingly cinema verité footage. In addition to many extras, all major characters of the film—Muslims and traditionalists—participate as Christians, with Prince Madior presiding as a bishop and the priest appearing as an honored corpse. We then return to the village and the shot of the priest that opened the communion sequence.

Conventional codes of editing and punctuation at the beginning and end of this sequence signify we are seeing something of the priest's subjectivity. That is, it appears to objectify his motivation and goals, the future of Africa for which he works, a Christian Senegal—in short, the priest's dream in the sense of the dream of his life. Yet, the sequence cannot be exhausted by this reading, partly because of the reality-effects. The twentieth-century detail—the clothing, the music—is too correct; how could the priest know how people would dress and sing in the twentieth century? We are seeing a version of the priest's "dream" that exceeds his knowledge and therefore psychological motivation in his interiority. Thus, the surprise of this sequence is not only formal, inasmuch as there had been no warning or preparation for a break in the film's straightforward narrative succession of story events. It is also that the scene gives us a kind of historically shocking *false flash-forward*, directed at a spectator who knows that modern Senegal is overwhelmingly Muslim and therefore recognizes the falsity of a scene depicting the contemporary triumph of Christianity.

This is a variant of Senegalese history that did not happen, a historical option lost.

This striking scene crystallizes a project of the film as a whole with respect to historicity. Narrative cinema normally converts the shot as indexical document into the recording of a performed diegesis; and, with varying degrees of intensity and elaboration, the historical film further converts the diegesis into a referential field, hence a quasi-document—that is, a "that's what it looked like," a reconstruction or restoration of something presumed to be real.[12] But the priest's dream in *Ceddo* interferes with the relations of pastness and present assumed in this process. Of course the sudden appearance of a present-oriented, twentieth-century mise-en-scène with attendant reality-effects sharply distinguishes itself from the diegetic reconstruction of pastness in the rest of the film. But on another crucial level, this opposition between past and present invades the film image itself, as in its cinema verité style.

Cinema verité style establishes its status as transmitter of the real by making indexicality signify itself. Taken altogether, its identifying markers (such as shaky camera, failures to anticipate the next center of interest, and so forth) emphasize the presentness of the camera to the profilmic at the moment of filming; hence, it refers itself back to an ideal of authentic indexicality and preservation of the event, even if practice can never completely measure up to it. But once this ideal is directly invoked with respect to film as document, then performance, diegesis, and historical restoration must come into question. It is impossible to make a cinema verité documentary of, say, late-eighteenth century Senegambia. In *Ceddo*, then, if the force of the narrative event of the priest's dream is that of a kind of counterfactual conditional, it takes the film straight to the basic claims of historical representation. The break between past and present that defines the founding need for historiography is suddenly held up for inspection. Historiographic positionality is announced as a problem and comes into play.

The priest's anticipatory pseudo-dream of a history that did not happen is answered by another, that of Princess Dior. As her Ceddo kidnapper is killed, we dissolve from a close-up of Dior to shots of her offering water to the kidnapper returning to a village home, in a traditional regional gesture of respect and love. Again, an interiorized reading is incomplete. This seemingly internalized vision does represent Dior's subjectivity, her changed attitude toward the Ceddo; however, the earlier false flash-forward—with its unique commingling of registers of document and documentary, preservation and restoration, indexicality and performance, past and present—suggests a simultaneous reading: from a position in the present, we know that this is another eventuality that did not occur historically, mutual respect between Wolof social strata that have been divided by caste, something that could have been a basis for staving off Islam in the name of indigenous tradition.

This "counterfactual" bears directly on the historiographic wish fulfillment of the finale, another historical falsity. This one, however, is not marked as dream or individual subjectivity, and its status is instead left ambivalent. The princess, as Wolof nobility and bearer of matrilateral succession, and as holder of a name similar to that of a famous nineteenth-century Senegalese anti-colonial leader (Lat-Dior), kills the imam while the Ceddo place their bodies in front of Muslim rifles. This enacts a peculiar sort of retrospective utopianism. In the microcosmic terms of the film, the traditional fetish religion defeats Islam. Yet, Senegal is today overwhelmingly Islamic and the narrative ends uneasily, with a freeze-frame centered on Dior looking directly at the camera in a mise-en-scène filled with Muslim disciples (Figure 7.8). *Ceddo*'s narrative resolution is achieved with another historical option defeated in Senegalese history—an actualized political and military alliance of the old nobility and the Ceddo to preserve indigenous ways.[13]

In fact, the inappropriate reality-effects and style of the priest's "dream" is only the most startling example of something that informs the film as a whole, namely strategies that invite spectators toward a consciously present-oriented consideration of options and consequences, even as they observe this enactment of the past. These can be overt references (for example, the new Muslim names given all the Ceddo by the imam—including Ousmane—are common in Senegal today) or subtle deviations from the normal expectations for historical cinema. Perhaps the most praised example is the film's music. Title music and nondiegetic background music are made up of contemporary African-oriented jazz by Manu Dibango. But aspects of this twentieth-century mode are directly based on "authentic music created by a griot more than a hundred years ago";[14] this is indicated early in the film when the nondiegetic music takes up a theme being played diegetically by Fara, the griot for the Ceddo. What is most forceful here is not a pure authenticity of period music from the Senegambian region used as movie music, for the jazz style reshapes even such themes mined from the past into a late twentieth-century mode. This alone is a signal of a historiography in the process of being written for current purposes. But more subtly, it is also as if the non-diegetic music of the film acts as a reminder of a historical sequence within music itself, from traditional Africa to modern jazz. The link in this musical history is the African-American gospel song, "I'll Make It Home Some Day," used as nondiegetic music correlated with narratively digressive sequences of slaves bought by the White slave trader. This song typifies a music produced neither in the geographical area, nor at the historical moment being depicted, but rather developed by these slaves and

Figure 7.8

their descendants when they reach the New World. Within music history, this gospel song mediates between indigenous African music and Dibango's jazz. But within the film's narration of national history, it manifests awareness of another historical consequence to the decisions being made in the narrative: the African diaspora.

Such tactics promote a certain fluidity of historical temporality in apprehending *Ceddo*, and in doing so they join the collective positionality of the film to an active historiographic one. If the film's representation of history is premised on the significance of collective forces, ultimately history can only be understood as a set of options in the play of those forces as they lead to differing futures including the present. Historical comprehension occurs in consideration of futures that did not occur, as opposed to those that did. Historiographically, the result is to loosen the inevitability of "this happened" or "this happened because," the third-person past and causal theses so familiar from classical narrative and historical representation. This has repercussions at the level of historical knowledge defined as explanation, for even as the film microcosmically explains how things happened, it does this by confronting the spectator with what did not happen, what choices were and were not made.

The culmination of this operation is a carefully constructed open-endedness reinforced by the uneasiness of the film's final shot, the freeze frame that isolates Dior from her new Ceddo allies as she stares at the camera. That Dior does not explain her action verbally leaves questions open, but it might be argued that this simply continues to pull the film away from individualized motivations, thus encouraging spectators to place her action within the overall sociopolitical framework of events. But this scene, which has a forcefully climactic impact, actually leaves much unsettled. First, the militant Muslim faction remains strong, so peaceful coexistence between religions demanded by the Ceddo is by no means secure (and, again, this is reinforced by the fact that Senegal is today predominantly Muslim). Second, the prerogatives of the White slave trader have never been questioned. Third, with both king and imam dead, the political problem has not been solved. Or rather, the solution poses its own questions.

Whatever modicum of satisfying resolution is provided has to do with bridging the gulf that has separated the aristocratic anti-Islamic forces from the Ceddo. Yet, the very tradition being defended cannot encompass that resolution, for it makes Dior the leader of the traditionalist forces. In that case, as a female descendant, she would represent a break with traditional practice by which the king's nephew should inherit the throne. It is important to emphasize that there is virtually no preparation for the idea that Dior should govern, which is to some degree promoted by the finale. Even discussions among the Ceddo never include women; in fact, Dior is the only woman who speaks in the entire film. Yet, male leaders—shrewd Madior, strong Saxewar, and admirable Diogomay—are all unable to conceive of the necessary conditions for a firm resistance on the part of tradition, which would be to place it in time, to temporalize it by admitting change into it.

As is typical in Sembene's written and cinematic corpus, ultimate success for indigenous African self-interest and resistance encounters a crucial nontraditional imperative: rethinking the sociocultural place of African women. Yet, if the logic of the strong action concluding the narrative is Dior's assumption of national leadership, contradictions around that solution remain outstanding. Therefore, while the story comes to a definite conclusion, the narrative world is not harmonized by the completed knowledge usual in a formally totalized narrative, nor, consequently, a completed historical sequence. This returns us to the present-oriented play on audience knowledge exploited by the film. For the solution offered by the film has not been historically effective. (Some of Sembene's films, especially *Mandabi* [1968] and *Xala*, include satiric probes of the dynamics of polygamy in the context of a modernizing, contemporary Senegal.) In this sense, the narrative solution in Ceddo represents another lost historical option and a challenge to the audience and its positionality.

African Histories

From another perspective, all of this indicates that *Ceddo* is not only a distinctive formulation of representative moments in a national history, but an experiment in modes of constructing historicity. While aspects of

Ceddo, such as the use of indigenous language, the foregrounding of certain regional cultural practices, the status of Islam, and so forth, are more or less anchored in Senegalese history and its researchable details, Sembene himself insists that the film is intended to stimulate a historical consciousness in all African ethnic groups.[15] In that case, the film's specific references to cultural and historical aspects of the Senegambian region outrun that specificity in order to suggest a set of relatively common issues that structure many African histories. At this level, for instance, even the decision to make the film in the Wolof language is a strategy of exemplification; instead of an exclusively Senegalese purport, it serves to emphasize the ubiquitous sub-Saharan fact of multilingualism, which seems, from the perspective of Western colonialism, to be a multiplicity of localized languages. This is all to suggest that a decisive context for the film is the most generalized problematic of African history.

Pervasive constructions of African history have explicitly or implicitly invoked an opposition between tradition and modernity that has become all too familiar. V. Y. Mudimbe has summarized some of the epistemic determinations, connotations, and consequences of this fundamental paradigm. It is linked to a number of others, such as agrarian, customary communities versus urbanized, industrial societies; subsistence economies versus highly productive economies; underdevelopment versus (over)development; and oral cultures versus written/print cultures. Historically, such paradigms are embedded in an imperialist object-subject, other-self dialectic with wide epistemological and ideological resonance. For example, one of the central discursive strains in definitions of Africa is classical anthropology, whose development coincided with the colonial division of the continent and which, like colonialist ideologies, defines itself by positing its object as other to "civilization." This problematic is a trap that catches concepts of African identity and nation in the opposition between two static, monolithic, mutually exclusive terms. But this opposition is not only a synchronic binary, for it implies a directional temporality and the sequencing drive of modern Western historicity. When this overriding sequence infiltrates historiography, the only movement possible to validate is along a unidirectional path out from traditional forms of culture and social organization toward modern, written cultures, an inescapable journey from the tribal nation to the centralized nation-state. The binary thus presents itself as the overriding narrative sequenciation of modernization or "development," and has its place in economics, social science, and policy formation.[16]

Nevertheless, the heritage of the tradition-modernity paradigm can sometimes seem ambivalent. While it continues to sustain regressive significations of Africa as Other, it has also supported influential attempts to formulate a distinctive African identity and development. One famous and controversial example is the theory of Negritude. The term was originally introduced by a group of Francophone Black poets and intellectuals. A leading figure in its theorization was Léopold Senghor, philosopher, poet, and founding president of Senegal, who was still in office when *Ceddo* was made and banned. Among other things, his version of the theory identifies contributions to human culture and consciousness lacking in White experience, but essential to Black experience. Not only the characteristics attributed to a specifically Black subjectivity, but the essentialism of the concept have led to important debates, polemics, and discussions.[17] Already by 1952 Frantz Fanon, another Black intellectual familiar with current French thought, asserted that "what is often called the black soul is a white man's artifact." He set out the terms of the problem by maintaining the search for position yet calling the project of an ontology of Negritude into question:

> In the *Weltanschauung* of a colonized people there is an impurity, a flaw that outlaws any ontological explanation. Someone may object that this is the case with every individual, but such an objection merely conceals a basic problem. Ontology—once it is finally admitted as leaving existence by the wayside—does not permit us to understand the being of the black man. For not only must the black man be black; he must be black in relation to the white man. Some critics will take it on themselves to remind us that this proposition has a converse. I say that this is false. The black man has no ontological resistance in the eyes of the white man. Overnight the Negro has been given two frames of reference within which he has had to place

himself. His metaphysics or, less pretentiously, his customs and the sources on which they were based, were wiped out because they were in conflict with a civilization that he did not know and that imposed itself on him.[18]

Mudimbe's overview of knowledges of Africa exemplifies a recent conception of this problem. Familiar with Foucauldian and poststructuralist thought, he argues that conceptions of African identity should be based less on delimiting a primordial African object of study or an essential African Being than on establishing an intermediary, ambiguous epistemological attitude that nevertheless recognizes the links between power and claims of knowledge. Yet the issue of identity remains politically and ideologically unavoidable. For Mudimbe, even an "ideology of otherness" (i.e., Negritude) can serve as an important historical counter to the primitivist anthropological heritage by constituting a "historical legend" providing a network of metaphors and concepts acceptable to African intellectuals and artists. Yet it is also subject to the kinds of critique mounted by those such as Fanon. Mudimbe suggests that one good definition of underdevelopment is marginality, conceived as a state of affairs between the two extremes of the paradigmatic opposition of traditional and modern. However, if African identities must be found here, the question becomes whether the instabilities of this discursive position can be turned to advantage.[19]

The forms in which historical accounts are usually presented presume identities—clearly identifiable historical agents, whether conceived individually or collectively. Making African constructions of identity both necessary and ambiguous thus has historiographic implications. This is first because if African identities necessarily reflect intermediary positions between the extremes of the various tradition-modernity oppositions, this means that they still assume that basic opposition and hence the Western historiographic paradigm. On the other hand, they would ultimately question the dialectic of self and other that grounds the oppositions in Western discourse. Although concerned with theoretical constructions of Africa, Mudimbe's formulation is reminiscent of Fanon's opposition to ontology in that it leads to a placement of African identities as always in transition, in time, in history. Thus, while the strategic bind around identity and nation has long been a prominent burden of Black African intellectuals and artists, it can also drive them politically and practically to the most searching confrontation with the ideologies of self that, from African perspectives, ground the massive historiographic reification by which the Western episteme has defined and positioned their practices and nations.[20]

As a construction of historicity by one of the most renowned Black African artists of the generation that experienced the transition to post-colonial status, *Ceddo* can be situated in this problematic. In *Ceddo* history appears as perpetual transition, as always in process, and consequently so are nation and identity. History comprehended as an ongoing play of collective forces presenting options for different histories and different futures is in opposition to history as the blocked or progressive path so persistently implanted—especially with respect to Africa—in Western philosophy, anthropology, and ideology. The active positionality of the film as described above certainly does not spring from a rejection of narrative as a historiographic form, but it is intricated with limitations on the unidirectionality and inevitability of a closed narrative enchainment or sequenciation associated not just with Western commercial cinema, but with Western historiographic knowledge.

Economically and culturally crucial as the opposition between the traditional and the modern is both for Africa's history and its recent politics, it has been a privileged concern of African cinema in general and *Ceddo* in particular. But Sembene counters the reification of these two extremes that anchor the paradigm's power as ideology. It is sometimes noted that *Ceddo* functions in part as an archeology, re-presenting and foregrounding precolonial political practices as well as social functions such as *jottali* and the griot. However, while Sembene's counterhistory is unthinkable without the researched recovery of repressed or denigrated African practices and events, it also refigures the tradition-modernity opposition that has been the basis for conceptions of Africa since the modern West defined the study of history in its own self-image.

More specifically, the film's historicity accepts the opposition of the old and the new, the indigenous and the foreign, but determines neither as static or monolithic. For example, not only are nonindigenous forces split into European/Christian and Arab/Muslim factions, but also the weakness of the Europeans, who never speak, pushes the anticolonialism struggle back in time. Although Senegal ultimately obtained independence as a state from France, the setting and subject matter of *Ceddo* make the non-European force of Islam an invader. To set the film at a transitional historical moment during which, microcosmically, a non-European foreign force is about to decimate indigenous African culture and politics, may have special resonance in the context of Senegalese history. However, it also emphasizes the permanent presence of transition, invasion, and conflict in African history. The encounter with the new and foreign was not a historically novel experience during the onslaught of European colonialism, but rather has been a complex historical constant. The radically critical implications of this perspective should not be underestimated, for it can lead even to problematizing the origins of non-European values most dear to some Africans, such as the status of Islamic clerics in Senegal. The militant imam with unquestioning disciples in *Ceddo* must call up some echoes of the Sufi brotherhoods that have been so important in West Africa and Senegal, and some of them can even claim a heritage of resisting French colonialism.

Furthermore, what the film defines as indigenous tradition is also split into factions and is by no means unambiguous. We have already seen the paradoxical inability of tradition to triumph without radical revision with respect to its placement of women. In addition, consider the film's most striking sign of tradition, the griot. The magnificently dressed Jaraaf is a court schemer, and ultimately a traitor not only to African tradition, but to the king, who honors him with his position. On the other hand, Fara, with his poor clothes and musical instrument, is allied with the people's travails. Thus, the presence of the griot in itself does not signify a primordial authenticity that is automatically beneficial. While the film's sympathies are clearly with the Ceddo, the indigenous tradition they defend is not uniformly and necessarily a virtuous lost world. The agencies of "tradition" are just as subject to the play of collective interests and

power as other agencies in the film. Indeed, insufficiencies within tradition are indicated by the fact that Sembene, who has sometimes discussed
his own cinema as an attempt to construct a modern equivalent of the
griot, refuses the socially integrative, harmonious resolutions of traditional African storytelling and in *Ceddo* and other works instead provides
endings with socially critical implications.[21]

Finally, consider the film's emphasis on the one major division
within the Wolof not explicitly and articulately explained in this highly
verbalized film: slavery. Slavery pervades all corners of the social world
of *Ceddo*, and some of its historical consequences are emphasized by the
African-American gospel song from another future, a future that—as
opposed to the priest's dream or the possibility implied in the film's ending—the audience knows did indeed occur. In *Ceddo*, slavery has two
determining contexts, one foreign and one indigenous. First, based on a
non-African market for slaves, the White trader promotes a nascent
European exchange economy, but one whose medium is Black bodies,
which are used as currency to buy his goods ranging from wine to rifles.
Yet if the worst of slavery is represented as the delivery of slaves to the
White, there is an insidious vulnerability to these methods of exchange
among even the most admirable of the Black figures.

For the second context of slavery is its complete naturalization
within Wolof society. Its presence never provokes formal discussion as
does, say, the choice between matrilateral and patrilineal inheritance. Yet
it is what fragments the forces defending tradition, making them tactically
vulnerable. An outraged Dior notes in the first conversation with her
captor that the Ceddo are slaves, and her final act of killing the imam is
possible only after she acquires new respect for these crown slaves and
thus overcomes the caste division that separates her from them. But this
climax—which, as we have seen, partakes of a historical vision that did not
happen—is the only moment in the film when such a social transformation becomes conceivable. Contempt or simple disregard for slaves is also
enacted by the other traditionalist aristocrats, Madior and Saxewar. Even
the majority of the Ceddo, finally driven to plan a fruitless rebellion, can
only imagine obtaining guns by reluctantly trading their own children to

the White slaver. A film knowingly influenced by oral cultural traditions, *Ceddo* has its narrative agents speak about many of the problems and options confronting them, often with eloquence and always with clarity; even the political option of having a woman ruler is briefly discussed in order to be dismissed by courtiers. Yet, Black-over-Black slavery and the trade of Black slaves to the White is a central element of the social world, whose validity remains unquestioned and unnoted by any character. This is a condemnation of a massive failure of traditional Africa to take care of its own. Here is a historical aspect of tradition that *needed* contradiction and change.[22]

A Radical Historicity

As an abstract historiographic structure, the relation between tradition and modernity can be conceived as an unchanging antinomy, in which case modernity becomes absolutely unavailable to traditional cultures ("primitive mentalities"), and the latter become absolutely other to the former. Alternatively, this relation can be conceived as a quasi-historical one, insofar as a mythic supernarrative of progressive ("modernization") or regressive passage, gradual or not, from one state of being to another is envisaged. Or rather, we can say that this alternative is historiographic, but not *radically* historical, because the two antipodes of the process retain atemporal identities; as beginning and end points of a temporal process, they are themselves static, outside of time, and therefore define the limits of modern historicity itself. This suggests a third possibility, wherein not only their relationship, but the two poles themselves are conceived as temporal entities, subject to constant internal contradiction and change. In this case, the relationship between tradition and modernity is conceived not just as historical, but as radically historical, for a de-essentialization of the extremes moves the entire configuration of anthropological historicity into time. It loosens the force of change inherent in modern historical temporality.

As a conclusion, then, we can propose that *Ceddo* bases itself on a radical historicity. While its narrative plays out a version of the confrontation between tradition and modernity, neither is an unfractured whole. The most striking aspect of this operation is the fluid complexity and sometimes the resultingly critical edge of the film's construction of tradition. Not even the indigenous assumes a seamlessly positive value to be defended and restored in its integrity. This marks the categorical depurification embodied in the film's historiography.[23]

It is also possible to ascribe a radical historicity to other levels of the film as discussed above. One kind of definition of an indigenous, or national, cinema seeks textual distinctiveness; hence, the interest of such components of *Ceddo* as its particular patterns of analytic editing. These patterns work first of all in ways specific to this text, for instance in connection with its mobilization of a culturally rooted stylization of speech that aids in collectivizing the issues being narrativized. Yet, this does not mean it is simply irrelevant to compare them to modes of editorial scene analysis familiar from a more internationalized perspective on the history of film style. As a methodological point, to establish distinctiveness requires a comparative outlook. But also in question is how one regards film history. As a moment in a textual commentary, to treat *Ceddo* in an international, film-historical context extends the basic impulse of the film's own historiography as depurification. Even textual distinctiveness is situated as a site of transition and transformation, of contradictory as well as unitarily collective determinants, as radically historical.

This radical history also applies to my descriptions of the film's aspirations for its spectator and affects even the status of the film image. As a "historical film," *Ceddo* includes something of a restorationist impulse. It constitutes the physical and social world of a carefully delineated past, with images and sounds of striking regional settings and reconstructed details and actions. On the other hand, the spectator is invited to reflect on contradictions and historical options, not only by the overtly stated dramatic rationales of characters, but also by a series of occurrences that, judged from knowledge available in the spectator's own time, might variously be false, possible, or actual. Thus, there are shifting, differential levels in narrative security possible in the contradiction between a truth of depicted archaeological detail and the conveying of narrative events and actions. This problematization of conventional relations between a historical past and a historicizing present bears directly on indexicality itself. For the indexical trace functions as a bridge between past and present, whether manifested as the document that grounds historical research or the normalized, photographically processed film image. The most striking moment in this regard is probably the priest's dream, where shifts in the register of indexicality and document-diegesis relations are put into play, but this crystallizes concerns of the film as a whole. There always remain ambivalences and limitations on any historical understanding solely on the basis of diegetic occurrences. No wonder narrative authority as a site of absolute historical knowledge never quite finds an adequate delegate—such as a Prince Salina in *The Leopard*—within the diegesis. Comprehension, as understanding a play of collective forces presenting options for differing futures, privileges historical knowledge, but as a confrontation with alternatives instead of as an integral and closed past. Ultimately, then, the spectator is also conceived as a historical agent, an agent asked to reflect on options for comprehending the history of Africa from his or her own historicized temporality.

But does not a radical historicity call any identity into question, precisely because it destabilizes historical sequencing, reference, and therefore positionality? If all terms in the opposition between tradition and modernity—and by extension, the indigenous and the foreign—are in perpetual transition, it might seem that *Ceddo* exceeds any simple placement as African cinema not only purely imitative of, but also purely other to Western cinema. This is a way of situating *Ceddo* in the framework of tradition versus modernity, but in order to propose that the film collapses this founding opposition. However, such a purely deconstructive description loses the historical and political basis of the film's radical historicity, the sense that it is answering to problems of special import in Africa. The dialectic of colonialism and liberation, and the tradition-modernity opposition, with its related paradigms such as indigenous versus foreign, are part and parcel of the very conditions of existence for a film such as *Ceddo*, conditions that come from a historical and political specificity.

Sembene is an artist who militantly bases his films in the signs and structures of African cultural tradition, so that, for example, his proclivity for partially indeterminate character motivation and partially open endings to promote discussion and reflection by the audience can be said to derive from the African dilemma tale; on the other hand, he can discuss Brechtian components in his work.[24] His emphasis on collectivity is associated with African cultural experience; but he also has a background in labor organizing and Marxism. *Ceddo* is a self-consciously African project drawing on African narrative traditions and Senegalese historical experience to tell its story; yet, these are mobilized and conveyed in a historical film made in the unprecedented political and ideological milieu of the postcolonial African nation-state—and cinema, the epistemological privilege of critical historiography, and the centralized nation-state (nationalism) were all Western developments during the colonialist period.

Nevertheless, there can be little doubt that *Ceddo* remains positional. If, based on such oppositions and contradictions, one described *Ceddo* as synthetic, this "synthesis" is not an ideal, balanced supercession of contradictories. Rather, the film is a reflection of and a reflection on its own status at a certain moment in African and film history. It is thus not just its subject matter that makes *Ceddo* a specifically Black African work; it manifests a reconceptualization of historical comprehension and address that answers questions crucial in the context of sub-Saharan Africa, where the confluence of transition and identity are unavoidable political issues. The radical historicity of *Ceddo* is rooted in and inseparable from the drive to construct a self-consciously postcolonial national cinema in Senegal, in the sense of a cinema rising from the specifics of African cultures, politics, and histories.

If nations as such are entities that must be culturally and discursively made and remade in order to exist, *Ceddo* exemplifies some of the ways in which the foundations of nationhood have been placed at issue in African cultural practices and thought. This chapter has repeatedly suggested that such discourses have wider implications for perspectives on conceptualizations of nation and historiography.[25] But it is the film's African concerns that ultimately lead to a historicization of the terms of identity and nation, for identity and nation are special and intertwined problems in Africa in the first place. This positionality explains why the film does not disavow the idea that historiography has a history, but insists on it. It is only because *Ceddo* deals with nation by making diverse African histories imaginable that it contributes to conceiving of different cinemas, and therefore can also contribute to making diverse film histories imaginable.

CHAPTER 8

Old and New:
Image, Indexicality, and
Historicity in the Digital Utopia

A veteran of the special effects industry recently estimated that
80 percent of studio feature films made today utilize some form of
digital image manipulation. It's not just films like *Jumanji*, *Babe*,
or *Apollo 13* that rely on a computer-generated streams of zeroes
and ones to give them their look; *Jefferson in Paris* made
extensive use of digital techniques to help the late 20th century
masquerade as the 18th.

—*Variety*, 1996

A new age does not begin all of a sudden.
My grandfather was already living in the new age
My grandson will probably still be living in the old one.

The new meat is eaten with the old forks.

—Bertolt Brecht, "New Ages" ("Die Neuen Zeitalter")

"Old and New": Indexicality versus Digitalization

For well over a century, indexicality was thought to be the ground for
the newest, most "advanced" forms of representation. During that time,
cultural theorists and critics constantly wrestled with media in which sign
production involves dependence on some minimum of the presence of the
real objects they represent. In image production, the key examples were
photography and film. Ideals of the indexical became culturally central in
arenas of epistemology (the historical document) as well as representation

(cinema). This book has sought to highlight and tease out some important implications of a kinship between cinema and historiography.

But recent arguments for the radical novelty of contemporary representational and epistemological fields often involve claims that ideals of indexicality have been displaced. "Postmodernism" is only one widespread code word for forwarding such a position in theories of culture and representation. In fact, there are a variety of tendencies taking up this position. One emphasizes digital encoding, as abetted by electronic and computer technologies, and it is the concern of this chapter.

What, then, is the digital? It is usually defined against a contrary or opposite, an "other," and the general name for that "other" is usually analog encoding. This distinction is primarily a matter of inscription. Whereas analog inscription is relatively continuous and depends on physical contact between different substances (artist's paint with canvas, for example), digital inscription is relatively discontinuous and depends on a seemingly arbitrary code of discrete, relational elements (numbers). In that case, indexicality becomes just a subset of analog inscription, for it is minimally defined as including some element of physical contact between referent and sign.[1]

With that said, there are a striking number of accounts of the digital that treat the indexical as the strongest or most significant type of analog inscription. In them, not the analog in general but the indexical becomes the opposing term, against which the digital may be defined and which it surpasses. This seems especially to be the case in analyses of digital imaging. This displacement is a first indication that we are not dealing here with abstract, "technical" definitions but ideals—claims aimed at sociocultural normativization.

This chapter examines some descriptions of digital encoding as embodying a historic break in the nature of media and representation, a kind of technological sea change in the production and processing of meanings. I will explore some key notions they repeatedly develop to describe this radical novelty, not necessarily to adjudicate their empirical truth or falsity, much less to "cover" fully the actuality of digitalization. Such descriptions are ultimately of sociocultural and representational ideals. My purpose is to sketch major elements of accounts of the digital as a set of such ideals, a kind of conceptual or theoretical utopia of the digital in the regime of representation, and to consider the requirements of this digital utopia. I will draw in most detail on a small selection of exemplary texts where the digital is theorized or conceptualized in opposition to the indexical.

The discourse of the digital utopia bears both on contemporary understandings of imaging media and on historicity. The emphasis on the image by those theorizing the digital against the indexical ties into the special attention increasingly being paid by cultural theorists and historians to "visuality" and its vicissitudes in definitions of both modern and postmodern culture. By associating representation in modernity more or less "purely" with the wide diffusion of visual discourses, cultural theorists run the danger of repressing the material, sensory, and technical hybridity of modern life and culture. Some cinema scholars, such as Rick Altman, have made a strong case against such a repression in film theory. Altman is particularly concerned with the historic and theoretical importance of the sound track for cinema, and it is certainly true that the digital sound should be a central component of any history of the digital in culture in general, including imaging practices in particular. But there are also levels of semiotic hybridity even within the single sensory register of the image, and emphases on visuality as a cultural category can result in their repression, just as any ontology could. In what follows I will suggest that there are sometimes explicit, sometimes implicit levels of hybridity in the register of the digital image. In important ways, such hybridities confuse the initiating opposition between digital and indexical. They therefore make claims for a ruptural historical break in representation more difficult, or at least more complicated, than they may seem at first.[2]

As for historicity, we need only consider how often accounts of the digital gravitate toward a postulate of radical change in arenas of representation, discourse, culture, and sometimes even society as a whole. This makes the opposition between the digital and its other, whether analog or indexical, into a matter of new and old. Furthermore, conceptions of the image are inseparable from conceptions of historicity. When indexicality was thought to be the ground for the newest, most "advanced" forms of representation, temporality—the past presence of the depicted object—was established as a foundation for both sign and its reference. Logically enough, recent assertions of the leading importance of the digital are often associated with claims for the transformation of temporality and reference, even among those who do not deal with the technology per se.[3]

The assertion of radical novelty recalls the problematic of modern historicity as outlined by Koselleck, and therefore the familiar conundrum of modern Western historicity. It depends on a perpetual lookout for the new and hence the permanent and universal possibility of change; therefore it requires some means of conceiving of itself historically, which means temporalizing itself. But what is the historical self-consciousness implicit in ideals of the digital? The very assertion of newness links this conceptualization to the "old" modernist historicity, and in profound ways. In that case, if digitalization is tied to postmodernist claims for a radically ruptural end to modern historicity, as it sometimes is, proclamations of the dissolution of historical representation may be a mere disavowal.

Of course, cultural theorists, artists, and technicians are not the only ones making significant claims about the radical novelty claimed by digital representation. So does consumer culture, whose advertising logic is in perpetual search of product differentiation, and hence a rhetoric of the new.

Some Fundamentals for a "New" Media Era: The Indexical Image, the Digital Image, and Digital Mimicry

Assertions of a new digital age do not rest on the fact of digital encoding alone, but also its association with the proliferation of computers designed to process the digital "stuff"—both the increasingly powerful personal computer and institutional machines with greater capacities. An array of binarized digits configures a logic, and such logics may be devised to enable specific computer programs to translate them into various forms that are "readable," that is, recognizable or codified for human receiver-operators. The terrain of such readabilities includes symbolic-logical "languages" and printed ordinary languages. It also includes many sorts of imaging, such as graphs, maps, the image components of airplane flight and military training simulators, holography, the Virtual Reality helmet-glove apparatuses that received a significant amount of publicity in the late 1980s, and so forth. But despite the publicity around holography and three-dimensional, immersive Virtual Reality displays, it is probable that the bulk of digital imagery that has reached larger publics to this point has been realized on two-dimensional surfaces—video monitors serving as computer screens, as well as television screens, film screens, and even photographic paper.

Claims for the radical novelty of digital imaging, as well as the digital in general, ultimately rest on the theoretical status of numbers, while assuming the development of high-speed computation. Theorists of the indexical image such as Bazin and Barthes fixated on light-sensitive chemicals as the key mediating materiality between an object and its depiction in the image. With photography or film as the usual examples, these are said to give an image its quality of a trace, imprint, or mold (Bazin) for the spectator. The basis of the digital image, on the other hand, is usually described as a configuration of numbers in binary sets, numerical operations, algorithms. Theorists of the digital image must emphasize the idea that numbers are something like *its* ground, its mediating "materiality."

This presumption can lead to numerous other distinctions. Here is one implication drawn by Timothy Binkley (whose theory of digital spectatorship will be privileged later in this chapter), with the Barthes of *Camera Lucida* in mind:

> A computer stores meta-pictorial information in a fragmented array of discrete numbers, which cannot communicate directly with the depicted or the observing world: some kind of translation is required before this set of abstruse digits can record or represent anything visual. In this *digital* format, defined not by a physical medium but by a conceptual structure, pictorial space is approached analytically, fragmented into regular rows and columns of small dots called *pixels* (picture elements). The concrete physical grains of chemicals in a photograph are replaced by an intangible array of numbers.... The end product [may be] a photograph, but it visually

"depicts" the numerical contents of a frame buffer, not necessarily the state of any real place at any particular time.[4]

Here the mathematical operations underlying the digital are to be understood as abstract conceptuality in opposition to physical substantiality. Bill Nichols encapsulates this premise with the remark, "The [memory] chip is pure surface, pure simulation of thought."[5] In these formulations, the quest for conceptual operationality displaces the quest for the concrete and the physical, so that the latter lose their force as determining the nature and quality of the image. Digital imaging is not just a matter of technically efficient inscription, but of sundering the contact between world and image, and between machine and reference, which is the very currency of the indexical. The digital can make any kind of an image, of the existent or nonexistent, out of whole cloth—or rather, whole algorithms.

Much could be said about this, but for now let us note two consequences. First, digital images are often differentiated from photographic or filmic images on the basis of a claim about their origins. Theorists of indexicality have often argued that the various compositional and selective choices made by filmmakers and photographers encounter a limit definitive of indexicality in the profilmic event: the material that is concretely present in front of the camera to be filmed. The very concept of indexicality is inapplicable if an object that will be depicted does not participate in the originary production of the image. Both indexical and the digital images are produced through machines, but the production of the digital begins from numbers as its mediating materiality. Therefore it can do without an origin in a profilmic "here and now" (or "there and then"); hence the ease with which the indexical imaging of photography and film can be used as the defining other to digital imaging.

A second consequence of the fact that a digital image is composed through the manipulation of numbers and not physical substances is that the digital appears to make an unprecedented range of image-configuring capabilities technically available. This is the case not only for specialists, but also, insofar as sufficiently "user-friendly" programs are practicable, to a wide variety of operators. The broad diffusion of machine-made imaging, one of the definitive characteristics of modernity, apparently leaps to a new level. Image making becomes as technically unencumbered by any necessary referentiality as a painting or sculpture, and yet complex image construction is possible at a speed that only machines can provide. The first digital ideal that I will discuss will be this extraordinary compositional malleability, which makes the picture seem infinitely manipulable and the possibilities of picture making limitless.

The sundering from origins and unprecedented manipulability of pictorial or compositional elements are two of the founding thematics in arguments for the radical novelty of the digital on the plane of images. (This is a kind of negative echo of the distinction between indexicality and perspective in Bazin's theory.)[6] Yet, embedded in the very theory and historiography of the digital, there are antitheses to both of these founding thematics of the digital image. As we will see, these produce internal contradictions in ideals of the digital.

With respect to origins, even if we temporarily go outside the realm of imaging, it becomes clear that the digital does not necessarily exclude something that seems very much like the profilmic event of indexicality. For example, take Manuel De Landa's description of how military spy satellites have evolved from photographic to digital surveillance: "[T]he imaging apparatus has left the plane of mechanical replication to become completely computerized, ceasing to create 'flat replicas' of the world and producing instead streams of pure data from which information of many kinds can be extracted." Yet, even if this example of the digital leaves coded pictorial resemblance behind, it has not given up concern with an indexical origin. The "purity" of "pure data" cannot mean the obliteration of referential origins, for without referential entities or events pre-existing the data itself, that data would have no informational value as surveillance. In this example, the target of satellite sensors, such as Soviet missile emplacements, is a kind of "pro-digital event." This suggests that if we consider such pragmatics or functions of digital information, the seeming oxymoron "digital indexicality" becomes necessary for understanding the history of digitalization.[7]

Indeed, to return to the image, in the less specialized realm of consumer goods there is already such a thing as a "digital camera." It gathers light like a traditional camera but does not record its presence by chemical reactions on photosensitive substances. Instead, it is a machine for encoding light intensities as numbers on a magnetized substrate, and the perceived image is actually composed of pixels with assigned color values arranged along Cartesian coordinates. Thus, George Legrady argues that a digital photograph is actually "a *simulated* photographic representation," no matter how much it may look like the product of a traditional, indexical camera.[8] But how is it that a digital camera can be sold not as a displacement, but as a replacement for a conventional still camera? How is it that, in the appropriate context, a digital photograph may take on the functions of an indexical photograph, such as family testament or photojournalism? The answer is that the digital camera does not necessarily exclude all the operations of a photochemical camera; it even uses a lens to gather light. Like De Landa's digitized surveillance satellite, it retains indexical import as a light-sensing device. If the digital image is configured to appear as a conventional photograph, this means that the digital camera is a machine for configuring its "pure data," according to a certain range of prior pictorial norms, namely those identified with photography. But this does not make it nonindexical.

In addition to such explicitly indexical functions, there are other ways that the regime of the digital is intertwined with the indexical rather than excluding it. Any analogical image—including conventionally produced photographic or film images—can be translated into a numerical logic for display on computer monitors. Thus digitized, they can also be manipulated and reshaped with great facility and with much more speed than in the developing laboratory, for computer programs enable the recomposition, reorganization, and significant transformation of all kinds of preexisting images. This capability has caused commentators to wonder about the contemporary truth status of the photograph, as in discussions of a classic example, the digital repositioning of one of the pyramids of Giza in a 1982 cover photograph for *National Geographic*. The relative ease and rapidity in the "postfilmic" manipulation of indexically produced images is a capacity that is generally adduced in support of the thesis of the radical distinctiveness of a digital age, and it has been one of the most important uses of the digital in cinema. But at this point, let us simply note that all these examples—surveillance satellites and digital photography, and digitized indexical images—have consequences of theoretical as well as descriptive importance: digital imaging as such does not absolutely rule out a profilmic origin, for the digital has means of incorporating the indexical.[9]

The instance of digitizing a photograph also suggests an antithesis for our second thematic of the numerically grounded image, its unprecedented compositional flexibility. Beyond incorporating indexical origins into the digital, there is the matter of pictorial composition. If I see a photograph on the computer screen, this means that the digital image has the ability to assume the exact compositional form of the conventional photograph. This is not only implicit in the digital camera, but also in the digital capacity to transform or fake photographs. The compositional flexibility of this imaging technology, which is supposed to be non- or even antiphotographic, includes imitating photograph form.

My term for the capacity of the digital to imitate such preexisting compositional *forms* of imagery is *digital mimicry*. Digital mimicry is not limited to photography or the indexical, for the digital possesses the capacity to mime any kind of nondigital image. However, given the importance of the opposition to indexicality in theories of digital imaging, it may be that mimicry of camera images holds special interest in the short history of the latter.[10]

Andy Darley has proposed dividing this history up to the present into two phases, which overlap but are defined by different dominant tendencies. The early phase peaked during the 1960s, when cutting-edge developments in computer imaging technologies and techniques often partook of the rhetoric and rationales of high modernist abstraction. Advanced research sometimes involved collaboration of artists and computer scientists; in fact, the best-known filmic uses of the computer during this period, celebrated in Gene Youngblood's 1970 book *Expanded Cinema*, were by independent filmmakers and do seem to fit in with this aesthetic tendency. This first phase seems congruent with theories that reason from the numeric grounds of the digital to the separation of image from concrete physical reality.

But following this early period, according to Darley, the dominant tendency in computer imaging turned depictive, emphasizing forms of pictorial verisimilitude to achieve what has come to be called simulation.[11] In discourses of the digital, simulation clearly has special meanings, and we will come to some of these. Here, however, I simply want to emphasize two points. First, this depictive turn means that decisive innovations in digital imaging were pointed toward modes of image composition that *already* could attract adjectives such as "accurate," "realistic," and "convincing." Second, this depictive turn either entails digital mimicry or at least finds it remarkably convenient. To make its "simulations," the digital had to mime previously known instruments that functioned as reliable imprints of the world. Of course, the camera-produced image, which is to say the indexical image, would be a leading candidate.

While the specific terms and history of such mimicry would require a highly technical and specialized exposition, the sheer fact of digital mimicry underlines how much computer scientists and artists have turned to visual codes already widely diffused. Thus, if it is true that the bulk of computer imaging so far has been on two-dimensional surfaces, then one important issue for the development of visual simulation would have to have been an old one: the projection of three-dimensional space on a two-dimensional plane. Indeed, in his authoritative book on the digital and photography, William J. Mitchell has gone so far as to call the development of algorithms for digitizing single-point perspective in the 1960s "an event as momentous, in its way, as Brunelleschi's perspective demonstration."

Take so-called 3-D digital imaging. A three-dimensional object— say, a building—is conceived as points, lines, and surfaces, and mapped according to Cartesian coordinates (x, y, and z axes representing breadth, height, and depth relations). These coordinates are numerically representable, which means that a three-dimensional model of the object can be stored in computer memory, but as a numerically coded, hence nonperceivable "virtual" object. This object only becomes perceivable by computations that translate it into an image. And if that image is on a two-dimensional surface, such as a computer monitor or some other flat support like printer paper or a conventional movie screen, the encoded solid object can only manifest its three-dimensionality by translation into a perspective projection. Not only is Renaissance perspective a culturally familiar and available solution, providing a basis for photographic norms, as well as painterly and other graphic traditions; it also had the further advantage of having originated in mathematical (geometric) conceptions of the image surface and of vision, which made it seem ready-made for the translations of number-based imaging.[12]

Of course cautions regarding the status of single-point perspective are in order: the credible depiction of depth on a two-dimensional plane entailed the digital encoding of complementary pictorial elements, such as shading and lighting; single-point is certainly not the only normalized form of linear perspective; forms of nonlinear perspective are well-known and practical in computer graphics; and there may well be significant practical and theoretical distinctions between miming linear perspective in images composed of a finite number of pixels (the computer screen) and those composed of an infinite number of points (such as a pencil drawing or oil on canvas). Nevertheless, the drive of digital image programming to utilize linear perspective as a baseline of recognizabilty has been so strong that at least some specialists believe that computer imaging embodies a "rebirth of perspective." Hence, Mitchell concludes that computer graphics "extends the tradition of mathematically constructed perspective that began with Brunelleschi and Alberti," even as it redefines that tradition. This reemplacement of perspective can stand as a central emblem of the importance within the digital universe of credible depth representation based on historically precedent models. And as such, it indicates that depictive credibility based on familiar codes in general retains greater sociocultural importance than is sometimes recognized.[13]

The digitization of perspective and supplementary compositional characteristics researched in the 1960s was one formal precondition for the depictive turn in computer imaging identified by Darley, but it was not the only one. Manuel De Landa provides a candidate for another such precondition when he notes that during this same period, "The whole imaging apparatus of film was modelled mathematically." He describes the spatial goal of this project as the production of "sculpted" objects on the computer screen, that is, depictions that seemed to possess optical properties familiar to cinematographers. But this was inextricable from a temporal goal, namely that such depictions include movement and change. The result was the digital "creation of synthetic camera movements through imaginary landscapes, which could be illuminated [sic] using the same techniques that a regular photographer would use."

De Landa emphasizes that a fundamental consequence of this synthetic motion picture camera was the incorporation of "real time" into digital imaging. He believes that this passage through a particular "simulation of a simulation" (digital mimicry of cinema) was crucial for the history of digital imaging partly because of the long-standing interest of the military in film and photographic surveillance images.[14] However, the massive naturalization of normalized photographic and cinematic codes in the nineteenth and twentieth centuries must have been a background factor, both in the appeal of photographic indexicality to the military along with its extension into computer imagery. Even De Landa's emphasis on temporality in connection with depictive credibility could be referred back to the sociocultural centrality of depicting (or indexically capturing), configuring, and thereby controlling time manifested in cinema.

It appears that two of the historic thresholds in the development of currently standard procedures for computer imaging were depth representation via perspective and corollary pictorial elements, and the combination of spatial movement and temporal duration—in short, an association of compositional components often thought to be fundamental to the quintessentially indexical medium of cinema. Of course one must be careful to remain aware of distinctions. There are crucial stages in the fashioning of a digital image wherein, as Binkley insists, "light and chemistry are replaced by algebra and digits." Thus, he contends, perspectival depth projection is mimed, but it "is purely formal and not based upon physical properties of a concrete straightedge" or actual light rays, as in a camera obscura.[15] Similar points might be made about movement, although they would be more complex because they involve both the duration of the image in relation to the spectator/operator's temporality and the perceptual illusions that produce movement on the screen in both media.

But if that is the case, the very fact of digital mimicry becomes even more striking. What can we say about the very ambition of producing an *impression*, an imitation, of the action of light, chemistry, a concrete straightedge, and so forth? Binkley treats the "virtual camera"—that is, the composition of digital images that look like camera images—as one of the supreme achievements of digital imaging. But his account makes the film image into the most perfect available model of credible imagery: "One tradition in computer graphics strives for *cinematic* realism, and its most prophetic adherents proclaim that total synthetic realism will be achieved in another few years" (my emphasis). On the other hand, digital image manipulability also implies something seemingly contrary, namely that the computer is also "a contriver of imaginary worlds." Yet, Binkley can also describe this digital capacity with reference to film, as involving "ultra-cinematic effects peculiar to the virtual camera which hold out the promise of new creative tools for film and video makers who want to explore fantasy as readily as reality."[16]

There is a cluster of pertinent suggestions here, all of which revolve around regimes of digital mimicry and complicate the opposition between digital and indexical. A criterion of credibility associated with indexical media is invoked to explain the goals of the digital image—even when simulation of the unreal is the point. (A similar paradox is a familiar idea in discussions of special effects in mainstream film.) The photographic medium of cinema is positioned as a key compositional model for the digital image. Most generally, digital mimicry signals the participation of digital imaging in already normalized forms of imagery. If one accepts Darley's chronology, since the 1970s, digital imaging has been very much implicated in large-scale efforts to reproduce nondigital image configurations, including a drive to look as convincing as photographic or filmic images are supposed to be. Given that the digital is supposed to afford an unprecedented range of possibilities for image composition and manipulation because it is mathematically grounded—and therefore, according to many, allows conceptuality to escape determination by the physical—why this should be so remains too little theorized or analyzed.[17]

In summary, it is common for theorists to treat indexicality as the defining difference for the digital, so that the photographic image often becomes the most exemplary "other" of the digital image. Yet, digital information and images can have indexical origins, the digital often appropriates or conveys indexical images, and it is common for the digital image to retain compositional forms associated with indexicality. In practice, then, digital imagery is often (but of course not exclusively) constituted by being propped onto certain culturally powerful image codes that preexisted it, and in this regard photography and film may be especially important examples. (Incidentally, this remains the case even when such codes only serve on norms that an image selectively deploys, or that it parodies, caricatures, transforms, and so forth.) The quest for digital mimicry has been one of the driving forces in the history of digital imaging. All of this means that, to a significant degree, digital imaging is not separable from prior histories of mediated representation on screen surfaces, but overlaps with them. Any argument that treats digital imagery as radically novel must deal with such overlaps.

A Utopia of the Digital

Discourses characterizing the digital are produced by a wide range of social agents, including artists, aesthetic theorists, and sociocultural theorists and critics, as well as journalists, corporate researchers, and publicists. Discourses of the digital include various tendencies, of course, but one strain that pervades many of them is that of the radical historical break between old and new. This is why the digital insistently seems to propose the question of its own history.

On the plane of imaging, this history is commonly located in the opposition between indexical and digital: the indexical is the old, the digital the new. But at some point such accounts will encounter the kinds of overlaps between the categories indicated above. These overlaps may take on the appearance of a variety of admixtures or hybrid cases, which imply, among other things, temporal or historiographic conflations. (Digital mimicry is always an indicator of such hybridity.) Such hybridities may be obvious or implicit and covert, but they go to the heart of definitions of the digital. On the one hand they make it difficult to define the digital by means of absolute categorization; on the other hand, it may turn out that these hybridities themselves characterize the digital as much as any "pure" nonindexicality.

In that case, the historiography of old and new, which is so often at the heart of conceptions of the digital, threatens to dissolve into a complex, "impure" historicity and a complex, "impure" historiographic temporality. The digital would have to be referred to a radical historicity without stable points of source and end, old and new. Historical sequencing would have to become provisional, and the categories enabling such sequencing would themselves have to be temporalized (historicized), de-idealized, returned to the complexity that characterizes the concrete rather than the conceptual, the nondigital as much as the digital. My point here is not that ideals should never be articulated or presented as purities, or that it is possible to completely avoid sequenciation; however, that said, one would have to seek the digital in the contradictory junctures of idealized purities and impure hybridities.

But discourses of the digital have strategies to counter hybridities and restore a historiographic temporality that can maintain the radical novelty of the digital against the indexical image. One of the most significant is a rhetoric of the forecast. With it the account of the digital locates itself in a moment of directional change. Hybridizations of old and new—as when the computer becomes a virtual camera, thus realizing the digital on the model of the indexical—are made into transitional phenomena on the way to an era of "purer" digitalization.

Examples are plentiful. When Binkley remarks that "the computer is initially made to emulate familiar genres for want of knowing offhand what else to do with it," the term *initially* is crucial. In the future, things will be different, and emulation—the digital mimicry that manifests hybridity—will eventually be minimized. Definitions of the digital and its capabilities are repeatedly made into a matter of the future. "With digitised photo-imagery," proclaims Anne-Marie Willis, "the index will be erased as the photo becomes pure iconicity." Opposing the view that the digital realm is "simply a set of rather complicated tools extending the range of painting and sculpture, performed music, or published literature," Roy Ascott predicts, "the further development of this field will clearly mean an interdependence of artistic, scientific and technological competencies and aspirations." Thus, Dan Slater points to something that goes well beyond his specific example when he complains that if one avoids "engaging in ungrounded prediction, it is not at all clear that domestic photography—in the sense of snapshooting—has been transformed in the slightest by digital technology." He hits upon one of the most typical—and perhaps *the* typical—mode for defining the digital, the forecast.[18]

The strategy of the forecast has a crucial function in freeing an account of the digital from having to deal with hybridities as constitutive. It delineates the characteristics of the digital as existing through pure ideals rather than impure actualities, things that will eventually be achieved, rather than an achieved state of things. Extrapolating from contemporary impurities, such accounts are written from a position "just before" an era of pure digitalization. In that sense, the forecast puts in place a temporal structure that suggests that such accounts are implicated not just in fetishizing digital technology, but in a kind of *historiographic* fetishization. Purely digital practices become something like an inevitability that is nevertheless "not yet." This fetish structure has a wide ambit. It can, for example, serve as the rationale for technical and profit-seeking practices and goals, just as it can conceivably ground an effect/affect for an individual computer operator. It also legitimates describing a technical and cultural phenomenon as if it existed outside socioeconomic determinations and functions.

The structure of the forecast constitutes the digital on the basis of a modern form of historical temporality. Reinhart Koselleck argues that the forecast, or rational extrapolation, is one of the progenitors of modern historicity.[19] In its assumption of an irrevocable linear temporality already in operation, the disavowal of hybridity through the forecast characterizes a mode of historicity underlying a certain theorization of the digital.

On this level, what is disavowed is temporal complexity and historical overlap. Like a symptom, the "not yet" of the forecast simultaneously conceals and yet suggests the extent to which historicity is not a contingent, but a necessary element of any account of the digital, and furthermore the extent to which that historicity exceeds temporal linearity and categorical purity in spite of itself.

This is not to say that such forecasts will always turn out to be wrong. For Koselleck, the rational forecast was developed as a pragmatic tool. It provided a method of feasible means-ends calculation that came into its own in the balance-of-power politics of the European Absolute State during the seventeenth and eighteenth centuries. Since then capitalism itself has generated a forecasting industry, and forecasts today sustain similar functions in everything from weather prediction to marketing research. But, of course, as they shade into utopian projections with a futurological bent, they will not necessarily turn out to be right either.

Within the discourse of the digital utopia, the rhetoric of the forecast unveils the extent to which definitions of the digital rely on ideals, much as Bazin's account of the history of film textuality posited perfect "realism" as an ideal. But Bazin made his ideal both subject to a variety of cinematic approximations and also asymptotic, ultimately unreachable. This is not always the case in accounts of the digital, where a state of transition and change is commonly invoked only in order to mummify the digital by means of a realization of the new that is, nevertheless, projected into a future never quite here and now.

Suppose we attempt to name some of the most important ideals that recur in accounts of digital imaging as radically new. Insofar as the writers are genuinely knowledgeable about existing digital imaging practices and goals, we will undoubtedly end up with categories of some descriptive and analytic value; and yet we will not necessarily end up with a map of the terrain of actually existing digital imagery. Rather, we will produce a kind of utopia of the digital heavily penetrated by the stratagem of the forecast, which disavows hybridity and temporal complexity. The digital utopia may be explicit or implicit in a given text aimed at conceptualizing digital imaging, and it may dominate that text or appear in it only implicitly, partially and/or contradictorily. In its strongest forms, it asserts that digital imaging does not just introduce a new element into representational cultures and practices, but it causes those cultures and practices to take a radically transformative turn.[20]

The digital utopia seems to call on the interplay of three fundamental characterizations of the novelty of digital imaging, which one repeatedly finds in discourses of theorists and practitioners. These three ideals taken together provide a provisional sketch for a utopia of the digital. They are (1) the *practically infinite manipulability* of digital images; (2) *convergence* among diverse image media; and (3) *interactivity*. It will quickly become clear that the three are mutually interdependent, but they can be separated for purposes of exposition. Each of them will be defined in opposition to older indexical (camera/photochemical) imaging practices. Speaking roughly, each may be predominantly associated with one phase of the orthodox breakdown of mainstream film production practices: production (practically infinite manipulability), distribution (convergence), and exhibition/reception (interactivity). Full implementation of these digital ideals would mean the realization of the claim for radical novelty.[21]

In what follows, I will discuss each of these three digital ideals in turn, noting some internal paradoxes or contradictions. In all cases, we will encounter digital mimicry, hybridity, and a constitutive historicity of the digital. There are two points to remember about this exercise. First, my position is that ideals such as these are neither necessarily and completely irrational, nor necessarily and completely rational; however, they are sociocultural phenomena at least as much as "technical" descriptions. This is especially clear after 150 years of theorizing the indexical, digital imaging's other. Indexicality has its own driving ideals, such as the provenance of the photographic and film images as referentiality in the realm of imagery.[22] Second, we should remember that the digital utopia need not claim that these three ideals are always and absolutely achieved in every actual case of digital imaging. This is what is so important about the rhetoric of the forecast, and it is what makes them *ideals* of the digital.

Production: Practically Infinite Manipulability

By practically infinite manipulability, I mean the unprecedented capability the digital is supposed to provide for an operator to implement his or her own conceptions of an image. Now, there are clearly constant pressures that channel the bulk of actual digital imaging practices in more or less disciplined ways. This is evident in the uses to which digital imaging is put by many kinds of professionals and their institutions, including fine artists and advertising graphic designers, computer programmers and cognitive scientists, and theme park designers and filmmakers, to name a few.

But the theoretical point typically made is that since digital imaging is split off from physical causality to an unprecedented degree, it is liberated from previously operative constraints on image making. Even a critic of the digital utopia like Kevin Robins can write, "The essence of digital information is that it is inherently malleable." As Binkley puts it:

> One of the most important features of digital media is that they can be manipulated with all the resources of a digital computer to create, filter, augment, refine, or alter the information they contain.... A creative imagination roams through digital domains unencumbered by the constraints of corporeal existence that are a way of life for analogue artists.[23]

The logic is clear. From a first principle that the underlying constitution of digital images is numerical, he establishes an opposition between conceptuality and physicality. The next step is to argue that the digital consists in subordinating the physical constraints of image production to the conceptual to an unprecedented degree; and conceptuality is identified with creativity. This logic underlies many accounts of the digital, and it is not only demonstrated but given substance by the opposition between the digital and the indexical.

The two great physical determinants on image making overcome by the digital are concrete reference and the physical characteristics of a medium. We have already seen that a fundamental difference between the digital and normalized photography or film is that the digital does not require the existence of a profilmic object for the apparatus to make an image of it. But also, as Gene Youngblood puts it, "the computer ... has no meaning, no intrinsic nature, identity, or use value until we talk it into becoming something by programming it."[24] The processes of high-speed computation are indifferent to the medium as well as the product in a way indexical cameras cannot be, for cameras are dedicated to the task of physio-chemical contact with a profilmic. The digital is not even dependent on the electronic computer, if more efficient means of high-speed computation can be devised. It has been forecast, for example, that electronic computers may some day be replaced by computing/storage entities made up of biological molecules.[25]

For the theoretically rigorous Binkley, these two positive lacks—lack of authority of the referent and of determination by the physics of the apparatus—follow from the abstract, conceptual nature of numbers: "The abstract structure [of digital encoding] precedes the source and stays independent of it, communicating only through an interface, and never brought into direct contact with an image or its referent."[26] They mean that the operator can instantiate any image conception she or he is able to dream up. They make the indexical image seem the appropriate opposing term for the digital ideal of practically infinite manipulability. But they also suggest something important about the very notion of manipulability.

It is true, as Philip Hayward and Tana Wollen remark, that "[d]igitisation has made the malleability of sounds and images seem like something new," but the reasons for their implicit skepticism are obvious to anyone with any knowledge of the histories of photography and cinema.[27] It was, after all, possible to fake photographs before digitization. Despite the sociocultural pressures that make these media repositories of referentiality, their histories are replete with examples of "manipulating" image configurations. A detailed rehearsal of means of such manipulation in photography and film—some of which fall within the range of the indexical and some outside it—is too extensive to undertake here. But it might be useful to remind ourselves of a few examples. These could include affecting tonality and hue by lens filters and film stock characteristics, painting on the image (as in some Indian domestic photography), stencil painting or tinting (as in silent films), fabricating cinema images by painting frames (as in some avant-garde films), unconventional lenses, such as prisms, which modify referential status by distorting compositional norms, and so forth. Postfilmic laboratory processes have sometimes included combinations of distinct images that may have differing referential statuses (composite printing, "Hollywood montage sequences," matting painted sets, animation, or other filmed actions into a standard film shot—which has also been much done for illusionistic effects in the history of filmic textuality). The list could go on, but the point is that the difference from photography and film claimed by the digital utopia cannot be the simple presence or absence of manipulability *per se*, or, as the example of painting on film shows, even of indexicality *per se*.

Given the possibility of manipulability in the stipulated realm of the indexical, then, it is more precise to try to describe the newness of image manipulability in the digital as a matter of degree rather than kind. There is an *increase*, in the ease and hence the "quantity" of manipulability. But then we must ask, quantities of what? Time is as good an answer as any. Just as theories of the indexical image tend to presuppose the film-developing process, theories of the digital presuppose the technological capacity for high-speed computation. If the flexibility of digital image-formation and transformation does have limitations, these consist only in the speed with which numerical operations can be processed. And in that case, as they say, speed is of the essence.[28]

In that sense, the sector of the digital utopia I call practically infinite manipulability is about the rapidity with which compositional choices can be implemented and made visible. If it seems to the digital artist that a new level of creative freedom is being breached, it is because the intention (imaginative or otherwise) of an operating subject can become more speedily determinant. So grounds for asserting practically infinite manipulability lie in the relation of the operating speed of the digital to the phenemonological temporality of the operating subject. This unprecedented temporality of image composition and production leads directly to claims for a new level of subjective freedom with respect to the construction of the space of the image. Restrictions of compositional manipulation and production time that have always impregnated imaging practices are overcome.

Of course, the rhetoric of the digital utopia may absolutize its difference from what preceded it, and this is registered in my adjective, *infinite*. But since it means "more instantaneous," the digital ideal of practically infinite manipulability is relative rather than absolute. And it is not only relative, but *historically* relative. That is, the claims of the digital utopia implicitly rest on assertions about a certain relation in historical time, a historical sequence; for in it, "more instantaneity" functions to mark a historical break to the unprecedented. The physical characteristics and restraints the digital overcomes are those imposed by older imaging technologies, that is, older media. The opposition between indexical and digital becomes one between a past and a present or, more typically given the prevalence of the forecast, a present-future. Here we come to the historicity definitive of all the digital ideals, which require a before and an after to constitute themselves.

Like all historicities, this one generates historiographies, whether explicit or implicit. One especially pertinent in comparisons of the digital and the indexical is what can be called a historiography of conquest. The digital ideal of practically infinite manipulability ultimately envisions technologies that can enable technically unfettered image production. But the ultimate demonstration of the unprecedented characteristics of digital imaging is arguably not in producing original kinds of images; it is in the fact that the ideal of infinite manipulability also applies to *preexisting* images. The full power of the digital regime is evidenced not simply by replacing other kinds of images, but by encompassing them.

As already noted, any kind of preexisting image—digital or not, technically produced or not—can be digitized and consequently be subject to a huge range of modifications: recompositions, combinations with other images, or any other imaginable transformations. This is also part of practically infinite manipulability. Practically infinite manipulability therefore implies that no image is necessarily stable, for any preexistent image is susceptible to an unending series of transformations with all the speed implied by infinite manipulability. In combination with the next digital ideal, convergence, this has given rise to a widespread notion summarized by Peter Wollen as "a vast image bank, an archive from which images can be taken and recontextualized at will."[29]

In a fully realized digital utopia, such an electronic archive would presumably consist of all previously made images, now digitized and permanently available for such later reuses. "In principle," writes Anne-Marie Willis, "every photograph that still remains in existence could become nothing more than raw material for image banks whose manipulators are free to do what they want" with them. Willis here seems to be discussing current applications, but her account is typical in being infiltrated by a rhetoric of the forecast. Hence she moves rapidly to complete unrestrictedness: "The new technologies make possible the storage of an endless range of imagery and ... the idea of the archive is transformed into a limitless decentered mirror-maze of images available to be used and transformed in countless ways."[30] In fact, the ideal of infinite manipulability entails an infinity of raw materials to be manipulated without limitation, including already existing images. The ideal terrain of digital imaging necessarily includes the capacity to incorporate other kinds of images—not just for reproduction, but to make them susceptible to practically infinite manipulability, *thereby subordinating them to the digital regime.*

In the historiography of conquest that is definitive of the digital utopia, digital imaging drives to overcome the authority of anything that it determines is old, that is, that preexists its own operations. There are at least three levels of preexistent authority that, in different ways, are to be invaded, occupied, and superceded by the digital. The first is the profilmic event itself. As I have noted, theorists of indexicality have often treated the profilmic event as possessing a certain recalcitrance based on the priority of its existence. For many theorists of indexicality, the recalcitrant pregivenness of the profilmic, its preexistent facticity in space and time, imposes necessary limits on image production and implies certain peculiarities about image reception. Bazin promoted this limitation as engendering an attitude of "respect," and for the Barthes of *Camera Lucida* it could provoke a special kind of subjective engagement. But in the discourse of the digital, the resistances that concrete space and time might offer to the abstractions of compositional manipulability become an object of assault. Any postulated profilmic event—of traditional as well

as digital photography—is definitionally vulnerable to almost instantaneous, practically infinite, "postfilmic" manipulations of the image.

The second preexistent whose authority is to be overturned is that
of any specific, preexisting image, digitally produced or not. In fact, as we
have just seen, it is crucial that nondigital images can be digitized and
stored electronically, thus becoming susceptible to a potentially unending
chain of digital manipulation and transformation. This leads directly to
the third preexistent, whose authority is overrun in the digital utopia: not
just specific images, but all genres and regimes of image making that
historically preceded digitalization, such as drawing, painting, engraving,
photography, cinema, and analog video, to name a few. In the digital
utopia, images are being perpetually recoded into numbers. Historically
precedent regimes of media and signification are thereby perpetually
appropriated and subjected to a unique capacity of the digital, practically
infinite manipulablity. Thus the digital spreads, infiltrates, overwhelms,
conquers all other media—but, like many modern conquerors, does so in
the name of liberation, liberation from constraint.

If practically infinite manipulability entails overcoming the authority of the preexistent—as the profilmic, as preexisting images, and especially as historically precedent regimes of image making—it follows that
the digital is not simply a more efficient supplement to older modes of
image making, but a radical obliteration of the categories by which they
have been delimited. This is one reason why it becomes important to
assert that the digital utopia is dependent on no specific technology, only
computation itself. "There are many fundamental differences between
photography and computer media," writes artist Richard Wright, "the
most important being that the computer is a nonspecific technology."
According to Binkley, the digital incorporates the techniques of other
image-making tools and thereby "transcends them," thus constituting
itself as "an incorporeal metamedium."[31] In its practices of incorporation
that make it incorporeal, the digital manifests an imperializing historiography of conquest, imposed by the winner—itself.

And yet, the vocation of the digital to appropriate nondigital images
has a major implication that tends to get overlooked within the digital's

own historicity. As we have seen, this historiography of conquest does not actually dispose of its others. This is registered at all levels by the prevalence of digital mimicry. It is not just that the digital requires an other against which to define itself and its radical novelty, nor just that it sometimes reduplicates the very capacities of those differential others, as with digital photography. It is that discourses of the digital utopia are simultaneously compelled to indicate that the digital interpenetrates and is interpenetrated by the very genres and regimes of imaging that it defines as the old. If the digital ideal of practically infinite manipulability obliterates the prior representational ideals connected to medium-specificities, then the digital can never be described through its own properties, can never claim to be just itself. The digital demonstrates its radically new capabilities and superior representational powers through its capacity to appropriate the old. But in that case, it is as if the digital is not able to allow the old regime to disappear. The ideal of practically infinite manipulability demands a hybridity of old and new.[32]

But this implies the persistence of all the preexistents attacked in the digital utopia: specific images, previous media, and, ultimately, the concrete itself. This persistence is embedded in the ideal of practically infinite manipulability itself. Simply beginning from the digitization of indexical images at the very least, the digital utopia involves a constitutive mixture of old and new—something it does not always acknowledge. As we will see when we come to interactivity, the new of the digital utopia may well remain caught in the dialectic of subjectivity and objectivity envisioned by theorists of "older" media. One wonders to what extent a master-slave dialectic is implicit in the historiography of digital conquest. This suggests that representational hybridity in general and digital mimicry in particular are necessary and permanent consequences of the digital utopia—not merely pragmatic, temporary necessities that can therefore be bypassed or repressed in accounts of the digital. Ron Burnett gets at this when he writes with respect to imaging:

> This is, I believe, a crucial historical interregnum. Older imaging technologies like the cinema and broadcast television remain in place while the

newer technologies adapt and adopt both substance and form of those media which preceded them. The combination carries traces of the past, present and future within a cultural and social context which is being recreated even at this moment.[33]

Only perhaps the "interregnum" should be conceived as being oxymoronically permanent. In that case even Burnett's stance includes elements of the digital utopia. With its insistence on a sharp break between old and new, the digital utopia seems to embrace the principle of perpetual transformation of *images;* and yet, it simultaneously tries to avoid the state of transition and consequent impurity, which is actually fundamental to its definitional *historicity.* The state of transition, instability, change bypassed by enthusiastic forecasts, may well have to be posited as a constant.

Distribution: Convergence and the Infinity of Machines

This brings us to the second ideal of the digital utopia, convergence. Convergence is the digital utopia's ideal characterization of distribution, although it is clearly inseparable from infinite manipulability and therefore production. While practically infinite manipulability is my own label, convergence is a term that has been widely used and in a variety of ways. In what follows, convergence means the capability the digital is supposed to possess for an unprecedented degree of communication, cooperation, and especially transmission among previously differentiated media.

Convergence is often characterized economically. As the digital ideal of distribution, it is ultimately grounded in the possibilities of delivery systems. Typically, there are forecasts associated with it, but these often have to do with new kinds of markets. Thus, in 1979 when Nicholas Negroponte sought funding for the influential Media Lab at the Massachusetts Institute of Technology, it was with the prediction that the broadcast/film, print/publishing, and computer industries would conjoin by the year 2000. But of course, he saw this as a technological fact. In 1994, he foresaw a domestic digital machine that would combine the functions of television and computer to coordinate, edit, select, and display from a vast reservoir of worldwide digital resources. This kind of conception, which evinces a certain subservience to consumerist economic and ideo-logical structures, as well as a technological naturalization of the long-term conglomerative pressures of big corporate capital, may belie utopian claims to radical novelty. Commentators who critique such ideologies with respect to the digital are also concerned with such projections.

The point to be emphasized here is that in these examples, the con-cept of convergence is centered on the forecast that many information-processing and imaging technologies are evolving into one production/display technology that does everything. As a typical passage has it:

> Previous technologies are beginning to converge. These new interactive digital multimedia signify the union of television with word processing, desktop publishing with high fidelity stereo, computer-based training with graphical arcade adventure.[34]

But this is only one pole of the digital ideal of convergence. At another pole, instead of envisioning the one machine that does everything, con-vergence has to do with transmissibility among several kinds of machines and media. Considering the notion of transmissibility among a variety of machines will show that these two poles are only different emphases, and not fundamentally opposed to one another.

For our purposes, the question is what it means to claim to transmit an identical image among a variety of machines for display and manipu-lation. Like practically infinite manipulability, convergence also assumes the grounding premise of the digital utopia, that its basic mediating mate-riality is numerical. As we have seen, numerical logics are abstract not only with respect to reference, but also with respect to the particularizing characteristics of a medium. One corollary with respect to images is that digital replication is qualitatively different than, say, photographically re-producing another photograph. Instead of indexically imprinting a first image in order to make a copy (as in rephotography), the digital simply repeats or "rewrites" the same numerical array in another memory bank. This array then functions as if it were a "first" input of data into another machine.

If we ask about the status of the transmitted image as a copy, we are faced with a kind of "duck-rabbit" ambivalence. From one angle, the digital obliterates the distinction between the first inscription of the numbers underlying the image and all others: "Copying of digital data is done by new inscription, not transcription."[35] In that case, *pace* Benjamin, the distinction between original and copy is located in photography after all, for once again the indexical is the implicit other. But from another angle, one can emphasize the potentially infinite *transmission* inherent in such replicability. Transmission does assume something like an "original," such as a specific image that is proliferated as that particular image (or an image of that first image). This "same" image, of course, is then subject to potentially infinite differentiation, since it becomes raw material subject to practically infinite manipulability any time it is transmitted to another machine and another operator.

Whatever status is attributed to the transmitted image in the endless theoretical discussions over originals and copies, however, the fact of transmission is the key to convergence. Digital encoding becomes a perfectly transparent translator among media, because once an image is encoded numerically, those same numbers can be infinitely written anew. This is the basis for envisioning an unprecedented, virtually universal transmissibility among several machines, as well as to a single machine that does everything. As Frank Rickett explains, "*Being digital* [my emphasis], the technology is capable of drawing on sources of data of all types (audio, visual, textual, numeric) and of presenting these disparate strands as a unified package within a single medium." Against the history of film theory, this looks something like an off-center realization of Eisenstein's idea that cinema could be organized around a common denominator shared by diverse sense impressions. Good materialist that he was, Eisenstein identified that common denominator as a physical phenomenon, but a quantifiable one—vibrations of air. In the digital utopia, however, the solution is to evacuate the physical and to find the common denominator in numbers as such, as a universal coding procedure. Hence the unity of the one and the many in the digital universe: "The digital code is a universal code," writes Florian Rötzer, "and the representation of the recorded or created phenomena also becomes arbitrary, because the acoustic can be converted into the visual and vice versa." So if one pole of convergence is the dream of a single machine that does everything, the other is free passage of any kind of "message" among a multiplicity of machines and media because all are rooted in numbers; thus the process takes on the universalist aura often claimed for mathematics.[36]

In fact, a hypothetical, fully realized convergence implies not only universal compatibility, but something like universal reach. Assume it is true that any given configuration of information, or images, can be perfectly transmitted among several media. This suggests that they are also capable of being distributed and infinitely redistributed anywhere in global space, where they may be viewed, copied, transformed, and further transformed with unprecedented speed and flexibility. That is, the idea of universal compatibility seems to feed and feed on an imaginary of a worldwide network of unhampered informational flow. Even those thinkers who are aware of long-term historical forces resort to the typical device of forecast to announce the new, as when Rötzer proclaims:

> The demise of the Berlin Wall ... is the sign of a general fluctuation as prescribed by the ramified media networks. We are now approaching a global society, prepared long ago by the capitalist system at the level of goods and capital flow.[37]

The ideal of convergence is thus closely connected not only to the idea of the electronic archive, but also to the much promoted metaphor of the information superhighway associated with the Internet. These are slogans and pragmatically significant lexical arenas in recent industrial, political, and show-business cultures that more or less vaguely connote a utopic notion of unblocked convergence.

Of course, all of this assumes certain supporting and subsidiary technologies, such as telephone lines, fiber-optic cable, communication satellites, and so forth. In fact, it is necessary to insist that the physical characteristics of such infrastructures present limitations that must be overcome to instantiate such forecasts. Speaking very broadly, hardware limitations have to do with speed of computation (which is related to digital storage capacity, leads to such technical strategies as data compression,

and is one of the motivations for bio-chip research). But such considerations are neither historically nor theoretically determinant for the digital
utopia, which perpetually forecasts more speed and more storage capacity.[38] Insisting on the determination of numbers as conceptuality, it must
bypass the infrastructural and physical characteristics of transmission,
thereby driving home the attack on media boundaries, which is basic to
the historiography of conquest in the digital utopia.[39]

Convergence suggests why it does not matter whether an image
was first produced directly through digital encoding or produced in a
nondigital medium and then digitized. The "same" image, no matter how
it was originally produced, can supposedly "travel" across many phenom-
enally distinct "media," because it is transmitted as numbers. It can then
be exhibited not only on a computer screen, but on a computer print-
out, video screen, movie screen, photographic print, and so forth. The
physical characteristics of the image or the display technology are no
longer determinant. As a summary term, Bellour's "virtual indifferentiation" seems especially appropriate here. But what links image-production
in a variety of media to image-exhibition in a variety of media is the
digitalization of distribution channels connecting the two. The digital
utopia conceives of an unprecedented flexibility in the distribution and
redistribution of images. Convergence is the name of this capacity.

But convergence also involves an interesting contradiction between
the constitutive ideals of practically infinite manipulability and itself. In
the first instance, these two ideals complement one another and together
support the breakdown of limitations promoted in the digital utopia. A
new plurality of imaging technologies and software, a new plurality of
exhibition venues for images, a new plurality of receivers and users of
images—surely all this adds up to an unprecedented diversity in the production of image-forms. However, matters are not this simple when we
consider convergence as distribution.

For transmissibility as such to operate freely and fully, an image
must be recognizable as the "identical" image across several media and/
or points on a network. Otherwise the receiver/operator will not be able
to view and manipulate images that count as the "same" as the image

that was transmitted in the first place. On the one hand, then, the ideal of practically infinite manipulability entails an absolute pliability as to image-formation and therefore image-form. On the other hand, the ideal of convergence drives toward an assumption of absolute similarity of image composition at all points on any postulated digital network and among all media. As we have just seen, this capacity for "communicating" absolute identities is supposed to be ensured by the digital "materiality" (that is, immateriality) of the image. The image is identically rewritable from machine to machine because it is constructed through a universal and arbitrary code.

Thus, while infinite manipulability suggests that digitalization makes an extreme diversity of image form and individualized uses available, convergence can imply a counterpressure *implicit within the digital utopia itself* toward compositional consistency. For this suggests that the distributional ideals of the digital utopia may militate toward a certain broad restriction of types of image configurations, at least as initializing norms, in order to support the need for similarity. In the actuality of the digital one could adduce additional determinants having to do with economics and social processes. Simon Penny forecasts that the digital will lead to new artistic modes, but he also dryly notes that "[t]he 'information superhighway' looks poised to become a gargantuan virtual Mall, with consumer commodity capitalism as its guiding philosophy."[40] Such a refreshingly countervailing forecast suggests something else about numbers as a universal code, namely the convenience of the fit between numerical codification on the one hand and the marketplace and ideologies of consumerism on the other. The ultimate quantitative universality grounding the digital may well be exchange value.

But even within the digital utopia itself, we have already encountered an overdetermining resource for establishing norms of compositional consistency, namely digital mimicry. Here is Mitchell summarizing the chief means of specifying pictorial values in digital image making:

> One way to assign pixel values is to employ some sort of sensor array or scanning device ... to record intensities in a visual field—to make an

exposure with a digital "camera": this appropriates digital imaging to the tradition of photography. A second way is to employ the cursor of an interactive computer-graphics system to select pixels and assign arbitrarily chosen values to them: this makes digital imaging seem like electronic painting, and indeed computer programs for this purpose are commonly known as "paint" systems. And a third way is to make use of three-dimensional computer-graphics techniques—to calculate values by application of projection and shading procedures to a digital geometric of an object or scene: this extends the tradition of mathematically constructed perspective that began with Brunelleschi and Alberti.

Such models or sources for digital image construction, already in place and widely naturalized, can provide norms that make transmissibility of the "same" image conceivable. Mitchell himself discusses transmissibility only in relation to the electronic archive—that is the storage of massive amounts of preexisting imagery that permits the retrieval of specific, identifiable images for viewing and/or transformation. (Interestingly, he seems to conceive of that transformation only as editing or recontextualization of an "original" image.)[41]

Thus, convergence adds yet another reason for miming preexisting image forms, though one that is generally implicit. Earlier I argued that digital mimicry is the contradictory mark of the digital's appropriation of the nondigital, and that one of its major functions is to promote image configurations that signify credibility to support the construction of simulations. This is overdetermined by the pressure implicit in the ideal of convergence toward a certain uniform range of normative image forms. Compositional norms, often on the basis of "older" media, serve to expedite reproduction as convergence, absent the physical "identities" sustained by indexical reproduction of an image. Of course, there is no reason that the two motivations of credibility and similarity cannot be mutually reinforcing.[42]

The ideal of convergence thus returns us to the hybridity of old and new characteristic of the digital. Convergence correlates with the ideal of infinite manipulability, but it also and simultaneously implies contradiction with that ideal, for the normalization of any set of image configurations restricts manipulability. This is because large-scale distribution of anything often requires the normalization of production and expectations about those things, no matter how vaguely defined and historically changeable this normalized terrain may turn out to be. (This is certainly something well understood by historians of the U.S. film industry.) Thus, the entire trope of a breakdown of limits that pervades the digital utopia, with its imaginaries of infinite manipulability and unblocked convergence, encounters a need for limits, which is manifested in the conventionalizing restriction of image codes exemplified by digital mimicry. And once again, the radical novelty of the digital utopia finds itself intricated with that which it claims to have surpassed.

Nevertheless, the digital utopia has another ideal that is the ultimate depository and proof of the new: the subject implied by digital interactivity.

Exhibition: Interactivity

The term *interactivity* in connection with the digital has become familiar outside specialized technological venues. It can be used in discourses associated with such social arenas as the art world, marketing promotion, and everyday speech, although often as a figurative term rather than a literal designation. Within theories of the digital, interactivity means a kind of exhibition in which a receiver is addressed as having some or all of the capacities of the sender or the programmer. When applied to the image, interactivity suggests that the image-receiver becomes an image-operator in the very act of reception. As a digital ideal, interactivity designates reception that fully possesses the breakthrough capabilities of practically infinite manipulability in conjunction with the unprecedented resources provided by convergence. In short, it proposes experiences of appropriating images that are radically novel.[43]

If the digital is a matter of manipulating arrays of numbers, and if convergence mandates that those numbers can cross through any number of points on a network, interactivity ultimately means that manipulation of an image need never stop. Roy Ascott formulates this key point:

[A]t the interface to telematic systems, content is created rather than received. By the same token content is disposed of at the interface by re-inserting it, transformed by the process of interaction, back into the network for storage, distribution, and eventual transformation at the interface of other users, at other access nodes across the planet.[44]

As a digital ideal, then, interactivity presupposes infinite manipulability and convergence, and unshackles all temporal and spatial limitations to image-formation. It makes the digital regime into one of perpetual process. One can never be certain that the image one is seeing at a specific time or point on the network has been definitively fixed or finalized. Indeed, the extent of the network is theoretically unlimited in time and in space. There is nothing in the concept of a network that restricts how long it will continue to carry transmissions, nor how long the transformations and retransformations of an image will go on; and there is nothing in the concept of a network that even restricts it to a planetary surface (despite Ascott's phrasing). But the full implications of this temporal and spatial unshackling can only be realized through interactivity.

Once again, the indexical often serves as the other, the old, which, it is forecast, the digital will supercede. Thus, when Ascott celebrates interactivity as artistic revolution, he writes:

[P]hotography as a stable medium is giving way to a practice which celebrates instability, uncertainty, incompleteness, and transformation.... What has changed ... from the old economy of the image, is that the processes of transformation I have described are now in the hands of the viewer as much as the artist.[45]

In the digital utopia, the old is fixation in the sense that the function of photography and film is to fixate things: fixation of the preexistent world in the image; fixation of the preexistent spectator captivated by desire for perception and knowledge of the world; and therefore fixation of stable identities of world and spectator. They are therefore opposed to the change, flux, unending process proposed by the digital utopia. By toppling the stable fixity of depiction attributed to an old era, interactivity seals in the sociocultural break to a new era and therefore the historiography of conquest that defines the digital.

Furthermore, the digital utopia defines interactivity as uniquely and specifically a digital capacity. Interactivity is therefore always available as a trump card proving the unique and radical novelty of the digital. For example, we have seen how the pervasiveness of digital mimicry could challenge assertions that the digital is radically new, simply because it implies the intrication of the digital with forms and functions of preexistent media. But the digital utopia can always respond that, regardless of how familiar are the compositional forms of digital imagery, no previous medium provides the spectator with a technical capacity to change the image.

At first it may seem a simple truism that interactivity is unique to the digital, if by interactivity one means technologically enabled capacities to affect the image in the act of reception. However, if interactivity is uniquely present in the digital, then why must it so often be characterized in the form of a forecast? One answer is that in actuality, current interactive capabilities remain highly finite and preprogrammed. At the most specialized levels of professional graphic art, verbal processing, and science, interactivity is subject to coding restrictions akin to those discussed above under the rubric of convergence, including the pervasive digital mimicry. And in the nonspecialized consumer markets, much of what is sold is interactivity of a greatly limited order: video games, educational programs, communications programs, and so forth. Even helmet-glove illusionistic environments involve phenomenologically "entering" and "acting" within a heavily preprogrammed mise-en-scène and set of scenarios. The general point applies as well to the art world. Those who believe that interactive art transforms the relation of spectator to the work must sometimes acknowledge, as does David Rokeby, that "The reactive behavior of most interactive works is defined by a computer program that is written in advance by the artist, or by a programmer realizing the artist's wishes." Thus, the number of pathways and choices open to the receiver may seem unprecedented, but as Lister puts it, "they are circumscribed by a multitude of prior decisions," having to do with "preconceptions of markets and audiences, and the ideologies and discourses *through* which they work and which inform their narratives, treatments and selections of content."[46]

But what is of interest here is not a debate over the fit or the lack of fit between discourses of the digital and some empirical reality, but rather the logic of the digital utopia. Interactivity is so often characterized through the form of a forecast because it is an ideal. As an ideal, it envisions bestowing both fully realized practically infinite manipulability and fully realized convergence on the spectator. But this means that *there has never been any such thing as interactivity.* No one has ever experienced interactivity as it appears, say, in the writings of someone like Ascott. As an ideal, it may function as a discursive figure, a technical goal. As a "not yet" in a certain kind of historical temporality, it may designate a trajectory of desire—a desired positionality of the subject receiving an image in the digital utopia. Shortly, I will discuss simulation and virtuality, considering them as terms that characterize technical means as attempting to instantiate that desire. But insofar as they depend on full-fledged interactivity, they do not exist either.[47]

Interactivity in this sense has implications on the terrain that 1970s film theory called spectatorship. Claims for the radical novelty of the digital include a radically new kind of position for the receiver of images. These claims therefore also entail assertions about the old kinds of subjects, those it attributes to precedent, indexical media, especially photography and film. But this is not necessarily an opposition between two kinds of theories, since the discourse of the digital can perfectly well accept discussions of spectatorship in, say, 1970s film theory, and may even embrace some of them in order to argue for the difference of the digital. The opposition is between two ideal spectators, two ideal subject-positions as the digital utopia needs to define them.

One name proposed for the new era of digital images under this description as one of unending, interactive flows is "post-photographic." Thus, Mitchell's authoritative book is entitled *The Reconfigured Eye: Visual Truth in the Post-Photographic Era.* He concludes that standardized photographic practices once "answered to a dominant conception of what the coinage of communication should be," but that digital imaging attacks the sediment of conventional, deadening relations implicit in such communicational norms: "The growing circulation of the new graphic currency that digital imaging technology mints is relentlessly destabilizing the old photographic orthodoxy, denaturing the established rules of graphic communication, and disrupting the familiar practices of image production and exchange."[48] Despite his sophistication (he calls on Foucault to indicate the importance of discursive norms), the normally careful Mitchell shifts from past to present-progressive tenses, registering the incompleteness of this history and his association with the digital utopia. The postphotographic, which is the very object of his book, is still in the haze of the "not yet," the perpetual state of transition on which the digital utopia depends in spite of itself.

However, the point of interest here is that, despite the label, the idea of a post-photographic era is anchored more in the presumptive state of a receiving subject than in formally conceived image characteristics. That state is usually identified with the decay of photographic credibility stemming from the possibilities for image modification and transformation in a digital age, as in the title of Mitchell's book. But what must be kept in mind, as Binkley remarks, is that the difficulties the digital presents to "judgements of faithful witness" reside "not in the technology, but in how it is understood" by receivers. A post-photographic spectator is technologically versed and media-wise. Living in a digital age, he or she will approach *any* image with claims to the truth of some originary event with some caution and wariness, and/or playfulness. But shifts in modes of appropriating images on this basis would have to do with ideology, culture, and subjectivity—again, a constellation familiar in film theory. For the digital utopia, the grounding standpoint on these issues is its ideal mode of image-spectator relations. Interactivity becomes less of a precisely delimited, technologically enabled capacity than a related but more general attitude of the receiving subject toward images in general. Thus, David Tomas can conclude, "With postphotography there is no longer a point of view, but visual context; no longer an eye, but a continuous *contextually* interactive, visually educative process in which biological eyes reflexively commune with the fragments and possibilities of their *cultures.*"[49] (In Tomas the utopianism of the digital is lent to a utopianism of the multicultural, that is, a more general social ideal.)

However, even within the digital utopia it becomes difficult to make the post-photographic attitude monolithic and coherent. To illustrate that difficulty, we can turn to other terms. In the end, "post-photographic" is not a completely satisfying name for digital imaging because it remains negative. It evokes the historiography underlying the digital utopia and suggests what is no longer done with images within it, but it does not name what is done (or can be done, or will be done). Perhaps this explains the currency of more positive terms for designating the terrain of the post-photographic image. Two of the most indicative are *simulation* and *virtuality*.

Digital simulation and virtuality are words not always used with uniformity and precision. But broadly speaking, they can be associated as terms that designate discourses or sets of signs that present themselves or are designed to be apprehended as explicitly coded constructions of nevertheless convincingly modeled environments available for interactive manipulation by the receiver. That is, they entail not only post-photographic modes of appropriating images, but interactive engagement. However, as usual with the digital, this can quickly expand into a more general description of a culturally pervasive attitude, as in N. Katherine Hayles's definition: "Virtuality is the cultural perception that material objects are interpenetrated by information patterns." Virtuality is also associated connotatively and metonymically with Virtual Reality devices, and it may have slightly stronger connection to the idea of a completely illusory mise-en-scène. Simulation, on the other hand, may place slightly greater weight on interactivity with that mise-en-scène (as in "flight simulator"). But the two are so closely linked in accounts of the digital as cultural transformation that it is often unproductive to disentangle them.[50]

It is misleading to identify Baudrillard's related concept of the simulacrum directly with computer simulations and virtuality. Baudrillard originally derived his own use of the term *simulacrum* in order to post an alternative to the category of representation, as part of a strategy for transforming modes of mass culture critique. According to Baudrillard, representation as such has to do with depicting or characterizing aspects of an actual world. It entails a complex play of inside the image (the represented world) and outside (the apprehender of the image) to the benefit of a subject or subjectivity-in-depth. The simulacrum, on the other hand, implies arbitrarily shifting or flexible subject positions, and therefore the radically novel irrelevance of both the subject-in-depth and the play of inside-outside oppositions on which it depends.[51]

But despite many claims to the contrary, neither the subject nor the inside-outside oppositions are necessarily irrelevant in digital simulation, which means that the digital remains in the realm of representation. This can be illustrated by going back to the compositional example of credible depth representation. As already noted, the history of digital simulation is replete with appropriations of Renaissance perspective and complementary subcodes. The digital utopia cannot conceive of such appropriation as mere imitation, for this would vitiate the claim to radical novelty that defines it. But the digital utopia can play its trump card, interactivity. The interactive sequenciation of several viewpoints as a spectator "moves through" the image is available in no other form of pictorial depth representation.

Thus, interactive simulation, virtuality, is often said to be immersive, in opposition to a spectatorial externality attributed to linear perspective. In painting and photography, writes Binkley, "the transparent window of perspective, for all its lucidity, is nevertheless an impenetrable barrier to our entreaties." A digital image, on the other hand, overcomes this exteriority of reception. In it, perspective is used to produce "environments we can inhabit." In her comparison of spectatorial engagement with cinematic space and spectatorial engagement with the space of the computer screen, Stone goes so far as to propose the following formula: "Interaction is the physical concretization of a desire to escape the flatness [of the screen] and merge into the created system." But note that the real proof of this immersion is that, through interactivity, spectatorial actions have effects in the interior of the image. Thus, according to Binkley, objects in simulated space "are rendered more real (interactive) since they can become aware of your presence and respond to you."[52]

We can interrogate some of the chief implications of interactivity in the digital utopia with two comments beginning from such formulations. First, although such accounts make the typical claim that interactivity collapses the inside-outside opposition, they actually illustrate how the problematic of inside and outside remains pertinent in accounts of digital imaging. Interactive virtuality tries to place the subject "inside" the image—or rather, inside the world represented in the image. This is literalized in many analyses of immersive three-dimensional Virtual Reality helmet-glove apparatuses, where descriptions and forecasts often focus on immersive experience grounded in sensory illusion (including such nonvisual elements as tactility). But such subjective immersion rests on a prior assumption, namely that the subject begins as an exteriority who must then be "moved" into the picture. Thus, writing about digital imaging for an art exhibition, Florian Rötzer proposes that "the virtualization of reality and realization of virtuality lead to the collapse of the traditional difference between an image and reality." And yet, he is constrained to emphasize that interactivity means "we are acting both in the 'real' world [i.e., manipulating the machine from outside the illusory mise-en-scène] and in the virtually present world in which our bodies are not actually present"; therefore, "although we experience changes in the image that occur because of our own physical movements, we still do not become an integrative part of the image," and "neither do we lose the position of external observer."[53]

This doubleness bears on the question of radical novelty, for it is not difficult to argue that the concern with inserting viewers whose bodies are "outside" an image "into" an image is a historically preexisting one that has been taken up by the digital. Erkki Huhtamo treats "the quest for immersion as a cultural topos," which can be found in a variety of precedent media, from the Victorian stereoscope to a number of cinematic forms ranging from *Hale's Tours* to extreme widescreen film processes, such as Cinerama and IMAX. The very concept of a virtual camera underpinned by interactivity illustrates that the figure of immersion actually pervades accounts of two-dimensional interactive images as well. Of course this does not mean that digital imaging or virtuality makes no difference. However, there is an underlying similarity that casts doubt on the radical novelty proposed in the digital utopia: the dialectic between subjective interiority and objective exteriority typical of representation remains in force.[54]

The second comment has to do with Binkley's parenthetical equation of "more real" with interactivity. This is especially pertinent for present purposes because Binkley provides an excellent example of something like a knowledgeable, fertile, and coherent theory of digital spectatorship, and it is worth pausing over. For one thing, it demonstrates that the ideal of interactivity does not necessarily exclude a rhetoric of realism. On the contrary, many discourses concerned with digital interactivity register a fascination with the spatial illusionism. Binkley homes in on interactivity as the key, asserting that "despite their infidelities, interactions with virtual environments feel oddly more real—not less real—than pictures of their real counterparts."[55] But the question, then, is how Binkley as theorist can hang on to the thesis of radical novelty, associated with the notion of a post-photographic attitude. So, he finds ways to make distinctions:

> When digital interfaces connect a user to a computer they accomplish something which is more like perceiving than picturing.... Simulations offer you experiences of a virtual reality which are more like experiences of reality pictured than experiences of pictures. Even though these exploits are often constructed with the aid of pictures, they transcend the simple display of imagery because of their interactivity.... Like art, [simulation] uses imagery to represent, but like life, it permits you to interact with what it represents.[56]

The unexpected peculiarity here is not only the return of an experience of reality and life in the digital image; it is also that that difference between the digital and the indexical is encapsulated in the surprising claim that the digital is more convincing than the indexical.

But this may not seem so surprising if we recall how the digital image is compositionally propped onto the forms of older media. Such propping can also support simulative interactivity. Virtuality and simulation presuppose a basic minimum of representational credibility, simply because the digital subject must recognize that he or she is entering a (virtual) world and must identify objects in that world in order to interact with them. In that case, such interactivity assumes the depictive imaging codes that Darley argues displaced the dominant alliance with a nonfigurative, modernist abstraction of early computer graphics. Digital mimicry will often be important here, which Binkley explicitly acknowledges:

> Digital media continue a tradition of surrogate reality inaugurated with the camera. The computer adds two novel twists: the reality behind the picture may be virtual, and it can interact.[57]

Since virtuality is only the name given for the particular kind of reality-modeling afforded by the digital image, it is interactivity that makes virtuality something different. Interactivity makes digital imaging so credible that it can be useful for prospective reality-testing; but it does not rule out more fantastic sorts of depiction. Even when the virtual environment is explicitly irreal, the model of the indexical is appropriate:

> The concoction of virtual experiences does not negate our photographic extension of seeing but is rather based upon it. Virtual realities are opened up by extending that [photographic] mode of seeing beyond the gateways to reality.

And, as already noted, one of Binkley's terms for irreal digital mises-en-scène is "ultra-cinematic effects." Once again, the digital is constituted in a hybrid historicity rather than the purity of a break.[58]

Further theoretical description of digital convincingness is therefore required, and it is directly on grounds of a theory (or at least a descriptive phenomenology) of digital subjectivity. Consider the following:

> What strange sort of experience is this interactive simulation? Is it like vicarious travel through pictures and travelogues? No. Voyeurism preys an

imaginary experience upon a real world; but the virtual world is imaginary while the experience of it is real: it is almost the exact inversion of the kinds of experiences we are accustomed to having in the cinema.[59]

This is an assertion about presumptive spectatorial knowledge in the digital utopia as opposed to the indexical. The digital spectator is a post-photographic subject and knows the image is only a realization of conceptuality generated by numerical codes. Crucially, however, the spectator is interactive. She or he also knows that *her or his own actions* on those objects *are* real, and not a fantasy. The result is that the reality of those actions may be projected onto the objects, investing them with an impression of reality. If the virtual environment "feels more real," this feeling derives from the spectator's own operations, his or her own agency as it has visible effects on and in the image. Hence, Binkley's insistence that "[n]umbers can materialize into objects only within the total interactive environment."[60]

This suggests an operational definition of interactivity: the real manipulation of unreal (virtual) objects. This real manipulation, the action on/in the image, is the key support for a rhetoric of reality. However, implicit in this is a simultaneous and reciprocal effect. If the objects are invested with a feeling of reality, so is the subject. It is not just that virtual space is infused by the real actions of the subject, but also that it provides that subject with a field for those actions. Furthermore, it is a certain kind of field, ideally one that instantaneously is affected by and displays an actualized subjective intent. Interactive simulation thus reconfirms that the spectator is a real subject: choosing, determining, exercising agency over objects within the mise-en-scène, at the interiority of the image.

It is interesting to note that this affirmation of the subject depends on a kind of indexicality and temporality, even though interactivity is often treated as a spatial category (the operator's actions in the "real space" of computer controls have effects in virtual or image space). Interactivity in imaging is achieved when the spectator's actions, which participate in manipulating the image, are perceivable in the image. This makes the image an indexical representation of the action of its spectator. Ideally, this would not be an indexical trace, for representation would occur instantaneously (or nearly so) with the spectator's actions. Once again, this is a matter of speed, hence computer memory capacity. Indeed, time is, arguably, the basis of the economics of the digital, the underside that is generally unacknowledged in the digital utopia. As Michael Benedikt remarks, "[T]ime is indeed the fundamental currency of computing, for it translates quite directly into data-processing capability and speed, and this in turn into the real-dollar cost of hardware, network on-line time, and access privilege."[61] But even technically, the extent to which this ideal is universally achievable is questioned by some. However, as with live television, the aspiration toward a phenomenal simultaneity of subjective cause and imaged effect seems clear.[62]

Interactive imaging thus leads toward the conception of an unprecedentedly powerful impression of reality in virtuality and simulation, and the conversion of the reality of the actions of the receiver into the contours of a powerful subject. In fact, if interactivity serves the digital utopia as its ultimate demonstration of radical novelty, there is a striking comparison in one of the most famous formulations of 1970s film theory, namely Christian Metz's contention that cinematic specificity is grounded in the spectator's real visual perception of an absent object. Metz reasoned from this that the cinematic spectator primarily identifies with itself (with its unconscious memory of narcissistic plenitude in the formation of the ego), and that the emplacement of the film camera is the textual stand-in for this primary cinematic identification. Like much 1970s film theory, Metz almost completely ignored the indexical characteristics of cinema, in his case perhaps because his version of the problematic of presence and absence tilted him toward spatial issues.

Binkley does not refer to Metz, but there is something similar in his conception of image and spectator. Binkley argues that interactive simulation is grounded in the subject's real action on a visible but really absent object. In his digital spectatorship, as in Metz's cinematic spectatorship, the subject identifies with itself, but as pure, effective, even formative activity, instead of as pure perception. While acknowledging elements of digital mimicry, Binkley is committed to establishing the novelty of the digital and so bypasses issues of digital hybridity, including a certain persistence of the indexical.

This suggests that the digital utopia is implicated in a kind of hypostasis of the category of the subject. As a digital ideal, interactivity is supposed to be the operation of a new kind of spectatorship and a new kind of subject. That is, the practice of this new subject is what is called interactivity. The digital utopia seems inexorably to push toward a closed circuit of individual subjectivity and image, the conceptuality of one defining the radical novelty of the other. In his article on the virtual camera, Binkley ventures some names for the kind of subjective investment entailed by digital interactivity: the philosophical name is solipsism, and the psychoanalytic name is narcissism. The digital utopia must insist on the difference between film and simulation. But how great is the difference between Metz's transcendental subject and the interactive one?[63]

However, if interactivity is the real manipulation of unreal objects, this returns us to the subject who operates digitally, but invests in the reality of the virtual world from a slightly different angle. The least that can be said is that interactive simulation demonstrates that spectatorship in the digital utopia is two-pronged. On the one hand, the post-photographic receiver is knowledgeable and wary of claims to originary representability associated with indexicality; on the other hand, that same receiver can invest the image with a certain reality-status, realizing itself interactively by manipulating it as if she or he were nevertheless part of the virtual universe. (And in principle, it does not matter whether this investment functions purely pragmatically, as in flight simulators, or in the realm of the fantastic.) By the standards of radical novelty that constitute the digital utopia, the reigning spectator of digital imaging is itself a hybrid of old and new, "photographic" and yet sharing the quest for the real attributed to the "post-photographic" era.

Or perhaps it is useful to understand that subject as divided instead of unified. Kevin Robins has dealt with the simultaneous placement of the digital spectator as outside and inside the simulation, first person and third person, subject and object, by proposing that "[t]he user is a split person."[64] This suggests a related theoretical description. The implicitly double-pronged, hybridized definition of the digital operator can be described perfectly well with reference to the concept of fetishism, with its simultaneity and splittings of knowledge and belief. "I know, but all the same . . ." is the often-cited motto of an approach that proposes that the structure of credible representation in general corresponds to the structure of fetishism. This theoretical path has sometimes been taken in film theory, not just to account for specific elements of cinematic texts, but to deal with the general appeal of an impression of reality.

In earlier chapters I argued that the idea of such splittings, along with the disavowals it implies, is useful for understanding cultural constructions of historicity and pastness, and also for describing something at the heart of even classical cinematic spectatorship that complicates notions of cinematic transparency. In the 1970s, film theorists often ignored regimes of knowledgeability assumed by that cinema. For example, the explicit artifice of the Hollywood musical displays an overt cinematic virtuosity and artificiality that can authorize a spectator to evaluate it as performance, construction. The "serious" historical film might seem an opposed example, locked into a closed diegetic universe of referentiality. But even the historical can authorize a variable range of spectatorial give-and-take whereby the spectator, far from being necessarily overwhelmed by a plethora of reality-effects, may feel authorized to assert knowledge by challenging the accuracy of those effects. True, the spectator of classical film does not possess technologically enabled interactivity, and this makes for significant degrees of difference. But, using terms of the fetishistic theory of representation, she or he may still be conceived as investing in knowledgeability and therefore "active" appropriation of the film text, as well as belief and involvement.[65]

What of post-photographic spectatorial knowledgeability in the digital image? In computer graphics there is a distinction between "image space" or "cyberspace," where the underlying numerical arrays are stored and manipulated, and "object space" or "virtual reality," which is the perceivable mise-en-scène generated in the output image.[66] Interactive simulation presumes a spectator aware of image space/cyberspace and at least some of its possibilities, and yet ready for various degrees of disavowal as she or he interacts with the perceived image as if it consisted of objects that constitute a field of actions. Simulation and virtuality closely tie interactivity to splittings between numbers and pictures, to being simultaneously "outside" *and* "inside" the image. As a digital ideal, interactivity makes the image remarkably susceptible to description under the old dialectic of knowledge and belief. It becomes the practice of that dialectic.

The convenience of this theoretical approach for handling the hybrid historicity implicitly constituting spectatorship in the digital utopia suggests, first, that the digital is conceivable within theories of representation that have always dealt with subjective investments and symbolic stand-ins. Second, since it is also applicable to the spectatorship in indexical media, it reconfirms that the historical "just before" of digital historiography—photography and film—should be imbricated in a more complicated way with ideals of the digital. This points up the benefits of a refusal to accept the self-defining historicity of the digital utopia, with its thesis of a radical break between old and new. If characterizing the two-pronged spectator of interactivity that the digital utopia itself generates is a problem within the digital utopia, this mandates leaving the digital utopia.

If interactivity is the trump card of the digital utopia, then its claim to radical novelty depends on a claim for new modes of subjectivity. Perhaps it is not so surprising that the historicity of the digital utopia resolves into a historiography of the human subject. The very idea of a post-photographic era embodies the construction of a historiography whose ground is not radically different from that of figures like Bazin and Barthes, who dealt with indexical spectatorship through accounts of subjective investment, irrationality and fantasy.[67] The ultimate point, then, does not have to do with the validity or limitations of psychoanalytic film theory, but with the fact that the digital does not escape that terrain marked out by the modern project of a theory of the subject. The claims for radical novelty made by the digital utopia remain on that terrain. Elements such as the forecast, digital mimicry, and the hybridity it reveals only indicate that the digital cannot be accounted for within its own closed circuit.

Concluding Remarks

There is much of descriptive value in the digital utopia. But the absolute liberations of practically infinite manipulability, convergence, and inter-activity inevitably find themselves limited by their own internal logic. These limitations invariably point to a constitutive hybridity that contradicts utopian claims to radical novelty. The digital utopia defines its novelty in opposition to precedent media, identifies precedent media with indexicality, and makes indexicality into a monolithic unity characterized by fixity of world, of representation, and of subject. This is wrong not only because, as Martin Lister puts it, *all* media involve "wider and complex forms of political, social and cultural interaction," something that interactivity as a digital ideal obscures.[68] It is also wrong on the level of theoretical frameworks and understandings.

The digital utopia sets up an opposition between indexical spectatorship as inactive and fixed, and digital spectatorship as active and mobile. The opposition between a passive and an active spectator is, of course, not specific to theories of the digital. (In fact, it has sometimes been used as a stick with which to beat 1970s film theory.) But it is always suspect, for it is redolent with theological connotations of determinism–free will debates but is never discussed on those grounds. I have invoked the fetishistic theory of representation as a wedge to demonstrate that the "new" and the "old" are susceptible to common theoretical frameworks and understandings, and therefore a more complex historicity.

But it is also informative for another reason. Fetishism is a structure of disavowal, and the digital utopia is shot through with disavowals. In their climactic concentration on the capabilities, satisfactions, and needs of the interactive subject, enthusiasts and theorists of the digital have been charged with a number of obfuscations: the emphasis on conceptuality ends up disavowing not only physicality, but the body and gender; the emphasis on subjective immersion ends up disavowing the materiality of the digital apparatus as well as the economics that guide its development; the emphasis on conceptuality of the individual operator ends up disavowing the ideological structures and the concrete histories that generate concepts in the first place. Such critiques are also ways of saying that the historicity of the digital utopia avoids historical self-consciousness. Defining itself through a historiography of conquest that can always be validated by a structure of the forecast, the digital utopia thus disavows its own historical emplacement. And in the present context, a final note is in order: this historical emplacement includes not only the current persistence of indexicality in a range of hybrid formations, but also the involvement of mainstream cinema as representational form and capitalist industry in the development and utilization of digital imaging. In this sense, at least, cinema is not the other of the digital, but finds itself, once more, as a historically hybrid entity.

Of course, as Bazin might have said, the digital is also a dystopia. Fully considering the relation between utopic and dystopic accounts of the digital will have to wait for another time.[69] It is a necessary step toward sublating the conceptuality of the digital in order to understand it as a matter of concrete historicities. To say this is to recognize the unavoidability of constructing histories, an unavoidability that is political, epistemological, and itself "historical."

Afterword

This book has been about modern historicity in relation to film theory, filmic textuality, and film history. From its emergence, it was possible to see the modern category of history as epistemologically unstable. Awareness of this problematicity and its implications has been heightened in important sectors of cultural theory and critique, theory of history, and, arguably, some related film theory of the past three decades. However, my general position has been that the category of history as inherited from the onset of modernity in the nineteenth century remains a crucial one. For one thing, it is crucial because any politically engaged approach to culture and theorized critique must be able to consider the possibility of change. Such an approach therefore must deploy, implicitly or explicitly, some attitude toward modern historicity. For the relation of change to stasis is centrally at stake in conceptions of historical knowledge as normalized in the West during the nineteenth century.

Hence my citation of Bazin's figurative definition of cinema—in translation, "change mummified"—in the title of this book. Considered as a trope, it is an oxymoron, which harshly yokes together mutability and stability. As a matter of film theory, it condenses the grounds for Bazin's entire account of cinema as a medium with an unprecedented vocation for the real, and it is linked to two of his fundamental "ontological" themes: the specific appeal of the indexical trace as possessing special referential force with respect to pastness, and the postulate of a subject radically anxious about the threat posed by the passage of time.

Bazinian realism has been subject to much criticism as film theory, some of it deserved but some of it, as I argued in chapter 1, limiting. More broadly, I suggested the usefulness of taking up and rethinking some ideas encapsulated in the phrase "change mummified": especially that there is something radically threatening or disordering about time, and that technically produced, mass-distributed images are heavily invested in the representation and management of temporality. "Change mummified" can therefore stand not only for Bazin's view of cinema, but also the project of modern historicity and the antinomies central to it. It becomes an entry into a terrain of overlaps and intersections between the two.

Thus, in Part I, I proposed that the ideal of the indexical trace, along with a preservative obsession, has pervaded modern Western cultural practices and projects of knowledge. And these do often entail imagining subjective positionalities as defenses and reassurances in the present against the instabilities inherent in modern temporality—instabilities focused through consciousness of the continual recession of presentness into pastness. In the most epistemologically prestigious institution engaging with pastness, modern disciplined historiography, the ideal indexical trace becomes the decisive historical document. Here historical knowledge is conceived as the construction of a coherent sequence evidenced by indexical traces; and anxiety about time is manifested as a problem of epistemological standpoint or positionality, ultimately expressed through the conundrum that historiography must conceive of itself as having a history. But in this broader context, such anxiety with respect to the destabilizing characteristics of temporality itself appears as social and "historical." The social organization of time is intimately connected to culture and therefore the production and dissemination of media such as film. Media times are socioeconomic and sociological as well as representational, discursive, and textual. This level of temporal management is indicated by the dependence of narrative cinema as institution on divisions and relations of labor time and leisure time.

Part II consisted of a series of case studies of vicissitudes of indexicality and historicity in cinema, with some attention to related media and discourses. All these studies revolve around problems of the relations of the indexical and sequenciation, but also point up issues of spectatorial and textual positionality with respect to pastness and time. This is one reason that they often refer back to 1970s film theory, which, among other things, placed questions of subjective positionality at the forefront of understandings of cinema. But they do so in a way that foregrounds aspects of cinema that 1970s film theory tended to repress, such as its claims to referentiality and the temporality of its operations. (A mark of this repression was the identification of Bazin as the key "other" in the canon of 1970s film theory; that is, as the old that had to be completely displaced by the new.)

More broadly, I hope the studies of Part II indicate the productivity and, for many questions, the unavoidability of understanding cinema and media not only "historically," but in relation to historicity. I also hope they indicate grounds for opposing the thesis of a general attenuation of modern historicity in and because of modern technical media. The chapters on mainstream cinema and the preclassical film, *A Policeman's Tour of the World*, circulate around the assumption that the institutionalization of the textual norms of mainstream U.S. cinema was not only a major threshold in the history of filmic textuality, but more generally, in media and cultural history. They address the implantation of historicity and the management of indexicality in mainstream film textuality while remarking on some consequences for film theory. The chapter on the documentary tradition carries these concerns from the establishment of the norms of mainstream film to the recent past and the present, which means acknowledging the interrelations of film with "newer" media and the kinds of indexicality they may idealize. The remaining chapters, on *Ceddo* as postcolonial film and on discourses of the digital utopia, continue this line in order to argue for the persistence of these concerns along with the variability of their manifestations in cinema and media culture. I think these studies only begin to suggest the range of differentiations among conceptions of historicity and relations to it in cinema, on the two planes that fundamentally define modern historiography: the indexical trace and the temporal sequence.

Something of my own historiographic attitude becomes more explicit with the appearance of two closely related ideas in the last two chapters. The first is what I called a radical historicity. This entails a historiography that knowledgeably confronts the instabilities of the relationships that modern historicity establishes between past and present. Such a historiography registers the corrosive premises of modern temporality and the problem of engaging with change and transformation; it also acknowledges that the positionalities in the present from which one constructs pastness cannot be extricated from historicity and those corrosive premises. It abandons neither sequenciation, nor the necessity of assuming a positionality (however complex) in the present. But this sequenciation and this positionality are, among other things, themselves understood as being temporalized, as being "in history."

Furthermore, this is to take up the modern imperative to historicize historicity, and with it the standpoint from which one writes history, but without pretending that it is possible to do so while avoiding the arena of referentiality that is at stake in historiography. In the particular case of *Ceddo*, for example, the standpoint rests on a self-conscious situatedness, which might be characterized in reductive shorthand as sub-Saharan African postcoloniality. This situatedness is associated with a certain (historical) arena of political awareness, for it is the consequence of the very history the film gives us. Certain kinds of political situatedness militate toward a radical historicity, and, conversely, even the most abstract kind of radical historicity one could imagine certainly has a politics embedded in it.

This is closely related to the second historiographic idea promoted in Part II, the hybridity of historical temporality. The construction of historiographic sequencing from past to present, old to new, is at the heart of modern historicity and even its other fundamental element, the indexical trace. (The very concept of something material that has persisted from past to present implies a sequence in the existence and status of the object, as it becomes historical evidence.) But the temporal commingling of the two extremes of past and present, old and new, suggests that all historical entities may be such mixtures, whose separate identities are established by sequenciation, which distinguishes them in its drive to order change.

Thus, in my presentation, hybrid temporality is introduced as such positively, through the postcolonial positionality of *Ceddo*, but also symptomatically, as the negative underside of discourses of the digital utopia. For the discourse of the digital utopia imagines the achievement of sociocultural and representational ideals through a historical sequence (of "new media" technologies) leading to a radical novelty, a purified historical break. But this very historiography unwittingly partakes of the "old," restaging and renovating scenarios of modern historicity, including historical temporality as the potential bearer of change and the new, and a triumph of subjective positionality over the flow of time expressed as the full realization of older representational ideals. Even variations on indexicality return in the digital and its discourses.

Within the straightforward historiographic sequencing of the digital utopia, this underside can only appear as a mixture of the old and the new. Such hybridities threaten the neat separation of past and present, exposing instabilities in their relations. This would make my example of the digital utopia the polar opposite of a radical historicity, for, as in *Ceddo*, the latter entails a historiography that explicitly engages with its own positionality. That is, the hybridity of historical temporality is another face of radical historicity.

An objection might be that if modern historicity persists even in that which claims to surpass it, then the modern itself, with its fundamental thesis of the possibility of change and radical novelty, could never be found in any pure state and so has never been actualized.[1] True enough. However, in my view the hybridity of historical temporality does not imply a free-floating miscellany, but is instead a historiographic construct. In this, it is like the idea of modernity itself, and is manifested in any specification of it. The modern is not a purity, but an interrelation of historical entities and forces in tendential relations of dominance and subordination. And it only has weight from a positionality in the present that constructs a sequence. The idea of the hybridity of historical temporality does not obliterate the temporal sequence, but rather can only be conceived in dialectical relation with it. It is grounded in and embodies the unavoidable interplay of present with pastness that modern historicity cannot overcome and that is basic to its rationale.

It may be worth pointing out that this notion of temporal hybridity has informed my attitude toward reading and writing film theory, including the opposition to Bazin set up by 1970s film theory, as well as the current status of the latter. It has also informed my references to other media besides cinema. Furthermore, modernity, with its presumption of perpetual change, has been marked by the regular introduction of "new media." Cinema was one, photography before it, television after it, and now digital interactive multimedia. All of them involve varied mixtures of pastnesses and presentnesses, encompassing diverse relations between objects of representation and subjects. As technologies seeking to produce mass-distributed images, all of them have had to negotiate and interact not only with their predecessors as representational and discursive modes, but relatedly with socioculturally dominant modes of temporal conception and organization. Again, "the new" is not only an aesthetic category, but a socioeconomic one.

And so, today, when the very phrase "new media" has become an idiolect of academia and show business, politics and ultimately capitalism itself, Bazin's trope "change mummified" may reverberate in unexpected ways. For it appears in an essay centrally concerned with how photography surpasses figurative painting, and with what is distinctive about film as compared to photography. In his own way Bazin was broadly concerned with the "history of imaging," as we now call it.

One can imagine rewriting and extending Bazin's sequence of new media into the present, so that it would go on to encompass television and the digital as well. Such a history would still focus on the status of indexical imaging and the internally unified sequence in each, keeping in mind that where presentnesses meet pastnesses are its crucial pressure points. However, within such a sequential schema, certain aspects of any "new" medium will appear as temporally hybrid. This certainly applies to cinema, which is more than indexicality, even if it makes sense to insist that the latter should be conceived as a "dominant" for some crucial questions. Bazin's own conception of the technically produced image is as a conjunction of old (perspective developed in painting) and new (technologies of the indexical trace). Television is nicely indicative as an example in this regard, with its explicitly heterogeneous intermixtures of types of indexicality (taking in liveness, videotaped actuality, films, and so forth) and sequenciations (a "flow" ranging from the succession of brief fragments to serialized longer narrativizations subject to constant interruption).

That the structure of historicity could be used to help define new media points toward the currency of issues involving temporality throughout the histories of those media. In the course of this book, I have referred to two large-scale shifts in temporality: The first, epistemological in character, was from an eschatological historiography based on a certain timelessness to a historiography filled with time and whose corollary is change. The second, socioeconomic in character, was from a socialization of labor and everyday life conceived according to a task-oriented, naturalized temporality, to one conceived according to a specialization of production tasks and a quantitatively rationalizable temporality. Among other things, the capitalist exigencies of the latter lead toward the economics of mass production and mass consumption along with the ideologies and divisions of labor time and leisure time. It was therefore a necessary condition for the dissemination of mass-distributed media as we know them.

I do not claim to have directly and fully addressed the question of how the long picture of one shift in temporality relates to the other. (And, it should be said, this question is only complicated by the fact that in both cases it is difficult to find either side of the opposition in pure form throughout a sociocultural formation.) But I have suggested that both of these temporal shifts do converge on media of mass-distributed imaging, among other social and cultural sites. I have also suggested that both involve the management and organization of time. If time needs to be managed, this implies that there is something potentially disturbing, disorienting, or dangerous in modern temporality, something always threatening to get out of control, to become culturally and/or socially problematic.

Bazin's "change mummified" has knowledge value in the way it brilliantly registers the drive to manage temporality. However, it does remain a symptom and product of that which it helps us to know. In the individualized anxiety that is its tenor, it is a fundamentally defensive and asocial conception. Simply as an indication of one possible alternative pathway, then, I will end by invoking a different trope, which moves toward anticipatoriness rather than defensiveness in the face of time, and is collective and social.

Walter Benjamin's final comment on modernity deals with historicity. In "Theses on the Philosophy of History," he conceives of the project of the materialist historian as grasping the suffering marginalized by bourgeois historiography. But, he notes, the past must be grasped from positionalities in the present that are themselves ever changing, for the present is also historical. The past is therefore evanescent, and access to it is itself socially and politically determined. Whereas Rankean methodology claimed it could solve this distinctively modern problem by establishing secure and definitive sequences, thus stabilizing change, Benjamin points toward hybrid temporalities. He embraces the idea that historiography consists in constantly shifting relations of present and past. Yet, he does not revert to a typical historical relativism. Benjamin concludes by comparing the temporality of the materialist historian to that of the traditional Jew, who was proscribed from predicting the future, but who knew that any instant of time could contain all the preconditions for the coming of the Messiah.[2]

At the risk of excessive grandiosity, I would suggest that Benjamin's trope, of a subject who lives profane time as if on the verge of a messianic break, points toward another configuration of the relations between the force of time and timelessness, and between pastnesses and presentnesses. In one sense, it is as oxymoronic as Bazin's "change mummified," for it reconceives modern temporality in relation to older notions that can be associated with eschatological time. The consciousness of time and change associated with modernity—and that defensiveness so acutely yet obscurely crystallized by Bazin—is rethought as one that may make the possibility of change into a matter of anticipation rather than anxiety. But this is not another utopia. It is to envision a *historicity* that encompasses the possibility of transformed social relations and subjectivities, and therefore the transformation of historical time.

Whatever else Benjamin's figure suggests, it consolidates an imperative informing his "Theses." On the one hand, the temporality of modernity, with its radical historicization of the world and hyperbolization of the new, *should* be taken on its own terms, as purchase to establish the possibility of the radically different and liberating.[3] On the other hand, it must *not* be taken on its own terms, insofar as one truly dissents from key social and economic conditions and effects with which it has been implicated in present and past. Whether one regards this as an aporia or a dialectic, coming to grips with it might enable a new history, and new practices, of "new media."

Notes

Introduction

1. Claude Lévi-Strauss, *The Savage Mind* (Chicago: University of Chicago Press, 1973), 248, 251–52, 254. Lévi-Strauss notes that this self–other construct is contradictory, for the historically knowledgeable "self" must make its definitive relation to the "other" ahistorical in order to sustain its position. Here he touches on the antinomy between change and stasis that is central to some of my own later points about historicity. I here leave aside subsequent charges that Lévi-Strauss's own theory reinstates the same opposition; see Johannes Fabian, *Time and the Other: How Anthropology Makes Its Object* (New York: Columbia University Press, 1983), 90–91. For Fabian's aggressive general critique of Lévi-Strauss on historicity, see 52–69.

2. Lévi-Strauss, *The Savage Mind*, 259–60.

3. This is the context of the famous methodological declaration: "I believe the ultimate goal of the human sciences to be not to constitute but to dissolve man." Lévi-Strauss, *The Savage Mind*, 256, 247; see also 262.

4. For canonical examples of arguments against unified, continuous temporality, see Louis Althusser, "The Errors of Classical Economics: An Outline for a Concept of Historical Time," chap. 4 in *Reading "Capital,"* Louis Althusser and Étienne Balibar, trans. Ben Brewster (London: New Left Books, 1970); Jacques Derrida, "Writing before the Letter," in *Of Grammatology*, trans. Gayatri Chakravorty Spivak (Baltimore, Md.: Johns Hopkins University Press, 1976), e.g., 66–67, 72–73, 85–86; Michel Foucault, "Nietzsche, Genealogy, History," in *Language, Counter-Memory, Practice: Selected Essays and Interviews*, ed. Donald F. Bouchard (Ithaca, N.Y.: Cornell University Press, 1977). See also Michel de

Certeau, *The Writing of History*, trans. Tom Conley (New York: Columbia University Press, 1988) for its many considerations of disciplinary historiography with respect to otherness.

5. See, "The Discourse of History" and "The Reality Effect" in Roland Barthes, *The Rustle of Language*, trans. Richard Howard (Berkeley and Los Angeles: University of California Press, 1989); Hayden White, *Metahistory: The Historical Imagination in Nineteenth-Century Europe* (Baltimore, Md.: Johns Hopkins University Press, 1973), as well as his later work, especially several essays collected in Hayden White, *The Content of the Form: Narrative Discourse and Historical Representation* (Baltimore, Md.: Johns Hopkins University Press, 1987). For a survey of the state of theory of history in 1960 from the perspective of analytic philosophy, see *Theories of History*, ed. Patrick Gardiner (Glencoe: The Free Press, 1959). It is divided into Part I, "Philosophies of History: Vico to Collingwood," and Part II, "Recent Views Concerning Historical Knowledge and Explanation." Part II is almost completely composed of current analytic philosophy, and the greatest portion of it is given over to "The Function of General Laws in History," Carl G. Hempel's famous account of historical explanation through a view of scientific explanation and debates it generated.

The rapidity with which conventional historical discourse was deprivileged in cultural and critical theory can be illustrated by the work of Roland Barthes. In "Myth Today" in *Mythologies*, trans. Annette Lavers (1957; reprint, New York: Hill and Wang, 1972), Barthes introduced semiology as a means of demonstrating that bourgeois ideology transformed historical entities into eternal, naturalized categories (the very inversion defined by Marx and Engels in their own attempt to historicize human consciousness). By agreeing that dehistoricization was the goal of bourgeois ideology, Barthes implicitly made the historical into the unquestionable evaluative standard of modern myth analysis. Yet, just ten years later in two influential articles, "The Discourse of History" and "The Reality Effect," Barthes took exactly the opposite tack, treating the very forms of conventional historical discourse itself as manifesting an overriding ideological and mythical operation.

6. Fredric Jameson, *The Political Unconscious: Narrative as a Socially Symbolic Act* (Ithaca, N.Y.: Cornell University Press, 1981); Paul Ricoeur, *Time and Narrative*, trans. Kathleen Blamey and David Pellauer, 3 vols. (Chicago: University of Chicago Press, 1984–88).

7. Jean-François Lyotard, *The Postmodern Condition: A Report on Knowledge*, trans. Geoff Bennington and Brian Massumi (Minneapolis: University of

Minnesota Press), xxiii, xxiv. For Jameson on narrative, see *The Political Uncon-scious;* on history, see his *Postmodernism or, The Cultural Logic of Late Capitalism* (Durham, N.C.: Duke University Press, 1991) especially the famous chapter 1, "The Cultural Logic of Late Capitalism," where postmodernism is identified as a key ideological turn in a socioeconomic drive to construct an experiential and rep-resentational universe that blocks knowledge of the social totality. One particu-larly useful encapsulation of the variegated status of the term *postmodern,* which emphasizes Jameson's role in capturing it for Marxism, is Perry Anderson, *The Origins of Postmodernity* (New York: New Left Books, 1998).

8. Once again, there are indicators of this connection in Lévi-Strauss, who linked his own awareness of the crucial function of codification procedures and the consequent recession of conventional historical consciousness to the invention of message-transmitting machines. But he had in mind recent ones closely tied to Information Theory (he mentions telecommunications, the com-puter, and the electron microscope), and he did not treat it in the context of a constant augmentation of technical media of representation since the nineteenth century, which concerns me here. See Lévi-Strauss, *The Savage Mind,* 268.

9. See, for example, several contributions to *Post-Theory: Reconstructing Film Studies,* ed. David Bordwell and Noël Carroll (Madison: University of Wis-consin Press, 1996), which has the avowed goal of proposing new "research programs" for Film Studies, but whose contributors attest to the continuing unavoidability of 1970s film theory by spending so many pages criticizing it.

10. The most influential call in the 1970s for reconceiving film history on the basis of new theories of historical temporality and textuality was probably Jean-Louis Comolli, "Technique et idéologie," published as a series in *Cahiers du cinéma,* nos. 229 (May 1971), 230 (July 1971), 231 (Aug.–Sept. 1971), 233 (Nov. 1971), 234–35 (Dec. 1971, Jan.-Feb. 1972), 241 (Sept.–Oct. 1972), which explic-itly appealed to Althusser and Julia Kristeva on these issues. Copies of British Film Institute translations of several installments were disseminated in budding Anglo-American circles of film scholarship. For an early example of their impact, see Edward Branigan, "Color and Cinema: Problems in the Writing of History," *Film Reader* 4 (1979): 16–34.

One important theorist who proposed to implement nonlinear film histori-ography was Nöel Burch; see, for example, "Porter, or Ambivalence," *Screen* 19 (winter 1978–79): 91–105. For a sense of the strength of this ambition at the time, see the critique of Burch on both traditional historiographic grounds and on grounds of insufficient nonlinearity in Kristin Thompson and David Bordwell, "Linearity, Materialism, and the Study of Early American Cinema," *Wide Angle* 5, no. 3 (1983). The underdevelopment of the conception of history in 1970s film theory is already noted in a generally sympathetic overview, Philip Rosen, "*Screen* and the Marxist Project in Film Criticism," *Quarterly Review of Film Studies* 2 (Aug. 1977): 273–87. For examples of film scholars who ally themselves with the postmodern turn and the deauthorization of modern historicity, see Giuliana Bruno, "Ramble City: Postmodernism and *Blade Runner*," in *Alien Zone: Cultural Theory and Contemporary Science Fiction Cinema*, ed. Annette Kuhn (New York: Verso, 1990), 183–95; Timothy Corrigan, *A Cinema without Walls: Movies and Culture after Vietnam* (New Brunswick, N.J.: Rutgers University Press, 1991), esp. chapter 1 on historical representation and contemporary cinema; and Anne Friedberg, *Window Shopping: Cinema and the Postmodern* (Berkeley and Los Angeles: University of California Press, 1993).

11. For an early review of work by the new generation of film historians in relation to historical methods, see Robert C. Allen and Douglas Gomery, *Film History: Theory and Practice* (New York: Knopf, 1985), which is, however, staged as an introductory textbook. Michèle Lagny, *De l'histoire du cinéma: Méthode historique et histoire du cinéma* (Paris: Armand Colin, 1992) takes in a wider range of scholarship (it was written later and deals with both French- and English-language film historiography) and more directly addresses recent theories of history and cinema. See also Francesco Caseth, *Theories of Cinema 1945–1993*, trans. Francesca Chiostri et al., (Austin, University of Texas Press, 1999), chap. 17. Theory of history is the real concern of an interesting consideration of the new discipline of film history; see Pierre Sorlin, "Cinema: An Undiscoverable History?" trans. Keith Reader, *Paragraph* 15, no. 1 (March 1992).

For an example of the language of "theory" versus "history," see Robert Sklar, "Oh! Althusser!: Historiography and the Rise of Cinema Studies," in *Resisting Images: Essays on Cinema and History*, ed. Robert Sklar and Charles Musser (Philadelphia: Temple University Press, 1990). Sklar finds recent cultural and film theory of minimal use to the historian, but also tries to establish distance from the new, conventionalized film historiography, which he calls "bourgeois," while promoting a refurbished social history of cinema; see especially 14ff. A more complex version of this impulse, but from the "theory" side more than the "history" side, is expressed in David Bordwell, "Contemporary Film Studies and the Vicissitudes of Grand Theory," in Bordwell and Carroll, *Post-Theory*. The climactic example of

Bordwell's argument for "middle-level research programs" (itself a variant on Sklar's claim to be mediating between abstract theoretical and empiricist extremes) is the new film historiography. It may be that a version of the appeal of critical historical method (see chapter 3 in this volume) is embedded in his approach. It certainly seems that an insistence that any theoretical account should encompass the historical pervades his important work. See, for example, *Narration in the Fiction Film* (Madison: University of Wisconsin Press, 1985). This project was already announced in David Bordwell, "Lowering the Stakes: Prospects for a Historical Poetics of Cinema," *Iris* 1, no. 1 (1983): 5–18.

12. A sense of the interest in historical cinema that emerged among those concerned with 1970s film theory and textual theory can be gleaned from *Edinburgh Magazine 2: History/Production/Memory* (1977), which includes translations of materials from *Cahiers du cinéma* (including an interview with Foucault), as well as articles by such figures as Stephen Heath. Prominent early examples of scholarly concern with historical representation in film around this period include Marc Ferro, *Cinema and History*, trans. Naomi Greene (Detroit: Wayne State University Press, 1988), and Pierre Sorlin's pioneering *The Film in History: Restaging the Past* (Totowa, N.J.: Barnes and Noble, 1980). Examples of significant later case studies published in the United States and informed by, or at least aware of, aspects of the critique of historicity in cultural theory or 1970s film theory include Anton Kaes, *From Hitler to Heimat: The Return of History as Film* (Cambridge, Mass.: Harvard University Press, 1989); Robert Burgoyne, *Bertolucci's 1900* (Detroit: Wayne State University Press, 1991); Robert Burgoyne, *Film Nation: Hollywood Looks at U.S. History* (Minneapolis: University of Minnesota Press, 1997); George Custen, *Bio/Pics: How Hollywood Constructed Public History* (New Brunswick, N.J.: Rutgers University Press, 1992); Angela Dalle Vacche, *The Body in the Mirror: Shapes of History in Italian Cinema* (Princeton, N.J.: Princeton University Press, 1992); Marcia Landy, *Cinematic Uses of the Past* (Minneapolis: University of Minnesota Press, 1996); several of the contributions to *The Persistence of History: Cinema, Television, and the Modern Event*, ed. Vivian Sobchak (New York: Routledge, 1996), which also registers acute awareness of the generalization of theoretical themes into descriptions of culture in postmodernist cultural theory; and *The Historical Film: History and Memory in Media*, ed. Marcia Landy (New Brunswick, N.J.: Rutgers University Press, 2001).

Disciplinary historians (as opposed to film scholars) have also increasingly taken up the question of historical cinema, sometimes as a supplement, sometimes as a challenge to the conventional historical scholarship. See, e.g., the forum in *American Historical Review* 30 (Dec. 1988): 1173–227. One of the most aggressive in this regard is Robert A. Rosenstone; see his *Visions of the Past: The Challenge of Film to Our Idea of History* (Cambridge, Mass.: Harvard University Press, 1995) and *Revisioning History: Film and the Construction of a New Past*, ed. Rosenstone (Princeton, N.J.: Princeton University Press, 1995).

1. Subject, Ontology, and Historicity in Bazin

  1. André Bazin, "The Evolution of the Language of Cinema," in *What Is Cinema?* trans. Hugh Gray, 2 vols. (Berkeley and Los Angeles: University of California Press, 1967 and 1971), hereafter cited as *WC*. These volumes contain selections from André Bazin, *Qu'est-ce-que le cinéma?* 4 vols. (Paris: Ed. du cerf, 1959–61), a collection of Bazin's most important articles, which he organized shortly before his death. "The Evolution of the Language of Cinema" is actually a composite of three articles previously published by Bazin between 1950 and 1955.

  2. For various types of commentaries on Bazin participating or stemming from 1970s film theory, see the following: on Bazin's ideological/metaphysical complicity, see James Roy MacBean, *Film and Revolution* (Bloomington: Indiana University Press, 1975), 101–3 and passim; on his contradictory logic, see Brian Henderson, "The Structure of Bazin's Thought," in *A Critique of Film Theory* (New York: Dutton, 1980); on the blockages of his realism from the perspective of semiotics and psychoanalysis, see Colin MacCabe, "Theory and Film: Principles of Realism and Pleasure," *Screen* 17, no. 3 (autumn 1976), esp. 9–17. On the partiality of Bazin's insights, see Peter Wollen, *Signs and Meaning in the Cinema*, rev. ed. (Bloomington: Indiana University Press, 1972), 125–36, 140–41; Christian Metz, *The Imaginary Signifier: Psychoanalysis and the Cinema*, trans. Celia Brittan et al., (Bloomington: Indiana University Press, 1982); Jean-Louis Comolli, "Technique et idéologie: Caméra, perspective, profondeur de champ," intermittent series in *Cahiers du cinéma*, nos. 229–41, especially the explication and comparisons of Bazin and Mitry in no. 230 (July 1971) and no. 231 (August–September 1971); the latter is translated in *Narrative, Apparatus, Ideology: A Film Theory Reader*, ed. Philip Rosen (New York: Columbia University Press, 1986), 422–30; Brian Henderson, "Bazin Defended against His Devotees," *Film Quarterly* 32, no. 4 (summer 1979), esp. 30–37. For later and different kinds of critical accounts, see Edward R. Branigan, *Point of View in the Cinema: A Theory of Narration and*

Subjectivity in Classical Film (New York: Mouton, 1984), 198–212; Noël Carroll, *Philosophical Problems of Classical Film Theory* (Princeton: Princeton University Press, 1988); and David Bordwell, *On the History of Film Style* (Cambridge, Mass.: Harvard University Press, 1997). For an admiring account, on the other hand, see the only book-length treatment of Bazin, Dudley Andrew, *André Bazin* (New York: Oxford, 1978).

It is striking how many of these critiques were established by 1976. Whatever their merits (in my view there are many), it is indeed as if the familiar constellation of breakthrough tendencies in post-1968 film theory required an "other" to help define their own radical novelty, and Bazin was found to be more than suitable. In the Anglo-American world, the translation of major works by Bazin in the two volumes entitled *What Is Cinema?* in 1967 and 1971 was undoubtedly a factor that both confirmed Bazin's importance and made him more generally available as a target.

3. Jean-Paul Sartre, "Existentialism Is a Humanism," in *Existentialism from Dostoevsky to Sartre*, ed. Walter Kaufmann (New York: Meridian, 1956), 302, emphasis in original; Andrew, *André Bazin*, 68–81. For an earlier American view of Bazin also sensitive to the connection with Sartre, see Annette Michelson's knowledgeable and presciently critical review of the first volume of English-language translations from *What Is Cinema?* in *Artforum* 6 (summer 1968): 67–70. Perhaps another kind of reading of Bazin might be derived by emphasizing, say, Merleau-Ponty.

4. See, e.g., Maurice Merleau-Ponty, "The Film and the New Psychology," in *Sense and Non-Sense*, trans. Hubert L. Dreyfus and Patricia A. Dreyfus (Evanston, Ill.: Northwestern University Press, 1964). This work was originally published in 1947, which means it is contemporary to "The Ontology of the Photographic Image."

5. André Bazin, *Jean Renoir*, ed. François Truffaut, trans. W. W. Halsey II and William H. Simon (New York: Delta, 1974), 85.

6. See the first part of Comolli's series, "Technique and Ideology," reprinted in *Movies and Methods*, vol. 2, ed. Bill Nichols (Berkeley and Los Angeles: University of California Press, 1985); Stephen Heath, "Narrative Space," in *Questions of Cinema* (Bloomington: Indiana University Press, 1981), esp. 24–54. For a more condensed but seminal version of this position, see Jean-Louis Baudry, "Ideological Effects of the Basic Cinematographic Apparatus," in Rosen, *Narrative, Apparatus, Ideology*.

7. David Bordwell, *Narration in the Fiction Film* (Madison: University of Wisconsin Press, 1985), 100–110, quotes on 107, 102. See also Bordwell, *On the History of Film Style*, 159–63, and esp. 181–83. In his argument about the scientific nature of perspective, Bordwell agrees that there was an original ideological project to Quattrocento perspective, namely to demonstrate that space is rational and the real is therefore subsumable under harmonious laws accessible to reason. He believes that this goes against the emphasis of 1970s theory on the stability of a centered spectator. My view is that 1970s theory would have little problem aligning this part of his account with its own, since the susceptibility of "real" space to human rationality would seem to be an idea congruent with the idea of a centered subject of knowledge. Furthermore, Bordwell agrees that the "monocular viewing point" is inevitable in photography or "any representation of depth in the moving image" because of the nature of the camera lens (*On the History of Film Style*, 181). But he strongly attacks 1970s film theory on linear perspective with several claims, including the following: whatever its ideological origins, so-called Renaissance perspective is a reliable mode of mapping certain regularities in the behavior of light; Renaissance theorists and spectators of paintings already understood the divergences of monocular perspective from real perception, and filmmakers deliberately play on these; in cinema, mise-en-scène and lens selection often result in a perceptual field that varies significantly from central projection.

8. Jonathan Crary, *Techniques of the Observer: On Vision and Modernity in the Nineteenth Century* (Cambridge, Mass.: MIT Press, 1990). On other uses of the camera obscura and its disjuncture from perspective, see 32ff, esp. 34; cf. 41. On the differences between nineteenth-century optical devices and the camera obscura, see chapter 4. Crary summarizes the view he opposes as one that, among other things, associates cinema with perspective; see 4 and 110, and notes 21 and 22. Unfortunately, this book does not have an account of photography, a monocular apparatus that, he notes, displaced the stereoscope. Nor does it have an account of the functioning of the "normal" lens, which reproduces perspective in photography. With respect to the ambivalent place of photography in Crary's argument, the following passage is worth noting: "Photography defeated the stereoscope as a mode of visual consumption as well because it recreated and perpetuated the fiction that the 'free' subject of the *camera obscura* was still viable." This is oddly congruent with the 1970s theory he begins by opposing. Crary has no account of the determinants of this operation or its necessity; hence his argument about the de-privileging of perspective is incomplete.

9. It is also interesting with respect to what will follow that while perspective has to do with representations of space, all three find moments to oppose spatial realism by appeal to the temporality of processes associated with a subject or a spectator, which is said to determine the actual apprehension of spatial relations. In Heath and in Comolli, this involves the dialectic of desire, for Bordwell the time required for perceptual processing, and, most elaborately, for Crary the modern "discovery" of temporality in the subject.

10. From *The World Walk*, a 1984 BBC production about the war criminals imprisoned at Spandau, written by Jonathan Smith:

HESS: Speer, I just realized my food can't be poisoned. After all, I could take any of the bowls offered. Yours, Schirach's . . .

SPEER: Or the Admiral's.

HESS: Quite.

SPEER: Good. So you're over that obsession at last.

HESS: Of course not. If I were, it wouldn't be an obsession.

11. Wollen, *Signs and Meaning*. The claim that Bazin deemphasizes "the agency of the human mind" is on 131. On the pages immediately following, however, Wollen makes points congruent with my argument. Another important reading of Bazin, which hits on some motifs of my argument, is Wollen's "'Ontology' and 'Materialism' in Film," in *Readings and Writings: Semiotic Counter-Strategies* (London: New Left Books, 1982), esp. 189–93, 205–6. But there Wollen concludes that cinematic "language" is opposed to ontology for Bazin, who is said to have desired meaning to emerge completely and naturally from the profilmic. This again misses the possibility that the ontology proceeds from the subject's desire rather than a supposedly direct relation between apparatus and filmed object.

12. "Likeness" or "resemblance" is itself a complicated notion for Peirce: "Peirce's theory of iconicity is not a sentimental appeal to 'natural resemblances' and, in fact, allows for changing mimetic conventions." Elizabeth W. Bruss, "Peirce and Jakobson on the Nature of the Sign," in *The Sign: Semiotics around the World*, ed. R. W. Bailey, L. Matejka, and P. Steiner (Ann Arbor: Michigan Slavic Publications, 1980), 88. For Peirce's definitions of indexicality and its relation to iconicity, see pertinent passages in *Philosophical Writings of Peirce*, ed. Justus Buchler (New York: Dover, 1955), 102, 108. "A genuine Index may contain Firstness," Peirce writes, "and so an Icon as a constituent part of it." (*Genuine* here is a technical term; Peirce distinguishes between *genuine* and *degenerate* indices.) On

pronouns and indexicality, see 110–11. Part of the appropriateness of consider-ing Bazin through Peirce is that Bazin's premise of the inevitability of a subjective project even in the apprehension of the most realistic media is paralleled by Peirce's insistence, emphasized by Teresa de Lauretis, that signification always includes the interpretant. See de Lauretis, *Alice Doesn't: Feminism, Semiotics, Cin-ema* (Bloomington: Indiana University Press, 1984), 179–80.

13. Since this argument regarding a special credibility of cinematic images is fairly abstract and restricted, two points might be glossed in passing. First, the question of synthesized movement, of which Heath and Bordwell are well aware, is not dealt with here. Briefly, depicted movement as a matter of spatial displace-ment is inconceivable outside temporality, and it is the centrality of temporality toward which I am moving.

Second, the decentering of spatial likeness in an account of cinematic real-ism might seem inappropriate in a discussion of Bazin given, for example, the ways in which he treats something like *The Cabinet of Dr. Caligari* as a film-historical "heresy" (*WC*, 1:26). But the most striking and famous visual "distortions" of such a film take place at the profilmic level (expressionistic sets, stylized acting, and so forth); these "distortions" are then conveyed to us with an impression of faithful transmission, as a preexisting configuration of the profilmic. For example, it is appropriate for a viewer of *Caligari* to appreciate the work of the expressionist artists who served as set designers. Such trust even in images whose appearance varies from ordinary conventions occurs on the assumption of an indexical rela-tion to a preexistent. (It also assumes an unconventionally designed profilmic field is being transmitted through lenses that refer to current perspectival norms; otherwise we would have no basis for seeing the sets as distorted.) Thus, it is how we take film images to be produced that might encourage this understand-ing of the image. Incidentally, a similar kind of comment might be made about Bordwell's example (*Narration in the Fiction Film*, 107) of a photograph depicting depth according to a non-Western system, achieved by arrangement of the pro-filmic in conjunction with a telephoto lens.

14. The temporality of the film image bears on a vacillation in this chapter between the theoretically familiar phrase "mechanically produced" images and "technically produced" or "automatically produced" images. While the former is applicable to photography and film, it is not, strictly speaking, quite appropriate for video imaging. Television certainly provides opportunities to extend Bazinian concerns, in that it is indexical and in its dominant forms partakes of graphic

procedures such as Quattrocento perspective. But the potential for "liveness" means that television is not restricted to bringing a subject something from the past, but also introduces the possibility of the simultaneity of sign and referent; hence, the mummy complex is not fully applicable for television, at least in theory. In actuality, of course, much mainstream television and other kinds of video are "prerecorded," whether on film or videotape. "Live" programming is restricted to certain genres, such as sporting events (but even these include prerecorded material, from videotape replays to footage of earlier games). Furthermore "live" programming is itself almost invariably recorded so it can be shown again after the actual event. The entire relation between prerecorded and "live" programming needs attention. To sample the range of concerns from a growing bibliography on liveness, see, for example, Jane Feuer, "The Concept of Live Television: Ontology as Ideology," in *Regarding Television*, ed. E. Ann Kaplan (Frederick, Md.: University Press of America and the American Film Institute, 1983); Mary Ann Doane, "Information, Crisis, Catastrophe," in *Logics of Television: Essays in Cultural Criticism*, ed. Patricia Mellencamp (Bloomington: Indiana University Press, 1990); Margaret Morse, "The Television News Personality and Credibility: Reflections on the News in Transition," in *Studies in Entertainment: Critical Approaches to Mass Culture*, ed. Tania Modleski (Bloomington: Indiana University Press, 1986). See also chapter 6 in this volume.

15. For comments on the paradox of the French theorist Bazin constructing his universals within Western art history by beginning from the older culture of a colonized "other," see Antonia Lant, "The Curse of the Pharaoh, or How Cinema Contracted Egyptomania," *October* 59 (winter 1992), esp. 86–112.

16. Since it is the spectator's being as subject that is at stake in the desire to bridge an unbridgeable representational gap, it is certainly possible to argue for kinds of kinship between certain psychoanalytic formulations and Bazin's. In this regard, the dominant concerns of 1970s film theory have a genealogy, for example, in phenomenology and even in film theory. For example, compare Metz, "The Imaginary Signifier," in *The Imaginary Signifier* to Bazin, "Theater and Cinema, part 2," in *WC*, esp. 1:96–102. Bazin's motifs in these pages include the presence-absence opposition, identification, and the use of striptease as a counterexample to cinematic spectatorship in relation to these.

17. Bazin also mentions a third category of adaptation, the "free adaptation" exemplified by Renoir.

18. See Bazin, *WC*, 1:35–36 for the passage in "The Evolution of the

Language of Cinema" that most concisely states this claim. However, a more extensive development of the argument is in the 1948 essay, "William Wyler ou le janséniste de la mise en scène," in Bazin, *Qu'est-ce que le cinéma?* vol. 1 (Paris: Ed. du Cerf, 1959). A translation without Bazin's expository footnotes appears in *Realism and the Cinema: A Reader,* ed. Christopher Williams (London: Routledge and Kegan Paul and the British Film Institute, 1980), 36–52.

19. Bazin, "William Wyler," 157; translation in Williams, *Realism and the Cinema,* 42, my emphasis.

20. In another exposition, this could also lead back to the thought of Henri Bergson. Andrew, *André Bazin,* 18–25, sketches the impact of the Bergsonian intellectual heritage on the formation of Bazin's thought, as well as Catholic thinkers read by the young Bazin, such as Béguin and Maritain. As Andrew puts it, the Bergsonian thought known by Bazin mainly through such critics "gave Bazin a deep feeling for the integral unity of a universe in flux," which led, among other things, to his critique of montage as part of the "analytical, spatializing tendency in man" (21).

21. On this basis. Roland Barthes (*Camera Lucida: Reflections on Photography,* trans. Richard Howard [New York: Hill and Wang, 1981], 77, 87) draws a sharper distinction between film and photography than Bazin; see chapter 4. On the pregivenness of the world, see, e.g., Bazin's discussion of *Paisà* in "An Aesthetic of Reality: Neorealism," *WC,* 2:35–38.

22. Henderson, "Bazin Defended against His Devotees," 32ff.

23. The translator's rendering is not quite literal. Bazin's French is "Pour la première fois, l'image des choses est aussi celle de leur durée et comme la momie du changement." André Bazin, "Ontologie de l'image photographique," in *Qu'est-ce-que le cinéma? Edition définitive* (Paris: Ed. du Cerf, 1975), 14. I have accepted this phrasing here and in the title of this book because it heightens the oxymoronic and defensive aspects of Bazin's conception.

24. Cf. Peter Munz, *The Shapes of Time: A New Look at the Philosophy of History* (Middletown, Conn.: Wesleyan University Press, 1977).

25. In Bazin, *WC,* 2:148, he equates the mythical function of the best Soviet cinema with that of the Western; therefore, his critique of Stalinist cinema should not be read as a reflexive anticommunism.

26. Bazin, "The Stalin Myth in Soviet Cinema," reprinted in Nichols, *Movies and Methods.* See also the discussion of this article in Janet Staiger, "Theorist, yes, but what of? Bazin and History," *Iris* 2, no. 2 (1984): 107–8.

27. Here is an unexpected but important cross-reference: When Lukács in 1967 criticized his own classic 1923 text of humanist Marxism, *History and Class Consciousness*, he considered an overvaluation of the Hegelian notion of a perfect unity of subject and object as his fundamental error within Marxist theory. Given the subsequent complex events in Lukács's own relation to Stalinism, one can note with some irony that Bazin shows how Stalinist cinema manifests this "deviation." But further, Lukács's 1923 account of the alienation of the subject, which he would soon repudiate, (a) had great impact (both pro and con) in the intellectual milieu of existentialism, from Heidegger to Sartre, and particularly in France where, for example, Bazin's mentor Mounier sought to overcome the subject-object split with his Personalism; and (b) was in part a response to fundamental difficulties in the theory of history in Western culture, such as the crisis of German historicism. (See chapter 3 of this volume.) What is interesting here is not just the chain of thinkers that might reveal structural kinship in the thought of Bazin and Lukács, but the general diffusion of certain problematics throughout the West. See "Preface to the New Edition (1967)," in Georg Lukács, *History and Class Consciousness: Studies in Marxist Dialectics*, trans. Rodney Livingstone (Cambridge, Mass.: MIT Press, 1971), esp. xxi–xxv, xxxv–xxxvi.

28. Bazin, "The Stalin Myth," 38–39.

29. Cf. Staiger, whose chronological discussion of Bazin's writings with respect to history places them in the political and social issues of his day.

30. The epitome of this stance in the theory of history was in the discussions of so-called covering-law explanatory form.

31. For a classic example of this view, see "Human Nature and Human History," in R. G. Collingwood, *The Idea of History* (New York: Oxford University Press, 1946) e.g. 215ff. I discuss the impulses behind this approach in chapter 3 of this volume.

32. See Comolli, "Technique et idéologie," *Cahiers du cinéma*, nos. 230, 231. For a summary of critiques of 1970s spectator theory as ahistorical, see Judith Mayne, *Cinema and Spectatorship* (New York: Routledge, 1993), 62ff.

2. Entering History

1. This narrative event is inexplicable in *The Man in the High Castle*. But some draft chapters of a sequel explain that two different histories or time lines coexist and there is an apparatus enabling travel between them. Such traditional science-fiction devices would have made the sequel much more generically and

causally conventional than *The Man in the High Castle* is, and to that extent less rich as an exploration of historicity. In fact, Dick abandoned the sequel. See the two completed chapters for the sequel in *The Shifting Realities of Philip K. Dick: Selected Literary and Philosophical Writings*, ed. Lawrence Sutin (New York: Vintage, 1995), 119–34.

2. André Bazin, *What Is Cinema?* vol. 1, trans. Hugh Gray (Berkeley and Los Angeles: University of California Press, 1967), 143.

3. Susan Sontag, *On Photography* (New York: Delta, 1977), 76.

4. Eugène-Emmanuel Viollet-le-Duc, *The Architectural Theory of Viollet-le-Duc: Readings and Commentary*, ed. M. F. Hearn (Cambridge, Mass.: MIT Press, 1990), 269–79, quoted sentence on 269. This essay on restoration was an entry in Viollet-le-Duc's *Dictionnaire raisonné de l'architecture française du XIe au XVIe siècle* (10 vols, 1854–68). See also his 1843 letter to the minister regarding the prospectus for the restoration of Notre Dame, 279–88, which includes different emphases and stronger passages against hypothesizing. For the general nineteenth-century debates, I have relied on Stephan Tschudi-Madsen, *Restoration and Anti-Restoration: A Study in English Restoration Philosophy* (Oslo: Universitetsforlaget, 1976), a useful monographic review of the polemics. These nineteenth-century controversies over restoration principles and practices were seminal. See, for example, the proceedings of a 1963 seminar on historic preservation sponsored by the U.S. National Trust for Historic Preservation, *Historic Preservation Today: Essays Presented to the Seminar on Preservation and Restoration*, Williamsburg, Virginia, September 8–11, 1963 (Charlottesville: University Press of Virginia, 1966), where they formed the basis for opening discussions. Cf. esp. papers by Jacques Dupont and Sir John Summerson and the response by George Mosse.

5. John Ruskin, *The Seven Lamps of Architecture* (New York: Farrar, Strauss and Giroux, 1988), 184 (emphasis in original).

6. Ibid., 186 (emphasis in original).

7. Ibid., 177.

8. Ibid., 184–85. See chapter 5, "The Lamp of Life," esp. 142–44, for a summarizing set of interlinked oppositions: life and death, activity and passivity, truth and falsity.

9. William Morris, "Restoration," in Tschudi-Madsen, *Restoration and Anti-Restoration*, 144–45.

10. On the changed meanings of the term *restoration*, architectural

societies, and the count of cathedral restorations, see Tschudi-Madsen, *Restoration and Anti-Restoration*, 13–18, 30–32, 25–26.

11. Thomas Hardy, *A Pair of Blue Eyes* (New York: Oxford University Press, 1998), 3. The novel includes depiction of a church restoration, and the 1895 preface incisively suggests the ethos and its contradictions, beginning with its first paragraph: "The following chapters were written at a time when the craze for indiscriminate church-restoration had just reached the remotest nooks of western England, where the wild and tragic features of the coast had long combined in perfect harmony with the crude Gothic Art of the ecclesiastical buildings scattered along it, throwing into extraordinary discord all architectural attempts at newness there. To restore the grey carcasses of a mediaevalism whose spirit had fled seemed a not less incongruous act than to set about renovating the adjoining crags themselves."

12. For British legislation with respect to old buildings, see Tschudi-Madsen, *Restoration and Anti-Restoration*, 24ff, and Nikolaus Boulting, "The Law's Delays: Conservationist Legislation in the British Isles," in *The Future of the Past: Attitudes to Conservation, 1174–1974*, ed. Jane Fawcett (London: Thames and Hudson, 1976). Comparable national laws protecting old edifices on the basis of national interest in the past were implemented throughout the nineteenth century, but especially after 1870; see Tschudi-Madsen, *Restoration and Anti-Restoration*, 102. The decree of Louis X is translated in John Harvey, *Conservation of Buildings* (London: John Baker, 1972), 27–28; for the original German, see Tschudi-Madsen, *Restoration and Anti-Restoration*, 104–5.

13. Nikolaus Pevsner, *An Outline of European Architecture*, rev. ed. (New York: Penguin, 1982), 377. See 375–89 for a survey of the appeal during this era to historical models. Himself a modernist, Pevsner opposes this historicism, but identifies the Ruskin-Morris impulse as a kind of precursor to more modern architectural views. Interestingly, this is also the line taken by some later defenders of Viollet-le-Duc's. Incidentally, even Ruskin agreed that elements of new buildings could be borrowed from older models, so long as they were subordinated to an overall conception of the building, so long as the borrowing embodied such moral qualities as frankness and honesty, thus avoiding the restorationist's sin of pretending to be the original, and so long as the architect used durable materials, since a building requires a few centuries of wear to achieve its prime (Ruskin, *The Seven Lamps*, 145–46, 183). For a survey of architectural historiography (which shows

that major architects of the period were often the historians), see David Watkin, *The Rise of Architectural History* (Chicago: University of Chicago Press, 1980).

14. Stephen Bann, *The Clothing of Clio: A Study of the Representation of History in Nineteenth-Century Britain and France* (New York: Cambridge University Press, 1984), 139.

15. Bann's actual analyses are inspired by Hayden White's tropology of historiography. On the development of irony with respect to lifelike representation of the past, see ibid., 122–23. Interestingly, Ruskin is a key figure here, but as one seeking an image of cultural integration from the past as a defense against irony about recovering the past. In this account, Ruskin's interest in photography (noted in relation to Fox Talbot) has to do with the problem of protecting a "naïve" attitude toward "the effect of resurrection." See idem, 122–37. Bann only considers cinema in a brief postscript.

16. Ibid., 133, 136. There is a passing reference to Bazin on 169.

17. Naedine Joy Hazell, "Gossip Gives Sturbridge an Edge," *Providence Sunday Journal*, 14 September 1997.

18. Useful accounts of the establishment of the genre include Charles B. Hosmer, Jr., *Preservation Comes of Age: From Williamsburg to the National Trust 1926–1949*, 2 vols. (Charlottesville: University Press of Virginia, 1981), 1: chapters 1 and 2; and Michael Wallace, "Visiting the Past: History Museums in the United States," in *Presenting the Past: Essays on History and the Public*, ed. Susan Porter Benson, Stephen Brier, Roy Rosenzweig (Philadelphia: Temple University Press, 1986). On the significance of the Skänsen movement for the genre, see Wallace, "Visiting the Past," 144–45. Hosmer mentions its influence on Henry Ford (1:75) and Wallace notes that the primary industrialist behind Old Sturbridge, A. B. Wells, visited Skänsen in 1938, just before Old Sturbridge began taking its final form (151). In one variant of the museum village, exemplified by Plimouth Plantation, Massachusetts, a fully "historical" population is supplied: interpreters take on the roles of actual historical individuals rather than types, and stay in character even when talking to tourists. Some idea of the contemporary profusion of the genre can be traced through tourist guides, such as Gerald Gutek and Patricia Gutek, *Experiencing America's Past: A Travel Guide to Museum Villages* (New York: John Wiley, 1986), which surveys forty-three of the most elaborate American living history museums east of the Rocky Mountains.

19. Wallace, "Visiting the Past," 142–49, 151–53, 156–57. In 1994 Colonial Williamsburg attempted to include a slave auction, but it became controversial. In

1999 it inaugurated a program that includes enactment of violent repression and escape attempts by slaves, entitled "Enslaving Virginia." See Eun Lee Kohl, "Exposing Another Side of History: Colonial Williamsburg Skits Cast New Light on U.S. Patriots: Their Roles as Slave Owners," *Boston Globe*, July 13, 1999, A4.

20. See Wallace, "Visiting the Past," and Hosmer, *Preservation Comes of Age.* For a discussion of some of these issues by professionals and scholars, see Jo Blatti, ed., *Past Meets Present: Essays about Historic Interpretation and Public Audiences* (Washington, D.C.: Smithsonian Institution Press, 1987), which originated in a 1984 conference on museum and historic site interpretation and education

21. "Sheep as They Used to Be 150 Years Ago," Providence *Journal-Bulletin*, 30 October 1986, B4.

22. I was told about the library by an Old Sturbridge interpreter during a 1985 visit. See also the special section on educational projects in Old Sturbridge in *Journal of Family History* 6 (spring 1981).

23. A. B. Wells, *Old Quinebaug Village*, quoted in Hosmer, *Preservation Comes of Age*, 1:114. For an account of the founding of Old Sturbridge Village, see idem, 1:109–21. For the family's version, see *The Wells Family: Founders of the American Optical Company and Old Sturbridge Village* (Southbridge, Mass.: privately printed, 1979), vii–x and 1–22; this is an account by Ruth Dyer Wells, who ran Old Sturbridge after Albert's heart attack in 1945.

24. Quoted in Wallace, "Visiting the Past," 139. In support of the campaign, the governor of Virginia said, "Dollars become as dust when compared to the inestimable patriotism inspired by a visit to the tomb," idem, 138.

25. Michael Wallace, "Reflections on the History of Historic Preservation," in Benson, Brier, and Rosenzweig, *Presenting the Past*, esp. 168–72. For a slightly different summary that still stresses the overwhelmingly private sources of support for preservation projects in the United States, see Charles B. Hosmer, Jr., "Private Philanthropy and Preservation," in *Historic Preservation Today*, 163–65. It should also be noted, as does Hosmer, that impetus for preservation of individual buildings could have other or overlapping rationales than preservationist ideologies of pastness, such as aesthetic or architectural worth; however, it is often difficult to separate such rationales from a high valuation of the past and history.

26. See Wallace, "Reflections," 173ff. for an account of more recent phases of architectural preservationism in the United States and an argument that alliances between preservationism and the marketplace have only an ambiguous advantage at best for the former. This argument is verified in Wallace's account of

the situation in the 1980s and 1990s; see Mike Wallace, "Preservation Revisited," in *Mickey Mouse History and Other Essays on American Memory* (Philadelphia: Temple University Press, 1995), 223–46.

27. On preservation and federal encouragement in the New Deal era, see Hosmer, *Preservation Comes of Age*, 1:3–6 and 2: chaps. 7 and 8. See also idem, "Private Philanthropy and Preservation," 163–64.

28. See Hosmer, *Preservation Comes of Age*, 1:75; and Wallace, "Visiting the Past," 147.

29. Wallace, "Visiting the Past," For the quote, see 382 n. 60. On 149 ff., Wallace outlines a set of subsequent transformations in the museum village genre, including new attention to social history and the history of minorities in the United States. However, he concludes that the shifts did not lead to a change in the static nature of the museum village.

30. See chapter 3 in this volume.

31. Sigmund Freud, "Fetishism," in *Collected Papers:* vol. 5, ed. James Strachey (New York: Basic Books, 1959), 198–204. While the masculine investment in the woman's body is the generative mechanism for the kind of fetishism that concerns Freud, there has been work on the relation of Freud's concept to notions of fetish and fetish-object associated with capitalism and colonialism. Laura Mulvey reviews some of these with film in mind in "The Carapace That Failed: Ousmane Sembene's *Xala,*" in *Fetishism and Curiosity* (Bloomington: Indiana University Press, 1996), 118–36.

32. For some idea of the international spread of such enterprises, see various contributions to *The Museum Time-Machine: Putting Cultures on Display,* ed. Robert Lumley (New York: Routledge, 1988), esp. Tony Bennett, "Museums and 'the People'," which draws on Wallace and includes a reading of the Welsh Folk Museum and the North of England Open Air Museum at Beamish in comparison to Hyde Park in Sydney and People's Palace in Glasgow. For more on England, see Robert Hewison, *The Heritage Industry: Britain in a Climate of Decline* (London: Methuen, 1987), and for a polemical survey of museum culture in Europe, see Donald Horne, *The Great Museum: The Re-presentation of History* (London: Pluto, 1984). For a comparison of the kinds of sites other than old buildings likely to be selected for preservation in the United States and other countries, see Robin Winks, "Conservation in America: National Character as Revealed by Preservation," in Fawcett, *The Future of the Past,* 143. The scholarly literature on museum culture, sometimes encompassing the museum village, has now mushroomed, and

it is impossible to do it justice here. In an internationalist context, it often shades into considerations of modernity, colonialism, and tourism. One of the most significant examples is Tony Bennett, *The Birth of the Museum: History, Theory, Politics* (New York: Routledge, 1995). A stimulating example is John Frow, "Tourism and the Semiotics of Nostalgia," *October* 57 (summer 1991).

33. Ruskin, *Seven Lamps*, 199–201, 187. There are many other examples in Ruskin. See, for instance, where any use of casted or machine-made ornamentation is listed as one of three major architectural deceits to be avoided (39). (The other two are giving the impression of a mode of support different from the actual one, and painting a surface to falsify it by suggesting a different material from the one actually used or suggesting nonexistent sculptured ornamentation.) On the appeal of the antimodern side of Ruskin and Morris to high status socioeconomic groups, along with an account of the dilution of their critical elements in the arts and crafts movement in the United States, see T. J. Jackson Lears, *No Place of Grace: Antimodernism and the Transformation of American Culture 1880–1920* (New York: Pantheon, 1981), chapter 2.

34. Tony Bennett, "The Shape of the Past," in *Nation, Culture, Text: Australian Cultural and Media Studies*, ed. Graeme Turner (New York: Routledge, 1993), esp. 87–88. Bennett's reference is to Dean MacCannell, *The Tourist: A New Theory of the Leisure Class* (New York: Schocken, 1976).

35. George L. Mosse, "Comment," in *Historic Preservation Today*, 38–42.

36. For examples of leftist interventions on these questions, see all the essays in Benson, Brier, and Rosenzweig, *Presenting the Past*; Popular Memory Group, "Popular Memory: Theory, Politics, Method"; and Michael Bommes and Patrick Wright, "'Charms of Residence': The Public and the Past," in the pathbreaking explorations of *Making Histories: Studies in History-Writing and Politics*, ed. Richard Johnson, Gregor McLennan, Bill Schwarz, and David Sutton (Minneapolis: University of Minnesota Press, 1982). Cf. Michael Wallace, "The Politics of Public History," in Blatti, *Past Meets Present*, 38–39.

37. "Past Comes Alive at OSV!" *The Villager* (published twenty-seven times a year by Worcester County Newspapers; n.d. [1986?]). The guide is Gutek and Gutek; see the back cover and 1.

38. "A Report on Principles and Guidelines for Historic Preservation in the United States," in *Historic Preservation Today*, 252. First penned in 1839 by the Frenchman A. N. Didron, this maxim was rapidly taken up by the new preservation movement in England, and was so widely repeated that in the United States

it became regarded as an American saying. Tschudi-Madsen, *Restoration and Anti-Restoration*, 80.

39. On the widespread impact of *Looking Backward*, see Darko Suvin, *Metamorphoses of Science Fiction: On the Poetics and History of a Literary Genre* (New Haven: Yale University Press, 1979), 178.

40. Ibid., 220.

41. Robert Scholes and Eric S. Rabkin, *Science Fiction: History, Science, Vision* (New York: Oxford University Press, 1977), 176.

42. On these issues in general, see Suvin, *Metamorphoses*, chapters 8–10. Suvin provides a commentary on late nineteenth-century utopias and dystopias, an analysis of Wells and the birth of "modern" science fiction, and a detailed analysis of the reverse-Darwinian plot model of Wells's "future history" in *The Time Machine*.

43. Michael Wallace, "Mickey Mouse History: Portraying the Past at Disney World," *Radical History Review* 32 (1985): 44. For an analysis of Disneyland as text, including its mythification of history, see "Utopic Degeneration: Disneyland," in Louis Marin, *Utopics: Spatial Play*, trans. Robert A. Vollrath (Atlantic Highlands, N.J.: Humanities Press, 1984). For further comments on relations between Disneyland and museum villages, see Bennett, "The Shape of the Past," 82–88. For a different but bracing perspective on the issues discussed here, see also Scott Bukatman, "There's Always Tomorrowland: Disney and the Hypercinematic Experience," *October* 57 (summer 1991): 55–78.

44. *Intolerance* could be analyzed to unpack a series of strategies that manifest temporal transcendence. These include not only the narrational intercutting of the four stories, but also such elements as the allegorical shots of the Fates and the "Woman rocking the cradle," both ahistorical entities that are supposed to bridge the sudden transitions among the different historical periods, and the overt promotion of such allegedly universal, and therefore transhistorical values as tolerance, love, and so forth. The point is not the uniqueness of *Intolerance*, but rather that such universalization processes, tied to implied spectatorship and so convenient ideologically, are easily available (if usually less explicit) even in the most conventional mainstream narrative formats.

45. This is, of course, analogous to the distinction between perspective and indexical traces in Bazin's "The Ontology of the Photographic Image."

46. Paul Ricoeur, *Time and Narrative*, vol. 3, trans. Kathleen Blamey and David Pellauer (Chicago: University of Chicago Press, 1988), 100.

3. Once upon a Time in the West

1. Lydia Maria Child, *The American Frugal Housewife: Dedicated to Those Who Are Not Afraid of Economy*, 12th ed. (1832; reprint, Bedford, Mass.: Applewood Books in cooperation with Old Sturbridge Village). As a facsimile edition, this version is a nice example of the categorical ambiguities produced by contemporary technologies of mechanical reproduction. No current publication date is given, presumably to maintain the facsimile status of the copyright page. One would call this a restored artifact, except that it might have been made using an actual 1832 edition as "camera ready copy" at Applewood Books and therefore retain some indexical (preservationist) linkage to the original thing.

2. E. P. Thompson, *The Making of the English Working Class* (New York: Vintage, 1966), 305–6.

3. Quotation from E. P. Thompson, "Time, Work-Discipline, and Industrial Capitalism," *Past and Present* 38 (December 1967): 86. My summary draws heavily on this classic overview of the institutionalization of temporal discipline in the workplace from the seventeenth to the nineteenth centuries, which focuses on Britain as the pioneering industrializing nation-state. For a gloss on the increase of "time awareness" and the factory that draws on Thompson, see David S. Landes, *Revolution in Time: Clocks and the Making of the Modern World* (Cambridge, Mass.: Harvard University Press, 1983), 227–30. For a view of this transition on the basis of an earlier, late medieval revolution in time consciousness (associated with the developments of central public clocks, hour-reckoning, and early modernization), see Gerhard Dohrn-van Rossum, *History of the Hour: Clocks and Modern Temporal Orders*, trans. Thomas Dunlap (Chicago: University of Chicago Press, 1996). For an important philosophical (rather than sociohistorical) conceptualization of the human organization of time through the calendar in relation to natural or cosmological cycles, see Paul Ricoeur, *Time and Narrative*, trans. Kathleen Blamey and David Pellauer (Chicago: University of Chicago Press, 1988), 3:104–8. A sociologically oriented overview is Eviatar Zerubavel, *Hidden Rhythms: Schedules and Calendars in Social Life* (Chicago: University of Chicago Press, 1981).

Thompson's argument has been much discussed among historians. Critics often argue that Thompson generalizes too much, and that the imposition of norms of time discipline should not be understood as a unified, undifferentiated uniformity. This form of critique is almost a reflex among professional historians, and even opponents usually accept some of Thompson's descriptions and/or conclusions. For example, see a series of articles published in the 1980s in *Past and Present* (which published Thompson's original article). One view is that Thompson underrates urbanization as a determinant of time discipline; see Mark Harrison, "The Ordering of the Urban Environment: Time, Work, and the Occurrence of Crowds, 1790–1835," *Past and Present* 110 (February 1986): 134–68. But it seems difficult to separate industrialization and urbanization, a point made in the exchange between Harrison and David Landes in "Debate: The Ordering of the Urban Environment: Time, Work, and the Occurrence of Crowds, 1790–1835," *Past and Present* 116 (August 1987): 192–205. Another view is comparative and Weberian; see Thomas C. Smith, "Peasant Time and Factory Time in Japan," *Past and Present* 111 (May 1986): 165–97, which argues that time discipline in Japanese industrialization was an inheritance from agricultural practices among Japanese peasants, based on family and collective ties. A related line also argues that even in England, workplace time discipline was important in daily life earlier than Thompson acknowledges; see Nigel Thrift, "*Vivos Voca:* Ringing the Changes in the Historical Geography of Time Consciousness," in *The Rhythms of Society,* ed. Michael Young and Tom Schuller (New York: Routledge, 1988), 53–94, which makes this case with reference to the thirteenth century and uncritically accepts all of Harrison's critique (86–87). Thrift's professional historiographic caution, however, provides enough qualifying distinctions between medieval and industrialized society to weaken his own case, and he never directly takes on Thompson's central distinction between task- and time-oriented labor. Cf. Keith Tribe, "'Industrialization' as a Historical Category," in his *Genealogies of Capitalism* (Atlantic Highlands, N.J.: Humanities Press, 1981), 101–20, which argues that accounts of economic history centered on technologies of production must be expanded to include distribution and consumption (116), such that technologically defined transformation (such as "industrial revolution") should be treated as the manifestation "of much deeper problems of supervision, authority and domination" (120). While Tribe attacks notions I use, such as the rationalization of production as well as industrialization, his general assumptions remain congruent with my own brief foray into industrialization history, which begins from a Marxist (Thompson) rather than a Foucauldian account. The seminal discussions are, of course, scattered through the accounts of labor, surplus value, and the workplace in Karl Marx, *Capital: A Critique of Political Economy,* vol. 1, trans. Ben Fowkes (New York: Vintage, 1977).

    4. Michel Foucault, *Discipline and Punish: The Birth of the Prison,* trans.

Alan Sheridan (New York: Vintage, 1979), 221. On the timetable, see 149ff. The immediately preceding section, on the development of spatial distributions in the new disciplinary techniques, includes some remarks on workshops and factories. For general comments on the relations of capitalism and the new disciplinary practices, see 221.

Foucault treats the medieval monastery, with its use of bells as time signals, as a precursor to modern scheduling and factory time. This is a long-established notion, found in the work of such varied scholarly predecessors as Louis Mumford and Jacques Le Goff (cf. Zerubavel, *Hidden Rhythms*, chapter 2). But Dohrn-van Rossum questions it, arguing that monastery discipline was task-oriented rather than time-oriented (monastery schedules were originally determined by the length of prayers and daily practical activities): "Talk of 'iron discipline' or the machine-like or clockwork rhythm of monastic life, even in a purely metaphorical sense, is misleading, because it suggests a time giver (a machine or clock) external to natural rhythms and the daily round of human life. In actual fact, life according to the Rule was bound in a very high degree to natural time givers, daylight and the seasons, and was by no means marked by ascetic resistance to the natural environment" (38); see 33ff. Dorhn-van Rossum also emphasizes additional early sources of clocked time-discipline, especially the urban public clocks. Yet, this does not negate Foucault's general view that such institutions provided models for the saturation of social forms with techniques of discipline, which came to a head after the seventeenth century, for they agree that there was a fundamental difference between the early modern transformation in time consciousness and that associated with the industrial revolution. See Dohrn-van Rossum, *History of the Hour*, chapters 9, 10.

5. Max Horkheimer and Theodor W. Adorno, *Dialectic of Enlightenment*, trans. John Cumming (1944; reprint, New York: Herder and Herder, 1972). For his own general conceptions, see Frederick Winslow Taylor, *The Principles of Scientific Management* (New York: Harper and Brothers, 1911). For figures on the accuracy of clocks since 1300, see the chart by F. A. B. Ward that is the frontispiece to G. J. Whitrow, *Time in History: The Evolution of Our General Awareness of Time and Temporal Perspective* (New York: Oxford University Press, 1988). In 1967, the international standard became a cesium atomic clock, accurate to within .0000001 second per day (a cesium atom oscillates 9,192,631,770 times per second). The Crowley Iron Works "Law Book" is described, along with other early examples of factory rationalization of time, in Dohrn-van Rossum, *History of the Hour*, 318–19.

6. For Ford's watchmaking, see Thompson, "Time, Work-Discipline," 89 n. 113. For "solar mean time," see Dohrn-van Rossum, *History of the Hour,* 346. H. G. Wells, *The Conquest of Time* (1941; reprint, Amherst. N. Y.: Prometheus Books, 1995), chapter 1.

7. Regarding temporal standardization, see Wolfgang Schivelbusch, *The Railway Journey: Trains and Travel in the Nineteenth Century,* trans. Anselm Hollo (New York: Urizen, 1979), 48–50; Landes, *Revolution in Time,* 93–95, 285–87; Stephen Kern, *The Culture of Time and Space 1880–1918* (Cambridge: Harvard University Press, 1983), 11–15; Whitrow, *Time in History,* 158ff.; Dohrn-van Rossum, *History of the Hour,* 342–50. There is a discussion of these factors in relation to the administrative coherence of the Western nation-state in Anthony Giddens, *The Nation-State and Violence,* vol. 2 of *A Contemporary Critique of Historical Materialism* (Berkeley and Los Angeles: University of California Press, 1985), chapter 7. They are also glossed more evocatively with reference to the emergence of modern historicity in the course of an influential conceptualization of nationness in Benedict Anderson, *Imagined Communities: Reflections on the Origin and Spread of Nationalism,* rev. ed. (New York: Verso, 1991), 192ff.

8. The totals on worldwide watch production are taken from Landes, *Revolution in Time,* 287. On mass production of watches, beginning in the United States and soon becoming an important industry in other countries, see idem, chapter 19. For comments on the earlier development of portable clocks and watches, see idem, 85–87, and Dohrn van-Rossum, *History of the Hour.*

9. Georg Simmel, "The Metropolis and Mental Life," in *The Sociology of Georg Simmel,* ed. and trans. Kurt H. Wolff (New York: The Free Press, 1950), 413. Note again, incidentally, the connection of the urban and temporal regulation; it is almost as if the personal timepiece is the culmination of an idea of urban coordination going back to the clock towers of the medieval city.

10. Max Weber, *The Protestant Ethic and the Spirit of Capitalism,* trans. Talcott Parsons (New York: Scribner's, 1958), 48ff. and passim. The 1893 science fiction novel, *A Cityless and Countryless World* by Henry Olerich, is an example of the narrativization of this sociological awareness. It describes a Martian society whose paper money was measured in units of time. It is discussed in Kern, *Culture of Time,* 15.

11. Lewis Mumford, *Technics and Civilization* (New York: Harcourt Brace, 1934), 14–15, 269–70.

12. Cf. Smith on Thompson. Mumford illustrates modern alienation by

reference to the scheduling of bodies in their physical functions (eating, eliminating, sexual intercourse, and so forth). In a typical overdetermination, femininity is associated with the body and requirements of the physical, and therefore the natural; hence it is either bound to or said to need "preindustrial" natural time more than masculinity does. For example, when Mumford objects to binding doctors "to a timetable almost as rigorous as that of a locomotive engineer," he does so with reference to "the mechanical interference of the obstetrician, eager to resume his rounds" despite the fact that childbirth requires patience (i.e., "natural" time) rather than a schedule (270). Traces of the same trope are in Thompson, writing three decades later, as when he asserts that the rural laborer's wife tended to remain less subject to clocked schedules and more task-oriented in an older sense. In his account, the child who may unpredictably cry no matter what the hour stands for women's work in general, which, he rather too quickly writes, has more of a "preindustrial" quality to it, even in the present (i.e., 1967); see "Time, Work-Discipline," 79. On the other hand, Thompson is interested in the unevenness of the transformation he is describing, identifying the rural laboring-class wife as the most exploited of all workers since she has to work both in the fields and in the domestic sphere. Yet, Thompson underemphasizes both the work of women in factories and the coming promotion of regularized scheduling in the domestic sphere, something illustrated by my citations from Child (see above).

13. Once it was well established as a mainstream sociocultural institution, of course, cinema could affect expectations about leisure and leisure time in its turn.

14. This is an often told story. Some of the particularities of this development in relation to conceptions of knowledge (rather than cultural history or history of science) are usefully traced out synthetically in the context of cosmology and scientific conceptualization since the ancient Greeks in Stephen Toulmin and June Goodfield, *The Discovery of Time* (1965; reprint, Chicago: University of Chicago, 1982), esp. chapter 10 for a survey of interrelations with the human sciences. It is also covered for the scientific layperson from the viewpoint of physics in Richard Morris, *Time's Arrows* (New York: Simon and Schuster, 1985). The term *deep time* was coined by John McPhee to denote the great number of years dealt with in modern geology; see Stephen Jay Gould, *Time's Arrow, Time's Cycle: Myth and Metaphor in the Discovery of Geological Time* (Cambridge, Mass.: Harvard University Press, 1987), 2. Gould provides a more detailed, if sometimes popularized, account of the British geological thinkers involved in formulating the deep

time of modern geology. See especially chapter 4, a lengthy, useful reading of Charles Lyell (but despite Gould's self-consciousness about conceptualizing history, his equation between historiography and the linear temporality symbolized as time's arrow seems overly simple to me).

15. Furthermore, there were closely related exhibitionary venues that normalized the temporality basic to these disciplines for wider publics. To take one that relates to chapter 2: "The birth of the museum is coincident with, and supplied a primary institutional condition for, the emergence of a new set of knowledges—geology, biology, archaeology, anthropology, history and art history—each of which in its museological deployment, arranged objects as parts of evolutionary sequences (the history of the earth, of life, of man, and of civilization) which, in their interrelations, formed a totalizing order of things and peoples that was historicized through and through." Tony Bennett, *The Birth of the Museum: History, Theory, Politics* (New York: Routledge, 1995), 96. Bennett's important study emphasizes the significance of Darwinism as a model for this ordering.

16. The preservationist-restorationist problematic is evinced relatively early in Freud's work: "Dreams and neuroses seem to have preserved more mental antiquities than we could have imagined possible; so that psycho-analysis may claim a high place among the sciences which are concerned with the reconstruction of the earliest and most obscure periods of the beginning of the human race." *The Interpretation of Dreams*, trans. James Strachey (New York: Avon, 1965), 588. For a study of emerging modern media such as cinema and related conceptions of temporality in scientific theory and philosophy during this period, see Mary Ann Doane, *Technologies of Temporality in Modernity* (Cambridge, Mass.: Harvard University Press, forthcoming).

17. Reinhart Koselleck, *Futures Past: On the Semantics of Historical Time*, trans. Keith Tribe (Cambridge, Mass.: MIT Press, 1985). I will draw on Koselleck selectively, without unpacking his often-noted central metaphors of the "space of experience" and "horizon of expectations," for example. For his own fuller accounts of issues I address here, see the following essays in *Futures Past:* "Modernity and the Planes of Historicity," "*Historia Magistra Vitae:* The Dissolution of the Topos into the Perspective of a Modernized Historical Process," and "'Neuzeit': Remarks on the Semantics of the Modern Concepts of Movement."

18. Koselleck, *Futures Past*, 246.

19. Ibid., 287.

20. In sociohistoric analyses of time, the concept of the cyclic has often

been used to designate an earlier or "other" society to that of the analyst, and so may come under suspicion about its ideological grounding. Some seek to bypass such problems by arguing that there is no society without some degree of both cyclic and linear temporalities. (As noted, Koselleck warns in a different context that all experiences of temporality are mixed. But of course, this does not relieve one of the responsibility for understanding degrees and balances among the different elements one postulates as part of the mixture.) For examples of both positions, see, respectively, Johannes Fabian, *Time and the Other: How Anthropology Makes Its Object* (New York: Columbia University Press, 1983), 41; and the summary in Barbara Adam, *Timewatch: The Social Analysis of Time* (Cambridge, Mass.: Polity, 1995), 34ff.

21. There are pertinent discussions of all these issues in Peter Osborne, *The Politics of Time: Modernity and Avant-Garde* (London: Verso, 1995); see chapter 1 for an overview of issues discussed here, including comments on Koselleck. See also Jürgen Habermas, *The Philosophical Discourse of Modernity: Twelve Lectures*, trans. Frederick G. Lawrence, (Cambridge, Mass.: MIT University Press, 1992), chapter 1, "Modernity's Consciousness of Time."

22. Leopold von Ranke, "Preface: Histories of the Latin and German Nations from 1494–1514," in *The Varieties of History, from Voltaire to the Present*, ed. Fritz Stern (New York: Vintage, 1972), 57. Compare, for example, the more cautious rendering of the same passage in Leopold von Ranke, *The Theory and Practice of History*, ed. Georg C. Iggers and Konrad von Moltke, trans. Wilma A. Iggers and Konrad von Moltke (New York: Bobbs-Merrill, 1973), 137: "It merely wants to show how, essentially, things happened." It is also possible to translate *wie* into "as" or "like"; for example, Koselleck's translator renders the phrase "to show the past as it once was" (Koselleck, *Futures Past*, 31). This opens the passage to a reading that proposes a figurative relation between the historiographic text and the past that is its object, something much favored in influential theories of history since the 1970s. Ricoeur exploits this ambivalence (e.g., *Time and Narrative*, 3:185) to support his own view that historiography is narrative discourse signifying a real past through analogy. For further remarks on this sentence, how it has been used, and some of its translations, see Stephen Bann, *The Clothing of Clio: A Study of the Representation of History in Nineteenth-Century Britain and France* (New York: Cambridge University Press, 1984), 8–14, 30–31.

23. Ranke, "Preface," 56.

24. For a much-cited example of Ranke's critical attitude toward sources

from the second volume, see "Critique of Guicciardini," in Leopold von Ranke, *The Secret of World History*, ed. and trans. Roger Wines (rev. ed., 1874; New York: Fordham University Press, 1981), 73–98.

25. Theodor Mommsen, "On the Training of Historians," in Stern, *Varieties of History*, 192ff.

26. "Preface: *Revue historique*," in ibid., 173.

27. J. B. Bury, "The Science of History," in ibid., 213–15 and passim.

28. A most powerful example is one of the most influential approaches in the theory of history for at least a generation, Hayden White, *Metahistory: The Historical Imagination in Nineteenth-Century Europe* (Baltimore: Johns Hopkins University Press, 1973). White's overall argument is that historiography tropologically prefigures any purported historical data. His work attacks the pretentions of the nineteenth-century critical method, the fundamental authority of authenticated sources, and the discipline it spawned. Quite consistently, his chapter on Ranke glosses the critical method in a couple of pages, and devotes most of its analysis to the implications of Ranke's modes of coherence. Many subsequent theorizations of historiography, through structuralist, poststructuralist, and rhetorical theory, have participated in this marginalization of the critical method, and continued the long-standing tendency among theorists of modern historiography to concentrate on the philosophical, ideological, metaphysical, and/or formal-aesthetic significances of the sequence.

As a result, theoretical discussions too often underplay the implications of normative disciplinary procedures with respect to sources and evidence stemming from the heritage of the critical method. For example, in a prestigious scholarly symposium on the notion of evidence in the late 1980s, those dealing with historiography or related fields tended to focus on the relation of evidence to overall argument, rather than the very notion of a historical source; see the important essay by Joan W. Scott, "The Evidence of Experience," in *Critical Inquiry* 17, no. 4 (summer 1991); and Carlo Ginzburg, "Checking the Evidence: The Judge and the Historian," in *Critical Inquiry* 18, no. 1 (autumn 1991). One contemporary theorist who does deal directly with the notion of the documentary source is Hans Kellner, *Language and Historical Representation: Getting the Story Crooked* (Madison: University of Wisconsin Press, 1989), chapter 2. See also Michel de Certeau, *The Writing of History*, trans. Tom Conley (New York: Columbia University Press, 1988).

29. Frederick Jackson Turner, "The Significance of History," in Stern,

Varieties of History, 201–2, Turner's emphasis. On archaeology, see also Bury, "Science of History," 221–22. Note that for both writers, historiography as a discipline is distinguished from mere antiquarian collection by the concept of unified development. However, critical evaluation of sources is prior. As Turner goes on to say about preserved prior chronologies and artifacts: "First he [the historian] must determine whether it is genuine; then whether it was contemporary, or at what period it was written" (202).

30. On document and documentary, see chapter 6 in this volume.

31. Gould, *Time's Arrow,* 154, 155. Incidentally, Gould fully endorses Lyell's vision of "the joy of history" (153), which suggests the persistent strength of these constructions into the late twentieth century. Cf. Toulmin and Goodfield, *The Discovery of Time:* "While the central concepts of Darwinism stimulated the human sciences, Darwinian theory was itself built on foundations laid by the geologists, notably Lyell; and Lyell in turn acknowledged a stimulus from the new school of critical historians founded by Niebuhr at Berlin" (232). Of course, in many respects the relation between geology and the dating of fossil remains is a chicken-egg question, for Lyell used fossil remains to solve some crucial problems in the dating of geological strata; see Gould, *Time's Arrow,* 157–67. Compare also Turner's American Historical Association presidential address, where he suggests analogies between historiography and geology on other grounds (that geology is not a science that constructs a priori laws), which does, however, go back to unpredictability, like Lyell; see Turner, "Social Forces in American History," in *The Frontier in American History* (New York: Henry Holt, 1921), 331.

32. Carl G. Hempel, "The Function of General Laws in History," in *Theories of History,* ed. Patrick Gardiner (Glencoe, Ill.: Free Press, 1959), 344–56, has been one of the single most discussed articles in the twentieth-century philosophy of history, but Hempel was undoubtedly less interested in historiography per se than in extending a deductive-nomological account of scientific reasoning. He does acknowledge the general failure of acceptable historiography to achieve the standards he set. He answers this with notions such as the "explanation sketch" (see 351ff.) probabalistic explanation; see the introductory passages, 90–93, of his 1963 paper, "Reasons and Covering Laws in Historical Explanation," in *The Philosophy of History,* ed. Patrick Gardiner (New York; Oxford University Press, 1978), 90–93.

33. It might be argued that this selectivity became less random as the era of modern historicity developed, with its broad dissemination of ideologies of

preservationism along with historical self-consciousness. (There is also the record of automatically produced indexical media, such as audio recording, film, and television.) But this assumes that historical thinking persists and is of a similar, predictable type between past and present.

34. Fernand Braudel, "History and the Social Sciences: The *Longue Durée*," in *On History*, trans. Sarah Mathews (Chicago: University of Chicago Press, 1980), 48.

35. A seminal analysis of the language of the disciplined historian for an entire generation of structuralist and poststructuralist cultural critics and theorists was done by Roland Barthes, "The Discourse of History," in *The Rustle of Language*, trans. Richard Howard (Berkeley and Los Angeles: University of California Press, 1989); its companion piece is "The Reality Effect" in the same volume (discussed more fully in chapter 4 of this volume). See also works of White cited elsewhere in this chapter, which in some respects take Barthes as their starting point.

Cf. Koselleck, "Perspective and Temporality: A Contribution to the Historiographical Exposure of the Historical World," in *Futures Past*, esp. 136–41. He finds the problem of historiographic positionality already formulated in the mid-eighteenth century by a transitional figure, J. C. Chladenius. One finds awareness of it throughout the nineteenth century; for example, in Johann Gustav Droysen, "Art and Method" (1868), an excerpt of which appears in Stern, *Varieties of History*, 142: "What we have to do is to find methods, in order to secure objective rules and control for this immediate and subjective grasp of events, especially as we now have before us, to represent the past, only the views of others or fragments of that which once existed. We need to ground, sound and justify our subjective knowledge. Only this seems able to assert itself as the sense of the historical objectivity so often named." While Droysen is often treated as an early critic of positivism in the critical method, note how this makes secure positionality a methodological issue for historiography rather than a fundamental epistemological difficulty. See also the discussion of this complex of issues and writers in Luiz Costa Lima, *Control of the Imaginary: Reason and Imagination in Modern Times*, trans. Ronald W. Sousa (Minneapolis: University of Minnesota Press, 1988), chapter 2 and esp. 90–97. On temporality, crisis, and film in relation to contemporaneous disciplines of physical science and philosophy, see Doane, *Technologies of Temporality*.

36. This is Dilthey's famous distinction between *Geisteswissenschaften* and *Naturwissenschaften*, and it is also connected to the classic formulation of methods supposedly specific to the former, such as that of *verstehen* (on *verstehen*, see notes

39 and 53). There is a detailed overview of the players and positions of the German "crisis of historicism" in Georg G. Iggers, *The German Conception of History: The National Tradition of Historical Thought from Herder to the Present* (Middletown, Conn.: Wesleyan University Press, 1968), 124–25, and chapters 6 and 7. For an international perspective on these matters, see idem, "The Crisis of the Conventional Conception of 'Scientific History,'" in *New Directions in European Historiography*, rev. ed. (Middletown, Conn.: Wesleyan University Press, 1984). Harry Elmer Barnes stressed World War I as a cause of positional uncertainty in his pioneering *A History of Historical Writing*, rev. ed. (New York: Dover, 1963), chapter 11. Cf. Ernst Breisach, *Historiography: Ancient, Medieval, and Modern* (Chicago: University of Chicago Press, 1983), 278–86, 326–30. There is nothing new in my treating German historical theory in relation to modernist relativism and subjectivism in social theory. See, for example, the once standard overview, H. Stuart Hughes, *Consciousness and Society: The Reorientation of European Social Thought 1890–1930* (New York: Vintage, 1958), esp. chapter 6.

37. Heinrich Rickert, *The Limits of Concept Formation in Natural Science: A Logical Introduction to the Historical Sciences*, abr. ed., trans. Guy Oakes (New York: Cambridge University Press, 1986), 47–48. This is a translation of a 1929 revision.

38. Ibid., esp. chapter 4.

39. See Koselleck, "Perspective and Temporality," 136ff. In discussing the German tradition, Koselleck gives credit for discovering the impossibility of an impartial perspective to J. S. Chladenius (1710–59). A more famous example from the first half of the same century was the Italian Vico, who was well known to Dilthey. Vico conceived of a new science that studied the history of human nations in a sequential temporality of beginnings, developments, finalities, breaks, and new beginnings—that is, as cycles, but of internally unified sequences. Furthermore, Vico, in effect, foreshadows the *verstehen* principle as a grounds for access to the distant past against change, as in the following much-noted passage: "But in the night of thick darkness enveloping the earliest antiquity, so remote from ourselves, there shines the eternal and never failing light of a truth beyond all question: that the world of civil society has certainly been made by men and that its principles are therefore to be found within the modifications of our own human mind. Whoever reflects on this cannot but marvel that the philosophers should have bent all their energies to the study of the world of nature, which, since God made it, He alone knows; and that they should have neglected the study of the world of nations, or civil world, which, since men had made it, men could come to

know" (Giambattista Vico, *The New Science of Giambattista Vico*, rev. ed., trans. Thomas Goddard Bergin and Max Harold Fisch [Garden City, N.Y.: Anchor, 1961], 52–53). Here he distinguishes the physical sciences from what would later be called the human sciences, and argues that the latter were not only possible, but more certain, because in them humanity studies that which it knows intimately—itself and its own civil society. Another innovation of Vico's that can be related to later attitudes was his interest in studying general cultural-ideological formations, which in some respects anticipates the historicization of ideas and worldviews that was later associated with theories of ideology and which he called common sense: "Common sense is judgment without reflection, shared by an entire class, an entire people, an entire nation, or the entire human race."

40. Bury, "Science of History," 218, 219. For a later, technical philosophical discussion of the idea that new historical sequenciations of the same existents become inevitable with the passage of time, see Arthur C. Danto, *Narration and Knowledge (including the integral text of* Analytic Philosophy of History) (New York: Columbia University Press, 1985), 149–53ff.

41. The standard reference is the first part of a relatively early manuscript critiquing Young Hegelian philosophers, which Marx and Engels abandoned unpublished. See Marx and Engels, *The German Ideology* (New York: International Publishers, 1976), Part I.

42. See Karl Mannheim, *Ideology and Utopia: An Introduction to the Sociology of Knowledge*, trans. Louis Wirth and Edward Shils (New York: Harcourt, Brace and World, 1936), 153–64, on the free-floating intelligentsia. One indication that temporality is the problem for Mannheim is his sometime use of spatializing metaphors for a totalizing positionality of knowledge, as when he writes that the epistemological goal is "not achievement of a super-temporally valid conclusion but the broadest possible extension of our horizon of vision." At other points, he explicitly rejects basic historicist theses as when, with reference to Ranke, he denies that historiography deals only in the unique. See idem, 3, 88, 106, 200–202.

43. Georg Lukács, *History and Class Consciousness: Studies in Marxist Dialectics*, trans. Rodney Livingstone (Cambridge, Mass.: MIT Press, 1971). Mannheim was well aware of this work. Compare, for example, Lukác's 1920 essay "Class Consciousness," on problems of historicism (47–49), its solution in the notion of imputed class consciousness (51), and its emphasis on a totalizing perspective (59ff). For complimentary remarks on Rickert (along with critique), see idem, e.g., 150–51 and 154ff.

44. Ibid., 154.

45. For the auto-critique, see ibid., "Preface to the New Edition (1967)."

46. For a good example of the persistence of these themes, see such later work as Georg Lukács, *Realism in Our Time: Literature and the Class Struggle*, trans. John and Necke Mander (New York: Harper, 1971). On the early intellectual relationship between Lukács and Mannheim, see Mary Gluck, *Georg Lukács and His Generation 1900–1918* (Cambridge, Mass.: Harvard University Press, 1985).

47. For what it is worth and for reasons that would take us too far afield here, Lukács's view that any claim of valid historical knowledge must be centered on the positionality of the most exploited social groupings still seems to me to be a significant insight, despite some danger of a romantic sentimentalization of the oppressed. But it is necessary to complicate his definitions of that exploitation.

48. Michel Foucault, *The Order of Things: An Archaeology of the Human Sciences* (New York: Vintage, 1973), 219–20.

49. White, *Metahistory*, 29. For his approach to the construction of historiographic coherencies as narrative, see Hayden White, *The Content of the Form* (Baltimore: Johns Hopkins University Press, 1987), esp. three essays: "The Value of Narrativity in the Representation of Reality," "The Question of Narrative in Contemporary Historical Theory," and "The Politics of Historical Interpretation: Discipline and De-Sublimation." Important studies of historiography informed by White's treatment of tropes as part-whole relations include Stephen Bann, *The Clothing of Clio*, and Kellner, *Language and Historical Representation*. F. R. Ankersmit, in "The Dilemma of Contemporary Anglo-Saxon Philosophy of History," in *History and Tropology: The Rise and Fall of Metaphor* (Berkeley and Los Angeles: University of California Press, 1994), draws on Rorty's view of analytic philosophy to provide a useful account of the shift in the theory of history.

50. White, *Metahistory*, 1, emphasis in original.

51. Niebuhr, preface to the second edition of his *History of Rome* (1827–32), in Stern, *Varieties of History*, 48.

52. Introduction to *History of the Reformation in Germany* (1839–47, in six volumes) in *The Secret of World History*, 70. Note the synecdoche by which "I" is figured as "eye."

53. The notion of contact between subjects in the past and the present can be found in many elaborated theories of history. An idea that historians establish a relationship of human empathy or understanding (if not identification) with historical agents in the past was formulated at least as early as Vico. It was highly

developed in the German theory of history as the much noted doctrine of *verste-hen*, and in Collingwood's argument that the historian mentally reenacts the thoughts of historical agents. Speaking generally, this tendency asserts that a successful or "objective" relation to the past is achievable through historiographic subjectivity—the historian's consciousness and imagination—in concert with the scientific protocols of authenticated sources. Once again, its solution is through an element of historicity that escapes temporality, namely the constants attributed to human subjectivity itself; however, the capacity of the trained historian may be privileged in this regard. For the (non-German) theoretical culmination of this tendency, see the explication of the historian's work, which is closely tied to a division between the human and natural sciences, such as geology, in R. G. Collingwood, *The Idea of History* (New York: Oxford University Press, 1946), e.g., 215–19, 282–302. Collingwood is somewhat acerbic about the critical method, but his analogy between the detective and the historian restates the primacy of indexical traces as the evidentiary basis for historiography.

54. Siegfried Kracauer, "Photography," in *The Mass Ornament: Weimer Essays*, ed. and trans. Thomas Y. Levin (Cambridge: Harvard University Press, 1995), 49–50.

55. In "Photography," Kracauer does often yoke photography and cinema together, judging them potentially superior to historicism's "barren self presentation of spatial and temporal elements" (61). Why this might be is indicated in other passages, such as "When the grandmother [in an old family photograph] stood in front of the lens, she was present for one second in the spatial continuum that presented itself to the lens. . . . A shudder runs through the viewer of old photographs. For they make visible not the knowledge of the original, but the spatial configuration of a moment; what appears in the photograph is not the person but the sum of what can be subtracted from him or her." Ibid., 56–57. This suggests an anti-Bazinian view of indexicality, for the photograph is insufficient in itself to promote an engagement investment by the subject in the authenticity of its depicted object. The divergence from Bazin is clear when Kracauer invokes the seemingly Bazinian "fear of death" in the apprehension of photographs. For he is discussing their use in illustrated newspapers—that is in the context of a highly capitalized, mass medium and not with respect to an individual subject's apprehension of the photograph as such, as in the mummy complex (59). As for the revelatory capacities of indexicality in modernity in relation to memory and subject-position, see the conclusion, 61–63.

At the end of his life, Kracauer returned to these questions and was trying to develop the analogy between historiography and photography/cinema more fully. See his posthumously published *History: The Last Things Before the Last* (New York: Oxford University Press, 1969), esp. chapter 2, "The Historical Approach," which is organized around this comparison and includes several references to *"wie es eigentlich gewesen."* See also his *Theory of Film* (New York: Oxford University Press, 1960) for a somewhat different late elaboration on the notion that cinema can propose a counter to modern, alienated interaction with reality.

56. For example, Foucault brings Husserl onto the scene at the conclusion of the chapter, which describes the nineteenth century as the age of History, and his summary of the phenomenological solution is that it wishes "to give empirical contents transcendental value, or to displace them in the direction of a constituent subjectivity." Foucault, *The Order of Things*, 219–20, 248.

57. Theodor W. Adorno, *Against Epistemology: A Metacritique; Studies in Husserl and the Phenomenological Antinomies*, trans. Willis Domingo (Cambridge, Mass.: MIT Press, 1983), 187–88. The context for this quote is the "surprising" appearance of Husserlian themes in *Being and Time:* "Both Husserl and Heidegger let the breach between necessity and contingency disappear by beginning with the principle of the ego, which Husserl called the transcendental ego and Heidegger being there (*Dasein*). In both philosophies there is an interplay of idea and fact. Heidegger's tendency to camouflage irresolvable contradictions, like those between timeless ontology and history, by ontologizing history itself as historicality and turning the contradiction as such into a 'structure of being' is prefigured in Husserl's epistemology. Husserl also sought to hypostatize irresolvability as a solution to the problem."

58. Ibid., 219–20, and see in general, 217–28. See also the remarks on "The Concept of Anxiety and Historicity," in Theodor W. Adorno, *Kierkegaard: Construction of the Aesthetic*, ed. and trans., Robert Hullot-Kentor (Minneapolis: University of Minnesota Press, 1989), 32–34. Incidentally, the quoted passage includes the following: "—or best of all [forbid] any thinking at all. Another trace of that can be found in the transformation of thought into 'seeing' (*Schau*) and the hatred of theorizing." It would be possible to spin this passage toward a tradition of conceiving of disciplined historiography and its insistence on authenticated documentary evidence through visual metaphors, and from there toward Adorno's interest in cinema and other media of mechanical reproduction.

59. Merleau-Ponty, "Film and the New Psychology," in *Sense and*

Non-Sense, trans. Hubert L. Dreyfus and Patricia A. Dreyfus (Evanston, Ill.: Northwestern University Press, 1964), esp. 59; Metz, "The Imaginary Signifier," in *The Imaginary Signifier: Psychoanalysis and the Cinema*, trans. Celia Britton et al., (Bloomington: Indiana University Press, 1982), 52–53. Note again that the former (cited by Metz) was almost contemporary with Bazin's ontological essays. A much-noted Marxist version of this view with reference to Husserl is Jean-Louis Baudry, "The Ideological Effects of the Basic Cinematographic Apparatus," in *Narrative, Apparatus, Ideology*, ed. Philip Rosen (New York: Columbia University Press, 1986).

60. This remark may seem to be just one more version of modernist self-reflexivity, which is a fair enough comment, for I do not pretend that it is currently possible to escape modern historicity. However, a variety of stances are possible within that historicity and even the figure of a debt to the dead; good examples are Michelet and Walter Benjamin's "Theses on the Philosophy of History."

61. My chronology has undoubtedly been at best a fuzzy shorthand; for example, deep time was taking hold in geology prior to the nineteenth century, and issues of historiographic perspective were also formulated earlier and were still important later, as my examples show. But this fuzziness was deliberate, for I am less concerned with a precise chronology of conceptual innovations than the dissemination and normalization of certain broad concerns with time, change, and history. This was a long process that lasted for many years. But so many of the key moments in articulating the intellectual and cultural premises of this awareness appeared during the 1800s that the shorthand of "the nineteenth century" still says something of significance.

62. There has been some controversy over whether Edison actually met his contractual commitment to exhibit the kinetoscope in Chicago. See Gordon Hendricks, *The Kinetoscope: America's First Commercially Successful Motion Picture Exhibitor* (New York: Theodor Gaus' Sons, 1966), 40–45, who concludes that Edison and his associates did do so. Bennett provides an important and useful account of the relation of grand international exhibitions and fairs to historicity and museum culture; see, e.g., 80–84. On the *historiographe*, see Germaine Lacasse, with Serge Duigou, "*L'Historiographe* (Les débuts du spectacle cinématographique au Québec)," *Les Dossiers de la Cinémathèque* 15 (Montréal: Cinémathèque québécoise, 1985). I owe this reference to André Gaudreault.

63. By the late twentieth century, such coincidences could become self-conscious. Even the flagship journal of the American Historical Association has

now devoted significant space to questions of film and history. See, for example, the forum on cinema and history in *American Historical Review* 30 (December 1988).

4. Detail, Document, and Diegesis in Mainstream Film

1. Research records mentioned in this chapter are in the Special Collections Department of the Doheny Library, University of Southern California. Information on hair in the ancient Middle East is in the research handbook for *Samson and Delilah*, entry under "Hair." Information on the Egyptian *sacrum* is in the caption of a photocopied photograph of a sacrum in the research files of *The Ten Commandments* (1956). For the emperor's forms of addressing Carlotta and his writing habits, see *General Research Record* for *Juarez*, query by Ellis dated 11.23.38; and memo/release included in production file. For gummed labels on bottles, *General Research Record* for *Dr. Ehrlich's Magic Bullet*, query by Goldie 11.14.39, reproduced in Figure 4.1.

2. The need to research necessary exclusions connects historical research to production determinants encompassing categories of legal identity and liability. This function of research departments is mentioned by Staiger in David Bordwell, Janet Staiger, and Kristin Thompson, *The Classical Hollywood Cinema: Film Style and Mode of Production to 1960* (New York: Columbia University Press, 1985), 323. Good examples of this function are in the production file for *Confessions of a Nazi Spy* in the Warner Brothers Collection, Doheny Library. It includes several memos from the research department with notations like, "There is a W. G. Hildebrandt, living in New York City, and I suggest that we spell the name Wilhelm Wildebrandt" (Lissauer to Robert Lord, 13 January 1939), and "There is a HOTEL ATLANTIC in New York City, we advise that it be changed to HOTEL ATLANTA" (Lissauer to Lord, 17 January 1939). This production file also includes a lengthy memo from Morris Ebenstein of the legal department to Hal Wallis, which summarizes some of the issues for the studio around right-to-privacy law in a film purporting to authenticity in the representation of recent public events.

3. George F. Custen, *Bio/Pics: How Hollywood Constructed Public History* (New Brunswick: Rutgers University Press, 1992), 128, 34–45, and chapter 3. See also his case studies of *Night and Day* and *The Story of Alexander Graham Bell*, 121–39. Research activities for nonbiopic films are noted by Custen (for example, *Meet Me in St. Louis* and *East of Eden*); however, he stays within bounds of his monographic constraints as opposed to my interest in the wider implications of

these research activities. Also, while Custen usefully points at "the typical research *minutiae* on which these [research] departments thrived" (128), his case studies of biopic production histories tend to emphasize decisions about story elements such as character and plot events, rather than such minutiae. Story elements probably generated the greatest amount of explicit and therefore documented internal memos under the strong producer apparatus of 1930s and 1940s Hollywood; yet, the *unspoken* routines of production, involving implicit norms of relating mise-en-scène to practical norms of historical accuracy deserve as much attention. For an interesting argument that Hollywood studios sought to evade censorship by *avoiding* claims of accurate research and authenticity, see Ruth Vasey, *The World According to Hollywood 1918–1939* (Madison: University of Wisconsin Press, 1997), 210–19.

 4. On Méliès and research, see the comments on *The Coronation of Edward VII* (1902) in André Gaudreault, "The Cinematograph: A Historiographical Machine," in *Meanings in Texts and Actions: Questioning Paul Ricoeur*, ed. David E. Klemm and William Schweiker (Charlottesville: University Press of Virginia, 1993), esp. 92–93, which takes its information from Jacques Deslandes and Jacques Richard, *Histoire comparée du cinéma*, 2, 455–60. Publicity trumpeting research and accurate detail with respect to "Indian and Western subjects" is noted as early as 1909 by Richard Abel, *The Red Rooster Scare: Making Cinema American: 1900–1910* (Berkeley and Los Angeles: University of California Press, 1999), 164–65.

 5. For accounts of industry strategies in the 1980s and 1990s, see Justin Wyatt, *High Concept: Movies and Marketing in Hollywood* (Austin: University of Texas Press, 1994), chapter 3; and Janet Wasko, *Hollywood in the Information Age: Beyond the Silver Screen* (Austin: University of Texas Press, 1994). Some of these tendencies are already discussed in Douglas Gomery, "Corporate Ownership and Control of the U.S. Film Industry," *Screen* 25, nos. 4–5 (July–October 1984): 60–69. According to Balio, the resurgence of vertical integration dates from 1986, when Columbia acquired a small theater chain in New York City; see Tino Balio, "Adjusting to the New Global Economy: Hollywood in the 1990s," in *Film Policy: International, National, and Regional Perspectives* (New York: Routledge, 1996), 24.

 6. The notion of a shift from modern to postmodern culture is often adduced in this respect. For particularly interesting and forceful statements of this position, see Timothy Corrigan, *A Cinema without Walls: Movies and Culture after Vietnam* (New Brunswick, N.J.: Rutgers University Press, 1991), 1–50; and

Miriam Hansen, "Early Cinema, Late Cinema: Transformations of the Public Sphere," in *Viewing Positions: Ways of Seeing Film*, ed. Linda Williams (New Brunswick, N.J.: Rutgers University Press, 1994). But there is also a strong argument for emphasizing the macroeconomic structure of the film industry in this regard. See Richard Maltby, "Nobody Knows Everything: Post-Classical Historiographies and Classical Entertainment," in *Contemporary Hollywood Cinema*, ed. Steve Neale and Murray Smith (New York: Routledge, 1998).

7. It will be noted below that mainstream media industry publicity often trumpets research as one of its virtues. Thus, the information in this paragraph was culled not from *Variety* or a work of professional film scholarship, but from articles in my local newspaper, picked up from the news services of other papers: John J. Archibald, "Screening out Errors in Television Script," *Providence Evening-Bulletin*, 3 July 1987, B8 (*St. Louis Post-Dispatch* service). Cf. Bill Steigerwald, "A Former Docudrama Fact Checker," *Providence Journal-Bulletin*, 4 November 1986, A13 (*Los Angeles Times* service).

8. Human bodies in films have been subject to a wide range of studies, especially feminist analyses and work on star codes. Some examples of more occasional kinds of probes of the profilmic are in *Fabrications: Costume and the Female Body*, ed. Jane Gaines and Charlotte Herzog (New York: Routledge, 1990); Brian Henderson, "Notes on Set Design and Cinema," *Film Quarterly* 42, no. 1 (fall 1988): 17–28; and the architecturally oriented Donald Albrecht, *Designing Dreams* (New York: Harper and Row, 1986). Charles Affron and Mirella Jona Affron, *Sets in Motion: Art Direction and Film Narrative* (New Brunswick, N.J.: Rutgers University Press, 1996) is a fertile work that bears directly on some of my concerns, but I cannot do justice to it here. Affron and Affron attempt a categorical systematization, defining five different "design intensities" or overall functionalities of the arrangement of the profilmic ("set design" includes location filming for them). These five functions are all defined in relation to narrative. It might seem that their first category, "denotation," is the one most pertinent to my discussion of profilmic detail and the historical film (see their chapter 2); however, their idea that denotative profilmic transparency is achieved essentially through meeting generic expectations is made on a different level than my argument. On the other hand, in my argument the term *transparency* becomes problematic because the two stances I identify, of detail and spectacle, are ultimately inseparable. Furthermore, they might well object that I tend to collapse the rest of their categories (set as punctuation, embellishment, artifice, and narrative) into one, whose synecdoche

is "spectacle." But some of this is because their concerns begin from the relations of narration to arrangements of the profilmic, and mine begin from the theoretical and historical status of filmic indexicality in relation to film theory and the theory of history. C. S. Tashiro, *Pretty Pictures: Production Design and the History Film* (Austin: University of Texas Press, 1998) is closer to my concerns, not only because of its approach to historical cinema, but because it foregrounds the question of the profilmic object. See, for example, chapter 8, "A Few Words about a Hat."

9. Letter of Charles Everett to Warner Brothers, 8 March 1938, Zola file, Dieterle Collection, Doheny Library.

10. Custen notes similar examples. Compare also the discussion of representational contradictions of the historical film in Jean-Louis Comolli, "Historical Fictions: A Body Too Much," trans. Ben Brewster, *Screen* 19, no. 2 (summer 1978): 46: "The spectacle is always a game. It requires the participation of spectators not as consumers but as players, accomplices, masters of the game, even if they are also its stakes." In the face of many critiques of psychoanalytic film theory as constructing a "passive" spectator, it is worth emphasizing Comolli's view that the knowledge of the active spectator makes the fetishistic structure of representation more intense, and that the historical film takes this tension to an extreme. I will return to this.

11. Draft signed "Warner Brothers Studio National Magazine Department," Doheny Library, emphasis added. This appears to be a draft press release.

12. Mario Chiari, "Production Designer," in *Barabbas: The Story of a Motion Picture*, ed. Lon Jones (Bologna: Cappelli, 1962), 159.

13. See Alicia Annas, "The Photogenic Formula: Hairstyles and Makeup in Historical Films," in *Hollywood and History: Costume Design in Film*, ed. Edward Maeder (Los Angeles and London: Los Angeles Museum of Art and Thames and Hudson, 1987).

14. "The Charge of the Light Brigade," *Photoplay Studies* 2, no. 11 (November 1936): 10. I'm grateful to Richard Maltby for making this material available. This issue also reprints two prestigious reviews that note and justify the historical inaccuracies of the plot, Frank Nugent's in the *New York Times* (2 November 1936) and Welford Beaton's in *The Hollywood Spectator* (24 October 1936). An example of an aesthetic constraint on set design was the impact of architectural modernism, discussed in Albrecht. Henderson is useful on some of this, but oddly evades the mass production aspects of the issues he raises.

15. Edward Maeder, "The Celluloid Image: Historical Dress in Film," in Maeder, *Hollywood and History*, 13. On these matters, see this entire catalog, especially Annas, for a suggestive survey of some of the compromise formations and strategies in Hollywood cinema over time.

16. Chiari, "Production Designer," 159.

17. Thus, Roy Rosenstone, an insurgent historian who aggressively promotes historiography in cinema, makes a case that inverts the traditional approach among his colleagues. He asserts that cinema has "its own rules of representation," which are distinct from those of scholarly written historiography in the different medium of verbal language; and that cinematic historiography therefore need not accede to the protocols and representational practices of professional historians. It is not mainstream cinema that provides him with positive examples, however, but its textual competitors such as art cinema, oppositional cinema, third cinema, and so forth. (He emphasizes what he calls the "new history film," whose "aim is less to entertain an audience or to make profits than to understand the legacy of the past.") Thus, even Rosenstone's argument does not go against those who, throughout film history, have complained about the historiography of commercial cinema, because he implicitly positions mainstream cinema outside "truly" cinematic rules and modes of historiography, even though mainstream cinema has constituted the norm for most audiences throughout film history. See his introduction to *Revisioning History: Film and the Construction of a New Past* (Princeton: Princeton University Press, 1995), 3, 4.

18. The bibliography on classical cinema is now very large. The original theoretical inspiration is in writings of André Bazin, such as, "The Evolution of the Language of Cinema," in *What Is Cinema?*, 1: 28–33 (though he describes French as well as Hollywood cinema of the 1930s as a "classical art"). A number of influential accounts of classical or mainstream textuality from 1970s film theory have been reprinted: see, for example, Stephen Heath, "Narrative Space," in *Questions of Cinema* (Bloomington: Indiana University Press, 1981); Christian Metz, "Story/Discourse: A Note on Two Voyeurisms," in *The Imaginary Signifier: Psychoanalysis and the Cinema* (Bloomington: Indiana University Press, 1982); and Laura Mulvey, "Visual Pleasure and Narrative Cinema," in *Visual and Other Pleasures* (Bloomington: Indiana University Press, 1989). For an alternative account, see David Bordwell, *Narration in the Fiction Film* (Madison: University of Wisconsin Press, 1985), esp. chapter 9, "Classical Narration: The Hollywood Example." A version of the latter as well as the articles by Heath and Mulvey are included in

Narrative, Apparatus, Ideology, ed. Philip Rosen (New York: Columbia University Press, 1986). Bordwell pluralizes the very concept of a classical cinema, arguing that from a narrational perspective, "the Hollywood cinema cannot be identified with classicism *tout court*," and principles of classical cinematic narration can be found in other historical periods and locales, albeit with some different mechanisms (he suggests 1930s Italy and 1950s Poland as possible examples); see Bordwell, *Narration in the Fiction Film*, 165–66. For a more sympathetic critique of some key texts of 1970s film theory that reject the mainstream/nonmainstream binary, see D. N. Rodowick, *The Crisis of Political Modernism: Criticism and Ideology in Contemporary Film Theory* (Urbana: University of Illinois Press, 1988). For a collection of scholarly essays attempting to rethink the category of classical cinema, see Jane Gaines, *Classical Hollywood Narrative: The Paradigm Wars* (Durham: Duke University Press, 1992). Another important reconsideration is Miriam Bratu Hansen, "The Mass Production of the Senses: Classical Cinema as Vernacular Modernism," *Modernism/Modernity* 6, no. 2 (1999): 59–77. The most important scholarly work on classical cinema as a historical/industrial product is Bordwell, Staiger, and Thompson, *The Classical Hollywood Cinema*. See also the review of related issues in Maltby, "Nobody Knows Everything."

19. I would argue that this process has been a relatively permanent one. Even arguments that postmodern social and cultural forces have been disarticulating the unifying semantic force of narrative in commercial cinema cannot account, it seems, for the fact that fictional feature films remain the leading commercial product of filmmaking and provide central cultural events that then get parceled and channeled through the media apparatus of video, cable, broadcast, theme park, digital multimedia, other blockbuster tie-ins, and so forth. For important examples of such arguments, see Timothy Corrigan, *A Cinema without Walls*, and Miriam Hansen, "Early Cinema, Late Cinema: Transformations of the Public Sphere." An argument for the continuing importance of classical narrative form (though not necessarily classical style) is Kristen Thompson, *Storytelling in the New Hollywood: Understanding Classical Narrative Technique* (Cambridge, Mass.: Harvard University Press, 1999).

20. Robert C. Allen, "Contra the Chaser Theory," in *Film before Griffith*, ed. John L. Fell (Berkeley and Los Angeles: University of California Press, 1983), 109–12. The point is not that there were no noncomic fictional films before 1903–4, but that they were not among the most numerous film types being produced.

21. See Robert C. Allen, *Vaudeville and Film 1895–1913: A Study in Media Interaction* (New York: Arno, 1980), where the author uses counts of film types from copyright records as one of his major sources of evidence. For example, Allen finds that as late as 1904, documentary-oriented films comprised over 40 percent of U.S. film titles, as did comic films, with dramatic narratives at only 8 percent (181). By this measure, the suddenness of the disappearance of the actuality is most striking. Allen also finds that even in 1907, documentary genres comprised 33 percent of films copyrighted in the United States, while in 1908 and 1909 the figures declined to 4 percent and 3 percent respectively (211). In 1907, the figure for dramatic narratives was only 17 percent but in 1908 it jumped to 66 percent (213). The numerical preponderance of actuality filmmaking through 1907 is proposed not only by Allen, but by a number of scholars. See, for example, David Levy, "Edison Sales Policy and the Continuous Action Film, 1904–1906," in *Film before Griffith*, 222. Paul C. Spehr, "Filmmaking at the American Mutoscope and Biograph Company 1900–1906," *Quarterly Journal of the Library of Congress* 37 (summer-fall, 1980), reports that between 1900 and 1906, Biograph made 1,035 nonfiction films and 774 fiction films. Tino Balio uses this figure to argue for the dominance of actuality films in "A Novelty Spawns Small Businesses, 1894–1908," introduction to Part I of *The American Film Industry*, rev. ed. (Madison: University of Wisconsin Press, 1985), and he flatly asserts that the shift to narrative occurred after the nickelodeon boom (20, 21). See also Allen, "The Movies in Vaudeville: The Historical Context of Movies as Entertainment," in Balio, *American Film Industry*, 78.

22. For Musser's argument, worded as a critique of Allen, see Musser, "Another Look at the Chaser Theory," *Studies in Visual Communication* 10, no. 4 (1984): 38ff. and passim, followed by an exchange between Allen and Musser: Allen, "Looking at 'Another Look at the Chaser Theory,'" 45–50, and Musser, "Reply to Allen," 51–52. See also Allen, "Motion Picture Exhibition in Manhattan 1906–1912: Beyond the Nickelodeon," in *Film before Griffith*; and Musser, "The Nickelodeon Era Begins: Establishing the Framework for Hollywood's Mode of Representation," *Framework* no. 22–23 (autumn 1983): 4–11. Musser has since published a fuller elaboration of his account in *The Emergence of Cinema: The American Screen to 1907*, vol. 1 of *History of the American Cinema* (Los Angeles: University of California Press, 1990); see esp. chapters 10–12. See also "Rethinking Early Cinema: Cinema of Attractions and Narrativity," *The Yale Journal of Criticism* 7, no. 2 (1994): 203–32, where Musser continues to object to the influence of Allen's

conclusion. Abel, *The Red Rooster Scare*, 1, points out that part of the debate is over the stability of the market for films from 1900 to 1903, suggesting that some differences arise from the fact that Allen's research centers on exhibition venues (especially vaudeville), while Musser's centers on production.

23. For seminal polemics about the status of preclassical filmic textuality, see the work of Noël Burch. One much-discussed formulation is his "Porter, or Ambivalence," *Screen* 19 (winter 1978–79): 91–105. See also his 1979 lecture, "Primitivism and the Avant-Gardes: A Dialectical Approach," in Rosen, *Narrative, Apparatus, Ideology*, and "Un mode de représentation primitif?" *Iris* 2, no. 1 (1984); his film *Correction Please, or How We Got into Pictures* (Arts Council of Great Britain), 1979; and his book-length summary of his views, *Life to Those Shadows*, trans. and ed. Ben Brewster (Los Angeles: University of California Press, 1990). For a critique of Burch's methods with respect to claims about textuality and film historiography, see David Bordwell and Kristin Thompson, "Linearity, Materialism, and the Study of Early American Cinema," *Wide Angle* 5, no. 3 (1983): 4–15. See also David Bordwell, *On the History of Film Style* (Cambridge, Mass.: Harvard University Press, 1997), chapter 4. Another influential scholar with respect to conceptions of preclassical textuality is Tom Gunning; see his much-cited article on preclassical textuality, "A Cinema of Attractions: Early Film, Its Spectator, and the Avant-Garde," *Wide Angle* 8, no. 3/4 (fall 1985), and "An Aesthetic of Astonishment: Early Film and the (In)Credulous Spectator," *Art and Text* 34 (1989). Most pertinent to my concerns here is Gunning's study of the transition to "the Narrator System" in Griffith's Biograph films, *D. W. Griffith and the Origins of American Narrative Film: The Early Years at Biograph* (Urbana and Chicago: University of Illinois Press, 1994). For a critique of Gunning, see Musser, "Rethinking Early Cinema." The most comprehensive collection of the new scholarship on preclassical cinema from the 1970s and 1980s, including textual analyses and theorizations, is *Early Cinema: Space, Frame, Narrative*, ed. Thomas Elsaesser (London: British Film Institute, 1990).

24. Allen first speculated that the transition to narrative may have been determined primarily by the need to regularize production in an early article, "Film History: The Narrow Discourse," in *Film: Historical-Theoretical Speculations* (*1977 Film Studies Annual*, Part 2), ed. Ben Lawton and Janet Staiger (Pleasantville, N.Y.: Redgrave, 1977), 13–15. He reviews his evidence for this view in his *Vaudeville and Film*, esp. 212–20. For some later caveats and refinements in response to Musser's critique, see Allen, "Looking at 'Another Look,'" esp. 47.

Musser, in "Another Look at the Chaser Theory," objects to some of Allen's inferences, but he does seem to agree on the idea that fiction is more rationalizable than actuality; nevertheless, he insists that part of the constellation of determinants for producers seeking rationalization was audience desires, and that narrative was attractive for audiences. See 37ff. for Musser's argument that the increase in narrative films was a strategy to attract audiences starting in 1902 after an industry slump. Interestingly, although Musser argues against the proposition that industrial rationalization determined the shift to narrative, he does believe that it determined the later, post-1908 development of classical cinema's textual procedures associated with D. W. Griffith. See Musser, "The Nickelodeon Era Begins," 11. Musser's important argument may have appeared too late to be taken into account by Janet Staiger, who takes Allen's view of the function of narrative in Bordwell, Staiger, and Thompson, *Classical Hollywood Cinema*, 115–16 and passim.

25. An advertisement for *Circulation of the Blood* is reproduced in Standish Lawder, *Cubist Cinema* (New York: New York University Press, 1975), 15. See Lauder's brief discussion of popular scientific films (12–14). For Allen on newsreels, see *Vaudeville and Film*, 217.

26. Walter Benjamin, "The Work of Art in the Age of Mechanical Reproduction," in *Illuminations*, ed. Hannah Arendt, trans. Harry Zohn (New York: Schocken, 1969), 223, 224. This tension is one source of some ambiguities in Benjamin's own evaluative attitude toward the concept of aura, which is more evident in his work as a whole than in the published version of this essay.

27. See chapters 5 and 6 of this volume.

28. See Janet Staiger, "Securing the Fictional Narrative as a Tale of the Historical Real," *South Atlantic Quarterly* 88, no. 2 (spring 1989): 393–413 for an analysis of the construction of historical authenticity that emphasizes the relation between narrative procedures and intertextual appeals. For her own historiography of the case, see Natalie Zemon Davis, *The Return of Martin Guerre* (Cambridge, Mass.: Harvard University Press, 1983). See also her comments on historical cinema in Natalie Zemon Davis, "Any Resemblance to Persons Now Living or Dead," *Yale Review* 76, no. 4 (1987): 457–82, where Davis promotes compromise formations between narration and reality effects in film.

29. Both essays are reprinted in Roland Barthes, *The Rustle of Language*, trans. Richard Howard (Berkeley and Los Angeles: University of California Press, 1989), 127–48. The influence of "The Discourse of History" sometimes seems

less obvious than that of "The Reality Effect," but segments of the former are clearly echoed and elaborated in accounts of historiography, such as those of Stephen Bann and Hayden White. Incidentally, its emphasis on shifters in historiography could be profitably compared to the appropriation of linguists like Roman Jakobson and especially Emile Benveniste in 1970s Film Studies; the most-cited example is "Story/Discourse: A Note on Two Voyeurisms," in Metz, *The Imaginary Signifier.*

30. One approach to the relation of classical cinema and novelistic form that includes discussion of preclassical cinema is Judith Mayne, *Private Novels, Public Films* (Athens: University of Georgia Press, 1988). A strong claim for the influence of the short story as well as the novel and the drama on the early development of narrative structures for classical cinema is made by Kristin Thompson, "From Primitive to Classical," in Bordwell, Staiger, and Thompson, *Classical Hollywood Cinema*, esp. 165–73. For an interesting instance of attention to the association of cinema and historicity, see Gaudreault, "The Cinematograph."

31. Roland Barthes, *Camera Lucida: Reflections on Photography*, trans. Richard Howard (New York: Hill and Wang, 1981), 87.

32. But editing in the sense of relationships among discrete shots is not necessary for the principle to hold; recall that even Bazin's hypothetical one-shot film is on the screen for a restricted period of time.

33. For comparisons of photography and cinema, see Barthes, *Camera Lucida*, 55, 76ff., esp. 78–79, 89–90, 111. On the private nature of photographic spectatorship, see, for example, 55, 97–100.

34. Ibid., 51.

35. From a different theoretical tradition, see Oskar Negt and Alexander Kluge, *Public Sphere and Experience: Toward an Analysis of the Bourgeois and Proletarian Public Sphere*, trans. Peter Labanyi et al. (Minneapolis: University of Minnesota Press, 1993) for a work that foregrounds fantasy as a political terrain with special interest in media.

36. One canonical conceptualization of these processes is Pierre Bourdieu, with Luc Boltanski, Robert Castel, Jean-Claude Chamboredon, and Dominique Schnapper, *Photography: A Middle-Brow Art*, trans. Shawn Whiteside (Stanford, Calif.: Stanford University Press, 1990); for example, "[O]rdinary practice seems determined, contrary to all expectations, to strip photography of its power to disconcert; popular photography eliminates accident or any appearance that dissolves the real by temporalizing it" (76). (The original French publication was in

1965, which makes it roughly contemporaneous with Barthes's earlier writings on photography.)

37. Barthes, *Camera Lucida*, 117. See 115–16, where Barthes finds some of the "photographic" craziness he values in a scene from Fellini's *Casanova*, a narrative film. See also 111, but compare 89–90.

38. The U.S. Attorney General's 1987 report on pornography even cites Bazin to argue for the social impact of indexical imaging. See the discussion in Linda Williams, *Hard Core: Power, Pleasure and the 'Frenzy' of the Visible* (Berkeley and Los Angeles: University of California Press, 1989), chapter 7, e.g., 184–89.

39. This recognizability is related to, but not as narrow as, the pioneering concept of "reference period" in Pierre Sorlin, *The Film in History: Restaging the Past* (Totowa, N.J.: Barnes and Noble, 1980), chapter 2. Tashiro, *Pretty Pictures*, has much of importance to say about this (passim), but still attributes its force to perspective rather than indexicality (e.g., 58–59).

40. Jean-Louis Comolli, "Historical Fiction: A Body Too Much," 41–53.

41. Hitchcock, of all *auteurs*, says, "I'm very concerned about the authenticity of settings and furnishings," apropos of the reproduction of the United Nations building lobby in *North by Northwest*. "When we can't shoot in the actual settings, I'm for taking research photographs of everything." He goes on to recall that the apartment of Scottie in *Rear Window* was based on photographic research covering the apartments of retired, college-educated San Francisco detectives, and that sets and costumes of characters in *The Birds* were based on an exhaustive series of photographs not only of Bodega Bay, but of its actual inhabitants. François Truffaut, with Helen B. Scott, *Hitchcock* (New York: Simon and Schuster, 1967), 192–93. Cf. Custen, *Bio/Pics:* 128: "It was not uncommon, then, to have invented characters moving implausibly, without a trace of irony, through historically accurate sets" (128).

42. And any spectatorial apprehension that the sets concretely existed as a profilmic field preserved on film is correct. See the comments and recollections of art, costume, and set designers in Hugh Fordin, *The Magic Factory: How MGM Made* An American in Paris (New York: Praeger, 1973), chapter 6.

43. Minnelli has recalled the great amount of work that went into researching both the actuality of Paris and the paintings set in Paris. He also recalls a contest in the MGM art department to see who could come up with the best Parisian scenes based on impressionist painters. See Vincent Minnelli with Hector Arce, *I Remember It Well* (New York: Berkeley, 1974), 239–40. See also Fordin, *The*

Magic Factory, for discussions of imitating the color style of particular painters, even when a specific painting was not being mimed. On the invocation, deployment, and significance of specific paintings in *An American in Paris,* see Angela Dalle Vache, *Cinema and Painting: How Art Is Used in Film* (Austin: University of Texas Press, 1996), chapter 1.

44. In *The Epic Film: Myth and History* (Boston: Routledge and Kegan Paul, 1984), Derek Elley writes that in the 1930s, "the costume picture took the side of the musical, with its glossy view of a privileged society at play.... Claudette Colbert in DeMille's *The Sign of the Cross* (1933) and *Cleopatra* (1934) might just as well have been cavorting around a New York hotel suite as a palace or an imperial barge" (20). For Elley, this is a point of critique rather than the basis for an insight about the possible relatedness of the two genres around issues of referentiality and performance.

45. Vivian Sobchack, "'Surge and Splendor': A Phenomenology of the Hollywood Historical Epic," *Representations* 29 (winter 1990): 28. Neale is discussing the quite different case of *Triumph of the Will,* but usefully emphasizes the spectatorial distinctions that the opposition between claims to accuracy and performance address: "Spectacle is content neither with simply rendering visible the observable nor with inscribing the spectating subject simply in position as observer. It is much more concerned with the processes of rendering visible and of looking themselves. What counts in spectacle is not the visible as guarantee of veracity (of truth, of reality) but rather the visible as mask, as lure. What counts is not the instance of looking as observation, but as fascinated gaze." (Steve Neale, "Triumph of the Will: Notes on Documentary and Spectacle," *Screen* 20, 1 [spring 1979]: 85).

46. Gordon Jennings, "Special-Effects and Montage for *Cleopatra,*" *American Cinematographer* 15 (December 1934): 350. I owe this reference to John Belton.

47. It is also a configuration with a cultural history and an important lineage in the function of the ornamental and spectacular in modern Western aesthetics. See Naomi Schor, *Reading in Detail: Aesthetics and the Feminine* (New York: Methuen, 1987), which also includes a perspicacious discussion of Barthes.

5. Disjunction and Ideology in a Preclassical Film

1. This is not meant to be an exhaustive summary of these distinctions. For example, pans seem to have been much more common in actuality shooting.

2. See esp. David Levy, "Reconstituted Newsreels, Re-enactments and the American Narrative Film," in *Cinema 1900/1906: An Analytical Study,* ed. Roger Holman (Brussels: FIAF, 1982), and "Edison Sales Policy and the Continuous Action Film, 1904–1906," in *Film before Griffith,* ed. John L. Fell (Berkeley and Los Angeles: University of California Press 1983); Charles Musser, "The Travel Genre in 1903–04: Moving toward Fictional Narration," *Iris* 2, no. 1 (1984). See also Stephen Bottomore, "Shots in the Dark: The Real Origins of Film Editing," *Sight and Sound* 57, no. 3 (summer 1988); and Tom Gunning, *D. W. Griffith and the Origins of American Narrative Film: The Early Years at Biograph* (Urbana and Chicago: University of Illinois Press, 1994), on the development of "the Narrator System" from preclassical cinema, e.g., 215–17.

3. In chapter 4 I discussed the detailed schema of preclassical transitions in the United States proposed in Charles Musser, "Another Look at the Chaser Theory," *Studies in Visual Communication* 10, no. 4 (1984), 24–44, as well as the debate between Musser and Allen: Robert Allen, "Looking at 'Another Look at the Chaser Theory,'" 45–50, and Musser, "Reply to Allen," 51–52. On the importance of Pathé, see Richard Abel, *The Red Rooster Scare: Making Cinema American 1900–1910* (Berkeley and Los Angeles: University of California Press, 1999); see, for example, the summary claims on 36–37.

4. Even in certain of the cases I count as tableaux shots, there are descriptive ambivalences. Some sense of continuity might be felt between scenes 3 and 4, since the action in 4 follows one of the characters in 3 and both scenes are along different sections of the Suez Canal. There also may be some sense of continuity between scenes 9 and 10, since the painted backdrop in 10 appears to possess graphic similarities to 9, which is an actuality shot. In addition to the shots listed above, it might be argued that shots 5 and 8 should be added to the list of tableaux. They are both actuality shots that might be seen as views of locales connected to the scenes that follow them or as detached views. Such ambivalences are themselves significant. This was undoubtedly a time of some experimentation; for example, the 1907 Pathé release, *Le Cheval Emballé,* already utilizes relatively extensive crosscutting. For an account of the development of preclassical approaches to continuity across the cut, see Tom Gunning, "Non-Continuity, Continuity, Discontinuity: A Theory of Genres in Early Films," *Iris* 2, no. 1 (1984), 101–12.

5. This is the only shot in the film that excludes setting and so is marked as extruding from the establishing tableau. It is difficult to imagine how the

embezzler-turned-banker's offer could be expressed otherwise without intertitles, and the film follows the common practice during this period of using intertitles only to introduce whole scenes by announcing locations and actions. Thus, the filmmakers "diegeticize" the offer by representing written words, which are filmable, instead of spoken words, which are invisible. They motivate the appearance of the word in the middle of a scene by means of point-of-view editing.

6. On the other hand, chase film editing itself can be treated as an important transitional innovation in the history of preclassical editing. See Gunning, "Non-Continuity, Continuity, Discontinuity," 108–9, for a succinct account of this type of editing as it relates to the breakup of tableau space.

7. See especially Ben Brewster, "A Scene at the Movies," *Screen* 23, no. 2 (July/August 1982), 5–15. While discussing earlier films, such as *Grandma's Reading Glass* (1902), Brewster treats optical point of view as a subset of the magnified insert, a device already known, and suggests that "POV began as a primitive rather than sophisticated use of cutting" (7). Although I am stressing the mobilization of a contiguous space rather than an insert, I am also dealing with a later and longer film precisely because it evidences the pressures of more complex narrativization, and Brewster's claim about the preclassical origins of point-of-view editing is in accord with my analysis.

For a brief introduction to issues of voyeurism and looking in preclassical cinema with special attention to sexuality, see Judith Mayne, "Uncovering the Female Body," in *Before Hollywood: Turn-of-the-Century Films from American Archives*, program for AFA film exhibition (New York: American Federation of the Arts, 1986), 63–67. See also Linda Williams, "Film Bodies: An Implantation of Perversions," in *Narrative, Apparatus, Ideology: A Film Theory Reader*, ed. Philip Rosen (New York: Columbia University Press, 1986). An important collection of original articles on point of view and voyeurism in preclassical cinema is *Ce que je vois dans mon ciné*, ed. André Gaudreault (Paris: Méridiens Klincksieck, 1988).

8. See Musser, "The Travel Genre." With respect to *A Policeman's Tour*, one can argue that the embezzler as source of the look is being established as a tour guide and/or delegate for the lecturer who would normally narrate such films. At any rate, the textual association of a look with narrational orientation and/or authority in a preclassical film is another mark of its transitional status.

9. Walter Benjamin, "The Work of Art in the Age of Mechanical Reproduction," in *Illuminations*, ed. Hannah Arendt, trans. Harry Zohn (New York:

Schocken, 1969), 223. Christian Metz, "The Imaginary Signifier," in *Narrative, Apparatus, Ideology*, esp. 260–67. But note how Metz suggests sociohistoric grounds for cinematic voyeurism, esp. on 265–67.

10. *Films et Cinématographs Pathé* (Pathé Frères, 1907), 202, my translation. I owe this reference to Tom Gunning. It is, of course, pertinent to an ideological analysis stressing colonialism that the catalog uses Asian scenes as its most attractive example of actuality.

11. For remarks on preclassical settings and disparities in mise-en-scène from a different viewpoint, see Paolo Cherchi Usai, "L'architecture du point de vue dans le cinéma des premiers temps," in Gaudreault, *Ce que je vois*, 67–71. The concept of "attractions" in preclassical film is introduced in Tom Gunning, "The Cinema of Attraction: Early Film, Its Spectator, and the Avant-Garde," *Wide Angle* 8, nos. 3–4 (1986): 63–70. For a narratological perspective on a similar distinction and a Pathé film, see André Gaudreault, "Récit singulatif, récit itératif: *Au bagne* (Pathé, 1905)," in *Les Premiers Ans du Cinéma Française*, ed. Pierre Guibert (Perpignan: Institut Jean Vigo, 1985), 233–41. Richard Abel, "From Spectacle to Story: Point-of-View Shots in Several Early Pathé Films," in Gaudreault, *Ce que je vois*, 73–76, is an account of tensions between attractions and narrativization in some contemporaneous Pathé films that employ point-of-view shots. In a wider-ranging survey that is suggestive of impulses at play in *A Policeman's Tour*, Tom Gunning, "What I Saw from the Rear Window of the Hotel des Folies-dramatiques, or The Story Point of View Films Told," argues that many early films use point of view as an attraction in itself rather than a narrative device, but that some such films include indications of "the means by which this scopic force was absorbed and channeled in later narrative films" (Gaudreault, *Ce que je vois*, 37). Gunning goes on to associate the narrativization of point of view with the construction of a moralized fictional universe in which the object of the gaze rather than the voyeur is punished. Guilt and villainy thus become melodramatic rather than comic problems, and climactic punishment (common in early peeping tom films) becomes "more than a comic attraction" (41). *A Policeman's Tour of the World* cheerfully inverts any generic or moralizing expectations about punishment; see the discussion of its ending at the conclusion of this chapter.

12. Among Pathé releases, the best known is probably *La Revolution en Russie* (*Revolution in Russia/Mutiny in Odessa*) (1905). In conversation Richard Abel has suggested additional titles I have not seen, including *L'incendiaire* (1905), *Le Contremaitre Incendiaire* (1907), and *Un Drame dans les Airs* (1904).

13. See Fatimah Tobing Rony, *The Third Eye: Race, Cinema, and Ethnographic Spectacle* (Durham, N.C.: Duke University Press, 1996), for a study of textualizations of colonialist anthropology in documentary and fictional cinema.

14. On lecturers, see Charles Musser, "The Travel Genre," 48. Musser argues for the exhibitor's creative role in earlier preclassical cinema. From this viewpoint, one of the major processes in the development of early cinema was a struggle between producer and exhibitor for control over meaning. Insofar as editing became predetermined before exhibition and the lecturer superfluous because meanings could be secured within the film, this diminished the power of the exhibitor over the text in favor of the producer.

15. The Pathé catalogue acknowledges the debt to Verne, and also one to Balzac (!). This may register the cultural appeal of the novel as an overdetermining factor in the pressures toward narrativization of views.

6. Document and Documentary

1. Actually, 1963 is a year that stands as a threshold in the development of the mise-en-scène of the U.S. network newsroom as a nerve center collecting and collating knowledge of national and international scope. It was only in 1961 that U.S. television network news departments began establishing bureaus outside of New York, Chicago, and Los Angeles. In the fall season of 1963, CBS expanded its nightly network news program from fifteen to thirty minutes, and NBC followed almost immediately. The status of this event is indicated by the fact that the first expanded evening of news on both networks featured exclusive interviews with President Kennedy.

2. Absolutely speaking, of course, the physics of these media are such that this simultaneity is not quite achieved; from the perspective of the spectator, sociocultural and economic relationships, and ideology, however, I would argue that the possibility of temporal simultaneity as an ideal is embedded in the self-presentation and functioning of such media. In fact, liveness is normalized and carefully structured in television in the context of a variety of other kinds of images; see Jane Feuer, "The Concept of Live Television: Ontology as Ideology," in *Regarding Television*, ed. E. Ann Kaplan (Frederick, Md.: University Press of America, 1983). This is true even (or especially) for its mobilization in crisis; see Mary Ann Doane, "Information, Crisis, Catastrophe," in *Logics of Television*, ed. Patricia Mellencamp (Bloomington: Indiana University Press, 1990). See also Margaret Morse, "The Television News Personality and Credibility:

Reflections on the News in Transition," in *Studies in Entertainment: Critical Approaches to Mass Culture*, ed. Tania Modleski (Bloomington: Indiana University Press, 1986).

3. John Grierson, *Grierson on Documentary*, ed. Forsyth Hardy, rev. ed. (New York: Praeger, 1966), 145–46, 201, 290.

4. For the influence of this approach in U.S. publications, see, for example, Joris Ivens, "Collaboration in Documentary," *Films* 1, no. 2 (spring 1940), e.g., 30, for the discussion of personal style, conception, and script as faced with actuality, and 35 on reenactment in documentary. Cf. several articles reprinted in *The Documentary Tradition: From Nanook to Woodstock*, ed. Lewis Jacobs (New York: Hopkinson and Blake, 1971), including Leo T. Hurwitz's 1934 anticapitalist, anti-Hollywood manifesto, "The Revolutionary Film—Next Step," which opposes the "synthetic documentary film" to the newsreel (91) but for whom "drama" remains a key term; Evelyn Gerstein, "English Documentary Films" (1936), which again begins by opposing documentary to the newsreel and goes on to make further distinctions in favor of the documentary's knowledge value; Ben Bellit, "The Camera Reconnoiters" (1937), which opposes Frontier Films to travelogues on the one hand and Hollywood on the other, quoting Paul Strand to indicate that documentary goes beyond newsreels and travelogues in finding the "basic dramatic meanings implicit in the documents" (143); and Herbert Kline, "Films without Make-Believe" (1942). The opposition of documentary versus newsreel and travelogue shows up again in Philip Dunne, "The Documentary and Hollywood" (1946), in *Nonfiction Film: Theory and Criticism*, ed. Richard Meran Barsam (New York: Dutton, 1976).

5. See chapter 3 in this volume. White's views on narrative closure and historicity are elegantly and definitively stated in three essays reprinted in Hayden White, *The Content of the Form: Narrative Discourse and Historical Representation* (Baltimore: Johns Hopkins University Press, 1987): "The Value of Narrativity in the Representation of Reality," "The Question of Narrative in Contemporary Historical Theory," and "The Politics of Historical Representation: Discipline and De-Sublimation." He extends and refines his argument in several of the essays included in Hayden White, *Figural Realism: Studies in the Mimesis Effect* (Baltimore: Johns Hopkins University Press, 1999). For an interesting conception of documentary film that invokes some of White's work on historical sequenciation and the construction of reality in relation to cinematic indexicality, see Bill Nichols, "History, Myth, and Narrative in Documentary," *Film Quarterly* 41, 1

(fall 1987): 9–20. Nichols ingeniously separates timelessness and identification out from narrative, which he associates with the configuration of temporal flux and historicity in ways reminiscent of Paul Ricoeur. However, it is worth noting that this is not an approach one would usually associate with White. Influenced by Northrop Frye as well as structuralist and poststructuralist narratology, White generally conceives of narrative form in a restricted number of archetypal, temporally overarching categories. For a major element of White's critique of modern historiography is precisely that narrative is not a reliable figuration of temporality, because a given category of narrative will tend to impose similar patterns and hence meanings on very different historical references.

6. Compare the discussion of Turner on evidence and Kracauer on historicism in chapter 3 of this volume.

7. Arthur C. Danto, *Narration and Knowledge (including the integral text of Analytic Philosophy of History,* rev. ed.) (New York: Columbia University Press), 148–53, 157–58. For reasons of space and my own exposition, which includes consideration of nonlinguistic representations of the past, I am taking these elements somewhat out of their context, which is Danto's explication of his concept of the narrative sentence. It is important, however, that Danto's analysis allows for cases in which endings change among successive generations of historians, because as time goes on additional events occur and different sequenciations become reasonable.

8. See chapters 4 and 5 of this volume.

9. Grierson, *Grierson on Documentary,* 199–201.

10. See chapter 4 in this volume. For the scholarly problematic of transitions leading to classicism, see some of the articles conveniently reprinted in *Early Cinema: Space, Frame, Narrative,* ed. Thomas Elsaesser with Adam Barker (London: British Film Institute, 1990), starting with the several by Charles Musser ("The Travel Genre in 1903–04: Moving Towards Fictional Narrative" and "The Nickelodeon Era Begins: Establishing the Framework for Hollywood's Mode of Representation") and Tom Gunning ("Non-Continuity, Continuity, Discontinuity: A Theory of Genres in Early Films" and "Weaving a Narrative: Style and Economic Background in Griffith's Biograph Films"). See also Musser, "Another Look at the 'Chaser Theory,'" *Studies in Visual Communication* 10, no. 4 (1984). A fuller elaboration of his account is in Charles Musser, *The Emergence of Cinema,* vol. 1 of *History of the American Cinema* (Los Angeles: University of California Press, 1990).

11. Paul Willemen, "The Third Cinema Question: Notes and Reflections," in *Questions of Third Cinema*, ed. Jim Pines and Paul Willemen (London: BFI, 1989), 5. Willemen also aligns Italian neorealism with the Griersonian documentary movement as offering a parallel model to third cinema.

12. "The Course of Realism" in *Grierson on Documentary*, 207. See also "Propaganda and Education," 288–90. Compare the following: "For the troubles of the press, like the troubles of representative government, be it territorial or functional, like the troubles of industry, be it capitalist, cooperative or communist, go back to a common source: to the failure of self-governing people to transcend their casual experience and their prejudice, by inventing, creating and organizing a machinery of knowledge. . . . This is the primary defect of popular government, a defect inherent in its traditions, and all its other defects can, I believe, be traced to this one." Walter Lippmann, *Public Opinion* (1922; reprint, New York: Macmillan, 1960), 364–65; see chapter 25 for an argument that the remedy is the interpolation of a cadre of professionalized experts between government and the citizen.

13. Walter Benjamin, "The Work of Art in the Age of Mechanical Reproduction," in *Illuminations*, trans. Harry Zohn (New York: Schocken, 1969), 224.

14. Cf. Karl Mannheim, *Ideology and Utopia: An Introduction to the Sociology of Knowledge*, trans. Louis Wirth and Edward Shils (New York: Harcourt, Brace, 1936), 154–61.

15. For Gramsci on the social processes involving intellectual and technical elites, see, for example, "The Intellectuals," in Antonio Gramsci, *Selections from the Prison Notebooks*, ed. and trans. Quintin Hoare and Geoffrey Nowell-Smith (New York: International Publishers, 1971), 5–25, and the remarks on the dialectic of intellectuals and the masses in the section entitled "The Study of Philosophy," 333–43. Examples of appropriations of Gramsci by different kinds of influential cultural theorists are Stuart Hall, "Gramsci's Relevance for the Study of Race and Ethnicity" and "The Problem of Ideology—Marxism without Guarantees," both in *Journal of Communication Inquiry* 10, no. 2 (summer 1986); and (sometimes more implicitly) Gayatri Chakravorty Spivak, "Can the Subaltern Speak," in *Marxism and the Interpretation of Culture*, ed. Cary Nelson and Lawrence Grossberg (Urbana: University of Illinois Press, 1988), and "Subaltern Studies: Deconstructing Historiography," in Spivak, *In Other Worlds: Essays in Cultural Politics* (New York: Routledge, 1987). A collection on the history of politically committed, leftist documentary cinema is Thomas Waugh, ed., *"Show Us*

Life": Toward a History and Aesthetic of the Committed Documentary (Metuchen, N.J.: Scarecrow, 1984).

16. Jean Baudrillard, *In the Shadow of the Silent Majorities . . . Or the End of the Social,* trans. Paul Foss (New York: Semiotext(e), 1983).

17. Jean Baudrillard, *Simulations,* trans. Paul Foss, Paul Patton, and Philip Beitchman (New York: Semiotext(e), 1983); see, e.g., 39–46.

18. Ibid., 49. On *An American Family* and what it is supposed to illustrate, see 49–58. In different versions of this text, some of the points about *An American Family* are different. See the version in Jean Baudrillard, *Simulacra and Simulations,* trans. Sheila Glaser (Ann Arbor: University of Michigan Press, 1994), 27–29, where the problem of causality is diminished to a mere hint. Nevertheless, I would argue that the problem does remain in the very notion of the contamination of the real by simulcra, so that the earlier version is truer to the implications of Baudrillard's conception.

19. For a sophisticated rather than a naive example, see Steve Neale, "Triumph of the Will: Notes on Documentary and Spectacle," *Screen* 20, no. 1 (spring 1979): 85: "[Spectacle] addresses the imbrication of looking and the visible not [as in documentary] *as the prior condition to the construction of a form of knowledge* about a particular subject or issue, but rather as that which hovers constantly across the gap between the eye and the object presented to it in the process of the scopic drive. Documentary *disavows this gap altogether,* subordinating both instances to that set of essentially empiricist codes of exposition required to promote its knowledge effect" (my emphasis). Note the quick slippage from the careful wording in the first italicized passage to the absoluteness of the second. I am suggesting such a widespread attitude elides too much within the history of documentary, but even theoretically there are problems. For example, what, within psychoanalysis, is it to disavow something "altogether"? Classically, this is treated as impossible, and disavowal involves some minimal degree of oscillation between knowledge and belief.

7. Toward a Radical Historicity

1. A seminal essay on African liberation as national that highlights the position of the indigenous intellectual and artist is Frantz Fanon, "On National Culture," in *Wretched of the Earth,* trans. Constance Farrington (New York: Grove Press, 1968); see also "The Pitfalls of National Consciousness" in the same collection, and Amilcar Cabral, "National Liberation and Culture," in *Return to the*

Source: Selected Speeches of Amilcar Cabral, ed. Africa Information Service (New York: Monthly Review Press, 1973).

2. This approach differs in emphasis from that of important commentators on Sembene's films. Françoise Pfaff, *The Cinema of Ousmane Sembene, a Pioneer of African Film* (Westport, Conn.: Greenwood, 1984), 51–52, notes his interest in juxtaposing contrasting spaces, but claims that Sembene's historical, rural films employ longer takes than do his contemporary, urban films. Yet, even if the takes in *Ceddo* are longer than in his other films, such as *Mandabi* or *Xala*, this usually does not affect spatial articulations to the extreme of leading to sequence shots or extended scenes composed only of a couple of shots. While there are occasional examples of such constructions in *Ceddo* (especially the long take, in which the court nobles decide to betray the king), for the most part scenes are edited according to a spatially analytical impulse. (*Emitai,* on the other hand, seems to better match her description.) Manthia Diawara goes further in his groundbreaking (at least in the United States) article, "Popular Culture and Oral Traditions in African Film," *Film Quarterly* 41, no. 3 (spring 1988), describing the court scene in *Ceddo* (whose analytical aspects are discussed below) as composed of deep focus long takes as opposed to "the fast editing style of European films" (11).

These writers, with Sembene himself, explain that editing and other rhythms in Sembene's films generally tend to seem slower than those of many Western aesthetics and practices because they originate in Black African traditions of narrative and temporality. This seems likely enough (although a younger generation of sub-Saharan African filmmakers appears to be becoming impatient with this aesthetic); however, it also seems problematic to use the long take as such as the representative device. The long take is well known elsewhere, and was an established option even in Hollywood at the time it was codified most influentially into French cinema aesthetics by Bazin's celebrations of such directors as Renoir and Welles. (One wonders if this shouldn't be a significant consideration for interrogations of oppositional components of films from Francophone Africa.) Perhaps the term *long take,* especially given its influential heritage from Bazin, is not sufficiently exact, or too limited a formulation, to describe the specificity of Sembene's distinctive practices with respect to temporal rhythms, for these have to do not just with absolute shot length, but *relations* of narrative, image, and sound.

3. In an interview that provides some of the most sophisticated formulations about the film, Sembene argues that the actions of the kidnapper must be read as those of a collective rather than a rebellious individual, in part because

hostage-taking as a tactic in disputes is known in several cultural traditions of the region. Françoise Pfaff, "Entretien avec Ousmane Sembène," *Positif* 235 (October 1980): 56.

4. For Sembene on the term *ceddo*, see ibid., 55–56. Elsewhere, Sembene seems to stress some of the precolonial grandeur of the Ceddo: "[I]t is ... a manner of being with rules and regulations. The Ceddo is a lively mind or spirit, rich in the double meaning of words and knows the forbidden meanings. The Ceddo is innocent of sin and transgression. The Ceddo is jealous of his/her absolute liberty." *Nations Nouvelles* 28 (1976), quoted in Teshome H. Gabriel, *Third Cinema in the Third World: The Aesthetics of Liberation* (Ann Arbor, Mich.: UMI Research Press, 1982), 87. On 86–87, Gabriel stresses that Ceddo denotes anti-Islamic "outsider." For additional perspectives, see also the entry under *cedo* (the officially legitimated spelling rejected by Sembene) in Lucie Gallistel Colvin, *Historical Dictionary of Senegal* (Metuchen, N.J.: Scarecrow,1981); on *tieddo*, see Cheikh Anta Diop, *Precolonial Black Africa* (Trenton, N.J.: Africa World Press, 1987), 46–47; and for a commentary on the *tyeddo*, anticolonialist conflicts, and Muslim-pagan struggles in the nineteenth century, see Donal B. Cruise O'Brien, *Saints and Politicians: Essays in the Organization of a Senegalese Peasant Society* (London: Cambridge University Press, 1975), 26ff. On the theme of the ceddo as applied to the anticolonial struggles in recent Senegalese literature, see Dorothy S. Blair, *Senegalese Literature: A Critical History* (Boston: Twayne, 1984), 27–30.

The suggestion that the imam has attributes of the trickster is made in Mbye Baboucar Cham, "Ousmane Sembene and the Aesthetics of African Oral Traditions," *Africana Journal* 13, nos. 1–4 (1982): 32–33. Cham points out that in oral traditions the trickster is a protagonist, but Sembene's protagonists are often victimized by tricksters. It is important that Sembene does not just reproduce an indigenous cultural configuration, but uses and reshapes it, in this case by inversion of values. See the commentary on the strength of Muslim institutions and power in Senegal and their political relations to the state and national identifications in Mar Fall, "La question islamique au Sénégal: Le regain récent de l'islam; la religion contre l'État?" *Présence Africain* 142 (1987): 24–35. The sociocultural potency of Islam is exemplified for Fall by the fact that a leader of the communist *Parti Africain de l'Indépendence* opens his meetings with a Muslim formula; see 28 n. 16. A dispute between Senegalese Christians and Muslims is the narrative premise of the late Sembene film *Guelwaar* (1992).

5. Pfaff, "Entretien avec Ousmane Sembène," 56.

6. Interview with Sembene in *Seven Days*, March 10, 1978, 27, quoted in Pfaff, *The Cinema of Ousmane Sembene*, 174. There are other markers of the importance of gender; for example, the prominent carving at the top of the *samp* is a feminine figure.

7. Cham, "Ousmane Sembene," 35ff.

8. Social complexities around the contemporary figure of the griot are analyzed in Christopher L. Miller, "Orality through Literacy: Mande Verbal Art before the Letter," chapter 3 in *Theories of Africans: Francophone Literature and Anthropology in Africa* (Chicago: University of Chicago Press, 1990). Cham, "Ousmane Sembene," 25–26, summarizes ambivalences in the social status of griots (or gewels), and also social distinctions among types of storytellers. On Sembene conceived as griot, see Pfaff, *The Cinema of Ousmane Sembene*, chapter 2.

9. Diawara, "Popular Culture"; Cham, "Ousmane Sembene," passim. Cf. Pfaff, *Cinema of Ousmane Sembene*, chapters 2 and 3, and Diawara, "Oral Literature and African Film: Narratology in *Wend Kuuni*," in *Questions of Third Cinema*, ed. Jim Pines and Paul Willemen (Bloomington: Indiana University Press, 1989), pp. 199-211. (Two articles by Teshome Gabriel in this same collection seem to bear on this conjunction of oral traditions and film, but their ambit goes well beyond African cinema: "Towards a Critical Theory of Third World Films," 30–52, and "Third Cinema as Guardian of Popular Memory: Towards a Third Aesthetics," 53–64.) The transition from oral to written authority is emphasized in Serge Daney, "*Ceddo*," *Cahiers du cinéma* 304 (October 1979): 51–53. The importance of the oral tradition for sub-Saharan African film aesthetics is also emphasized in Nwachukwu Frank Ukadike, *Black African Cinema* (Berkeley and Los Angeles: University of California Press, 1994).

10. One wonders whether this national arena, suggesting at least a partial ring of onlookers around the debaters/performers, does not also bear some relation to the figure of the griot. The word *gewel* (meaning the formally functioning griot) is said to derive from *geew* (circle), based on the practice of forming a circle around the praise-singer/musician. See the glossary in Sembene Ousmane, *The Last of the Empire*, trans. Adrian Adams (London: Heineman, 1983).

11. One confrontation in this scene, that between the Ceddo spokesperson Diogomay and Prince Biram, is edited mostly with 180-degree cuts along an axis bisecting the enclosure at right angle to the court. The alternation includes cuts from frontal medium shots of the speakers to medium long shots from behind Diogomay with the king and court in extreme background. In the

420 – NOTES TO PAGES 285–92

name of technical precision, someone might want to treat this as being close to a reverse shot construction within the enclosure. But, at least in Western shot/reverse shot editing, 180-degree reversals have generally been unusual, at least since the early sound period. This pattern, incidentally, has a number of functions, ranging from covering Biram's entrance into the enclosure to placing the camera, for the only time in the entire scene, in a position close to that of the Ceddo people.

12. See chapter 4 in this volume.

13. See Pfaff, *The Cinema of Ousmane Sembene*, 176, on Dior's gesture. Pfaff notes the reference to Lat-Dior (175)

14. Sembene in Pfaff, "Entretien avec Ousmane Sembène," 57.

15. Ibid., 55.

16. See in general V. Y. Mudimbe, *The Invention of Africa: Gnosis, Philosophy, and the Order of Knowledge* (Bloomington: Indiana University Press, 1988), passim. On the paradigmatic opposition between the traditional and the modern, see, e.g., 3–5, 16–18. In the present context, it is perhaps worth noting that this constellation was present from the beginning of the canon of modern Western historicity. See, for example, the offensive exclusion of Africa from history, the universal, and therefore the human in the work of Ranke's great German rival in the conceptualization of history. Georg Wilhelm Friedrich Hegel, *The Philosophy of History*, trans. J. Sibree (New York: Dover, 1956), 91–99, esp. 99. A widely discussed consideration of the historical temporality of these oppositions in anthropology is Johannes Fabian, *Time and the Other: How Anthropology Makes Its Object* (New York: Columbia University Press, 1983).

17. For a brief response to such critiques, see Léopold Sédar Senghor, *On African Socialism*, trans. Mercer Cook (New York: Praeger, 1964), 72–75. In this 1960 lecture, Senghor continues to associate African knowledge with closeness as opposed to distance, touch as opposed to sight, and feeling and intuition as opposed to analytic reason. Senghor finds a vindication for valuing this kind of knowing in the critiques of classic modes of Western rationalism by French phenomenologists and existentialists, concluding his defense with an appeal for an integration of the two modes of knowledge. Senghor attributes to the "young people" who criticize him a "complex" for believing that such purportedly Negro-African modes of reasoning are inferior to European modes.

18. Frantz Fanon, *Black Skin, White Masks*, trans. Charles Lam Markmann (New York: Grove Press, 1967), 14, 109–110. In general, see the essay, "The Fact of Blackness," from which the latter passage is excerpted.

19. Mudimbe, *Invention*, 5. Cf. Mudimbe's discussion of Fanon and Senghor on 92–94. Given that he utilizes later anti-essentialist Western theory from Lévi-Strauss through Foucault, Mudimbe is more sympathetic to Senghor than one might expect, partly in reaction against critiques of the latter and partly in alliance with a view of historical constructions as myths. On "historical legend," see 191–94.

20. To compare the considerations of these issues of the historical instability of Black identity in relation to cinema, see Stuart Hall, "Cultural Identity and Cinematic Representation," *Framework* 36 (1989): 68–81. Also, cf. Teshome H. Gabriel, "Thoughts on Nomadic Aesthetics and the Black Experience of Independent Cinema: Traces of a Journey," in *Blackframes: Critical Perspectives on Black Independent Cinema*, ed. Mbye B. Cham and Claire Andrade-Watkins (Cambridge, Mass.: MIT University Press, 1988), esp. the section entitled "Axis and Not Poles," 72–73.

While historical and experiential differences must be kept in mind, it might be productive to compare the binds around identity and essentialism encountered in decades of such Black theoretical discourses and controversies with those found in feminist theory.

21. On different kinds of griots marking the ambivalences of tradition, see Diawara, "Popular Culture," passim and esp. 9–12 on Sembene. See also Diawara, "Oral Literature and the African Film." The point about resolutions in Sembene is taken from a discussion of delimitations on narrative linearity in his work in Cham, "Ousmane Sembene," 27–28.

22. Slavery was a centuries-old practice in the Senegambian region when the French gradually delegitimated it between 1848 and 1905. By the nineteenth century and stimulated at first by the Atlantic slave trade (already outlawed by France in 1815), the export of people captured in raids on neighboring kingdoms was a leading economic factor in the politics of the area. However, it should be noted that in this region, slavery was a more complex system than in New World plantations. There were distinctions between menial and aristocratic slaves, such as the Ceddo, and slaves had certain rights, such as holding property, including their own slaves. Hence in the film, the Ceddo seek to reclaim certain older privileges, abrogated by the new power of Islam, that might make their status as slaves seem equivocal to a Western audience. See Colvin, *Historical Dictionary*, entries under "slave" and "slave trade," and O'Brien, *Saints and Politicians*, 25–30. For the most optimistic perspective on precolonial slavery in this area, see Diop, *Precolonial*, 1–5.

A commentary on *Ceddo* emphasizing slavery as well as other themes stressed here, such as the representation of history and the theatricalization of discourse, is Th. Mpoyi-Buatu, "Sembene Ousmane's *Ceddo* and Med Hondo's *West Indies*," in John D. H. Downing, ed., *Film and Politics in the Third World* (New York: Praeger, 1987), esp. 55–63.

23. This is to reject the kind of reading of the film exemplified by Jean-Luc Pouillaude: "Sembène Ousmane dismisses Islam and Catholicism, all forms of conversion being a reduction of the African soul to something other than itself" ("L'emblème: sur *Ceddo*," *Positif* 235 [October 1980]: 53 [my translation]). Clearly the film values African history and practices; but the idea of an African "soul," an essence or coherent and noncontradictory identity that preexists encounters with forces exterior to itself, and that can and should be preserved without change and outside history, is exactly what, in my reading, the film surpasses.

24. Pfaff, *The Cinema of Ousmane Sembene*, 37; Margaret Tarratt, "The Money Order," *Films and Filming* 20, no. 4 (1974), quoted in idem, 139.

25. Cf. Mudimbe, *Invention*, 196, during a concluding discussion of African identity, the perpetuality of transition, and history: "[A]cculturation is not only an African disease but the very character of all histories. In the sequences, mutations and transformations that we can read, all histories deploy in effect a dispersion of the violence of the Same, which from the solid grounding in the present invents, restores or endows meaning to the Other in a past or in geographically remote synchronic cultures."

8. Old and New

1. One could go further, for there are senses in which *any* analog inscription is an index of something; for example, a painter's brushstroke is readable as an index, but of her or his operation on the canvas rather than the depicted object. But it seems clear that the overall referential status of a figurative painting such as a portrait is not the same as that of, say, a portrait photograph. A more nuanced commentary on these definitions, or even the case of the painter, would have to contend with questions of performed "virtuosity," raised in earlier chapters in relation to filmic spectacle.

2. By the mid-1990s, the linkage of visuality and modernity was a standard thesis in influential cultural criticism and theory. For some examples, see the theoretically innovative Jonathan Crary, *Techniques of the Observer: On Vision and*

Modernity in the Nineteenth Century (Cambridge, Mass.: MIT University Press, 1992); a synoptic (but surprisingly conventional) intellectual history of the theoretical context, Martin Jay, *Downcast Eyes: The Denigration of Vision in Twentieth-Century French Thought* (Berkeley and Los Angeles: University of California Press, 1993); and, on cinema and modernization in a non-Western case, Rey Chow, *Primitive Passions: Visuality, Sexuality, Ethnography, and Contemporary Chinese Cinema* (New York: Columbia University Press, 1995). Examples of Rick Altman's polemic against the repression of sensory hybridity in film theory and historiography are included in the introductions to *Sound Theory/Sound Practice*, ed. Rick Altman (New York: Routledge, 1992).

3. To take just one prominent example, see Jacques Derrida, *Specters of Marx: The State of the Debt, the Work of Mourning, and the New International*, trans. Peggy Kamuf (New York: Routledge, 1994). Especially in chapters 2 and 3, Derrida's philosophy of deconstruction and characteristic calls for a new mode of historicity are explicitly linked to new technologies of signification and transmission, as well as changes in the geopolitical world system, which are related back to "tele-techniques" and "the media."

4. Timothy Binkley, "Camera Fantasia: Computed Visions of Virtual Realities," *Millennium Film Journal* 20/21 (fall–winter 1988–89), 10–11.

5. Bill Nichols, "The Work of Culture in the Age of Cybernetic Systems," *Screen* 29: no. 1 (winter 1988). Nichols's account is different in tone and standpoint from Binkley's. It is judiciously critical and includes an account of the fetishism provoked by the digital. It is therefore all the more striking that even Nichols's account of this fetishism partakes of the historiographic problematic of old and new, and tends to bypass digital mimicry and hybridity, which I emphasize later in this chapter.

6. I have already made much of this distinction in chapter 1.

7. Manuel De Landa, *War in the Age of Intelligent Machines* (New York: Zone Books, 1991), 180–81; see also 189. For a similar argument with respect to remote sensors, see Kevin Robins, "The Virtual Unconscious in Postphotography," in *Electronic Culture: Technology and Visual Representation*, ed. Timothy Druckrey (New York: Aperture, 1996), 158.

8. George Legrady, "Image, Language, and Belief in Synthesis," in *Critical Issues in Electronic Media*, ed. Simon Penny (Albany, N.Y.: State University of New York Press, 1995), 190, my emphasis. For a more precise description of differences as well as similarities between digital and traditional photography, see

William J. Mitchell, *The Reconfigured Eye: Visual Truth in the Post-Photographic Era* (Cambridge, Mass.: MIT Press, 1992), 60ff.

9. The indexical also has means of incorporating the digital, for example through rephotography, but the issues this raises are of a different order. On the *National Geographic* cover, see Mitchell, *Reconfigured Eye*, 16, and see also chapter 9 for a systematically conceived set of related examples. For a typical summary of the discussions of photography and digitization, see Fred Ritchen, "Photojournalism in the Age of Computers," in *The Critical Image*, ed. Carol Squiers (Seattle: Bay Press, 1990), 28–37, but cf. Rosalind Krauss, "A Note on Photography and the Simulacral," also in *The Critical Image*, 15–27.

10. For another perspective, see Bellour's interesting essay for the Pompidou Center program on analogy in painting, photography, film, video, and computer graphics. He characterizes what I call digital mimicry with the term *virtual indifferentiation:* "[O]n the one hand, more and more differentiations [among media], and, on the other, a virtual indifferentiation." Raymond Bellour, "The Double Helix," in Druckrey, *Electronic Culture*, 177.

11. Andy Darley, "From Abstraction to Simulation: Notes on the History of Computer Imaging," in *Culture, Technology, and Creativity in the Late Twentieth Century*, ed. Philip Hayward (London: John Libbey, 1990), esp. 52–56. Darley insists on the importance of relating the shift in goals of computer imaging to social, economic, and political context. To illustrate Darley's claim with respect to cinema, one need only compare an early text by Gene Youngblood to a later one: the visionary promotion of abstraction in discussion of the Whitneys in his *Expanded Cinema* (New York: Dutton, 1970), and the visionary promotion of simulation in "The New Renaissance: Art, Science, and the Universal Machine," in *The Computer Revolution and the Arts*, ed. Richard L. Loveless (Tampa: University of South Florida Press, 1989), 8–20.

12. Implicit in this is something that will also be important later, when we come to interactivity. Perspective projections require the construction of a point of view. One of the great advantages of having the 3-D virtual object as the basis of the image is that one may "move" the viewpoint for the computer user, changing points of view, apparent distance from the object, and so forth. If such changes in viewpoint are combined with motion imaging, they will appear as continuous movement around and through the object.

13. Mitchell, *Reconfigured Eye*, 118, 6. See chapter 6 for a knowledgeable account of perspective and computer imaging. Mitchell also deals with the

digitization of complementary image characteristics necessary for convincing depiction of depth on a two-dimensional surface. See also Kim H. Veltman, "Electronic Media: The Rebirth of Perspective and the Fragmentation of Illusion," in Druckrey, *Electronic Culture*, 209–28. The argument that digital imaging partakes of a dominant Western pictorial tradition that originated in the Renaissance has even been extended to virtual reality imaging. See, for example, Simon Penny, "Virtual Reality as the Completion of the Enlightenment Project," in *Culture on the Brink: Ideologies of Technology*, ed. Gretchen Bender and Timothy Druckrey (Seattle: Bay Press, 1994), 231–48; and Sally Pryor and Jill Scott, "Virtual Reality: Beyond Cartesian Space," in *Future Visions: New Technologies of the Screen*, ed. Philip Hayward and Tana Wollen (London: British Film Institute, 1993), 168: "[T]he representation of 'reality' in VR is actually a highly specific view of the world, a view which unthinkingly assumes a Western tradition and ideology. VR rests on an unstated foundation of conventions such as Cartesian space, objective realism, and linear perspective." For the contrary argument, that digital imaging is leading inexorably to "the retreat of perspective" and toward something like a direct mapping of space without this code, see Lev Manovich, "The Automation of Sight: From Photography to Computer Vision," in Druckrey, *Electronic Culture*, 237ff. Manovich seems to envision something like the "pure data" of De Landa's spy satellites.

For a history of the interaction of the art world with the digital, see the knowledgeable (if sometimes conceptually fuzzy) survey by Margot Lovejoy, *Postmodern Currents: Art and Artists in the Age of Electronic Media*, 2d ed. (Saddle River, N.J.: Prentice-Hall, 1997). An earlier general account is Cynthia Goodman, *Digital Visions: Computers and Art* (New York: Abrams, 1987); chapter 4 is on depth representation.

14. He also emphasizes the stake of animation artists in computer imaging. Manuel De Landa, "Real Time," *Millennium Film Journal* 20–21 (fall-winter, 1988–89), 71, 73ff.

15. Binkley, "Camera Fantasia," 22.

16. Ibid., 30. Mitchell's chapter on perspective is titled "Virtual Cameras."

17. But for some fertile probes into this question, see Bellour, "Double Helix."

18. Timothy Binkley, "The Quickening of Galatea: Virtual Creation without Tools or Media," *Art Journal* 49, no. 3 (fall 1990): 234. Anne-Marie Willis, "Digitisation and the Living Death of Photography," in Hayward, *Culture*,

Technology, and Creativity, 201–2. Roy Ascott, "Is There Love in the Telematic Embrace?" *Art Journal* 49, no. 3 (fall 1990): 247. Dan Slater, "Domestic Photography and Digital Culture," in *The Photographic Image in Digital Culture*, ed. Martin Lister (New York: Routledge, 1995), 133. Slater argues the contemporary increase in the flow of images is intimately tied to consumerist culture as it intersects with modified domestic contexts. See also the sketch of the close relations between accounts of the digital and science-fiction narratives in Philip Hayward, "Situating Cyberspace: The Popularization of Virtual Reality," in Hayward and Wollen, *Future Visions*. This affinity for science fiction is undoubtedly linked to the prevalence of the forecast in the digital. Incidentally, Binkley has a more interesting way to deal with hybridity, and he sometimes acknowledges the irreducibility of some analog element in the digital. See "Transparent Technology: The Swan Song of Electronics," *Leonardo* 28, no. 5 (1995): 427.

19. Reinhart Koselleck, *Futures Past: On the Semantics of Historical Time*, trans. Keith Tribe (Cambridge, Mass.: MIT Press, 1985), 13ff.

20. Several variations of the digital utopia are recognized and subject to significant critique in *Fractal Dreams: New Media in Social Context*, ed. Jon Dovey (London: Lawrence and Wishart, 1996); see especially Kevin Robins, "Cyberspace and the World We Live In," 1–30, and Sean Cubitt, "It's Life Jim, But Not as We Know It," 31–58. One example of an informative account not limited to imaging, but with a strong utopian component is Richard Lanham, *The Electronic Word: Democracy, Technology, and the Arts* (Chicago: University of Chicago Press, 1993).

21. To put it like this suggests an elegantly exhaustive schema of underlying claims for the novelty of the digital, but I am neutral as to whether additional defining characteristics of the digital utopia could be adduced. And there may also be a wide range of digital utopias, some of which may begin from more intensive sociopolitical considerations rather than claiming to begin from a technological given.

22. See chapter 1 in this volume.

23. Kevin Robins, "The Virtual Unconscious in Postphotography," in Druckrey, *Electronic Culture*, 156. Timothy Binkley, "Refiguring Culture," in Hayward and Wollen, *Future Visions*, 100.

24. Youngblood, "The New Renaissance," 11.

25. "We are witnessing a dramatic shift in the physical basis of computing from electrons to light to DNA." Timothy Binkley, "Transparent Technology," 427–28. For related, even more visionary remarks, see Paul Brown, "Metamedia

in Cyberspace: Advanced Computers and the Future of Art," in Hayward, *Culture, Creativity, Technology,* 231ff.

26. Binkley, "Camera Fantasia," 18.

27. Hayward and Wollen, "Introduction: Surpassing the Real," in *Future Visions,* 7.

28. "Computers don't do anything you couldn't do," remarks Binkley. "They are just faster at it" ("The Quickening of Galatea," 239). However, he elsewhere notes, "Although computers are fast, they are not instantaneous and never will be" ("Transparent Technology," 431). Cf. Michael Benedikt, "Cyberspace: Some Proposals," in *Cyberspace: First Steps,* ed. Michael Benedikt (Cambridge, Mass.: MIT Press, 1991), 170–71, where he intimates that because of temporal restrictions, access to computer time bears exchange value.

29. Peter Wollen, "Modern Times: Cinema/Americanism/The Robot," in *Raiding the Icebox: Reflections on Twentieth-Century Culture* (Bloomington: Indiana University Press, 1993), 65.

30. Anne-Marie Willis, "Digitisation and the Living Death of Photography," 206, 205.

31. Richard Wright, "Technology as the People's Friend: Computers, Class, and the New Cultural Politics," in Penny, *Critical Issues,* 89. Binkley, "The Quickening of Galatea," 235, 234. A few years later, he modified his terminology: "[T]he computer is not a transcendent technology. It is a *transparent* technology" (Binkley, "Transparent Technology," 431).

32. In recent articles, Binkley notes a similar problem with respect to the conceptuality at the heart of the digital ideal. "A mathematical equation can still be lucid when modeled in a physical system, but its pristine state must be compromised at least a little to the contingencies of real space and time in order for it to have any efficacy in our lives" ("Transparent Technology," 431). That is, the digital has to presume the physical need to appeal to a preexisting body. Thus Binkley moves toward acknowledging that a basic hybridity of analog and digital is unavoidable: "As a result of this dependence on interfaces, digital media augment rather than undermine their analog forebears" ("The Vitality of Digital Creation," *Journal of Aesthetics and Art Criticism* 55, no. 2 (spring 1997): 112.

33. Ron Burnett, "A Torn Page, Ghosts in the Computer Screen, Words, Images, Labyrinths: Exploring the Frontiers of Cyberspace," in *Connected: Engagements with Media,* ed. George E. Marcus (Chicago: University of Chicago Press, 1996), 91.

34. Stewart Brand, *The Media Lab: Inventing the Future at M.I.T.* (New York: Penguin, 1988), 10–11. For Negroponte's 1994 views, cited during a discussion of convergence and the interests of multinational electronic corporations, see Andrew Dewdney and Frank Boyd, "Television, Computers, Technology, and Cultural Form," in Lister, *The Photographic Image*, 153–54. For an example of a critical stance toward the consumerist ideologies driving important developments in the digital, see the remarks on the "impending unification of the television, telephone and computer" in Simon Penny, "Consumer Culture and Its Technological Imperative," in Penny, *Critical Issues in Electronic Media*, 67; and Frank Rickett, "Multimedia," in Hayward and Wollen, *Future Visions*, 89.

35. Binkley, "Transparent Technology," 430. There is a fuller exposition of the distinction as one between photographic recursion and the "heteromorphic" character of interfaces in Binkley, "Refiguring Culture," 111–16. Poststructuralists would note that digital "writing" here stands for the paradoxically anti-originary nature of all copying, and therefore the copied nature of all that claims to be originary. See Nichols, "The Work of Culture," for a meditation on Benjamin and the "cybernetic" universe.

36. Rickett, "Multimedia," 74. Sergei Eisenstein, *Film Form*, ed. and trans. Jay Leyda (New York: Harcourt, Brace, 1968), e.g., 52, 70. Florian Rötzer, "Virtual Worlds: Fascinations and Reactions," in Penny, *Critical Issues*, 120.

37. Rötzer, "Virtual Worlds." 126.

38. Here is a typical passage from a widely read account: "ARPANET used 56,000-bit-per-second lines for over a decade.... In 1987 NSFNET (the successor to Internet) moved to communication lines capable of transporting 1.5 million bits per second. By 1992 NSFNET had moved to 45-million-bit-per-second lines—a seven-hundredfold increase in speed in five years. At that speed you can send five thousand pages per second, a couple of encyclopedias per minute. The next quantum leap in speed is the gigabit level—billions and hundreds of billions of bits per second; at the multigigabit-per-second level, you are talking about how many Libraries of Congress you can transmit every minute. Gigabit-rate networking is one of the projects of the present NREN testbed.... And research into terabit—trillions of bits per second—networking is well under way." Howard Rheingold, *The Virtual Community: Homesteading on the Electronic Frontier* (Reading, Mass.: Addison-Wesley, 1993), 79.

39. Cf. Binkley: "Optical fiber and electrical copper, in conjunction with a host of related technologies, are spinning out a World Wide Web that will readily

encompass us all. But the web is not woven of high-technology fibers the way a basket is woven of reeds. It is not a material but a conceptual entity" ("Transparent Technology," 427–28).

40. Penny, "Consumer Culture," 67.

41. Quotation in Mitchell, *Reconfigured Eye*, 6. Mitchell is careful to preserve the novelty of the digital by also arguing that the digital not only continues, but also "redefines" these older traditions. For his comments on transmissibility, see 80–85. He has dealt at greater length with digital transmissibility and networking in *City of Bits: Space, Place, and the Infobahn* (Cambridge, Mass.: MIT Press, 1995), which, however, is written in a freer forecasting mode, indulges in a McLuhanistic rhetoric of metaphoric description, and is unproblematically congruent with the digital utopia.

42. While I am here dealing with the logic of the digital ideal, not an "actually existing" digital realm, it should be uncontroversial to note that there are also pressures toward normalized regularities of image production "external" to this logic. I have already suggested that, as in all institutionalized professions, those utilizing computer graphics tend to normalize a range of options, which means limiting practically infinite manipulability. I have also noted in passing the immense importance of market economics and consumerist ideologies.

I have seen no account by specialists that substantiates my linking transmissibility/convergence with the conventionalization of digital imaging, but there are some straws in the historical wind that lend impressionistic support. For example, the predecessor of the internet, ARPANET, went online in 1969, which makes its growth coincident with the depictive turn in computer imaging in Darley's periodization. Allucquere Rosanne Stone, "Will the Real Body Please Stand Up?: Boundary Stories about Virtual Cultures," in Benedikt, *Cyberspace*, esp. 85ff., poses a different schema for a history of the digital and imaging. She still locates a general move toward emphasis on simulation about the same time, but then finds the key moments in the diffusion of multiuser systems such as Bulletin Board Services in the 1970s, and the emergence of virtual reality and cyberspace in the mid-1980s.

Also, there are biographical intertwinings of digital networking and depictive imaging, in that individuals important in the immediate prehistory and history of digital interactive simulation, such as Ivan Sutherland, worked at the U.S. Advanced Projects Research Agency, which developed ARPANET, something also noted by Stone (95–96) and Rheingold (*Virtual Community*, 70–74).

43. There are two broad emphases around interactivity in discourses of the digital: interaction with machines, and interaction with other human operators as mediated by interaction with networked machines. The latter range from multiuser text-based services to the science-fiction depictions of cyberspace in such influential novels as *Neuromancer* and *Snow Crash*. I will be concerned mainly with the first, because it seems logically (if not always practically or imaginatively) prior; and because it is the focus of so many theoretical discussions of digital imaging as radically novel, my concern here.

44. Roy Ascott, "Is There Love," 243.

45. Ascott, "Photography at the Interface," in Druckrey, *Electronic Culture*, 166–67. Ascott continues, "Or are implicitly so." This hedging once more marks a description as a forecast of that which is not yet.

46. David Rokeby, "Transforming Mirrors: Subjectivity and Control in Interactive Media," in Penny, *Criticial Issues*, 136. Lister, *The Photographic Image*, 19. Lister's specific example here is CD-ROM interactivity, but he means it to be a general point.

47. It is also possible to make an oddly complementary argument that there has *always* been interactivity, or at least that older media are more "interactive" in some significant sense than discourses of the digital utopia admit.

48. Mitchell, *Reconfigured Eye*, 222, 223. Mitchell's important monograph on these issues sometimes ventures into the digital utopia, especially when he makes politicized claims. For him the emergence of "post-photographic" regime is an opportunity "to deconstruct the very ideas of photographic objectivity and closure, and to resist what has become an increasingly sclerotic pictorial tradition" associated with socially dominant journalistic, legal, and scientific faith in the objectivity of recording instruments (8). Compare the more critical, distanced stance toward the digital utopia and the notion of the post-photographic generally taken by contributors to Lister, *The Photographic Image*.

49. Binkley, "Camera Fantasia," 12, 32, 38. David Tomas, "From the Photograph to Postphotographic Practice," in Druckrey, *Electronic Culture*, 153 (emphasis added).

50. N. Katherine Hayles, "The Condition of Virtuality," in *Language Machines: Technologies of Literary and Cultural Production*, ed. Jeffrey Masten, Peter Stallybrass, and Nancy J. Vickers (New York: Routledge, 1997), 184. The histories of the two terms with respect to the digital are closely linked. See Pryor and Scott, "Virtual Reality," 152.

51. Jean Baudrillard formulated his notion of the simulacrum influentially and polemically during the early 1980s. See *In the Shadow of Silent Majorities, or, the End of the Social and Other Essays*, trans. Paul Foss, John Johnston, and Paul Patton (New York: Semiotexte, 1983), and *Simulations*, trans. Paul Foss, Paul Patton, and Philip Beitchman (New York: Semiotexte, 1983). For Baudrillard on cinema, see two of his other works: *The Evil Demon of Images* (Sydney: The Power Institute of Fine Arts, 1987) and *Simulacra and Simulation*, trans. Sheila Faria Glaser (Ann Arbor: University of Michigan Press, 1994). See also the remarks on Baudrillard and documentary cinema in chapter 6 of this volume. Examples of a cultural and film critic productively employing the term *simulation* (as a sociocultural dominant) can be found in Scott Bukatman, *Terminal Identity: The Virtual Subject in Postmodern Science Fiction* (Durham: Duke University Press, 1993), e.g., 106–8. Binkley also distances digital simulation from the simulacrum in "Camera Fantasia," 31–32.

52. Binkley, "Refiguring Culture," 118; "The Vitality of Digital Creation," 113, 114. (Again, it should be noted that Renaissance perspective methods are only one kind of depth projection that digital imaging may employ.) Stone, "Will the Real Body," 107. Stone is strategically critical of dominant discourses of the digital, but sometimes becomes compatible with them, probably because she accepts the idea of radical novelty. Binkley, "The Vitality of Digital Creation," 113. This limited discussion of being positioned "inside" an image has wider resonance for the digital display in general. The idea of immersion "in" the image probably applies to any digital image configuration, including even the seemingly flat "desktop" screens of currently dominant personal computer operating systems, with cursor and iconic stand-ins for the operator in the image and overlap cues (e.g., placing text elements "on top of" one another).

53. Florian Rötzer, "Images within Images, or, From the Image to the Virtual World," in *Iterations: The New Image*, ed. Timothy Druckrey (Cambridge, Mass.: MIT Press, 1993), 68; cf. Benedikt, "Cyberspace: Some Proposals," 151: "[I]t is out of a rapproachement of the two systems—physical space and data space—that cyberspace is born."

54. Erkki Huhtamo, "Encapsulated Bodies in Motion: Simulators and the Quest for Total Immersion," in Penny, *Critical Issues in Electronic Media*. See also the discussion of an "archeological" approach to the image in work by several digital artists who explore the continuities rather than the differences between the digital and earlier imaging technologies and cultural forms in Erkki Huhtamo, "Time Traveling in the Gallery: An Archeological Approach in Media Art," in

Immersed in Technology: Art and Virtual Environments, ed. Mary Anne Moser with Douglas MacLeod (Cambridge, Mass.: MIT Press, 1996), 233–69. For a detailed description of *Hale's Tours* see Raymond Fielding, "Hale's Tours: Ultrarealism in the pre-1910 Motion Picture," in *Film before Griffith*, ed. John L. Fell (Berkeley and Los Angeles: University of California Press, 1983), 116–30. On envelopment and cinema, see John Belton, *Widescreen Cinema* (Cambridge, Mass.: Harvard University Press, 1992), esp. chapter 9, including Belton's summary of changes in spectatorship according to industrial practices and discourses, e.g., 187ff. For systematic consideration of viewpoint and signifying a subject who "moves through" cinematic mises-en-scène, see Edward Branigan, *Point of View in the Cinema: A Theory of Narration and Subjectivity in the Classical Film* (New York: Mouton, 1984).

55. Binkley, "Camera Fantasia," 34; see also 32, 36. From the earliest conception of an immersive Virtual Reality apparatus, which is based on perspectival imaging to each eye via video goggles, the hybridity of the system was deemphasized in favor of the superiority of interactivity with respect to illusionism: "The fundamental idea behind the three-dimensional display is to present the user with a perspective image which changes as he moves. The retinal image of the real objects which we see is, after all two-dimensional. . . . Although stereo presentation is important to the three-dimensional illusion, it is less important than the change that takes place in the image when the observer moves his head. The image presented by the three-dimensional display must change in exactly the way that the image of the real object would change for similar motions of the user's head." Ivan E. Sutherland, "A Head-Mounted Three-Dimensional Display," *Proceedings of the Fall Joint Computer Conference* (1968), 757–64, cited in Mitchell, *The Reconfigured Eye*, 79.

56. Binkley, "Refiguring Culture," 117–18.

57. Ibid., 118.

58. Binkley, "Camera Fantasia," 34, 30.

59. Ibid., 41. In the immersion of spectatorial actions within virtual space, imaginative distance between subject and object is negated, but voyeurism is classically said to require a real distance between the subject and object of vision. This supports Binkley's contention that voyeurism is appropriate as a description of indexical spectatorship, but not as digital spectatorship. However, it is necessary to remember that the negation of distance is itself only virtual, something a post-photographic digital operator supposedly is never permitted to forget in the digital utopia.

60. Ibid., 38.

61. Benedikt, "Cyberspace: Some Proposals," 170–71. There is, of course, much more to the economic and material underside of the digital that is not admissible to the digital utopia. For example: "[T]he production [of cyberspace] depends on the material space beyond its interfaces. Yet even those who assemble the computer chips may not have access to the worlds that computers engender. Since electronic networks involve a choice about who will be connected and who will not, a network consists of its gaps as well as its links and nodes. There is a negative or shadow cyberspace—material and devoid of technological resources—that those who seek to understand electronic culture must take into account" (Margaret Morse, "*Nature Morte:* Landscape and Narrative in Virtual Environments," in *Immersed in Technology: Art and Virtual Environments,* ed. Mary Anne Moser with Douglas MacLeod [Cambridge, Mass.: MIT Press, 1996], 200).

62. The same can be said about the convincingness of the image, which is tied to interactivity in this discourse: "Anything less than infinite computing power will deliver less sensory realism than ordinary reality, and less than we are apt to want. Therefore *the question is not whether or not cyberspace should be symbol-sustained, but how much it should be so.* VR pioneer Jaron Lanier's dream of 'post-symbolic communication' simply will not happen in any short term, if ever.... It may not even be possible." Benedikt, "Cyberspace: Some Proposals," 191.

63. Binkley, "Camera Fantasia," 37, 41. This view is not unique to Binkley. See, for example, Derek Foster, "Community and Identity in the Electronic Village," in *Internet Culture,* ed. David Porter (New York: Routledge, 1997), 26–27.

64. Kevin Robins, "The Virtual Unconscious," in Druckrey, *Electronic Culture,* 162.

65. On the general theory of the fetishistic structure of representation, see Stephen Heath, "Lessons from Brecht," *Screen* 15 (summer 1974).

66. For the cyberspace-virtual reality pair, see Rebecca Coyle, "The Genesis of Virtual Reality," in Hayward and Wollen, *Future Visions,* 148.

67. And they both had accounts, although of quite different kinds, of how the image might have a narcissistic or solipsistic function that erases the object. See the discussion of Bazin and the myth of Stalin in chapter 1 of this volume and the discussion of Barthes's *Camera Lucida* in chapter 4.

68. Lister, *The Photographic Image,* 20.

69. But such accounts are available. For example: "My argument is that computers were born and introduced as forces of production.... First, they

enabled military competition to proceed apace, and the arrival of the Cold War at the end of the 1940s revved this engine almost uncontrollably. Second, they enabled the effective bureaucratisation of information, which in turn enabled massive expansion and monopolisation of commercial sectors. Third, they functioned to undermine trade union power in crucial sectors of employment through selective automation. But in all three cases, one of the enabling contributions was the representation of computers *as the good future*. The imagery of computers, arguably, constitutes the imagery of American capital stripped of its overt political coating, operating like a computer virus by disguising its own intentions." Martin Barker, "Drawing Attention to the Image: Computers and Comics," in Lister, *The Photographic Image*, 193. See also other contributions to this volume. For some politicized approaches to the digital in general, see James Brook and Iain A. Boal, eds., *Resisting the Virtual Life: The Culture and Politics of Information* (San Francisco: City Lights, 1995). See also Vivian Sobchak, "Toward a Phenomenology of Cinematic and Electronic Presence: The Scene of the Screen," *Post Script* 10, no. 1 (1990), 50–59, for a brief article by a film theorist who considers the digital in relation to Fredric Jameson's Marxist categories of cultural history through a body-centered phenomenology. Unfortunately, from my perspective, Sobchak ends up with the rather un-Jamesonian project of separating rather than interrelating aspects of the social totality—in this case, cinema and the digital.

Afterword

1. Compare Bruno Latour, *We Have Never Been Modern*, trans. Catherine Porter (Cambridge, Mass.: Harvard University Press, 1993).

2. "We know that the Jews were prohibited from investigating the future. The Torah and the prayers instruct them in remembrance, however. This stripped the future of its magic, to which all those succumb who turn to the soothsayers for enlightenment. This does not imply, however, that for the Jews the future turned into homogeneous, empty time. For every second of time was the strait gate through which the Messiah might enter." Walter Benjamin, "Theses on the Philosophy of History," in *Illuminations*, trans. Harry Zohn (New York: Schocken, 1968), 264.

3. And, in my view, this also applies to postmodernity, if there is such a thing at this level of discussion.

Index

Actuality film, 164–66, 177, 202, 206, 207–10, 213–19, 242–45, 247
Adorno, Theodor, 137–40, 195–96, 252; *Minimia Moralia*, 147
Africa: histories, 289–96; postcolonial intellectuals, 267–68
Allen, Robert, 163–66
Althusser, Louis, 8
Altman, Rick, 303
American Family, An (film), 256–60
American Historical Association, 143
American in Paris, An (film), 184–86, 198
Anachronisms, 158–160, 287–88
Anapurna (film), 30–31
Ancient Monuments Protection Act (1882), 54
Andrew, Dudley, 10
Annales school, xiv
Anti-Scrape Society. *See* Society for the Protection of Ancient Buildings
ARPANET, 429n.42

Arts and Crafts Movement, 76, 98
Ascott, Roy, 333–34
Authenticity: in detail, 147–149, 157–59, 407n.41, 250, 280–87; distance from, 180; and pastness, 76–77; in restorationism, 64–67

Bann, Stephen, 84; *Clothing of Clio*, 56–57
Barabbas (film), 157, 159
Barthes, Roland, xv, 170–73, 195–97; *Camera Lucida*, 171–76, 244, 305, 323–24, 362n.5
Baudrillard, Jean, 253–60, 268, 338–40
Bazin, André, xxiii, 3–41, 84, 100, 109, 135, 167–68, 313, 322, 349, 352, 356, 357; "Aesthetic of Reality," 12, 32; on change, 37–38; critiques of, 8–14; "Evolution of the Language of Cinema," 3–5, 11, 13, 25–26, 32; "French Renoir," 12–13; and

Philip Rosen is professor of modern culture and media at Brown University. He was previously director of the Screen Studies Program at Clark University and has published widely on film, film and media theory, and cultural theory. He is editor of *Narrative Apparatus Ideology: A Film Theory Reader* and coeditor of *Cinema Histories/Cinema Practices*.